William Schouler

A History of Massachusetts in the Civil War

William Schouler

A History of Massachusetts in the Civil War

ISBN/EAN: 9783337411190

Printed in Europe, USA, Canada, Australia, Japan

Cover: Foto ©ninafisch / pixelio.de

More available books at **www.hansebooks.com**

A HISTORY.

OF

MASSACHUSETTS IN THE CIVIL WAR.

BY

WILLIAM SCHOULER.

LATE ADJUTANT-GENERAL OF THE COMMONWEALTH.

———•———

BOSTON:
E. P. DUTTON & CO., PUBLISHERS,
135 WASHINGTON STREET.
1868.

TO THE HONORABLE

LEVI LINCOLN,

OF WORCESTER,

THE MOST VENERABLE AND DISTINGUISHED LIVING CITIZEN OF MASSACHUSETTS,

This Volume

IS RESPECTFULLY DEDICATED BY

THE AUTHOR.

PREFACE.

THE original plan of this work would have included a brief narrative of each Massachusetts regiment which had served in the war, and a sketch of the meetings held in the several cities and towns in the Commonwealth to encourage recruiting, and to raise money and provide for the families of the soldiers. I soon found it was impossible to carry out this plan so as to do any thing like justice to the subjects. The mass of papers, letters, and reports bearing upon them placed in my hands, convinced me that one volume should be devoted exclusively to the three years' regiments, and one to the cities and towns.

There are several thousand letters in the files of the Governor, Adjutant-General, and Surgeon-General, written from the front by officers and enlisted men, which contain information both interesting and valuable; and many more are doubtless in the possession of the families of those who served in the war. From these and other sources, material can be furnished to make an interesting volume; and it is due to the veteran regiments that it should be written.

I have received new and valuable material from nearly every city and town in the Commonwealth, showing what was done by them in carrying on the war; and from this could be compiled a work which would reflect the highest honor upon the municipalities of this Commonwealth.

Should the present volume be received with favorable regard

by the people of Massachusetts, it is my purpose to write a volume of the same size and style, devoted exclusively to the three years' regiments and batteries, to be followed by another, devoted to the cities and towns.

WILLIAM SCHOULER.

LYNN, March 17, 1868.

CONTENTS.

CHAPTER I.

Massachusetts — Civil Government — Election, 1860 — Legislature — President of the Senate — Speaker of the House — State of the Country — Farewell Address of Governor Banks — Governor Andrew's Inaugural — Their Views of the Crisis — Sketch of Governor Andrew — Lieutenant-Governor — Executive Council — Adjutant-General — Military Staff — Congressmen — The Volunteer Militia — Military Equipment — Early Preparations — Salutes, 8th of January — General Order No. 2 — Report of Adjutant-General — General Order No. 4 — Proceedings of the Legislature — Regular Session — Emergency Fund — Loan Credit of State — Delegates to Peace Convention — South Carolina to Massachusetts — Two thousand Overcoats — Order of Inquiry — Letter of Adjutant-General — Letter of Colonel Henry Lee, Jr. — Meeting of Officers in Governor's Room — Colonel Ritchie sent to Washington — His Letters to the Governor — Secretary Seward's Letter — Letter of Colonel Lee — Charter of Transports — John M. Forbes, Esq. — Meeting in Faneuil Hall — Meeting in Cambridge — Speech of Wendell Phillips, Esq., at New Bedford — Remarks — The President calls for Troops — The Eve of Battle 1–48

CHAPTER II.

The Call for Troops — The Marblehead Companies first in Boston — The Excitement of the People — Headquarters of Regiments — Four Regiments called for — General Butler to command — New Companies organized — Liberal Offers of Substantial Aid — Dr. George H. Lyman, Dr. William J. Dale, Medical Service — Action of the Boston Bar — The Clergy, Rev. Mr. Cudworth — The Women of the State — The Men of the State — Liberal Offers of Service and Money — Robert B. Forbes, Coast Guard — Colonel John H. Reed appointed Quartermaster — The Personal Staff — Executive Council — Mr. Crowninshield appointed to purchase Arms in Europe — An Emergency Fund of Two Hundred Thousand Dollars — Letter of the Governor to Secretary Cameron — General Butler consulted — The Route by Annapolis — Narrative of Samuel M. Felton — Mr. Lincoln's Journey to Washington — His Escape from Assassination — The Third Regiment — Speech of Ex-Governor Clifford — The Fourth Regiment — Address of Governor Andrew — Departure for Fortress Monroe — The Sixth Regiment — Departure for Washington — Reception in New York and Philadelphia — The Eighth Regiment — Departure — Speeches of Governor Andrew and General Butler — Reception on the Route — Arrival in Philadelphia — The Fifth Regiment sails from New York for Annapolis — Major Cook's Light Battery ordered to Washington — The Third Battalion of Rifles sent forward — The Massachusetts Militia — Arrival of the Third Regiment at Fortress Monroe — Attempt to save Norfolk Navy Yard — The Fourth Regiment the first to land in Virginia — Fortress Monroe — Big Bethel — The Fifth Regiment — Battle of Bull Run — The Sixth Regiment — Its March through Baltimore — The Nineteenth of April — First Blood shed — The Eighth Regiment — Lands at Annapolis — Saves the Frigate Constitution — Arrives in Washington — The Rifle Battalion at Fort McHenry — Cook's Battery at Baltimore — End of the Three Months' Service — Conclusion . . 49-108

CHAPTER III.

The People of the Towns — The Press — The Pulpit — Edward Everett — Fletcher Webster offers to raise a Regiment — The Sunday Meeting in State Street — Mr. Webster's Speech — Meeting in the Music Hall — Speech of Wendell Phillips — Meeting in Chester Park — Speeches of Edward Everett and Benjamin F. Hallett — Meeting under the Washington Elm in Cambridge — Ex-Governor Banks, George S. Hillard, and others — Letters received by the Governor — Extracts — Reception of the Dead Bodies of the Killed in Baltimore — Mr. Crowninshield goes abroad to buy Arms — Ex-Governor Boutwell sent to Washington — Letter of John M. Forbes to Mr. Felton — Letter to General Wool — To Rev. Dr. Stearns — To Robert M. Mason — Offer of a Ship Load of Ice — Purchase of the "Cambridge" — Provisions sent to Fortress Monroe and Washington — Governor to President Lincoln — Attorney-General Foster — The Ladies of Cambridge — Call for Three Years' Volunteers — Letter of John M. Forbes — Letters received by the Adjutant-General — Extracts — Letters from Dr. Luther V. Bell and Richard H. Dana, Jr. — Ex-Governor Boutwell arrives at Washington — Letters to the Governor — State of Affairs at Washington — Letter from Mr. Foster — Cipher Telegram — Judge Hoar at Washington — Letters to the Governor — The War Department will accept no more Troops — Charles R. Lowell, Jr., Massachusetts Agent at Washington — His Instructions — Letter of Governor to Dr. Howe — Appointed to examine the Condition of the Regiments — His Report — Colonel Prescott — Letters of the Governor and General Butler — Slavery 109-161

CONTENTS.

— The Republican State Convention — Interesting Debate — Democratic Convention — Thanksgiving Proclamation — Thanksgiving in the Massachusetts Camps — Major Wilder Dwight — The Second Regiment at Harper's Ferry — Full Account of the Controversy between Governor Andrew and Major-General Butler about recruiting and raising Regiments in Massachusetts 216–282

CHAPTER VI.

The Campaign of 1862 — Meeting of the Legislature — Ex-Governor Clifford elected President of the Senate — His Speech — Alexander H. Bullock elected Speaker of the House — Speech of Mr. Bullock — Of Caleb Cushing — Proceedings of the Legislature — Abstracts of Military Laws passed — Massachusetts Prisoners in Richmond — Clothing sent — Letter from Adjutant Pierson — Expedition of General Burnside — Capture of Roanoke Island — Massachusetts Troops first to land — Care of the Sick and Wounded — Dr. Hitchcock sent on — The Wounded in New York — Colonel Frank E. Howe — Establishment of the New-England Rooms — Care of the Sick and Wounded — The Army of the Potomac — The Wounded at Williamsburg — Letters of Colonel Howe — Every Assistance given — The Agencies of the State for the Care of the Men — The Office in Washington — Colonel Gardiner Tufts, Mrs. Jennie L. Thomas, Robert C. Corson, William Robinson, appointed Agents — Visits of the Adjutant-General, Colonel Ritchie, and Colonel John Q. Adams, to the Front — Report to the Governor — The Appearance of Washington — Reports of Edward S. Rand and Dr. Bowditch — First Massachusetts Cavalry at Hilton Head — Our Troops in North Carolina — Appointment of Allotment Commissioners — Their Valuable Services — Letters of the Governor — Rule for making Appointments — Illegal Recruiting — Colonel Dudley — Thirtieth Regiment — Captured Rebel Flags — Death and Burial of General Lander — Letters of Governor to Secretary of War — Secretary of the Navy — To the President on Various Subjects — Letter to General Burnside — Secretary Chase — The Retreat of General Banks — Great Excitement — Troops sent forward — Militia called out — The Position of our Regiments — The War in Earnest 283–337

CHAPTER VII.

Recruiting for the New Regiments — The Position of the Armies in the Field — Letters from the Adjutant-General to Different Persons — Establishment of Camps — Departure of New Regiments — Recruits for Old Regiments — Letter to Secretary Seward — Suggestions adopted — Foreign Recruits — Letter to General Couch — Deserters — Want of Mustering Officers — Letter from General Hooker — Our Sick and Wounded — Letter to General McClellan — General Fitz-John Porter — Call for Nineteen Thousand Soldiers for Nine Months — Appointment of Major Rogers — Preparing for a Draft — Militia

CONTENTS. xi

Volunteers — Letter to the President — Great Activity in Recruiting — Liberality of John M. Forbes — Colonel Maggi — Town Authorities ask Civilians to be commissioned — First Attempt to raise Colored Troops — Letter to Hon. J. G. Abbott — Recommends Merchants and Others to devote Half of each Day to Recruiting — Hardship to Seaboard Towns — Attempt to have Credits allowed for Men in the Navy — Difficulties — Earnest Letter — Surgeons sent forward — Several Recommendations — Battle of Antietam — Dr. Hitchcock sent forward — His Report — Affairs at the Front — Recruiting Brisk — Republican Convention — Sharp Debate — Nominations — People's Convention — General Devens nominated for Governor — Speeches — Letter to General Dix — Contrabands — Complaints — Quotas filled — Departure of Regiments — Invasion of Texas — Major Burt — State Appointments, &c. 338–390

CHAPTER VIII.

The Proclamation of Freedom — Colored Regiments — Letter to Samuel Hooper — The California Battalion — Meeting of the Legislature, January, 1863 — Organization — Address of the Governor — Delay of the Government in paying the Soldiers — The Commission of Mr. Crowninshield — His Claim not allowed — Reports of the Adjutant, Surgeon, and Quartermaster Generals — Abstract of Military Laws — Letter to Hon. Thomas D. Eliot — Western Sanitary Commission — Confidential Letter to General Hooker — Efforts to reinstate Major Copeland — The Pirate "Alabama" — Curious Coincidence — Authority to recruit a Colored Regiment — The Governor's Policy in the Selection of Officers — Colonel Shaw — The Passage of the Fifty-fourth (colored) Regiment through Boston — Departure for South Carolina — Death of Colonel Shaw at Fort Wagner — Letter of the Governor to Captain Sherman — Letter to General Hamilton, of Texas — Major Burt — Plan to invade Texas — Mortality of Massachusetts Regiments in Louisiana — War Steamers — Rights of Colored Soldiers — Temperance — General Ullman's Expedition — Coast Defences — General Wilde — John M. Forbes writes from London — Colonel Ritchie — A Rebel Letter — Robert C. Winthrop — Letter to Mr. Gooch, M.C. — Army Officers in Boston — Cases of Suffering — Useless Detail of Volunteer Officers — Letter to General Wool — Suggestions about Recruiting — About Deserters — Staff Appointments — Complaints — Nine Months' Men — Letter to J. H. Mitchell, Massachusetts Senate — Claims for Money in the Legislature — Case of Mr. Maxwell, of Charlemont — Sergeant Plunkett, of the Twenty-first Regiment — Soldiers to be shot — Troubles in the Department of the Gulf, &c. 391–440

CHAPTER IX.

The Military Condition — Reverses and Successes of the Union Arms — Service and Return Home of the Nine Months' Regiments — List of Casualties — Deserters — The July Riot in Boston — Prompt Action — An Abstract of the Orders — Alarm in other Cities — The Attack in Cooper Street — The Eleventh Battery — The Word to fire — The Riot suppressed — The Draft — Appointment of Provost-Marshals — The Fifty-fifth Colored Regiment — Letters from Secretary Stanton — Injustice to the Colored Troops — Letters of the Governor on the Subject — Difficulties with the Draft — Major Blake sent to Washington — Request to allow Bounties to Drafted Men refused — John M. Forbes in Washington — Letters to the Governor — Heavy Ordnance — Colonel Lowell — The Attack on Wagner — Death of Colonel Shaw — Instances of Bravery on the Part of Colored Troops — Letters to General Dix — Troops for Coast Defence — Governor writes to Governor of Ohio — Formation of Veteran Regiment — Massachusetts Militia — Letters to Colonel Lee — Colored Cavalry — Letter of Secretary Stanton — Confidential Letter on the Exposed Condition of the Coast — Telegraph Communication with the Forts — Letters to Senator Sumner — Exact Condition of the Defences — Letter of the Adjutant-General — Reports of General William Raymond Lee — Colonel Ritchie sent to England — Democratic State Convention — Republican State Convention — Re-election of Governor Andrew — The President calls for Three Hundred Thousand more Volunteers — Extra Session of the Legislature called — Governor's Address — Bounties increased — Abstract of Laws 441–506

CHAPTER X.

The Military Camps in Massachusetts — Number of Troops Jan. 1, 1864 — Where Serving — Letter of Governor to Lewis Hayden — From Miss Upham — Soldier's Scrap-book — Letter to Samuel Hooper — Sale of Heavy Ordnance — The Condition of our Defences — Colonel Ritchie in England — Meeting of the Legislature — Organization — Addresses of Mr. Field and Colonel Bullock — Address of the Governor — Eloquent Extract — Abstract of Military Laws — Members of Congress — Letter to John B. Alley — The Springfield Companies — Secretary Stanton refuses to pay them Bounties — Correspondence in Regard to it — Letters from General Butler — Governor to Miss Upham — Complaints about Soldiers at Long Island — Re-enlisted Veterans — Order of War Department — Returns of Veteran Regiments — Their Reception — Letter to General Hancock — General Burnside reviews the Troops at Readville — Letter to the Christian Watchman — General Andrews — Surgeon-General Dale — Confederate Money — Letter from General Gordon — Battle of Olustee — Letter to Selectmen of Plymouth — A Second Volume of Scrap-book — Letter from Mr. Lovejoy — Lieutenant-Colonel Whittemore — Correspondence — The Heavy Artillery — Condition of Fort Warren — Misunderstanding — Secretary Stanton and the Governor — Colonel William F. Bartlett — His Promotion — Earnest Letter to Mr. Sumner — Troubles about Recruiting — Complaints made — A Convention held — Letter of the Adjutant-General — The Recruiting of New Regiments — Forwarded to the Front — The Advance of General Grant 507–559

CHAPTER XI.

General Position of Affairs at the Beginning of 1864 — Credits in the Navy — Law of Congress — Appointment of Commissioners — Circular Letter — Agents to Recruit in Rebel States — Letter to Mr. Everett — Governor Andrew in Washington — Pay of Colored Troops — Letter to the President — Letter to Mr. Stanton — Expectation of Rebel Attack on our Coast — Present of a Turtle — Brigadier-General Bartlett — Letter to Governor Seymour, of New York — Letter to the Secretary of War — Letter to the Attorney-General — Letter to Andrew Ellison — Colonel N. A. M. Dudley — Letter of Governor Yates, of Illinois — Case of Otis Newhall, of Lynn — Case of Mrs. Bixby, of Boston — Letter to the President — Plan to burn the Northern Cities — Speech of Mr. Everett — Destruction of the "Alabama" — Honors paid to Commodore Winslow — Donations for our Soldiers — Letter of Mr. Stebbins — Letter to the Union League Club, New York — Colored Officers — Letter to James A. Hamilton — Battle before Nashville — Case of Jack Flowers — National Conventions — Nominations — Republican State Convention — Proceedings — Renomination of Governor Andrew — Democratic State Convention — Nominations — Report of the Adjutant-General's Journey to the Front — Staff Appointments during the Year — Conclusion 560–608

CHAPTER XII.

Public Confidence — Meeting of the Legislature — Organization — Address of Governor Andrew — Acts passed by the Legislature — General Sargent — Death of Edward Everett — Frontier Cavalry — Governor and Secretary Stanton — Abolition of Slavery — Boston Harbor — Fast Day — Currency Question — Proclamation of President Lincoln — Case of a Deserter — Letter from Secretary Seward — Foreign Enlistments — The End of the Rebellion — Capitulation of General Lee — Rejoicings throughout the State — Governor sends a Message to the Legislature — Meeting in Faneuil Hall — Proposition for a National Thanksgiving — Death of President Lincoln — Action of the Legislature — Governor's Letter to Mrs. Lincoln — Original Copy of General Lee's Farewell Address, sent to the Governor by General Russell — Death of General Russell — Monument to the First Martyrs in Lowell — Address of the Governor — Letter to F. P. Blair, Sen. — Meeting at Faneuil Hall — Letter of the Governor — Reconstruction — Colonel William S. Lincoln — Memorial Celebration at Harvard — Letter to Mr. Motley, Minister to Austria — Miss Van Lew — Alexander H. Stephens — Governor to President Lincoln — Relics of Colonel Shaw — Letter to Colonel Theodore Lyman — State Prisoners in Maryland — Letter to James Freeman Clarke — Freedman's Bureau — Emigration South — Letter to General Sherman — Governor's Staff — Governor declines Re-election — Republican Convention — Democratic Convention — Reception of the Flags — Forefathers' Day — Speech of General Couch — Speech of Governor Andrew — Compliment to the Adjutant-General — General

CONTENTS.

Grant visits Massachusetts — Mrs. Harrison Gray Otis — Her Services — New-England Women's Auxiliary Association — What it did — New-England Rooms, New York — Massachusetts Soldiers' Fund — Boston Soldiers' Fund — Surgeon-General's Fund — Number of Men sent from Massachusetts to the War — Governor Andrew's Valedictory Address — Governor Bullock inaugurated — Last Military Order — Close of the Chapter 609–670

CIVIL AND MILITARY HISTORY

OF

MASSACHUSETTS IN THE REBELLION.

CIVIL AND MILITARY HISTORY

OF

MASSACHUSETTS IN THE REBELLION.

CHAPTER I.

Massachusetts — Civil Government — Election, 1860 — Legislature — President of the Senate — Speaker of the House — State of the Country — Farewell Address of Governor Banks — Governor Andrew's Inaugural — Their Views of the Crisis — Sketch of Governor Andrew — Lieutenant-Governor — Executive Council — Adjutant-General — Military Staff — Congressmen — The Volunteer Militia — Military Equipment — Early Preparations — Salutes, 8th of January — General Order No. 2 — Report of Adjutant-General — General Order No. 4 — Proceedings of the Legislature — Regular Session — Emergency Fund — Loan Credit of State — Delegates to Peace Convention — South Carolina to Massachusetts — Two thousand Overcoats — Order of Inquiry — Letter of Adjutant-General — Letter of Colonel Henry Lee, Jr. — Meeting of Officers in Governor's Room — Colonel Ritchie sent to Washington — His Letters to the Governor — Secretary Seward's Letter — Letter of Colonel Lee — Charter of Transports — John M. Forbes, Esq. — Meeting in Faneuil Hall — Meeting in Cambridge — Speech of Wendell Phillips, Esq., at New Bedford — Remarks — The President calls for Troops — The Eve of Battle.

To write the part taken by Massachusetts in the civil war which began in April, 1861, and continued until the capture, by General Grant, of Lee and his army in Virginia, and the surrender of Johnston and his forces to General Sherman in North Carolina, in 1865, requires patient research, a mind not distracted by other duties, and a purpose to speak truthfully of men and of events. Massachusetts bore a prominent part in this war, from the beginning to the end; not only in furnishing soldiers for the army, sailors for the navy, and financial aid to the Government, but in advancing ideas, which, though scouted nt in the early months of the war, were afterwards accepted by the nation, before the war could be brought to a successful end.

Massachusetts is a small State, in territory and in population. With the exception of Maine, it lies the farthest eastward of all the States in the Union. Its capital is four hundred and fifty miles east of Washington, and is separated from it by the States of Rhode Island, Connecticut, New York, New Jersey, Pennsylvania, Delaware, and Maryland. It contains seven thousand eight hundred square miles of land, river, lakes, and sea. In 1860, it had a population of 1,231,066, engaged in farming, manufacturing, fishing, and mercantile pursuits. Less than one-half the land is improved. It is about $\frac{1}{380}$ part of the whole Union, ranking the thirty-sixth in size among the forty States and Territories. It is divided into fourteen counties, and three hundred and thirty-five cities and towns. Its governor, lieutenant-governor, eight councillors, forty senators, and two hundred and forty representatives, are elected every year, in the month of November, by the free suffrage of the qualified voters.

The executive department of the Government is vested in the governor and Executive Council, — the governor, however, being the supreme executive magistrate, whose title is, *His Excellency;* the legislative, in a Senate and House of Representatives, each having a negative upon the other, and known and designated as the General Court. The judicial department is composed of different courts, the judges of which are appointed by the governor, and hold their offices during good behavior, and can only be removed upon the address of both houses of the Legislature, or by the abolishment of the court; this to " the end, that it may be a government of laws, and not of men."

In the election for governor, in 1860, there were four candidates and four political parties. John A. Andrew, of Boston, was the candidate of the Republicans; Erasmus D. Beach, of Springfield, of the Douglas wing of the Democrats; Amos A. Lawrence, of Boston, of the conservative party; and Benjamin F. Butler, of Lowell, of the Breckenridge wing of the Democratic party. John A. Andrew received 104,527 votes; Erasmus D. Beach, 35,191; Amos A. Lawrence, 23,816; Benjamin F. Butler, 6,000; all others, 75. Mr. Andrew's majority over all the opposing candidates was 39,445.

The eight councillors elected were all Republicans, as were all the members of Congress. The presidential electors in favor of the election of Abraham Lincoln and Hannibal Hamlin, for President and Vice-President of the United States, received about the same majority Mr. Andrew did for Governor. Nearly all of the members of the Senate and House of Representatives were of the Republican party.

The newly elected Legislature met on the first Wednesday in January, 1861. Hon. William Claflin, of Newton, was chosen President of the Senate, and Stephen N. Gifford, Esq., of Duxbury, clerk. Hon. John A. Goodwin, of Lowell, was chosen Speaker of the House of Representatives, and William Stowe, Esq., of Springfield, clerk.

On assuming the duties of President of the Senate, Mr. Claflin made a brief address, in the course of which he said, —

"While we meet under circumstances auspicious in our own State, a deep agitation pervades other parts of our country, causing every true patriot to feel the greatest anxiety. Disunion is attempted in some States, because, as is alleged, laws have been passed in others contrary to the Constitution of the United States. Massachusetts is accused of unfaithfulness in this matter in some of her enactments, although she has always been ready to submit to judicial decisions, and is so still. She has ever guarded jealously the liberties of her citizens, and, I trust, ever will. We cannot falter now without disgrace and dishonor. Whatever action we may take, let us be careful of the rights of others, but faithful to our trust, that we may return them to our constituents unimpaired."

Mr. Goodwin, on taking the Speaker's chair, referred to national affairs in the following words: —

"The session before us may become second in importance to none that has been held in these halls, since, threescore years ago, our fathers consecrated them to popular legislation. For the second time in our history, we see a State of our Union setting at naught the common compact, and raising the hand of remorseless violence against a whole section of her sister States, and against the Union itself. But for the *first* time in our history are unrebuked traitors seen in the high places of the nation, where, with undaunted front, they awe into treasonable inaction the hand the people have solemnly deputed to hold the scales of justice, and wield her imperial sword. To what points this ignominious crisis may compel our legislative attention, cannot now be stated; nor is it for the Chair to allude to particular measures of legislation. But it is to be remembered, that Massachusetts sacrificed much to establish the Union, and to defend and perpetuate it. She is ready to sacrifice more, provided it touch not her honor or the principles of free government, — principles interwoven with her whole history, and never dearer to the hearts of her people of all classes and parties than they are to-day. Let us approach this portion of our duties with coolness and deliberation, and with a generous patriotism."

Not since the days of the Revolution had a legislature assembled at a time of more imminent peril, when wise counsels, firm resolution, and patriotic devotion to the Constitution and the Union, were imperatively demanded. James Buchanan was still President of the United States; Floyd was Secretary of War; Cobb, Secretary of the Treasury; Thompson, Secretary of the Interior; and Toucey, who, although a New-England man, was believed to sympathize with the South, Secretary of the Navy. John C. Breckenridge was Vice-President of the United States, and presided over the deliberations of the Senate, of which Jefferson Davis, Judah P. Benjamin, John Slidell, James M. Mason, and Robert Toombs were members; all of whom proved traitors to the Government, were plotting daily and nightly to effect its overthrow, and to prevent the inauguration of Abraham Lincoln on the fourth of March. South Carolina had already voted itself out of the Union, and had assumed a hostile front to the Union garrison in Fort Sumter, in Charleston harbor. Other Southern States had called conventions to consider what steps they should take in the emergency which had been precipitated upon them by the South-Carolina secession ordinance. Our navy was scattered over far-off seas, the United-States arsenals were stripped of arms by orders from the Secretary of War, and the treasury of the General Government was well-nigh depleted by the Secretary of the Treasury.

The debates in Congress were warm and exciting. The speeches of the disunionists were rank with treason. The power of the North to prevent, by armed force, the South from seceding was sneered at and derided. Some of the Republicans in Congress replied with equal warmth and animation to the threats of the Southern men; others counselled moderation, and expressed a hope that the difficulties which threatened our peace might yet be adjusted. Prominent among those who expressed these views were Mr. Adams, of Massachusetts, and Mr. Seward, of New York. To gain time was a great point,— time to get Mr. Buchanan and his Cabinet out of power and out of Washington, and to get Mr. Lincoln and his new Cabinet into power and into Washington. I have good reason to believe, that neither of the distinguished statesmen whom I have named had a full belief that an appeal to arms could, for a great length of time, be avoided; but they felt, that, when it did come, it was all important that the Government should be in the hands of its friends, and not of its enemies. They argued, that, if the clash of arms could be put off until the inauguration of the new President on the fourth of March, the advantage to the Union side would be incalculable. It was wise strategy, as well as able statesmanship, so to guide the debates as to accomplish this great purpose; and to these two gentlemen acting in concert, one in the Senate and the other in the House, are we, in a great degree, indebted for the wise delay. Mr. Lincoln was inaugurated, and the Union ship of state was fairly launched, not indeed with fair winds and a clear sky, but with stout hands and wise heads to guide her course; and after long years of terrible disaster, and amid obstacles which at times appeared insurmountable, finally weathered them all, and was brought safely to a peaceful haven.

Hon. Nathaniel P. Banks was Governor of Massachusetts the three years immediately preceding the election and inauguration of John A. Andrew. His administration had been highly successful and popular. He had met public expectation on every point. Many important measures had been passed during his term; and, upon retiring from office, he deemed it proper "to present to the Legislature a statement of the condition of public affairs, with such considerations as his experience might suggest;" and enforced this departure from the course pursued by his predecessors in the gubernatorial office, with many cogent reasons. He delivered his valedictory address on the 3d of January, 1861, in which he gave a review of the legislation, and a statement of the finances of the State for the three years during which he had been the chief executive officer.

It is my purpose to speak upon but two of the topics discussed in the address, which have a direct bearing on the war which was so soon to open, and in which Governor Banks was to take a prominent part, as a major-general in the Union army.

The Legislature of 1858 had passed what was known as an act for the protection of personal liberty. It was intended to mitigate the harsh and unjust provisions of the act of Congress passed in 1850, known as the Fugitive-slave Law. Several persons, held in the South as slaves, had made their way to Massachusetts; and, being afterwards arrested, had been returned to their masters. The entire provisions of that act were abhorrent to our people, notwithstanding its friends and supporters claimed for it an exact conformity to the provisions of the Constitution of the United States.

The opinion of the Supreme Court of the United States, pronounced by Judge Story, himself a Massachusetts man, declared that the Constitution contemplated the existence of "a positive, unqualified right, on the part of the owner of the slave, which no State law or regulation can in any way qualify, regulate, control, or restrain." This opinion of the Supreme Court, Governor Banks said, "has been approved by the Legislature of this State, and confirmed by its Supreme Judicial Court." He then invited the attention of the Legislature to the sections of the State act relating to the writ of *habeas corpus* and the State act for the protection of personal liberty, which he thought conflicted with the act of Congress regarding fugitive slaves; and said "It is not my purpose to defend the constitutionality of the Fugitive-slave Act. The omission of a provision for jury trial, however harsh and cruel, cannot in any event be supplied by State legislation. While I am constrained to doubt the right of this State to enact such laws, I do not admit that, in any just sense, it is a violation of the national compact. It is only when unconstitutional legislation is enforced by executive authority, that it assumes that character, and no such result has occurred in this State."

He then remarked, that Massachusetts had given unimpeachable evidence of her devotion to law; and it was because she had been faithful that he wished to see her legislation in harmony with her acts. "It is because I do not like to see her representatives in Congress, and her sons everywhere, put upon the defensive when they have just cause to be proud of her loyalty; . . . it is because, in the face of her just claims to high honor, I do not love to hear unjust reproaches cast upon her fame, — that I say, as I do, in the presence of God, and with a heart filled with the responsibilities that must rest upon every American citizen in these distempered times, I cannot but regard the maintenance of a statute, although it may be within the extremest limits of constitutional power, which is so unnecessary to the public service and so detrimental to the public peace, as an inexcusable public wrong. I hope, by common consent, it may be removed from the statute-book, and such guaranties as individual freedom demands be sought in new legislation."

I have referred to these matters because they were prominent pretexts, made by the disunion party to justify a dissolution of the Union. The State acts named were condemned by many of our wisest men, who never had a thought unfriendly to the Union, nor would, by their acts or votes, sanction the existence of human slavery, or extend the area of its domain. The views of Governor Banks at this time are also important and interesting as in contrast to those expressed, a few days after, in the inaugural address of Governor Andrew.

Governor Banks, in concluding his address, referred in direct terms to the secession ordinance of South Carolina, and said, "While I would not withhold from the South what belongs to that section, I cannot consent that we should yield what belongs to us. The right to the Territories, so far as the people are concerned, must be a common right; and their *status* should be determined upon the rights of men, and not upon privileges of property." He was opposed to founding government upon the right to hold slaves. "There is no species of property entitled to such protection as will exclude men from Territories, aside from all considerations of property. Neither do I believe that a geographical line will give peace to the country. The lapse of time alone will heal all dissensions. There can be no peaceable secession of the States. The Government has pledged its faith to every land, and that pledge of faith cannot be broken." He drew encouragement from the thrill of joy which touched every true heart, when Major Anderson moved his little garrison from Fort Moultrie to Fort Sumter. "Certainly, never an act, so slight in itself, touched the hearts of so many millions of people like fire from heaven, as the recent simple, soldier-like, and patriotic movement of Major Anderson at Fort Moultrie." He closed this part of his address with these grand words: "But no such result can follow as the destruction of the American Government. The contest will be too terrible, the sacrifice too momentous, the difficulties in our path are too slight, the capacity of our people is too manifest, and the future too brilliant, to justify forebodings, or to excite permanent fears. The life of every man is lengthened by trial; and the strength of every government must be tested by revolt and revolution. I doubt not that the providence of God, that has protected us hitherto, will preserve us now and hereafter."

Throughout the entire address a hopeful feeling prevailed. The Governor evidently did not believe that we were so nigh the verge of civil war. He made no recommendation for the increase of the military force of the State, or to prepare that already organized for active service. It may properly be said, however, in this connection, that Governor Banks, upon retiring from office, did not deem it in good taste or proper to recommend legislative action to a body with which he was so soon to sever all official connection.

Shortly after retiring from the gubernatorial chair, Governor Banks made arrangements to remove to Illinois, having accepted a responsible executive position in the Illinois Central Railroad; but, in a few months, the country required his services as a military commander, which post he accepted, and continued in high command until the end of the war, when he returned to Massachusetts, and was elected to Congress by the people of his old district.

John A. Andrew, Esq., of Boston, was inaugurated Governor of the Commonwealth, Jan. 5, 1861, and immediately delivered his address to the Legislature, in which he gave a statement of the financial condition of the Commonwealth, its liabilities, and its resources to meet them. The State was practically free of debt. The aggregate valuation of taxable property was within a fraction of nine hundred millions, a computation of which had been made by a special committee appointed for the purpose, whose labors had closed on the 1st of January, 1861, only five days before the address was delivered. After asking the attention of the Legislature to matters of a purely local character, Governor Andrew devoted the remainder of his address to matters of more general interest. He discussed the right of the Legislature to pass the statutes concerning personal liberty and the *habeas corpus*, and contended that Massachusetts had a clear right to pass them; and that, if properly understood and rightfully carried out, there could not be any conflict of jurisdiction between the State and Federal officers. The argument upon these questions extends through nine pages, and concludes as follows: —

"Supposing, however, that our legislation in this behalf is founded in mistake, the Legislature will only have endeavored to perform their duty towards the citizens whom they were bound to shield from unlawful harm. The power to obtain the judgment of the court affords ample redress to all claimants. Should a critical examination disclose embarrassments in raising and reserving questions of law for the appropriate tribunals, the Legislature will readily repair the error.

"In dismissing this topic, I have only to add, that in regard, not only to one, but to every subject bearing on her Federal relations, Massachusetts has always conformed to her honest understanding of all constitutional obligations; that she has always conformed to the judicial decisions; has never threatened either to nullify or to disobey; and that the decision of one suit, fully contested, constitutes a precedent for the future."

The concluding ten pages of the address give a graphic, condensed, truthful, and eloquent review of the condition of the country, of the danger and wickedness of a civil war, and of the position which Massachusetts and her great statesmen have always held in regard to them. He said, —

"Inspired by the same ideas and emotions which commanded the fraternization of Jackson and Webster on another great occasion of public danger, the people of Massachusetts, confiding in the patriotism of their brethren in other States, accept this issue, and respond, in the words of Jackson, ' *The Federal Union : it must be preserved !* '

"Until we complete the work of rolling back this wave of rebellion, which threatens to engulf the Government, overthrow democratic institutions, subject the people to the rule of a minority, if not of mere military despotism, and, in some communities, to endanger the very existence of civilized society, we cannot turn aside, and we will not turn back. It is to those of our brethren in the disaffected States, whose mouths are closed by a temporary reign of terror, not less than to ourselves, that we owe this labor, which, with the help of Providence, it is our duty to perform.

"I need not add, that whatever rights pertain to any person under the Constitution of the Union are secure in Massachusetts while the Union shall endure; and whatever authority or function pertains to the Federal Government for the maintenance of any such right is an authority or function which neither the Government nor the people of this Commonwealth can or would usurp, evade, or overthrow; and Massachusetts demands, and has a right to demand, that her sister States shall likewise respect the constitutional rights of her citizens within their limits."

I have given these extracts from the addresses of Governors Banks and Andrew, that their official opinions in regard to important national questions, expressed on the eve of a great war, might be made fresh in the memories of men. Both gentlemen expressed the true sentiment of Massachusetts. I have taken their words as a base or starting-point to begin the long, grand story of Massachusetts in the Rebellion.

As Governor Andrew was at the head of the State Government during the entire period of the war, he of course was and ever will be the prominent, central figure in the galaxy of gentlemen, civil and military, who, by their services and sacrifices, gave renown to the Commonwealth, and carried her with imperishable honor through the conflict.

John A. Andrew was the twenty-first Governor of Massachusetts since the adoption of the Constitution of the State in 1780. He was born at Windham, in the District of Maine, about fifteen miles from Portland, on the 31st of May, 1818. The family was of English origin, descending from Robert Andrew, of Rowley village, now Boxford, Essex County, Mass., who died there in 1668. He was connected with most of the ancient families of the Colony of Massachusetts Bay. The grandmother of Governor Andrew was the grand-daughter of the brave Captain William Pickering, who commanded the Province Galley, in 1707, for the protection of the fisheries against the French and Indians; and the mother of her husband was Mary Higginson, a direct descendant of the Reverend Francis Higginson, the famous pastor of the first church in the colony. The grandfather of Governor Andrew was a silversmith in Salem, who removed to Windham, where he died. His son Jonathan was born in Salem, and lived there until manhood, when he also removed to Windham. There he married Miss Nancy G. Pierce, formerly preceptress of Fryeburg Academy, where Daniel Webster was once a teacher. These were the parents of Governor Andrew.

At an early age, he entered Bowdoin College, from which he graduated in the class of 1837. He then removed to Boston, and entered, as a law student, the office of Henry H. Fuller, Esq. Being admitted to the Suffolk Bar in 1840, he commenced the practice of his profession, and adhered to it without interruption until his election as Governor in 1860, establishing in later years a reputation as an advocate second to no lawyer at that distinguished bar since the death of Rufus Choate. Attractive in personal appearance and bearing, with an excellent flow of language and variety of expression, and possessed of that sympathetic disposition which identifies an advocate in feeling and in action with the cause of his client, his merits were eminent as an advocate before juries; but the causes in connection with which his reputation as a lawyer had become chiefly known beyond legal circles, were those of arguments before Massachusetts courts, and the United-States courts for the district and circuit, on questions of political significance. He defended the parties indicted in 1854, for an attempt to rescue the fugitive slave Burns, and succeeded in quashing the indictments on which they were arraigned. The following year, he successfully defended the British consul at Boston against a charge of violating the neutrality laws of the United States during the Crimean War. In 1856, co-operating with counsel from Ohio, he made a noted application to Judge Curtis, of the United-States Supreme Court, for a writ of *habeas corpus*, to test the authority by which the Free-State prisoners were held confined in Kansas by Federal officers. More lately, in 1859, he initiated and directed the measures to procure suitable counsel for the defence of John Brown in Virginia; and, in 1860, was counsel for Hyatt and Sanborn, witnesses summoned before Senator Mason's committee of investigation into the John-Brown affair. Upon his argument, the latter was discharged by the Supreme Court of Massachusetts from the custody of the United-States marshal, by whose deputy he had been arrested under a warrant issued at the instigation of that committee. Being himself, about the same time, summoned before the committee, he appeared at Washington, and rendered his testimony. Nor had he hesitated, under his theory of his duties as a lawyer, to defend causes appealing less directly to his sympathies, or even positively repugnant to them. Among others, besides the instance of the British consul before mentioned, may be named his advocacy, in 1860, of the right of Mr. Burnham, against the inquisition of a committee of the Massachusetts Legislature; and also his defence, the same year, in the United-States District and Circuit Courts, of the notorious slaver-yacht "Wanderer" against forfeiture.

This brilliant legal career was a result of uninterrupted devotion to a profession which always demands constancy as a condition of success. Although warmly interested from an early age in the course of public affairs, and often taking part in political assemblies, — until 1848 as a Whig, in that year passing into the Free-Soil party, and in 1854 uniting naturally with the Republicans, — it was not until 1858 that he consented to accept political office. In the autumn campaign of the pre-

nificance. He defended the parties indicted in 1854, for an attempt to rescue the fugitive slave Burns, and succeeded in quashing the indictments on which they were arraigned. The following year, he successfully defended the British consul at Boston against a charge of violating the neutrality laws of the United States during the Crimean War. In 1856, co-operating with counsel from Ohio, he made a noted application to Judge Curtis, of the United-States Supreme Court, for a writ of *habeas corpus*, to test the authority by which the Free-State prisoners were held confined in Kansas by Federal officers. More lately, in 1859, he initiated and directed the measures to procure suitable counsel for the defence of John Brown in Virginia; and, in 1860, was counsel for Hyatt and Sanborn, witnesses summoned before Senator Mason's committee of investigation into the John-Brown affair. Upon his argument, the latter was discharged by the Supreme Court of Massachusetts from the custody of the United-States marshal, by whose deputy he had been arrested under a warrant issued at the instigation of that committee. Being himself, about the same time, summoned before the committee, he appeared at Washington, and rendered his testimony. Nor had he hesitated, under his theory of his duties as a lawyer, to defend causes appealing less directly to his sympathies, or even positively repugnant to them. Among others, besides the instance of the British consul before mentioned, may be named his advocacy, in 1860, of the right of Mr. Burnham, against the inquisition of a committee of the Massachusetts Legislature; and also his defence, the same year, in the United-States District and Circuit Courts, of the notorious slaver-yacht "Wanderer" against forfeiture.

This brilliant legal career was a result of uninterrupted devotion to a profession which always demands constancy as a condition of success. Although warmly interested from an early age in the course of public affairs, and often taking part in political assemblies, — until 1848 as a Whig, in that year passing into the Free-Soil party, and in 1854 uniting naturally with the Republicans, — it was not until 1858 that he consented to accept political office. In the autumn campaign of the previous year, resulting in the overthrow of the Know-Nothing party, by which Massachusetts had been ruled since 1854, he had sustained an active part. The former political issues being revived by the dissolution of that organization after its defeat, he consented to be chosen to the Legislature of 1858. Mr. Andrew was at once recognized as the leader of his party in the House. The leader of the opposition was Hon. Caleb Cushing, of Newburyport, formerly member of Congress, and the Attorney-General of the United States under President Pierce. At the close of the session, Mr. Andrew returned to his profession, refusing to permit his name to be used as a candidate for Governor, and declined also an election to the Legislature, and an appointment, tendered him by Governor Banks, of a seat on the bench of the Superior Court. In the spring of 1860, he was unanimously selected to head the delegation from Massachusetts to the Republican National Convention at Chicago. As chairman of the delegation, he cast the vote of the State for Mr. Seward until the final ballot, when it was thrown for Mr. Lincoln. That fall he was nominated by the Republican State Convention for Governor, and was elected by the majority we have already stated, in the largest popular vote ever cast in the State.

This, in brief, was the life of Governor Andrew, up to the time he entered upon the duties of 'Governor of this Commonwealth.

Associated with him on the ticket as Lieutenant-Governor was Hon. John Z. Goodrich, of West Stockbridge, who, being afterwards appointed Collector of the Port of Boston, resigned on the 29th of March, 1861. Oliver Warner, of Northampton, was elected Secretary of State; Henry K. Oliver, of Salem, Treasurer and Receiver-General; Dwight Foster, of Worcester, Attorney-General; and Levi Reed, of Abington, Auditor of Accounts. Jacob Sleeper, of Boston; John I. Baker, of Beverly; James M. Shute, of Somerville; Hugh M. Greene, of Northfield; Joel Hayden, of Williamsburg; James Ritchie, of Roxbury; Oakes Ames, of Easton; and Eleazer C. Sherman, of Plymouth, — were elected Councillors. William Schouler, of Lynn, was Adjutant-General, to which office he had been appointed by Governor Banks; he was also acting Quartermaster and Inspector-General of the Commonwealth, — the entire duties of which offices he performed with the assistance of William Brown, of Boston, clerk, and one man, who had charge of the State arsenal at Cambridge, in which were deposited the arms and munitions of war belonging to the Commonwealth, except those which were loaned to the companies of active militia, and cared for in their several armories.

The personal military staff of the Governor was limited by law to four aides-de-camp, each with the rank and title of lieutenant-colonel. Governor Andrew appointed, as his military aids, Horace Binney Sargent, of West Roxbury (senior aid); Harrison Ritchie, of Boston; John W. Wetherell, of Worcester; and Henry Lee, Jr., of Brookline. Colonel Sargent had served on the staff of Governor Banks. He remained on the staff of Governor Andrew until he was commissioned lieutenant-colonel of the First Regiment of Massachusetts Cavalry, in August, 1861, when Colonel Ritchie became senior aid, and John Quincy Adams, of Quincy, was appointed to fill the vacancy.

Massachusetts was represented in the Thirty-sixth Congress, which ended March 4, 1861, by Charles Sumner and Henry Wilson, in the Senate, and by Thomas D. Elliot, James Buffinton, Charles Francis Adams, Alexander H. Rice, Anson Burlingame, John B. Alley, Daniel W. Gooch, Charles R. Train, Eli Thayer, Charles Delano, and Henry L. Dawes, in the House of Representatives.

Before the war, and during the war, Mr. Sumner was chairman of the Committee on Foreign Affairs, and Mr. Wilson of the Militia and Military Affairs, two of the most important committees of that body, which positions they now hold.

In the Thirty-seventh Congress, which terminated March 4, 1863, Benjamin F. Thomas succeeded Mr. Adams, who resigned his seat upon receiving the appointment of Minister to England, Samuel Hooper succeeded Mr. Burlingame, who was appointed Minister to China, and Goldsmith F. Bailey succeeded Mr. Thayer.

In the Thirty-eighth Congress, which terminated March 4th, 1865, Oakes Ames succeeded Mr. Buffinton, George S.

Boutwell Mr. Train, James D. Baldwin Mr. Bailey, (deceased) and William B. Washburn Mr. Delano.

In the Thirty-ninth Congress, Mr. Gooch having accepted a government appointment, Ex-Governor Banks was elected to fill the vacancy.

These Congresses extend over the period immediately preceding the war, and that of its duration and close. The Massachusetts Senators and Representatives served with distinction on several of the most important committees, and thus were prominent in perfecting bills and shaping the legislation of Congress. It does not, however, come within the scope of this volume to speak of their varied and valuable services in behalf of the Union, although, if properly recorded, they would add materially to the renown of the Commonwealth. The story of their services will hereafter be told by the historian of the nation, for it was the nation, and not merely a part, that they served.

The whole number of enrolled militia of the Commonwealth, in 1860, was 155,389; and the number of the active or volunteer militia, 5,593. The active force was organized into three divisions and six brigades; nine regiments and three battalions of infantry; three battalions and eight unattached companies of riflemen; one battalion and five unattached companies of cavalry. Officers and men found their own uniforms. The State furnished arms and equipments, except to officers. Each company had an armory for the deposit of its arms, and for drill purposes, the rents of which were paid by the Commonwealth.

The State, on the 1st of January, 1861, had at the arsenal at Cambridge, and distributed to the active militia, seventy-one field-pieces, of various calibre, and about ten thousand serviceable muskets, twenty-five hundred of which were of the most approved pattern of the Springfield rifled musket, which, as a muzzle-loading arm, is the best in the world.

It was plain, from the tenor of his inaugural address, that Governor Andrew believed war between the North and South was imminent. He advised, among other things, an inquiry, whether, in addition to the active volunteer militia, the dormant militia, or some considerable portion of it, should not be placed on a footing of activity. "For how otherwise," he asks, "in the possible contingencies of the future, can we be sure that Massachusetts has taken care to preserve the manly self-reliance of the citizens, by which alone, in the long-run, can the creation of standing armies be averted, and the State also be ready, without inconvenient delay, to contribute her share of force in any exigency of public danger?"

But it was not alone in his address that he foreshadowed his belief of the approach of war. It would not have been wise to make known publicly his inmost thoughts. Let actions speak. On the evening of the very day on which his inaugural address was delivered (Jan. 5), he despatched confidential messages, by trustworthy messengers, to each of the Governors of the New-England States, urging preparation for the approaching crisis. Early in December, soon after the meeting of Congress, he had visited Washington, and personally acquainted himself with the aspect of national affairs, and with the views of the principal representatives both of North and South. After his return, he had opened a confidential correspondence on matters transpiring there, with Hon. Charles Francis Adams, who kept him minutely acquainted, from day to day, with the progress of events. One of the suggestions of Mr. Adams was, that there should be public demonstrations of loyalty throughout New England, and it was proposed by him to have salutes fired in each of the States on the 8th of January, the anniversary of General Jackson's victory at New Orleans. Colonel Wardrop, of New Bedford, Third Regiment Massachusetts Volunteer Militia, was sent to Governor Fairbanks, of Vermont; and other messengers were sent to Rhode Island, Connecticut, New Hampshire, and Maine, for this purpose. One of these messengers was the gentleman who afterwards became Governor Andrew's private military secretary, — Colonel Albert G. Browne, of Salem, — and who served him during the entire war; and who, for ability as a ready writer, truthfulness, sturdy independence, reticence, and undoubted patriotism, deserved, as he received, the respect and confidence of the Governor, the entire staff, and of gentlemen holding confidential and important relations with His Excellency. Colonel Browne's mission was to confer with Governor Goodwin, of New Hampshire, and Governor Washburn, of Maine. Besides the mere duty of organizing public demonstrations, he was intrusted, as to the Governor of Maine with a mission of a far more important character. Maine and Massachusetts, being subject to a common State government until 1820, sustained peculiar relations to each other, by similarity of legislation, institutions, and, in later years, of political sentiment. Colonel Browne was intrusted with the whole of the private correspondence with Mr. Adams before mentioned, and was directed to lay it confidentially before Governor Washburn; to advise him, that, in Governor Andrew's judgment, civil war was the *inevitable* result of the events going on at Washington and in the South; that the safety of Washington was already threatened; that the policy of the Executive government of Massachusetts, under the new administration, would be to put its active militia into readiness at once for the impending crisis, and persuade the Legislature, if possible, to call part of the dormant militia into activity; and to urge Governor Washburn to adopt the same policy for Maine. Leaving Boston on the evening of Saturday, Jan. 5, Colonel Browne, after an interview with Governor Goodwin, at Portsmouth on Sunday, reached Augusta on Jan. 7, and held his interview with Governor Washburn. By him, Adjutant-General John L. Hodsdon, and United States Senator Lot M. Morrill were called into consultation, and the answer was returned; that, "wherever Massachusetts leads, Maine will follow close, if she can't keep abreast."

Thus Governor Andrew, on the very day of his inauguration, placed himself in confidential relations with each of the Governors of New England, which continued through the entire rebellion, and were of mutual benefit.

On the 6th of January, the day after the inauguration, Governor Andrew directed the Adjutant-General to issue General Order No. 2, which was promulgated the next day, and properly executed on the eighth.

HEAD-QUARTERS, BOSTON, Jan. 7, 1861.

GENERAL ORDER NO. 2.

In commemoration of the brave defenders of New Orleans, Jan. 8, 1815, by the deceased patriot, General Jackson, and in honor of the gallant conduct and wise foresight of Major Anderson, now in command of Fort Sumter, in the State of South Carolina, His Excellency John A. Andrew, Governor and Commander-in-chief, orders, that a salute of one hundred guns be fired on Boston Common, at twelve, meridian, on Tuesday, Jan. 8th inst., and a national salute be fired, at the same time, for the same purposes, in Charlestown, Lexington, Concord, Waltham, Roxbury, Marblehead, Newburyport, Salem, Groton, Lynn, Worcester, Greenfield, Northampton, Fall River, and Lowell.

. . . .

By command of His Excellency John A. Andrew, Governor and Commander-in-chief.

WILLIAM SCHOULER, *Adjutant-General.*

The purpose of firing these salutes was to revive old patriotic memories. The 8th of January had been held a holiday by the Democratic party since the presidency of General Jackson; though of late years it had been, in a great measure, passed over without special regard. The association of the first battle-fields of the Revolution with the last and most brilliant action of the war of 1812 and the patriotic movement of Major Anderson in Charleston Harbor, would, it was believed, revive pleasant recollections of the past, and serve to unite the North in support of the Constitution and the Union.

As required by law, the Adjutant-General had made his annual report in December., It was addressed to Governor Banks, and is dated Dec. 31, 1860. On pages 37 and 38 he says, —

"Events have transpired in some of the Southern States and at Washington, which have awakened the attention of the people of Massachusetts, in a remarkable degree, to the perpetuity of the Federal Union, which may require the active militia of the Commonwealth to be greatly augmented. Should our worst fears be realized, and this nation plunged into the horrors of civil war, upon Massachusetts may rest, in no inconsiderable degree, the duty of staying the effusion of blood, and of rolling back the black tide of anarchy and ruin. She did more than her share to achieve the independence of our country, and establish the Government under which we have risen to such unparalleled prosperity, and become the Great Power of the American Continent; and she will be true to her history, her traditions, and her fair fame. Should it become necessary to increase the number of her active militia to a war footing, the present organization offers an easy and a good means. The present companies could be filled to their full complement of men, and the regiments to their full complement of companies; new regiments of infantry, new battalions of riflemen, new companies of artillery and cavalry, could be formed, with which to fill the several brigades, and make our present divisions five thousand men each, with proper apportionment of the several military arms. This, of course, would require a large outlay of money, which would doubtless be cheerfully met by our people, if their honor and the welfare of the country demand it of them."

The Adjutant-General then suggested, "that a board of officers be called, as provided in section one hundred and sixty-three, chapter thirteen, of the General Statutes, to consider and recommend such changes as their judgment shall approve, and their experience suggest."—"In the mean time," he said, "I would suggest, that a general order be issued, calling upon commanders of the active force to forward to head-quarters the names of the persons composing their commands, also their places of residence, so that a complete roll of each company may be on file in this department. The companies that have not their full quota of men should be filled by new enlistments to the number fixed by law; and, whenever new enlistments are made or discharges given, the names of the persons enlisted and discharged should be forwarded immediately to head-quarters, and placed on file."

Governor Banks, to whom the report was addressed, retired from office four days after it was printed, and before any action could be taken upon the recommendations made. They looked to a greatly increased active militia force, and are the first suggestions that were made in an official form for strengthening the military force of the Commonwealth, and placing it upon a war footing.

Governor Andrew adopted these suggestions; and on the 16th of January, eleven days after his inauguration, directed the Adjutant-General to issue General Order No. 4, which created a great interest throughout the State, and especially among the active militia.

COMMONWEALTH OF MASSACHUSETTS.
HEAD-QUARTERS, BOSTON, Jan. 16, 1861.

GENERAL ORDER NO. 4.

Events which have recently occurred, and are now in progress, require that Massachusetts should be at all times ready to furnish her quota upon any requisition of the President of the United States, to aid in the maintenance of the laws and the peace of the Union. His Excellency the Commander-in-chief therefore orders, —

That the commanding officer of each company of volunteer militia examine with care the roll of his company, and cause the name of each member, together with his rank and place of residence, to be properly recorded, and a copy of the same to be forwarded to the office of the Adjutant-General. Previous to which, commanders of companies shall make strict inquiry, whether there are men in their commands, who from age, physical defect, business, or family causes, may be unable or indisposed to respond at once to the orders of the Commander-in-chief, made in response to the call of the President of the United States, that they be forthwith discharged; so that their places may be filled by men ready for any public exigency which may arise, whenever called upon.

After the above orders shall have been fulfilled, no discharge, either of officer or private, shall be granted, unless for cause satisfactory to the Commander-in-chief.

If any companies have not the number of men allowed by law, the commanders of the same shall make proper exertions to have the vacancies filled, and the men properly drilled and uniformed, and their names and places of residence forwarded to head-quarters.

To promote the objects embraced in this order, the general, field, and staff officers, and the Adjutant and acting Quartermaster General will give all the aid and assistance in their power.

Major-Generals Sutton, Morse, and Andrews will cause this order to be promulgated throughout their respective divisions.

By command of His Excellency John A. Andrew, Governor and Commander-in-chief.

WILLIAM SCHOULER, *Adjutant-General.*

The order was generally well received, and immediately acted upon. Some of the newspapers attacked it, as unnecessary and sensational; but it was sustained as proper. The active militia responded with alacrity. Meetings were held in their armories, the rolls called; and the men who could not respond, should a call be made to march, were honorably discharged, and their places filled by active men who could. The corrected rolls were forwarded to head-quarters. Only one company sent in a political argumentative answer, which was drawn up with ability, and was evidently written by a Southern sympathizer. The document made several pages of manuscript. The Adjutant-General returned it to the officer, with the remark, that the paper was disrespectful in its tone and language to the Commander-in-chief, and in violation of the first principles of military law. He would give him an opportunity either to modify it or to withdraw it entirely. If a satisfactory response was not received within a reasonable time, the matter would be laid before His Excellency the Governor; and the probability was, the officers of the company would be discharged, and the company disbanded. In a few days, a proper answer was made; and the officer with his company, before the end of the year, were mustered into the service for three years, and were sent to the Department of the Gulf, where they did good service.

From the day that General Order No. 4 was issued, a new spirit and zeal imbued our volunteer force. Applications also came from different parts of the Commonwealth for permission to raise new companies. A general impression prevailed, that we were on the perilous edge of battle, and it was the duty of Massachusetts to be ready to meet the crisis. In the mean time, the Governor, who believed from the first that war would ensue, was obtaining information, from every available source, that would be of use, and which could guide him wisely in his course.

The first movement made in the Legislature in relation to national or military matters was a resolution which was offered in the House on the 11th of January, six days after Governor Andrew's inauguration, and a day or two after the Speaker had announced the standing committees; which was in effect, " that it is the universal sentiment of the people of Massachusetts, that the President should enforce the execution of the laws of the United States, defend the Union, protect national property; " and, to this end, the State " cheerfully tenders her entire means, civil and military, to enable him to do so." This was referred to the Committee on Federal Relations.

Jan. 12. Mr. Slocum, of Grafton, offered a resolution, directing the Committee on the Militia to inquire whether the militia laws of this State were in accordance with the Constitution and laws of the United States.

In the Senate, Jan. 14, the Committee on the Militia reported a bill of three sections to increase the volunteer force, which was discussed on the 15th and 16th, and finally recommitted to the committee, together with all the amendments that had been proposed.

On the same day (14th), Mr. George T. Davis, of Greenfield, introduced a bill " to prevent hostile invasions of other States ; " the purpose of which was to prevent, by fine and imprisonment, persons who should set on foot any unlawful scheme, military or naval, to invade any State or Territory of the Union. This was referred to the Committee on Federal Relations, but never was passed.

Jan. 18. *In the Senate.* — Mr. Cole, of Berkshire, from the Committee on Federal Relations, reported a series of resolutions, the purport of which was, to stand by the Union, and tendering to the President of the United States such aid, in men and money, as he may require. On motion of Mr. Northend, of Essex, the rules were suspended, and the resolves passed the Senate by a unanimous vote.

On the same day, Mr. Parker, of Worcester, introduced in the House a new militia bill, which was referred to the committee on that subject.

Jan. 19. *In Senate.* — Mr. Northend introduced a series of resolutions, to the effect that the Constitution of the United States was the supreme law of the land ; that the recent acts of South Carolina are revolutionary and treasonable ; and that this Government must be maintained at all hazards.

Referred to the Committee on Federal Relations.

The same day, a long debate took place in the House, on a bill to increase the militia, but without coming to a vote.

Jan. 21. *In Senate.* — Mr. Walker, of Worcester, introduced a resolution to inquire whether there were parties in this

Commonwealth making arms or ammunition, to be sold to the agents of States now or likely to be in rebellion, with power to send for persons and papers. Adopted.

Same day, a debate occurred in the House on the Militia Bill; but, without taking a vote, the bill was recommitted.

Jan. 23. *In Senate.* — Mr. Schouler, of Middlesex, offered an order, which was adopted, directing the Adjutant-General to furnish estimates, for the use of the Legislature, of the cost of furnishing 2,000 overcoats, 2,000 blankets, 2,000 knapsacks, and camp equipage for a force of 2,000 men, when in active service.

In the House, same day, Mr. Coffin, of Newburyport, reported the Militia Bill in a new draft.

Same day, the Governor sent a communication to the House, informing it of the tender of the Sixth Regiment, by Colonel Jones, for immediate service, if required.

Jan. 24. *In Senate.* — A message was received from the Governor, transmitting the proposition from the Legislature of Virginia, for the appointment of commissioners to meet at Washington on the 4th of February, to agree upon a compromise of the national difficulties. Referred to the Committee on Federal Relations, and ordered to be printed.

Jan. 26. *In Senate.* — Mr. Davis, of Bristol, offered this order: —

"That the Committee on the Judiciary be instructed to forthwith report a bill authorizing the authorities of this Commonwealth to indorse and guarantee the treasury notes of the United States to the full amount of the surplus revenue received by Massachusetts in the year 1837."

Some opposition was made to the order, but it was adopted.

Jan. 28. *In the House.* — Mr. Pierce, of Dorchester, introduced resolutions to sustain the Union; and that all attempts to overthrow it, with the expectation of reconstructing it anew, were vain and illusory.

Referred to the Committee on Federal Relations.

Jan. 29. *In Senate.* — A message was received from the Governor, transmitting certain resolutions passed by the States of Pennsylvania and Tennessee; also the Ordinance of Secession of the State of Georgia, adopted by a convention of the people of that State, and forwarded to Governor Andrew by George W. Crawford, president of that convention. After some debate, it was voted to print the message of Governor Andrew and the resolutions from the two States, but not to further notice the Secession Ordinance.

A debate then arose upon passing the bill for Massachusetts to indorse the notes of the United States to the amount of our indebtedness on account of the surplus revenue, which, after debate, was rejected, — yeas 14, nays 19. The reason for rejecting the bill was stated by Mr. Hardy, of Norfolk. "He did not like to have it put on record that old Massachusetts came to the Federal Government in the hour of distress, and said that she would loan her all she owed, and no more. He was in favor of giving all that the Government needed, as far as it was possible, — two, three, or four millions."

Same day, in the House, the bill to increase the militia was further debated, and a substitute for the whole bill, offered by Mr. Banfield, of West Roxbury, was adopted, and passed to a third reading by a vote of 116 to 40. This bill, however, did not become a law.

Jan. 30. *In Senate.* — On motion of Mr. Hardy, of Norfolk, the bill in relation to loaning the State credit to the United States, which was rejected yesterday, was re-considered; and he offered a new proposition, as follows: —

"That the Treasurer and Receiver-General of the Commonwealth be and hereby is authorized to guarantee, upon the request of the Secretary of the Treasury of the United States, the treasury bonds of the United States to the amount of $2,000,000, on such conditions as shall be agreed upon by the Secretary of the Treasury of the United States, and the Governor and Council of this Commonwealth."

Mr. Boynton, of Worcester, thought the passage of the bill would indicate that the credit of the United States is not good, and we must indorse it to make it good. He did not think it necessary to take such a step before it is called for. He thought it was "a Union-saving" movement, and would do more to our discredit than to the good of the country.

Mr. Hardy said it was not only a movement in behalf of the

Union, but a matter of business. It is true, the General Government is bankrupt. Massachusetts can help by her notes or her indorsement; and, instead of bending the knee or rolling in the dust before the South, it is putting backbone into the Government. It shows that Massachusetts has faith in the General Government.

Mr. Boynton was opposed to giving any aid to the present Administration (Buchanan's). When we have a new Administration that we can trust, he thought it would be time enough to talk about lending money.

Mr. Davis, of Bristol, moved to amend the bill so that it would take effect immediately upon its passage. The amendment was carried, and the bill was passed to a third reading.

On motion of Mr. Schouler, of Middlesex, the bill was ordered to be printed.

Jan. 30. *In the House.* — The Senate Militia Bill came up in order. Mr. Durfee, of New Bedford, moved to strike out all after the enacting clause, and to substitute a bill of his own. The subject was then laid on the table, and the bill and amendment ordered to be printed.

Jan. 31. *In Senate.* — A communication was received from the Adjutant-General, in accordance with a joint resolution of the Legislature, adopted on the 23d inst., giving the following estimates of equipping 2,000 men for active service: 2,000 overcoats, at $9 each, $18,000; 2,000 knapsacks, at $2.25 each, $4,500; 2,000 blankets, at $3 each, $6,000; camp equipage (exclusive of tents), $3,000, — total, $31,500.

On motion of Mr. Schouler, of Middlesex, the communication was laid on the table, and ordered to be printed.

Feb. 1. *In Senate.* — Mr. Whitney, of Plymouth, from the Committee on Federal Relations, reported a bill to create an emergency fund for the Governor of $100,000, to take effect upon its passage. The bill was immediately passed through the several stages, under a suspension of the rules.

The communication of the Adjutant-General was taken from the table, and referred to the Joint Standing Committee on the Militia.

In the House, the Militia Bill was discussed. Several amendments were offered by Mr. Quincy, of Boston, which were lost. The substitute offered by Mr. Durfee, of New Bedford, was also voted down; and the bill in the draft offered by Mr. Banfield, of West Roxbury, was ordered to be engrossed.

Mr. Parker, of Worcester, moved to reconsider the vote by which the bill was passed. Placed on the orders of the day.

Saturday, Feb. 2. *In the House.* — The motion to reconsider the vote by which the Militia bill was ordered to be engrossed was carried; and, on motion of Mr. Hills, of Boston, it was recommitted to the Committee on the Militia.

On leave, Mr. Smith, of Boston, introduced a new bill in relation to the militia; and that also was referred to the Committee on the Militia.

Mr. Tyler, of Boston, from the Finance Committee, reported to the House the Senate bill creating an emergency fund of $100,000. He moved that the rules be suspended, that it might take its several readings at once.

Mr. Parsons, of Lawrence, opposed the suspension of the rules, on the ground that a bill of so much importance should be carefully considered.

Mr. Slack, of Boston, thought extraordinary circumstances demanded extraordinary measures, and alluded briefly to the present state of national affairs.

On motion of Mr. Davis, of Greenfield, the House went into secret session. During the secret session, the motion to suspend the rules prevailed; and the bill took its several readings, and was ordered to be engrossed.

Feb. 2. — The Senate debated the resolves for the appointment of seven commissioners to proceed to Washington to confer with the General Government, or with commissioners from other States, upon the state of the country. These resolves were reported in accordance with the invitation of the General Assembly of Virginia. The debate in the Senate was very able: the proposition being sustained by Messrs. Northend and Stone, of Essex; Davis, of Bristol; and Hardy, of Norfolk; and opposed by Mr. Whiting, of Plymouth. The resolves passed, — yeas 24, nays 6. The bill provided, that the commissioners should be appointed by the Governor, and should make their report to the Legislature.

In the House, resolutions of a similar character were introduced by Mr. Parker, of Worcester. They were supported by Mr. Davis, of Greenfield, and Mr. Parker; and opposed by Mr. Branning, of Lee. Before coming to any conclusion, the resolves which had passed the Senate reached the House. Mr. Parker's were laid on the table, and the Senate resolves were discussed. After a long debate on a motion to suspend the rules, which was lost, — yeas 104, nays 65, not two-thirds, — the House adjourned.

Tuesday, Feb. 5. *In the House.* — The Senate resolves for the appointment of commissioners were, on motion of Mr. Davis, of Greenfield, taken from the orders of the day, and considered. He said the resolves met with his entire approbation.

Mr. Slocum, of Grafton, said, with all respect for Virginia, he could not abide by her opinions, since they might desecrate the soil of Massachusetts to slavery; rather than that, said he, let blood come. He moved an amendment.

Mr. Wallis, of Bolton, favored the amendment.

Mr. Gifford, of Provincetown, opposed it, and favored the resolutions. "He had no fears that Massachusetts would act at the bidding of Virginia or any other State."

Mr. French, of Waltham, favored the amendment, which was, in substance, that Massachusetts did not agree with Virginia that the Constitution required amendment to guarantee to each State its rights.

Mr. Hyde, of Newton, opposed the amendment. He did not see any good reason why it should be adopted. He did not think Virginia needed to be told where Massachusetts stands to-day.

Mr. Pierce, of Dorchester, did not want the matter forced through by outside influence. He was opposed to the resolves, and hoped they would be rejected.

Mr. Fisk, of Shelburne, advocated the proposition, and would forward it with his hand and vote.

Mr. Prentiss, of Marblehead, opposed the measure in a speech of considerable length, and asked if we would send commissioners to a convention of traitors? Let us rather send the sword.

Mr. Slack, of Boston, spoke in opposition. He foresaw that the convention would act contrary to the desires of the people of Massachusetts, and that this Commonwealth would be partly responsible for its acts.

Mr. Durfee, of New Bedford, moved to amend by instructing the commissioners not to recognize the resolutions presented in Congress by Mr. Crittenden, of Kentucky, as a proper basis for adjustment or compromise of difficulties.

Mr. Sears, of Boston, and Mr. Gibbs, of New Bedford, spoke in favor of the original resolves, and against the amendments.

The amendments were voted down, and the resolves were passed to be engrossed by a vote of yeas 184, nays 31.

Feb. 6. — The House voted to substitute the Senate bill for the increase of the militia for the bill of Mr. Banfield, of West Roxbury, — yeas 96, nays 60.

The bill was as follows : —.

CHAPTER 49. — *An Act in Relation to the Volunteer Militia.*

SECTION 1. The volunteer militia companies, as now organized, with their officers, shall be retained in the service; and hereafter, as the public exigency may require, the organization of companies of artillery may be authorized, on petition, by the Commander-in-chief, with advice of the Council, and the organization of other companies may be authorized, on petition, by the Commander-in-chief, or by the mayor and aldermen or selectmen, by his permission ; and said companies, so retained and so organized, shall be liable, on a requisition of the President of the United States upon the Commander-in-chief, to be marched without the limits of the Commonwealth ; but all additional companies, battalions, and regiments which may be organized under the provisions of this act, shall be disbanded whenever the Governor or the Legislature shall deem that their services are no longer needed. Companies of cavalry shall be limited to one hundred privates, and a saddler and a farrier; companies of artillery to forty-eight cannoneers, twenty-four drivers, and a saddler and farrier; the cadet companies of the first and second divisions to one hundred, and companies of infantry and riflemen to sixty-four, privates.

SECT. 2. The fourteenth section of the thirteenth chapter of the General Statutes, and all laws or parts of laws now in force, limiting the number of the volunteer militia, are hereby repealed.

SECT. 3. This act shall take effect upon its passage.

The resolves to appoint commissioners to attend a convention to be held in Washington, Feb. 5, were approved by the Governor, and were as follows: —

"Whereas, the Commonwealth of Massachusetts is desirous of a full and free conference with the General Government, and with any or all of the other States of the Union, at any time and on every occasion, when such conference may promote the welfare of the country; and

"Whereas questions of grave moment have arisen touching the powers of the Government, and the relations between the different States of the Union; and

"Whereas the State of Virginia has expressed a desire to meet her sister States in convention at Washington; therefore —

"*Resolved*, That the Governor of this Commonwealth, by and with the advice and consent of the Council, be, and he hereby is, authorized to appoint seven persons as commissioners, to proceed to Washington to confer with the General Government, or with the separate States, or with any association of delegates from such States, and to report their doings to the Legislature at its present session; it being expressly declared, that their acts shall be at all times under the control, and subject to the approval or rejection, of the Legislature."

On the same day, Feb. 5, the Governor, with the consent of the Council, appointed the following named gentlemen as commissioners: —

   Hon. JOHN Z. GOODRICH, of Stockbridge.
   Hon. CHARLES ALLEN, of Worcester.
   Hon. GEORGE S. BOUTWELL, of Groton.
   Hon. FRANCIS B. CROWNINSHIELD, of Boston.
   THEOPHILUS P. CHANDLER, Esq., of Brookline.
   JOHN M. FORBES, Esq., of Milton.
   RICHARD P. WATERS, Esq., of Beverly.

These gentleman immediately proceeded to Washington, and took part in the deliberations of the "Peace Congress." It was a very able delegation.

There was great interest felt in regard to the action of the Peace Congress, and how far its acts would bind the States which the delegates represented.

Feb. 8. *In the House.* — Mr. Albee, of Marlborough, offered the following resolution: —

"That our commissioners at Washington are hereby instructed to use every effort to prevent the adoption of the Crittenden Compromise, or any similar proposition, by the Convention now in session in Washington."

Passed, — yeas 112, nays 27; and the Governor was requested to forward a copy to each of the commissioners.

After the adjournment of the House, the members retained their seats, and the Clerk read the following communication : —

Extract from the Proceedings of the House of Representatives of South Carolina, Jan. 23, 1861.

"Mr. Holland offered the following, which were unanimously adopted : —

"Whereas a certain Mr. Tyler, of Boston, has introduced a resolution in the Massachusetts Legislature, 'that, in view of the great suffering in South Carolina, the immediate consequence of the citizens of that State acting under a mistaken idea of their rights and obligations, and in view of the abundance of this Commonwealth, a sum be appropriated from the State treasury, to be invested in provisions and stores for the relief of our suffering fellow-countrymen of that State;' therefore be it —

"*Resolved*, That the report now current in Massachusetts or elsewhere, that any part of South Carolina is suffering, or likely to suffer, for the want of provisions, is a lie as black as hell, and originated nowhere but amongst negro-worshippers at the North.

"*Resolved*, That the Legislature of Massachusetts be respectfully requested to appropriate the money to the relief of her own suffering, starving, poor thousands.

"*Resolved*, That we can attend to our own affairs without the aid of Massachusetts."

Mr. Speaker, — The foregoing is a true copy of the proceedings of the South Carolina Legislature. You are respectfully requested to have them read in open session.

W. F. COY KENDALL, *Assistant Clerk.*

March 19. *In the House.* — Mr. Tyler, of Boston, from the Committee on Finance, reported a resolve relating to the equipment of troops for active service in a new draft, reducing the sum from $35,000 to $25,000; which, on motion of Mr. Jewell, of Boston, was referred to the Committee on the Militia, with instructions "to inquire and report whether any contracts have been made or liabilities incurred in regard to any of the matters mentioned in the resolve; and, if so, what and when, and by what officer, and under what authority."

March 23. *In the House.* — Mr. Coffin, of Newburyport from the Committee on the Militia, reported that the resolve for the equipment of troops for active service ought to pass; also the following communication from the Adjutant-General: —

BOSTON, March 21, 1861.
Colonel FREDERICK J. COFFIN, *House of Representatives.*

SIR, — In answer to the inquiry made by the Honorable House of Representatives, "whether any contracts have been made or liabilities incurred in regard to any of the matters mentioned in the resolve reported to the House, relating to the equipment of troops for active service, and, if so, when, and by what authority," I have the honor to say: —

Under the direction of His Excellency the Governor and the Honorable Council, the following contracts have been made by me as Adjutant and Acting Quartermaster General: —

1st. With the Middlesex Company, Lowell, for 6,000 yards of cloth, six-fourths wide, to make 2,000 military overcoats, at $1.37 a yard.

2d. With William Deacon, to make 2,000 military overcoats at $2.15 each, he finding the trimmings, except the buttons.

3d. With James Boyd & Sons, to make 1,000 knapsacks, army pattern, and with Edward A. G. Roplstone, to make 1,000 knapsacks, army pattern, severally at $1.88 each.

4th. With Converse, Harding, & Co., for 1,000 pairs of blankets, army size, at $3.75 a pair.

5th. With the Rubber Clothing Company, Beverly, for 2,000 haversacks, at 75 cents each.

6th. The buttons for the coats have been contracted for with the manufacturer at Attleborough, and will cost about $740.

7th. I was also authorized to contract for 200,000 ball-cartridges to suit the new rifled musket. The lowest market price for these cartridges is $14 a thousand. At the State Arsenal, at Cambridge, there have been for many years upwards of 200,000 musket-balls suitable for the old smooth-bore musket. I have caused these to be recast, and the cartridges made at the Arsenal; so that the entire cost to the Commonwealth for the 200,000 new musket cartridges will not exceed $1,500.

The aggregate cost to the Commonwealth to fulfil these contracts will be $23,770; to which should be added $150 to pay a proper person or persons to inspect the work when finished, to ascertain whether the parties contracted with have faithfully fulfilled their several agreements. The resolve appropriating $25,000 will cover the entire expense, and will leave a surplus sufficient to purchase 300,000 percussion caps, which it will be necessary to buy, if the troops of the Commonwealth are called into active service.

With great respect, I have the honor to be your obedient servant,

WILLIAM SCHOULER,
Adjutant and Acting Quartermaster General.

Monday, March 25. *In Senate.* — A message was received from the Governor, transmitting a report of the commissioners appointed to represent the Commonwealth in the Peace Congress at Washington, which was read. Without taking action, the Senate adjourned.

The report gave a careful record of the proceedings of the Convention, which commenced its sessions in Washington on the 4th of February, and adjourned on the 27th of the same month. It sat with closed doors, and no full or consecutive report of its proceedings was ever made. It appears, however, from the report of our Commissioners, that most of the time was consumed in considering seven distinct propositions for amending the Federal Constitution, each of which was intended to strengthen the institution of slavery, by giving it additional guarantees and enlarged privileges. These propositions were reported by a committee composed of one from each State represented. Mr. Guthrie, of Kentucky, was made chairman. Massachusetts was represented on the committee by Mr. Crowninshield, who appears to have called for a specific statement of the grievances complained of by the discontented States. This request led to discussion, but failed to obtain the desired information. Mr. Guthrie's report was adopted by the committee by a majority of five, but the report, as a whole, never received the sanction of a majority of the Convention. Massachusetts voted against all of the propositions except the last, and on that, the delegation declined to vote, either for or against. As this Congress failed to accomplish any practical purpose, or to make an impression upon the country, either for good or for evil, it is not necessary at this late day to exhume from its secret records the crude conceits and extravagant demands which were pressed by Southern members, by which they hoped to prevent civil war, but which, if adopted, would have added strength and permanency to slavery, which was the weakness and the crime of the republic, and the fruitful cause of all our national woes. It does not appear that the Massachusetts members submitted any plan of adjustment, but contented themselves with debating such as were offered by others, and voting as their judgments dictated.

Same day. *In the House.* — Colonel Coffin, of Newburyport, introduced a bill to limit the number of privates in infantry and rifle companies to fifty, except when, in the opinion of the Governor, the number should be extended to sixty-four, which was subsequently passed.

The bill also to provide for the equipment of troops in active service was passed to be engrossed.

April 3. *In the House.* — The Committee on the Militia reported it was inexpedient to legislate upon the appointment of a commissary and surgeon-general, and of amending chapter 13, section 144, of the General Statutes, in relation to the mileage of the militia.

April 5. *In Senate.* — A resolve in favor of calling a national convention was discussed. It was opposed by Mr. Whiting, of Plymouth, and Mr. Walker, of Worcester, and advocated by Mr. Northend, of Essex, and Mr. Hardy, of Norfolk. It was finally, on motion of Mr. Davis, of Bristol, referred to the next Legislature.

The session closed Thursday, April 11, 1861.

The most important acts of the session, having for their object the preparation of the State for war, were "the act in relation to the volunteer militia," the appropriating of $100,000 as an emergency fund, and of $25,000 to provide overcoats and equipage for 2,000 men. The militia law of the General Statutes limited the active militia to 5,000 men: the act already quoted gave the Governor authority to organize as many companies and regiments as the public exigency might require.

While the Legislature was considering and passing preparatory measures, the Governor was not idle. A constant correspondence was kept up with our members of Congress and the Governors of other States. Leading merchants, and other gentlemen of experience and wisdom, were daily consulted. The militia was strengthened. A cipher key was arranged, to be used in transmitting messages which required secrecy.

The defenceless condition of the forts in Boston harbor was considered. In Fort Warren there was but one gun; in Fort Winthrop none at all; and, in Fort Independence, hardly twenty guns, and most of them were trained on the city itself. The casemates were unfit for human occupation. The grounds inside the forts were covered with workshops and wooden shanties; and, instead of being a defence to the city and harbor, the fortifications of Boston were a standing menace to them, and invited seizure by the enemy. The entire coast of Massachusetts was open to attack from sea; not a fort or an earthwork or a gun was in proper condition. There were neither officers nor troops in garrison. Our entire reliance, should war come, was in the patriotism of the militia and the people of the Commonwealth.

If troops were to be sent to Washington, the best and safest way of forwarding them was a question for discussion. Two Southern States lay between Boston and Washington; which, in case of civil war, were as likely to array themselves against the Government as for it. The danger of sending troops through Baltimore was very fully considered. The ease with which the passage of the Susquehanna could be impeded, and the long railroad bridges over the creeks between that river and Baltimore destroyed, was foreseen, and on the other hand the facility with which the approach by transports up the Potomac could be stopped by batteries, seemed to render that route impracticable. A meeting was held in the Governor's room on the 2d of February, and was adjourned to the 6th, at which Major-Generals Sutton, Morse, and Andrews, of the State militia; Colonel Thayer, U.S.A.; the Adjutant-General of the State; the aides-de-camp of His Excellency; and others, were present.

Colonel Henry Lee, of Governor Andrew's staff, in a letter dated July 9, 1867, to me, says, —

"With regard to the preparations for war made by Governor Andrew, I recollect, for my part, collecting information respecting steamers, and reporting the names and capacities and whereabouts of all which plied between Boston and other ports, on Feb. 2, 1861. On Feb. 4, the Governor called a meeting at his chamber in the State House, at which were present some of the chief officers of the militia: also, General Thayer, of the United-States Engineers, and Messrs. Gordon and Andrews, ex-United-States-army officers, both major-generals of volunteers in the late war. I recorded the replies, and drew up a memorandum of the items of clothing, equipment, arms, and ammunition needed, to prepare the militia for service in the field.

"On Feb. 6, a second meeting was called by the Governor. I cannot remember distinctly how much of the discussion took place at the first, and what at the second; but the result of the two was, the Governor's order for two thousand overcoats, equipments, &c., which was for two months the subject of so much ridicule. Feb. 9, a report was made by the Committee on Militia, of the Council, and a communication received by His Excellency from the Adjutant-General, giving estimates for clothing and equipments for two thousand troops in service."

The same order passed by the Council referred to by Colonel Lee, respecting the overcoats, speaks also of forwarding troops to Washington, "the mode of transit to be governed by circumstances that may arise hereafter; rail being preferred, if practicable."

Immediately after the meeting on the 2d of February, Governor Andrew detailed Colonel Ritchie, of his staff, to visit Washington, to confer confidentially with the Massachusetts senators and representatives, and General Scott, in regard to the prospect of a requisition being made for troops, and especially to learn from the general by what route in case of such a call he would wish the troops to be sent, and whether they would have to carry field equipage with them. He arrived at Washington on the 6th; and, on that evening, wrote to the Governor as follows: —

WASHINGTON, D.C., Wednesday, Feb. 6, 1861.

I received your instructions on Monday, at 1, P.M. I found, that, if I left Boston that afternoon, I could get here on Tuesday evening, but too late to attend to any business. I therefore determined to start on Tuesday morning, which gave me an opportunity of discussing the objects of my mission with Colonel Sargent, who took the same train as far as Springfield, Mass., and enabled me to reach this city this morning by daybreak.

Immediately after breakfast, I called on the Hon. Charles Sumner. He at once understood the object of my mission, and favored me with a statement on the present state of affairs. I also met him again later in the day in the Senate Chamber, when he went over again, with me, the same ground.

He gives as serious an account of the conspiracy to take possession of this city by the secessionists as any you have received; but he thinks the danger has been steadily diminishing since the 2d of January, — the day on which the President gave General Scott power to concentrate troops for the defence of the capital. The President has had several relapses since that date; and at times has seemed about to recall all the confidence he had placed in General Scott, and oblige him to undo all that had been done. The most extraordinary scenes have taken place in the Cabinet: only last week it was on the point of breaking up entirely, and the danger seemed to be as great again as at any previous time; but the general has triumphed in all particulars, excepting in his desire to have the militia of the Northern States called out: to that the President will not even now consent.

Mr. Sumner thinks there was a crisis in the Cabinet last week, and that, even after the general had overcome the hesitation of the President, there was a most serious danger to be apprehended from the revolutionary threats of the Democratic leaders in Maryland, in which the leaders of both wings of the Democratic party united. He thinks, however, that, the first schemes of the conspirators having been disconcerted, there was nothing to be apprehended in the way of an attack upon this city, unless the conspirators should have been enabled to lean upon State authority for their action. Therefore he thinks that the result of the election of delegates to the convention in Virginia has postponed the danger from this source. He is convinced that the conspirators counted upon a different result in Virginia; that, by the 18th, the Virginia Convention would have pronounced for secession; and that they were therefore safe in calling the Maryland Convention for that day, being sure that in that event Maryland would follow suit. If the result of the Virginia election had been in favor of the secessionists, the attack on the Capitol might have been carried out without waiting for the formal action of the Virginia Convention. Mr. Sumner now thinks there is no immediate danger to be feared of such an attack.

He is by no means confident of the determination to which that convention will ultimately come, but thinks that a delay has been gained which will carry us over the 4th of March in safety. Mr. Adams and Mr. Seward, with both of whom I have had long conversations, agree with Mr. Sumner fully as to any danger of an immediate attack. Mr. Seward thinks all danger is past. Mr. Sumner thinks Mr. Seward has never been aware of the real peril; and is evidently of the opinion that the crisis is only postponed. Mr. Adams thinks there will be no need of troops before the 6th of March, but thinks we shall have to fight after that date.

Mr. Sumner thinks Congress would be now sitting in Independence Hall, Philadelphia, but for General Scott's action. Mr. Seward seems to think this concentration of troops has been unnecessary. General Wilson appears to be of the opinion that Massachusetts and New York will have to furnish money, but doubts if they will be called upon for any troops. Mr. Seward urged me to write to you, and beg you to secure the passage of the resolutions by which Massachusetts would endorse the bonds of the United States to the extent of the deposit of surplus revenue in her hands, made in 1837. He says this is *all* they now ask of Massachusetts; that she will never have to pay a cent on account of such indorsement, but that the indorsement *must* be given, as the new Administration will be without funds. I have also conversed with Mr. Burlingame, Mr. Thayer, and Mr. Alley, of Massachusetts, and particularly with Mr. Stanton, of Ohio, the chairman of the committee who have been inquiring into this conspiracy.

Mr. Adams, Mr. Burlingame, Mr. Thayer, and Mr. Stanton, all talked the matter over together in my presence; and all were of opinion that no call would be made on Massachusetts before March 4.

Mr. Seward is the only one I have seen who stated that he thought all danger was now at an end, owing to the action of Virginia. And even Mr. Seward, at dinner this P.M., at Mr. Adams', stated that the South must succumb, or we should have to exterminate them, or they would have to exterminate us. He thinks the South are anxious to creep out of the movement of their own creation.

I have had to give you as rapid a resumé of the opinions of these civilians as possible, as I have hardly time to reach the mail. The only point of immediate importance is, that all agree that there is no probability of an immediate call upon us for militia.

Mr. Stanton thought, that, if a call were made, it would be for volunteers; and that there would be time to enlist special regiments for the war, as in the Mexican war. After leaving Mr. Sumner, I called on General Scott. He is avowedly very anxious even now, and would at once call for ten thousand men, if empowered to do so. He says the President, however, will never issue such a requisition. The President doubts his power; and, while I was with the general, Mr. Stanton came to consult with him about a bill, which I inclose, introduced for the purpose of meeting this objection of the President's.

But even if this bill passes, — and it will pass, unless the Republicans are satisfied that the President already possesses the power hereby intended to be given him, — still the President thinks that a call for Northern militia would at once set Virginia and Maryland in a blaze.

They have declared in Maryland, only last week, that the Susquehanna should flow with blood, if the attempt were made to bring Northern troops across it.

General Scott therefore agrees that there is no probability of any call being made on you by President Buchanan. He, however, would himself issue such a call at once if he had the power, and would have issued it a month ago.

With Colonel Keyes, of General Scott's staff, I discussed all the points at length, which were considered at the meeting of officers convened by you on Monday last.

Colonel Keyes is General Scott's right-hand man, and is the officer who has been charged with ferreting out this whole matter. He also says there will be no call at present, but that we *must be prepared*. I telegraphed at once, after my interview with Mr. Sumner, General Scott, and Colonel Keyes, to Mr. Albert G. Browne, Jr., " There is not the slightest probability of any immediate call; particulars by mail; take no further steps." Colonel Keyes approved of this despatch; and so did Messrs. Sumner, Wilson, Adams, Burlingame, and Thayer.

Colonel Keyes thinks it would not be safe to come, either by land or by the Potomac, but that the United States *must* hold the forts at Baltimore; and that the troops must come by sea to Baltimore, and land there under cover of the forts.

As to this, however, as also the other details, I will give you oral information; and Colonel Keyes will furnish me with much at a later day to which he could not give answers at once. There are also many things which will depend upon circumstances at the date of the call. I shall see to-morrow if affairs assume any different aspect; and, if they do not, I shall leave here to-morrow afternoon.

I shall not think it expedient, under the circumstances, to approach the Mayor of Baltimore.

Please excuse this hurried note, as I have been writing to save the mail, and been obliged to disregard form. I believe I have given you the substance of all that I have learned here.

Your Excellency's most obedient,
HARRISON RITCHIE,
Lieutenant-Colonel and Aide-de-Camp.

P.S. It is thought that the delay gained by the result of the Virginia election will give time for at least one thousand of the troops from Texas to get here before they are wanted. General Scott thinks he can count upon two thousand of the volunteers of this district. Colonel Keyes says, be prepared; organize your regiments, and drill them; furnish them with the new rifle-musket, knapsacks, canteens, blankets, and proper clothing, one hundred rounds of ammunition per man, and a supply of camp-kettles.

As to other camp equipage, it may be necessary: that he cannot tell at present.

Colonel Ritchie left Washington the next day, and, on arriving at New York, wrote another letter from that city, dated February 8th, in which he discusses again the position of affairs at Washington, and makes certain suggestions in regard to getting troops to Washington, which in time became of great practical service: —

"You will have perceived by my first letter that I had already made the acquaintance of Colonel Keyes. In fact we became great friends. When General Scott referred me to his two aides, — Colonels Leigh and Keyes, — I made up my mind after a very short conversation, that Colonel Leigh was a man of 'Southern proclivities,' who did not look with any favor upon my mission, though I had a letter of introduction to him from a mutual friend. He was disposed I thought to prevent my interview with General Scott, — and interrupt it after I had obtained it by introducing other people and other matters, — and he showed evident marks of dissatisfaction at my quiet persistence until I had accomplished my object. Of course I did not appear to notice this.* Keyes, on the other hand, went into the matter with his whole heart. He said he was bored to death with inquiries on these points — but where they were direct and to the point, he would answer them by the hour with pleasure. I had also heard of Mr. Goddard's errand, and conversed with him before receiving your

---

* Leigh afterwards deserted to the enemy, taking with him many of General Scott's plans and confidential papers.

Excellency's note. I, however, had another conversation with him yesterday morning, when he informed me that the answer given to his request for a detailed plan, was, in effect, that none such could be furnished at present. Some regulars, one company of artillery from Augusta, and one company of dragoons from Carlisle barracks, arrived yesterday; and, as I believe I mentioned in my first, a draft of infantry arrived at Washington in the train in which I reached the city.

"General Scott and Colonel Keyes are evidently anxious, and would like more men; but the President will never issue the requisition . . . Floyd has so plundered the United-States magazines, arsenals, and depots of munitions of war and warlike stores, that they do not know yet what is left, and so cannot tell what we must bring with us. It is clear, that, if we move, it must be by sea, landing at Baltimore or *Annapolis;* that pilots must be secured in advance, as they will be seized by the secessionists; and that the ships must go to sea with sealed orders, while a false destination is publicly reported.

. . . .

"I shall take the liberty to recommend one other caution, to be adjusted when I can speak with you in private, and which actual experience has shown me is necessary, if you desire that certain Boston papers should not divulge all your plans, as they have done hitherto. On Thursday morning (yesterday), I saw Mr. Sumner, Mr. Wilson, Mr. Burlingame, Mr. Adams, and others. They had nothing new to communicate, but adhere to their conviction, that there is no prospect, or possibility indeed, of an immediate call upon you. I mentioned in my first, that Mr. Seward was the only person I saw who pretended to think the danger more than postponed. I happened to be present at a conversation between him and some of his most intimate and confidential friends, when he evidently spoke out his sincere conviction. I was much impressed with what he said, which satisfied me that his optimist views are assumed, as necessary in his relation to the new Administration, and that in reality he is no more hopeful than Mr. Sumner. I will repeat his remark to you on my return. Mr. Adams also heard this remark; and when I asked him, yesterday, if he noticed it, he seemed surprised at my having marked it also, and confessed that it *impressed* him very forcibly.

"Mr. Adams was on his way to find me yesterday, as I was going to his house. He came to ask me to inform your Excellency that the Secretary of the Treasury had sent for him that morning, to beg him to urge upon you the extreme importance of our Legislature passing the resolves authorizing the indorsement by Massachusetts of the bonds of the United States to the amount of the shares of the surplus revenue deposited with her in 1837. Mr. Adams said that the Secretary wished to issue his proposals on Monday, if possible, and hoped these resolves would be passed before that time.

"I told Mr. Adams that Mr. Seward and Mr. Wilson had impressed me with the importance of this on the previous day, and that I had conveyed their request already to your Excellency. Mr. Adams then said I could do no more, and that he would write to you at once. I, however, saw Mr. Wilson about it yesterday morning, and he said he would consult the Massachusetts delegation yesterday, if possible, and get them all to sign a letter to you on the subject, for you to show to the Legislature.

"I should mention that I called the attention of our delegation to the unsatisfactory state of the United-States militia laws, and the questions that have arisen with us already. I left a copy of Lothrop's opinion with Mr. Wilson. He will read it, and read again the debates in our Constitutional Convention, and see what can be done. They all saw the delicacy of the points, and their importance, and will do what they can.

"Finding I could do nothing more, I decided to leave Washington last night, though, for my own pleasure, I should have liked to have remained some time longer at the centre of action in this great crisis. I accordingly came here last night. We were detained by ice and the extreme, savage cold; and I found this morning that my baggage, though properly checked and shipped at Washington, had not come through; indeed, none of the baggage did. This will detain me here; but I can only repeat in more detail what I have already written to your Excellency, when I have the pleasure of reporting my return to you in person. I hope your Excellency will not think my journey has proved entirely unprofitable. I think, at any rate, that an understanding and communication has been opened that may prove very useful in the future."

In connection with the letters of Colonel Ritchie, the following extract from a letter addressed to me by Secretary Seward, dated Washington, June 13, 1867, is of interest and importance: —

"In regard to February, 1861, I need only say, that, at the time the secession leaders were all in the Senate and House, with power enough, and only wanting an excuse, to get up a resistance in the capital to the declaration of Mr. Lincoln's election and to his inauguration; in other words, to have excuse and opportunity to open the civil war here before the new Administration and new Congress could be in authority to subdue it. I desired to avoid giving them that advantage. I conferred throughout with General Scott and Mr. Stanton, then in Mr. Buchanan's Cabinet. I presume I conversed with others in a way that seemed to me best calculated to leave the inauguration of a war to the secessionists, and to delay it, in any case, until the new Administration should be in possession of the Government. It was less military demonstration that was wanted at that particular moment than political discretion.

"Discretion taught two duties; namely, to awaken patriotism in the North, and to get the secessionists, with Buchanan's Administration, out of Washington. Mr. Adams well and thoroughly understood me. On the 22d of February, in concert with Mr. Stanton, I caused the United-States flag to be displayed throughout all the Northern and Western portions of the United States."

Colonel Ritchie did not leave Washington until he had come to a definite understanding in regard to the route by which to forward troops to Washington, should a call for them be made. He had been cordially received by General Scott, to whom the purpose of his mission was made known, and he was referred to Colonel Keyes of General Scott's staff for information upon matters of detail. It was then arranged, that, in case of a call, the troops should be forwarded by sea to Annapolis or Baltimore. Colonel Keyes stated, that all other routes to Washington would be unsafe; that, for this reason, General Scott had placed an officer in command of Fort McHenry in Baltimore Harbor, upon whom he could rely to hold it to the utmost. Immediate measures were taken by the Governor to have the necessary transports in readiness, and Colonel Lee, of his staff, was detailed to attend to this duty. The following extract from a letter dated Boston, Feb. 2, 1861, addressed to the Governor, by Colonel Lee, relates a conversation he had held that day with John M. Forbes, Esq., in regard to chartering steamers to be used as transports, which shows that the attention of the Governor had been given to this subject before Colonel Ritchie had returned from Washington:—

"Mr. Forbes assures me that he and others will have the transports ready as soon as the men can be, waiting until orders come before the vessel is chartered, so as to keep as quiet as possible. And he thinks, with me, that we had better wait for New York, as we can get ready and move quicker; and any forwardness on the part of Massachusetts would be more offensive than that of New York. He urges also to write or telegraph to General Scott, that we can at once send three hundred men to relieve the garrison at Fortress Monroe, if he desires to have the present garrison march to Washington. The cost of steamer per month, with crew, would be three to four thousand dollars, probably. I send a list in order of merit."

A very large and respectable meeting of the citizens of Boston was held in Faneuil Hall, on the 5th of February, to indorse the resolutions of Mr. Crittenden, of Kentucky, in favor of a compromise with the South. J. Thomas Stevenson, Esq., presided, and made a strong and able speech in favor of compromise, in the course of which he said "he would almost pray for a foreign war, that it might bind us again as one, and prevent the shedding of fraternal blood. He would give up every thing but honor." B. R. Curtis, Esq., ex-judge of the United-States Supreme Court, made the leading speech, which was received with great favor. The resolutions were read by Colonel Jonas French. Speeches were made by Mr. Wightman, mayor of the city, Mr. Saltonstall, Mr. G. S. Hillard, and others, some of whom afterwards distinguished themselves as officers in the war.

This meeting spoke the sentiments of the conservative citizens, who regarded war and disunion as evils greater than the existence of slavery, or even of its further extension; and yet they were anti-slavery men, and regarded slavery as a great moral and political wrong, and would gladly have seen it abolished.

A few days later, on the 11th of February, a great meeting was held in Cambridge. The City Hall was crowded. The meeting was called without distinction of party. Hon. John G. Palfrey spoke briefly. He said, " South Carolina has marshalled herself into revolution; and six States have followed her, and abandoned our Government." Richard H. Dana, Jr., Esq., made the speech of the occasion. He said the South was in a state of mutiny; he was against John-Brown raids, and uncompromisingly for the Union. He was opposed to the Crittenden compromise, and held to the faith of Massachusetts. This meeting uttered the sentiments of the majority of the State, and was designed as a counterblast to the meeting held the week before at Faneuil Hall.

The speeches made and resolutions passed at these meetings expressed the sentiments of the people of the State. Those who were at Faneuil Hall would rather compromise the issues than have bloodshed and civil war. The men who were at Cambridge would risk the chance of civil war rather than compromise.

There was another party, which, though small in number, was powerful in eloquence, moral character, and cultivated intellect. Its zeal never flagged, its leaders never faltered. Its hatred of slavery was chronic. Its martyr spirit was felt and acknowledged. Its policy was aggressive. It made no compromises; it sought no office; it asked no favor; and it gave no quarter. This was the abolition party. The leaders of it were Mr. Garrison and Mr. Phillips. The Federal Constitution, as interpreted by them, was a pro-slavery instrument: they would not, therefore, support it. The Union was "a covenant with hell:" therefore they would break it. For a quarter of a century they had thus spoken, and consistently acted, and held their ground up to the very day that the rebels fired on Sumter.

The following extract from a speech delivered in New Bedford by Mr. Phillips, on the evening of the 9th of April, 1861, is curious and remarkable, when we consider the positions held by that gentleman before the war, during the war, and since the war. It shows that learned men and orators are sometimes false prophets; and what is visible to plain men is hid from them : —

"The telegraph," said Mr. Phillips, "is said to report to-night, that the guns are firing, either out of Fort Sumter or into it; that to-morrow's breeze, when it sweeps from the North, will bring to us the echo of the first Lexington battle of the new Revolution. Well, what shall we say of such an hour? My own feeling is a double one. It is like the triumph of sadness, — rejoicing and sorrow. I cannot, indeed, congratulate you enough on the sublime spectacle of twenty millions of people educated in a twelvemonth up to being willing that their idolized Union should risk a battle, should risk dissolution, in order, at any risk, to put down this rebellion of slave States.

"But I am sorry that a gun should be fired at Fort Sumter, or that a gun should be fired from it, for this reason: The Administration at Washington does not know its time. Here are a series of States girding the Gulf, who think that their peculiar institutions require that they should have a separate government. They have a right to decide that question, without appealing to you or me. A large body of people, sufficient to make a nation, have come to the conclusion, that they will have a government of a certain form. Who denies them the right? Standing with the principles of '76 behind us, who can deny them the right? What is a matter of a few millions of dollars, or a few forts? It is a mere drop in the bucket of the great national question. It is theirs, just as much as ours. I maintain, on the principles of '76, that Abraham Lincoln has no right to a soldier in Fort Sumter.

"But the question comes, secondly, 'Suppose we had a right to interfere, what is the good of it?' You may punish South Carolina for going out of the Union: that does not bring her in. You may subdue her by hundreds of thousands of armies, but that does not make her a State. There is no longer a Union: it is nothing but boy's play. Mr. Jefferson Davis is angry, and Mr. Abraham Lincoln is mad, and they agree to fight. One, two, or three years hence, if the news of the afternoon is correct, we shall have gone through a war, spent millions, required the death of a hundred thousand men, and be exactly then where we are now, — two nations, a little more angry, a little poorer, and a great deal wiser; and that will be the only difference: we may just as well settle it now as then.

"You cannot go through Massachusetts, and recruit men to bombard Charleston or New Orleans. The Northern mind will not bear it; you can never make such a war popular. The first onset may be borne; the telegraph may bring us news, that Anderson has bombarded Charleston, and you may rejoice; but the sober second thought of Massachusetts will be, 'wasteful, unchristian, guilty.' The North never will indorse such a war. Instead of conquering Charleston, you create a Charleston in New England; you stir up sympathy for the South. Therefore it seems to me that the inauguration of war is not a violation of principle, but it is a violation of expediency.

"To be for disunion, in Boston, is to be an abolitionist: to be against disunion is to be an abolitionist to-day, in the streets of Charleston. Now, that very state of things shows, that the civilization of the two cities is utterly antagonistic. What is the use of trying to join them?

Is Abraham Lincoln capable of making fire and powder lie down together in peace? If he can, let him send his army to Fort Sumter, and occupy it.

"But understand me: I believe in the Union, exactly as you do, in the future. This is my proposition: 'Go out, gentlemen; you are welcome to your empire; take it.' Let them try the experiment of cheating with one hand, and idleness with the other. I know that God has written bankruptcy over such an experiment. If you cannonade South Carolina, you cannonade her into the sympathy of the world. I do not know *now* but what a majority there is on my side; but I know this, that, if the telegraph speaks true to-night, that the guns are echoing around Fort Sumter, that a majority is against us; for it will convert every man into a secessionist. Besides, there is another fearful element in the problem; there is another terrible consideration: we can then no longer extend to the black race, at the South, our best sympathy and our best aid.

"We stand to-night at the beginning of an epoch, which may have the peace or the ruin of a generation in its bosom. Inaugurate war, we know not where it will end; we are in no condition to fight. The South is poor, and we are rich. The poor man can do twice the injury to the rich man, that the rich man can do the poor. Your wealth rides safely on the bosom of the ocean, and New England has its millions afloat. The North whitens every sea with its wealth. The South has no commerce, but she can buy the privateers of every race to prey on yours. It is a dangerous strife when wealth quarrels with poverty.

"Driven to despair, the Southern States may be poor and bankrupt, but the poorest man can be a pirate; and, as long as New England's tonnage is a third of that of the civilized world, the South can punish New England more than New England can punish her. We provoke a strife in which we are defenceless. If, on the contrary, we hold ourselves to the strife of ideas, if we manifest that strength which despises insult and bides its hour, we are sure to conquer in the end.

"I distrust these guns at Fort Sumter. I do not believe that Abraham Lincoln means war. I do not believe in the madness of the Cabinet. Nothing but madness can provoke war with the Gulf States. My suspicion is this; that the Administration dares not compromise. It trembles before the five hundred thousand readers of the New-York 'Tribune.'

"But there is a safe way to compromise. It is this: seem to provoke war. Cannonade the forts. What will be the first result? New-York commerce is pale with bankruptcy. The affrighted seaboard sees grass growing in its streets. It will start up every man whose livelihood hangs upon trade, intensifying him into a compromiser. Those guns fired at Fort Sumter are only to frighten the North into a compromise.

"If the Administration provokes bloodshed, it is a trick, — nothing else. It is the masterly cunning of the devil of compromise, the Secretary of State. He is not mad enough to let these States run into battle. He knows that the age of bullets is over. If a gun is fired in Southern waters, it is fired at the wharves of New York, at the bank-vaults of Boston, at the money of the North. It is meant to alarm. It is policy, not sincerity. It means concession; and, in twelve months, you will see this Union reconstructed, with a constitution like that of Montgomery.

"New England may, indeed, never be coerced into a slave confederacy. But when the battles of Abraham Lincoln are ended, and compromises worse than Crittenden's are adopted, New England may claim the right to secede. And, as sure as a gun is fired to-night at Fort Sumter, within three years from to-day you will see thirty States gathered under a Constitution twice as damnable as that of 1787. The only hope of liberty is fidelity to principle, fidelity to peace, fidelity to the slave. Out of that God gives us nothing but hope and brightness. In blood there is sure to be ruin."

The lecture " was interrupted by frequent hisses."

In the preceding pages, we have sketched the position held and the measures adopted by Massachusetts during the four months immediately preceding the advent of war. Sumter had been fired upon; hostilities had commenced; nothing remained but the arbitrament of battle. By the wisdom and foresight of her Governor and Legislature, Massachusetts was better prepared for it than other loyal States. Her militia had spent the winter and spring nights in drilling, recruiting, and organizing. The requirements of Order No. 4 had been enforced. The young men who filled the ranks of the volunteer force had kept alive the military spirit and martial character of the Commonwealth. They had remained faithful to duty, despite the taunts and jeers of open enemies, and the neglect and parsimony of professed friends. They were now to give the world an exhibition of ready devotion and personal sacrifice to duty and country seldom equalled and never surpassed in any age or nation. They had been bred in the delightful ways of peace, unused to war's alarms and the strifes of battle. The common schools of Massachusetts were their Alma Mater. In their homes by the shores of the sea, and in the pleasant fields and valleys of the interior, they had been nurtured in Christian morals and the ways of God. They had beheld with anxiety, but without fear, the dark clouds of war settling upon the face of the nation, which they knew must be met and dispelled, or it would remain no longer a nation to them. Through the long and anxious years of the war, they never hesitated, doubted, or wavered in their faith that the Union would stand the shock which menaced it; and that, through the sacrifice of noble lives and the baptism of precious blood, it would emerge from the smoke and fire of civil war with unsubdued strength, and with garments glittering all over with the rays of Liberty. It was to be a contest between right and wrong, law and anarchy, freedom and despotism. He who could doubt the issue of such a war could have no abiding faith in the immortality of American progress, or the eternal justice of Christian civilization.

On the 15th day of April, 1861, Governor Andrew received a telegram from Washington to send forward at once fifteen hundred men. The drum-beat of the long roll had been struck.

CHAPTER II.

The Call for Troops — The Marblehead Companies first in Boston — The Excitement of the People — Headquarters of Regiments — Four Regiments called for — General Butler to command — New companies organized — Liberal Offers of Substantial Aid — Dr. George H. Lyman, Dr. William J. Dale, Medical Service — Action of the Boston Bar — The Clergy, Rev. Mr. Cudworth — The Women of the State — The Men of the State — Liberal Offers of Service and Money — Robert B. Forbes, Coast Guard — Colonel John H. Reed appointed Quartermaster — The Personal Staff — Executive Council — Mr. Crowninshield appointed to purchase Arms in Europe — An Emergency Fund of Two Hundred Thousand Dollars — Letter of the Governor to Secretary Cameron — General Butler consulted — The Route by Annapolis — Narrative of Samuel M. Felton — Mr. Lincoln's Journey to Washington — His Escape from Assassination — The Third Regiment — Speech of Ex-Governor Clifford — The Fourth Regiment — Address of Governor Andrew — Departure for Fortress Monroe — The Sixth Regiment — Departure for Washington — Reception in New York and Philadelphia — The Eighth Regiment — Departure — Speeches of Governor Andrew and General Butler — Reception on the Route — Arrival in Philadelphia — The Fifth Regiment sails from New York for Annapolis — Major Cook's Light Battery ordered to Washington — The Third Battalion of Rifles sent forward — The Massachusetts Militia — Arrival of the Third Regiment at Fortress Monroe — Attempt to save Norfolk Navy Yard — The Fourth Regiment the first to land in Virginia — Fortress Monroe — Big Bethel — The Fifth Regiment — Battle of Bull Run — The Sixth Regiment — Its March through Baltimore — The Nineteenth of April — First Blood shed — The Eighth Regiment — Lands at Annapolis — Saves the Frigate Constitution — Arrives in Washington — The Rifle Battalion at Fort McHenry — Cook's Battery at Baltimore — End of the Three Months' Service — Conclusion.

THE call for troops, mentioned in the last paragraph of the preceding chapter, came from Washington by telegraph, through Henry Wilson, of the United-States Senate; which was dated April 15, 1861, and asked for twenty companies, to be sent on separately. In the course of the day, formal requisitions were received from the Secretary of War and the Adjutant-General of the Army for two full regiments. By command of Governor Andrew, Special Order No. 14 was immediately issued by the

Adjutant-General, and was forwarded, by mail and by special messengers, to Colonel Wardrop of the Third Regiment, at New Bedford; Colonel Packard of the Fourth, at Quincy; Colonel Jones of the Sixth, at Pepperell; and Colonel Monroe of the Eighth, at Lynn. The order was to muster the regiments under their command in uniform on Boston Common forthwith, " in compliance with a requisition made by the President of the United States: the troops are to go to Washington." An order was also issued to fill all existing vacancies in regimental and line officers, waiving the usual notice.

The reason for ordering four regiments when only two had been called for was, that, by detaching strong companies from weak regiments, the two called for might be filled to the maximum.

The call aroused the people of the entire State to instant action. The State House became the great centre of interest. The Governor's room and the Adjutant-General's quarters were crowded with citizens, tendering their services in whatever capacity they could be made useful. Telegrams were received from military and civil officers, living in remote parts of the Commonwealth, making the same generous and patriotic offers. As if by magic, the entire character of the State was changed: from a peaceful, industrious community, it became a camp of armed men; and the hum of labor gave place to the notes of fife and drum.

On the morning of the 16th of April, the companies began to arrive in Boston; and, before nightfall, every company that had received its orders in time reported at headquarters for duty.

There has been some controversy in military circles as to which company can claim the honor of first reaching Boston. I can answer, that the first were the three companies of the Eighth Regiment belonging to Marblehead, commanded by Captains Martin, Phillips, and Boardman. I had been at the State House all night; and, early in the morning, rode to the Arsenal at Cambridge, to ascertain whether the orders from headquarters, to send in arms, ammunition, overcoats, and equipments, had been properly attended to. Messengers had also been stationed

at the different depots, with orders for the companies, on their
arrival, to proceed at once to Faneuil Hall, as a north-easterly
storm of sleet and rain had set in during the night, and had not
abated in the morning. On my return from Cambridge, I
stopped at the Eastern Railroad Depot. A large crowd of men
and women, notwithstanding the storm, had gathered there, expecting the arrival of troops. Shortly after eight o'clock, the
train arrived with the Marblehead companies. They were received with deafening shouts from the excited throng. The
companies immediately formed in line, and marched by the flank
directly to Faneuil Hall; the fifes and drums playing "Yankee
Doodle," the people following and shouting like madmen, and
the rain and sleet falling piteously as if to abate the ardor of the
popular welcome. And thus it was the Marblehead men entered Faneuil Hall on the morning of the 16th of April.

It is impossible to overstate the excitement which pervaded
the entire community through this eventful week. The railroad
depots were surrounded with crowds of people; and the companies, as they arrived, were received with cheers of grateful
welcome. Banners were suspended, as if by preconcerted arrangement. The American flag spread its folds to the breeze
across streets, from the masts of vessels in the harbor, from the
cupola of the State House, the City Hall, in front of private
dwellings; and men and boys carried miniature flags in their
hands or on their hats. The horse-cars and express-wagons were
decked with similar devices; and young misses adorned their
persons with rosettes and ribbons, in which were blended the
national red, white, and blue. In the streets, on 'Change and
sidewalk, in private mansion and in public hotel, no topic was
discussed but the approaching war, the arrival and departure
of the troops, and measures best adapted for their comfort and
welfare. Every one was anxious to do something, and in some
way to be useful. Young men, wishing to raise new companies and proffer services, pressed to the offices of the Governor and the Adjutant-General. These offices, the rotunda,
and the passages leading to the State House, were filled with
zealous and determined people. Faneuil Hall, Boylston Hall,
the hall over the Old-Colony Railroad Depot, where companies

were quartered, had each its living mass of excited spectators. Every train which arrived at Boston brought in relatives, friends, and townsmen of the soldiers, to say a kind word at parting, to assure them that their families would be well cared for while they were absent, and to add to the general enthusiasm and excitement of the occasion.

During the entire week, wagons were bringing in, from the State Arsenal at Cambridge, clothing, arms, ammunition, and other munitions of war, to be deposited, prior to distribution, in Faneuil Hall and the State House. On Saturday, the 13th of April, two days prior to the call for troops, the Adjutant-General, by direction of the Governor, had written to the Secretary of War, asking the privilege of drawing, from the United-States Armory at Springfield, two thousand rifled muskets in advance of the annual quota becoming due; also urging the President to order two regiments of volunteers to garrison Fort Warren and Fort Independence in Boston harbor, to be there drilled and exercised, until called by the President for active service in the field. Neither request was granted.

While the troops ordered out were getting to Boston with all diligence, and making ready for instant departure, another telegram was received (April 16) from Senator Wilson, stating that Massachusetts was to furnish immediately four regiments, to be commanded by a brigadier-general; on receipt of which, orders were issued for the Fifth Regiment to report, and, on the 17th, Brigadier-General Benjamin F. Butler was detailed to command the troops.

By six o'clock on the afternoon of the 16th, the Third, Fourth, and Sixth Regiments were ready to start. The headquarters of the Third was in the hall over the Old-Colony Railroad Depot; that of the Fourth at Faneuil Hall; that of the Sixth in the armory of the Second and Fourth Battalions, at Boylston Hall, over the Boylston Market.

While these regiments were getting ready, offers to raise new companies of militia came from all parts of the State. The Adjutant-General, in his Report for 1861, says, "From the 13th of April to the 20th of May, one hundred and fifty-nine applications were granted to responsible parties for leave to raise companies. In nearly every instance, the application was signed by the requisite number of men for a company. These applications came from every part of the Commonwealth, and represented all classes, creeds, and nationalities. The authorities of the several cities and towns acted with patriotic liberality toward these companies, furnishing good accommodations for drilling, and providing for the families of the men." In the aggregate, they numbered full ten thousand men, eager for orders to march. Drill companies were also formed of men past the military age, and of citizens who desired to learn the manual of arms. To these companies two thousand seven hundred old muskets were loaned by the State. Most of these new militia companies were organized between April 13 and the 4th of May. Numerous letters, offering pecuniary aid to soldiers' families, were received by the Governor and the Adjutant-General. William Gray, of Boston, sent his check for ten thousand dollars; Otis Norcross, of Boston, sent his for five hundred; Gardner Brewer, also of Boston, offered the State ten thousand dollars; and many other gifts, of less amount, were received.

The Boston Banks offered to loan the State three million six hundred thousand dollars, without any security for repayment, but faith in the honor of the Legislature, when it should meet. They also offered the Secretary of the Treasury to take Treasury notes to the full extent of their power. The banks in other parts of the State made offers of loans equally generous, according to their capital. Gentlemen of the learned professions showed the same liberal and patriotic spirit. Dr. George H. Lyman, who was afterwards medical inspector in the United-States Army, with the rank of lieutenant-colonel, had, in anticipation of civil war, prepared himself, by a study of rules and regulations of the medical department of the army, for the expected emergency. Therefore, on the call for troops, he tendered his services to the Governor, to prepare medicine chests, and act as medical purveyor in fitting out the regiments. Dr. William J. Dale writes thus: " On the sixteenth day of April, 1861, I was called from my professional pursuits, by Governor Andrew, to assist Dr. George H. Lyman in furnishing medical supplies for the Sixth Regiment; and I continued, under the direction of the Governor, to perform, conjointly with Dr. Lyman, such duties as were incidental to a medical bureau, until the 13th of June, 1861, when I was commissioned Surgeon-General of Massachusetts, with the rank of colonel." Thus early in the war, steps were taken to form a military medical department for the State, which was of great value and importance during the whole of the war, reflecting honor upon the Commonwealth and upon the distinguished gentleman who was placed at its head. Many of the first physicians of the Commonwealth volunteered to give their professional services to the families of the soldiers, free of charge. A meeting of the Boston Bar was held, at which it was voted to take charge of all cases of other attorneys while absent in the war, and that liberal provision be made for their families. Many applications were made by clergymen to go out as chaplains, to take care of the sick and wounded, and protect the physical, moral, and religious welfare of the soldiers. Conspicuous among these was Rev. Mr. Cudworth, pastor of the Unitarian Church in East Boston. On Sunday, April 21, he preached a sermon on the crisis, in which he said he had already offered his services to the Governor as chaplain. He hoped his society would furnish at least one company to defend the flag. In case his services as chaplain were not accepted, he should devote his year's salary to the common cause; and he announced that the sexton and organist would do the same. He advised that the money raised by the parish to build a new church should be appropriated to the families of the soldiers, and that they should worship in the old house until the war was over. He recommended the ladies of the parish to form a society to make under-clothing for the soldiers. He showed a handsome necklace, which a lady had given him to be sold for the benefit of the soldiers' families. On this occasion, the pulpit was draped with the American flag. Mr. Cudworth, soon after, was commissioned chaplain of the First Massachusetts three-years Regiment, and left with it for the front on the 15th of June, and continued in the service, and the regiment, until the 28th of May, 1864.

During the week, and particularly after the Sixth Regiment

had been attacked in Baltimore, the enthusiasm and resolution of the people were intense. Many ladies of the most refined and tender culture offered their services as hospital nurses; and many of them subsequently went forward on their mission of humanity, and ministered with tender hands and feeling hearts to the comfort of our sick and wounded men in the hospitals. The letters of these true Christian women are on file at the State House. They speak one language, and express one thought,— opportunity to do good, and to comfort those who are afflicted. Among these letters is one dated April 19, from Mrs. Frances Wright, of Foxborough, and signed by one hundred young ladies of that town, offering their services as nurses, or to make soldiers' garments, to prepare bandage and lint, to do any thing for the cause in their power to do. The Governor, in his answer, writes, "I accept it as one of the most earnest and sincere of the countless offers of devotion to our old Commonwealth, and to the cause of the country;" and concludes by asking them "to help those who are left behind, and follow those who have gone before with your benedictions, your benefactions, and your prayers."

Benjamin F. Parker, and Whiton, Brown, & Wheelright, "tender the use of their sail-loft, and all such assistance of workmen as may be necessary to do any work on the tents, free of expense to the Commonwealth." John H. Rogers, offers "twenty cases of boots, as a donation for the soldiers now enlisting." Captain Francis B. Davis offers "his barque 'Manhattan,' to take men and munitions of war to any part of the United States." As arrangements had been already made, this offer was declined for the present. James M. Stone and Newell A. Thompson offered their services to superintend the distribution of quartermaster's stores and ordnance, which were accepted. Robert B. Forbes, on the 17th, made a proposal to raise a Coast Guard, which met with the cordial approval of the Governor; but as there was no provision, in the militia law, by which material aid could be given by the State, the Governor wrote to the Secretary of War on behalf of the project. On the 19th, thirty thousand dollars was subscribed by a few gentlemen in Boston, as a fund to organize a volunteer regiment, which was subsequently raised, and known as the Second Regiment of Massachusetts Volunteer Infantry. The subscription paper was headed by David Sears, James Lawrence, Thomas Lee, Samuel Hooper, George O. Hovey, and Mrs. William Pratt, each of whom subscribed one thousand dollars.

The call for troops, and their organization and equipment, rendered a division of military duties, and the enlargement of the staff of the Governor, a necessity. By law, the Adjutant-General, in time of peace, was Inspector-General and acting Quartermaster-General of the Commonwealth. In time of war, the triple duties of these offices could not be performed by one person; and therefore Colonel John H. Reed, who had experience in military affairs, and had served as senior aide-de-camp on the staff of Governor Banks, was commissioned, on the nineteenth, Quartermaster-General of Massachusetts, with the rank of brigadier-general. General Reed entered upon his duties immediately, and relieved the Adjutant-General of all quartermaster's duties and responsibilities. Many of the duties had previously been performed, during the week, by the aides-de-camp of the Governor, and by private gentlemen, who had volunteered their services.

From the hour the telegram was received by the Governor, the pressure of business upon the executive and military departments of the State became more and more urgent. Colonels Sargent, Ritchie, Lee, and Wetherell, of the Governor's personal staff, were on duty, answering inquiries, writing letters, and attending to the multiplicity of details which the duties of the executive rendered necessary. The Executive Council was also in session; and, on the 20th of April, it " was ordered that the Treasurer be authorized to borrow two hundred thousand dollars, to be held as an emergency fund for military purposes;" also, "that an agent be sent to Europe with authority to purchase, on account of the Commonwealth, twenty-five thousand rifles and army pistols, to be imported as soon as may be, for the use of the militia in defence of the State and of the nation, and that the Governor issue a letter of credit to such agent for the purpose of fulfilling this order." The Governor appointed Hon. Francis B. Crowninshield the agent to proceed to Europe and purchase arms, and gave him a letter of credit to the amount of fifty thousand pounds sterling. Mr. Crowninshield sailed in the next steamer from New York for England.

On the day that orders were received to send forward troops, the Governor wrote the following letter: —

BOSTON, April 15, 1861.

To Hon. SIMON CAMERON, *Secretary of War.*

SIR, — I have received telegrams from yourself and Brigadier-General Thomas, admonishing me of a coming requisition for twenty companies of sixty-four privates each; and I have caused orders to be distributed to bring the men into Boston before to-morrow night, and to await orders. Allow me to urge the issue of an order to the Springfield (Mass.) Armory, to *double the production of arms at once,* and to push the work to the utmost. If any aid by way of money or credit is needed from Massachusetts, I hope to be at once apprised. An extra session of our General Court can be called immediately, if need be; and, if called, it will respond to any demand of patriotism.

And I beg you would permit, in addition to suggesting the utmost activity at Springfield Armory, to urge that the armory at Harper's Ferry be discontinued, and its tools, machinery, and works be transferred elsewhere, or else that it be rigidly guarded against seizure, of the danger of which I have some premonitions. If any more troops will certainly be needed from Massachusetts, please signify it at once, since I should prefer receiving special volunteers for active militia to detail any more of our present *active militia*, especially as many most efficient gentlemen would like to raise companies or regiments, as the case may be, and can receive enlistments of men who are very ready to serve.

Allow me also to suggest that our forts in Boston Harbor are entirely unmanned. If authorized, I would put a regiment into the forts at any time. Two of my staff spent last Saturday in making experiments of the most satisfactory character, with Shenkle's new invention in projectiles; and so extraordinary was the firing, that I have directed eighteen guns to be rifled, and projectiles to be made. May I commend this invention to the examination of the United-States Government?

I am happy to add that I find the amplest proof of a warm devotion to the country's cause, on every hand to-day. Our people are alive. Yours, JOHN A. ANDREW.

General Butler was appointed on the 17th to command the Massachusetts Brigade. He established temporary headquarters in the State House. He was consulted by the Governor in regard to the movement of the troops; the letters which Colonel Ritchie had written from Washington, in February, were read to him; and the arrangements which had been agreed upon by General Scott and the Governor, that troops, when called for, should be sent by sea to Annapolis or by the Potomac River to Washington, were made known. He was put in possession of all the information which had been obtained respecting the movement of troops to Washington by way of Annapolis. On the day the requisition for troops came to Governor Andrew, he telegraphed, in reply, that the troops would be at once forwarded to Annapolis by sea; to which an answer was received from the Secretary of War, to "send the troops by railroad: they will arrive quicker, the route through Baltimore is now open." In consequence of this despatch, the route was changed, and the Sixth Regiment was forwarded by rail, although, through the activity and foresight of John M. Forbes, steamers were in readiness to take the regiment by sea. Had the route not been changed, the bloodshed in Baltimore on the ever-memorable 19th of April would have been avoided. How the Secretary of War could have believed the route through Baltimore was safe, it is difficult to understand, if, as may have been supposed, he was aware of the schemes which were planned in Baltimore to assassinate Mr. Lincoln, when on his way to Washington to be inaugurated, and which were thwarted by the prudence, vigilance, and accurate knowledge of one man.

The true history of Mr. Lincoln's perilous journey to Washington in 1861, and the way he escaped death, have never been made public until now. The narrative was written by Samuel M. Felton, of Philadelphia, President of the Philadelphia and Baltimore Railroad Company, in 1862, at the request of Mr. Sibley, Librarian of Harvard University; but it was not completed until lately, when it was sent to me, with other valuable material, by Mr. Felton. It has a direct bearing upon events which transpired in forwarding the Sixth Massachusetts Regiment to Washington, and which are now to be narrated. Mr. Felton is a native of Massachusetts, and a brother of the late President of Harvard University. He was born in West Newbury, Essex County, Mass., July 17, 1809, and graduated at Harvard in the class of 1834. His services in the cause of the Union and good government, therefore, are a part of the renown of this Commonwealth, and should properly find a place in these pages. His narrative is as follows : —

"It came to my knowledge in the early part of 1861, first by rumors and then from evidence which I could not doubt, that there was a deep-laid conspiracy to capture Washington, destroy all the avenues leading to it from the North, East, and West, and thus prevent the inauguration of Mr. Lincoln in the capital of the country ; and, if this plot did not succeed, then to murder him while on his way to the capital, and thus inaugurate a revolution, which should end in establishing a Southern Confederacy, uniting all the Slave States, while it was imagined that the North would be divided into separate cliques, each striving for the destruction of the other. Early in the year 1861, Miss Dix, the philanthropist, came into my office on a Saturday afternoon. I had known her for some years as one engaged in alleviating the sufferings of the afflicted. Her occupation had brought her in contact with the prominent men South. In visiting hospitals, she had become familiar with the structure of Southern society, and also with the working of its political machinery. She stated that she had an important communication to make to me personally ; and, after closing my door, I listened attentively to what she had to say for more than an hour. She put in a tangible and reliable shape, by the facts she related, what before I had heard in numerous and detached parcels. The sum of it all was, that there was then an extensive and organized conspiracy throughout the South to seize upon Washington, with its archives and records, and then declare the Southern conspirators *de facto* the Government of the United States. The whole was to be a *coup d'état*. At the same time, they were to cut off all modes of communication between Washington and the North, East, or West, and thus prevent the transportation of troops to wrest the capital from the hands of the insurgents. Mr. Lincoln's inauguration was thus to be prevented, or his life was to fall a sacrifice to the attempt at inauguration. In fact, troops were then drilling on the line of our own road, and the Washington and Annapolis line, and other lines ; and they were sworn to obey the commands of their leaders, and the leaders were banded together to capture Washington. As soon as the interview was ended, I called Mr. N. P. Trist into my office, and told him I wanted him to go to Washington that night, and communicate these facts to General Scott. I also furnished him with some data as to the other routes to Washington, that might be adopted in case the direct route was cut off. One was the Delaware Railroad to Seaford, and then up the Chesapeake and Potomac to Washington, or to Annapolis and thence to Washington; another, to Perryville, and thence to Annapolis and Washington. Mr. Trist left that night, and arrived in Washington at six the next morning, which was on Sunday. He immediately had an interview with General Scott, who told him he had foreseen the trouble that was coming, and in October previous had made a communication to the President, predicting trouble at the South, and urging strongly the garrisoning of all the Southern forts and arsenals with forces sufficient to hold them, but that his advice had been unheeded; nothing had been done, and he feared nothing would be done; that he was powerless; and that he feared Mr. Lincoln would be obliged to be inaugurated into office at Philadelphia. He should, however, do all he could to bring troops to Washington sufficient to make it secure; but he had no influence with the Administration, and feared the worst consequences. Thus matters stood on Mr. Trist's visit to Washington, and thus they stood for some time afterwards. About this time, — a few days subsequent, however, — a gentleman from Baltimore came out to Backriver Bridge, about five miles this side of the city, and told the bridge-keeper that he had come to give information which had come to his knowledge of vital importance to the road, which he wished communicated to me. The nature of this communication was, that a party was then organized in Baltimore to burn our bridges, in case Mr. Lincoln came over the road, or in case we attempted to carry troops for the defence of Washington. The party, at that time, had combustible materials prepared to pour over the bridges; and were to disguise themselves as negroes, and be at the bridge just before the train in which Mr. Lincoln travelled had arrived. The bridge was then to be burned, the train attacked, and Mr. Lincoln to be put out of the way. This man appeared to be a gentleman and in earnest, and honest in what he said; but he would not give his name, nor allow any inquiries to be made as to his name or exact abode, as he said his life would be in peril were it known that he had given this information; but, if we would not attempt to find him out, he would continue to come and give information. He came subsequently several times, and gave items of information as to the movements of the conspirators; but I have never been able to ascertain who he was. Immediately after the development of these facts, I went to Washington, and there met a prominent and reliable gentleman from Baltimore, who was well acquainted with Marshal Kane, then the chief of police. I was anxious to ascertain whether he was loyal and reliable, and made particular inquiries upon both these points. I was assured that Kane was perfectly reliable; whereupon I made known some of the facts that had come to my knowledge in reference to the designs for the burning of the bridges, and requested that they should be laid before Marshal Kane, with a request that he should detail a police force to make the necessary investigation. Marshal Kane was seen, and it was suggested to him that there were reports of a conspiracy to burn the bridges and cut off Washington; and his advice was asked as to the best way of ferreting out the conspirators. He scouted the idea that there was any such thing on foot; said he had thoroughly investigated the whole matter, and there was not the slightest foundation for such rumors. I then determined to have nothing more to do with Marshal Kane, but to investigate the matter in my own way, and at once sent for a celebrated detective, who resided in the West, and whom I had before employed on an important matter. He was a man of great skill and resources. I furnished him with a few hints, and at once set him on the track with eight assistants. There were then drilling, upon the line of the railroad, some three military organizations, professedly for home defence, pretending to be Union men, and, in one or two instances, tendering their services to the railroad in case of trouble. Their propositions were duly considered; but the defence of the road was never intrusted to their tender mercies. The first thing done was to enlist a volunteer in each of these military companies. They pretended to come from New Orleans and Mobile, and did not appear to be wanting in sympathy for the South. They were furnished with uniforms at the expense of the road, and drilled as often as their associates in arms; became initiated into all the secrets of the organization, and reported every day or two to their chief, who immediately reported to me the designs and plans of these military companies. One of these organizations was loyal; but the other two were disloyal, and fully in the plot to destroy the bridges, and march to Washington, to wrest it from the hands of the legally constituted authorities. Every nook and corner of the road and its vicinity was explored by the chief and his detectives, and the secret working of secession and treason laid bare, and brought to light. Societies were joined in Baltimore, and various modes known to, and practised only by, detectives, were resorted to, to win the confidence of the conspirators, and get into their secrets. The plan worked well; and the midnight plottings and daily consultations of the conspirators were treasured up as a guide to our future plans for thwarting them. It turned out, that all that had been communicated by Miss Dix and the gentleman from Baltimore rested upon a foundation of fact, and that the half had not been told. It was made as certain as strong circumstantial and positive evidence could make it, that there was a plot to burn the bridges and destroy the road, and murder Mr. Lincoln on his way to Washington, if it turned out that he went there before troops were called. If troops were first called, then the bridges were to be destroyed, and Washington cut off, and taken possession of by the South. I at once organized and armed a force of about two hundred men, whom I distributed along the line between the Susquehanna and Baltimore, principally at the bridges. These men were drilled secretly and regularly by drill-masters, and were apparently employed in whitewashing the bridges, putting on some six or seven coats of whitewash, saturated with salt and alum, to make the outside of the bridges as nearly fireproof as possible. This whitewashing, so extensive in its application, became the nine days' wonder of the neighborhood. Thus the bridges were strongly guarded, and a train was arranged so as to concentrate all the forces at one point in case of trouble. The programme of Mr. Lincoln was changed; and as it was decided by him that he would go to Harrisburg from Philadelphia, and thence over the Northern Central road by day to Baltimore, and thence to Washington. We were then informed by our detective, that the attention of the conspirators was turned from our road to the Northern Central, and that they would there await the coming of Mr. Lincoln. This statement was confirmed by our Baltimore gentleman, who came out again, and said their designs upon our road were postponed for the present, and, unless we carried troops, would not be renewed again. Mr. Lincoln was to be waylaid on the line of the Northern Central road, and prevented from reaching Washington; and his life was to fall a sacrifice to the attempt. Thus matters stood on his arrival in Philadelphia. I felt it my duty to communicate to him the facts that had come to my knowledge, and urge his going to Washington privately that night in our sleeping-car, instead of publicly two days after, as was proposed. I went to a hotel in Philadelphia, where I met the detective, who was registered under an assumed name, and arranged with him to bring Mr. Judd, Mr. Lincoln's intimate friend, to my room in season to arrange the journey to Washington that night. One of our sub-detectives made three efforts to communicate with Mr. Judd while passing through the streets in the procession, and was three times arrested and carried out of the crowd by the police. The fourth time he succeeded, and brought Mr. Judd to my room, where he met the detective-in-chief and myself. We lost no time in making known to him all the facts which had come to our knowledge in reference to the conspiracy; and I most earnestly advised that Mr. Lincoln should go to Washington privately that night in the sleeping-car. Mr. Judd fully entered into the plan, and said he would urge Mr. Lincoln to adopt it. On his communicating with Mr. Lincoln, after the services of the evening were over, he answered that he had engaged to go to Harrisburg and speak the next day, and he would not break his engagement even in the face of such peril, but that, after he had fulfilled the engagement, he would follow such advice as we might give him in reference to his journey to Washington. It was then arranged that he should go to Harrisburg the next day, and make his address; after which he was to apparently return to Governor Curtin's house for the night, but in reality go to a point about two miles out of Harrisburg, where an extra car and engine awaited to take him to Philadelphia. At the time of his retiring, the telegraph lines, east, west, north, and south from Harrisburg were cut, so that no message as to his movements could be sent off in any direction. Mr. Lincoln could not probably arrive in season for our regular train that left at eleven, P.M., and I did not dare to send him by an extra for fear of its being found out or suspected that he was on the road; so it became necessary for me to devise some excuse for the detention of the train. But three or four on the road besides myself knew the plan. One of these I sent by an earlier train, to say to the people of the Washington Branch road that I had an important package, I was getting ready for the eleven, P.M., train; that it was necessary I should have this package delivered in Washington early the next morning without fail; that I was straining every nerve to get it ready by eleven o'clock, but, in case I did not succeed, I should delay the train until it was ready,— probably not more than half an hour; and I wished, as a personal favor, that the Washington train should await the coming of ours from Philadelphia before leaving. This request was willingly complied with by the managers of the Washington Branch; and the man whom I had sent to Baltimore so informed me by telegraph in cipher. The second person in the secret I sent to West Philadelphia, with a carriage, to await the coming of Mr. Lincoln. I gave him a package of old railroad reports, done up with great care, with a great seal attached to it, and directed in a fair, round hand, to a person at Willard's. I marked it 'Very important; to be delivered without fail by eleven o'clock train,' indorsing my own name upon the package. Mr. Lincoln arrived in West Philadelphia, and was immediately taken into the carriage, and driven to within a square of our station, where my man with the package jumped off, and waited till he saw the carriage drive up to the door, and Mr. Lincoln and the detective get out and go into the station. He then came up, and gave the package to the conductor, who was waiting at the door to receive it, in company with a police officer. Tickets had been bought beforehand for Mr. Lincoln and party to Washington, including a tier of berths in the sleeping-car. He passed between the conductor and the police-officer at the door, and neither suspected who he was. The conductor remarked as he passed, 'Well, old fellow, it is lucky for you that our president detained the train to send a package by it, or you would have been left.' Mr. Lincoln and the detective being safely ensconced in the sleeping-car, and my package safely in the hands of the conductor, the train started for Baltimore about fifteen minutes behind time. Our man No. 3, George ———, started with the train to go to Baltimore, and hand it over, with its contents, to man No. 1, who awaited its arrival in Baltimore. Before the train reached Gray's Ferry Bridge, and before Mr. Lincoln had resigned himself to slumber, the conductor came to our man George, and accosting him, said, 'George, I thought you and I were old friends; and why did you not tell me we had Old Abe on board?' George, thinking the conductor had in some way become possessed of the secret, answered, 'John, we are friends, and, as you have found it out, Old Abe is on board; and we will still be friends, and see him safely through.' John answered, 'Yes, if it costs me my life, he shall have a safe passage.' And so George stuck to one end of the car, and the conductor to the other every moment that his duties to the other passengers would admit of it. It turned out, however, that the conductor was mistaken in his man. A man strongly resembling Mr. Lincoln had come down to the train, about half an hour before it left, and bought a ticket to Washington for the sleeping-car. The conductor had seen him, and concluded he was the veritable Old Abe. George delivered the sleeping-car and train over to William in Baltimore, as had been previously arranged; who took his place at the brake, and rode to Washington, where he arrived at six, A.M., on time, and saw Mr. Lincoln, in the hands of a friend, safely delivered at Willard's, where he secretly ejaculated, 'God be praised!' He also saw the package of railroad reports, marked 'important,' safely delivered into the hands for which it was intended. This being done, he performed his morning ablutions in peace and quiet, and enjoyed with unusual zest his breakfast. At eight o'clock, the time agreed upon, the telegraph-wires were joined; and the first message flashed across the line was, 'Your package has arrived safely, and been delivered,' signed 'William.'

Then there went up from the writer of this a shout of joy and a devout thanksgiving to Him from whom all blessings flow; and the few who were in the secret joined in a heartfelt Amen. Thus began and ended a chapter in the history of the Rebellion, that has been never before written, but about which there have been many hints, entitled 'A Scotch Cap and Riding-cloak,' &c., neither of which had any foundation in truth, as Mr. Lincoln travelled in his ordinary dress. Mr. Lincoln was safely inaugurated; after which I discharged our detective force, and also the semi-military whitewashers, and all was quiet and serene again on the railroad. But the distant booming from Fort Sumter was soon heard, and aroused in earnest the whole population of the loyal States. The seventy-five thousand three-months men were called out; and again the plans for burning bridges and destroying the railroad were revived in all their force and intensity. Again I sent Mr. Trist to Washington to see General Scott, to beg for troops to garrison the road, as our forces were then scattered, and could not be got at. Mr. Trist telegraphed me that the forces would be supplied; but the crisis came on immediately, and all, and more than all, were required at Washington. At the last moment, I obtained, and sent down the road, about two hundred men, armed with shot-guns and revolvers, — all the arms I could get hold of at the time. They were raw and undisciplined men, and not fit to cope with those brought against them, — about one hundred and fifty men, fully armed, and commanded by the redoubtable rebel, J. R. Trimble."

Such was the condition of affairs along the line of that road when the Sixth Regiment reached Philadelphia, on the 18th of April. I now proceed with the narrative.

The Third and Fourth Regiments were composed of companies belonging to towns in Norfolk, Plymouth, and Bristol Counties. The Sixth and Eighth were almost exclusively from Middlesex and Essex Counties. The field-officers of the Third were David W. Wardrop, of New Bedford, colonel; Charles Raymond, of Plymouth, lieutenant-colonel; John H. Jennings, of New Bedford, major; Austin S. Cushman, of New Bedford, adjutant; Edward D. Allen, Fairhaven, quartermaster; Alexander R. Holmes, of New Bedford, surgeon; Johnson Clark, of New Bedford, assistant-surgeon; Alberti C. Maggi, of New Bedford, sergeant-major; and Frederick S. Gifford, of New Bedford, quartermaster-sergeant.

Company A, "Halifax Light Infantry." Joseph S. Harlow,

of Middleborough, captain. The lieutenants were Cephas Washburn, of Kingston, and Charles P. Lyon, of Halifax.

Company B, "Standish Guards," of Plymouth. Charles C. Doten, of Plymouth, captain; Otis Rogers, of Plymouth, and William B. Alexander, of Boston, lieutenants.

Company B, "Cambridge City Guards," of Cambridge. This company was the first company raised for the war in Massachusetts, and was organized in January, 1861, and attached temporarily to the Fifth Regiment. It was recruited out of the Cambridge "Wide Awake Club." Its officers were James P. Richardson, captain; Samuel E. Chamberlain and Edwin F. Richardson, lieutenants, — all of whom belonged to that part of the city of Cambridge known as Cambridgeport.

Company G, the "Assonet Light Infantry," Freetown. John W. Marble, captain; Humphrey A. Francis and John M. Dean, lieutenants, — all of Freetown.

Company H, "Samoset Guards," Plympton. Lucian L. Perkins, of Plympton, captain; Oscar E. Washburn, of Plympton, and Southworth Loring, of Middleborough, lieutenants.

Company K, "Bay State Light Infantry," Carver. William S. McFarlin, of South Carver, captain; John Dunham, of North Carver, and Francis L. Porter, of New Bedford, lieutenants.

Company L, "New Bedford City Guards." Timothy Ingraham, captain; and James Barton and Austin S. Cushman, lieutenants, — all of New Bedford.

This company left New-Bedford early on the morning of the 16th. Its departure was witnessed by thousands of citizens. Addresses were made by ex-Governor John H. Clifford and the Mayor of the city. The following is an extract from Governor Clifford's speech: —

"You, New-Bedford Guards, — guards of honor and safety to your fellow-citizens! We know, that, when brought to the test, you will be justified and approved. It was a severe trial to be summoned away in time of peace and prosperity; but it may be the discipline of a beneficent Providence, to remind us of our blessings, and that as a people we might show to the world whether we are worthy of liberty. We remain: you go forth. The ties of affection, the tenderness of mother, wife, sister, and friends, cluster around this hour. All these ties you cheerfully yield to the call to patriot conflict and our country's welfare.... All bid you God-speed, even the families who are to be left alone; as the wife of one of you said this morning to the question if her husband was going, 'My husband going? Yes; and I would not keep him back for all that he could gain at home. I will welcome him on his return, if he should return; and, if that should not be, I will for ever bless and honor his memory.' Go in peace, my friends. Disturb not your minds about the care of your families. Your fellow-citizens will see to it that those you leave behind shall want nothing while you are gone. We shall hear from you on the field of duty, and that not one has failed, wherever he may be. God keep you safe under his care, and bring you back with untarnished glory, to be received by your fellow-citizens with heartfelt joy and honor!"

At the conclusion of this speech, an impressive prayer was made by Rev. Mr. Girdwood. An escort of citizens, headed by ex-Governor Clifford, conducted the company to the cars, which started for Boston amid the cheers of the assembled thousands.

The Third Regiment was destined for Fortress Monroe; and, the steam transport being ready, the regiment left its quarters about six o'clock on the afternoon of Wednesday the 17th, marched to the State House to receive its equipments, and from thence to Central Wharf, where it embarked. The regiment was cheered the whole length of its march, and a national salute was fired on the wharf. The steamer cast off about seven o'clock, and anchored in the stream, where it remained until noon the next day, when it sailed, bearing to Virginia its patriot freight. It arrived at Fortress Monroe on the 20th.

The field and staff officers of the Fourth Regiment were Abner B. Packard, of Quincy, colonel; Hawkes Fearing, Jr., of Hingham, lieutenant-colonel; Horace O. Whittemore, of Boston, major; Henry Walker, of Quincy, adjutant; William H. Carruth, of Boston, quartermaster; Henry M. Saville, of Quincy, surgeon; William E. Faxon, of Quincy, "surgeon's mate;" Alvin E. Hall, of Foxborough, sergeant-major; and George W. Barnes, of Plymouth, quartermaster-sergeant.

Company A, "Union Light Guards," Canton. Officers: Ira Drake, of Stoughton, captain; Henry U. Morse and Walter Cameron, of Canton, lieutenants. At this time, Lieutenant

Cameron was in New Orleans; and John McKay, Jr., of Canton, was chosen to fill the vacancy. Lieutenant Cameron, however, soon after returned home, and joined his company at Fortress Monroe.

Company B, "Light Infantry," Easton. Officers: Milo M. Williams, captain; Linton Waldron and William E. Bump, Jr., lieutenants, — all of Easton.

Company C, "Light Infantry," Braintree. Officers: Cephas C. Bumpus, captain; James T. Stevens and Isaac P. Fuller, lieutenants, — all of Braintree.

Company D, "Light Infantry," Randolph. Officers: Horace Niles, captain; Otis S. Wilbur and H. Frank Wales, lieutenants, — all of Randolph.

Company E, "Light Infantry," South Abington. Officers: Charles F. Allen, captain; Lewis Soule and John W. Mitchell, lieutenants, — all of South Abington.

Company F, "Warren Light Guards," Foxborough. Officers: David L. Shepard, captain; Moses A. Richardson and Carlos A. Hart, lieutenants, — all of Foxborough.

Company G, "Light Infantry," Taunton. Officers: Timothy Gordon, captain; Zaccheus Sherman and Frederick A. Harrington, lieutenants, — all of Taunton.

Company H, "Hancock Light Guards," Quincy. Officers: Franklin Curtis, captain; Edward A. Spear and Benjamin F. Meservey, lieutenants, — all of Quincy.

Company I, "Lincoln Light Guards," Hingham. Officers: Luther Stephenson, Jr., captain; Charles Sprague and Nathaniel French, Jr., lieutenants, — all of Hingham. This company was named in honor of Major-General Benjamin Lincoln, of revolutionary renown.

This regiment was ready to march on the 16th; but transportation could not be arranged until the next day. Its destination was Fortress Monroe. It left Faneuil Hall at three o'clock on the afternoon of the 17th, and marched to the State House, where it was addressed by Governor Andrew, who said, —

"It gives me unspeakable pleasure to witness this array from the good Old Colony. You have come from the shores of the sounding sea, where lie the ashes of Pilgrims; and you are bound on a high and noble pilgrimage for liberty, for the Union and Constitution of your country. Soldiers of the Old Bay State, sons of sires who never disgraced their flag in civil life or on the tented field, I thank you from the bottom of my heart for this noble response to the call of your State and your country. You cannot wait for words. I bid you Godspeed and an affectionate farewell."

Colonel Packard made a brief and fitting response; and the regiment filed down Park Street, and marched to the depot of the Old Colony Railroad, where a train was ready to receive it. In a few minutes, the regiment was on the way to Fall River, where it was put on board the steamer "State of Maine," and arrived at New York the next afternoon. Its departure was delayed until four o'clock on the morning of the 19th, in adjusting ballast and taking in coal, when it started for Fortress Monroe, and arrived there at break of day on the morning of the 20th. In its march through Boston and along the route to Fall River, the regiment was received with cheers of approval from the men, and by the waving of handkerchiefs by the women, who turned out to greet it.

The Sixth Regiment mustered on the 16th at Lowell, at nine o'clock in the morning. Before leaving the city for Boston, it was addressed by the Mayor and others, and cheered by the populace. Four of the companies belonged in Lowell. The inhabitants in mass came from their dwellings, mills, and workshops, to witness the regiment depart. It arrived in Boston at one o'clock, where it met with a cordial reception. The crowd followed it to Faneuil Hall, and from thence to Boylston Hall, where its headquarters were established.

The field and staff officers of the Sixth were Edward F. Jones, of Pepperell, colonel; Benjamin F. Watson, of Lawrence, lieutenant-colonel; Josiah A. Sawtell, of Lowell, major; Alpha B. Farr, of Lowell, adjutant; James Monroe, of Cambridge, quartermaster; Charles Babbidge, of Pepperell, chaplain; Norman Smith, of Groton, surgeon; Jansen T. Paine, of Charlestown, "surgeon's mate;" Rufus L. Plaisted, of Lowell, paymaster; Samuel D. Shattuck, of Groton, sergeant-major; Church Howe, of Worcester, quartermaster-sergeant; John Dupee, of Boston, commissary-sergeant; Frederick Stafford, of Lowell, drum-major; William H. Gray, of Acton, hospital steward. The Sixth had a full staff and regimental band.

Company A, "National Greys," Lowell. Officers: Josiah A. Sawtell, captain; Andrew J. Johnson and Andrew C. Wright, lieutenants, — all of Lowell.

Company B, "Groton Artillery," Groton. Officers: Eusebius S. Clark, captain; George F. Shattuck and Samuel G. Blood, lieutenants, — all of Groton.

Company C, "Mechanics' Phalanx," Lowell. Officers: Albert S. Follansbee, captain; Samuel D. Shipley and John C. Jepson, lieutenants, — all of Lowell.

Company D, "City Guards," Lowell. Officers: James W. Hart, captain; Charles E. Jones and Samuel C. Pinney, Llewellyn L. Craig, lieutenants, — all of Lowell.

Company E, "Davis Guards," Acton. Officers: Daniel Tuttle, captain; William H. Chapman and George W. Rand, Silas B. Blodgett, Aaron S. Fletcher, lieutenants, — all of Acton.

This company was named in honor of their brave townsman, Captain Isaac Davis, who commanded an Acton company to defend the North Bridge, across Concord River, on the 19th of April, 1775, where he fell a martyr to liberty and American independence.

Company F, "Warren Light Guard," Lawrence. Officers: Benjamin F. Chadbourne, captain; Melvin Beal, Thomas J. Cate, and Jesse C. Silver, lieutenants, — all of Lawrence.

Company G, "Worcester Light Infantry," Worcester. Officers: Harrison W. Pratt, captain; George W. Prouty, Thomas S. Washburn, J. Waldo Denny, and Dexter F. Parker, lieutenants, — all of Worcester.

This company was originally organized in 1803, by Hon. Levi Lincoln, and served in the war of 1812, under command of his brother, Captain John W. Lincoln.

Company H, "Watson Light Guard," Lowell. Officers: John F. Noyes, captain; George E. Davis, Andrew F. Jewett, and Benjamin Warren, lieutenants, — all of Lowell.

Company I, "Light Infantry," Lawrence. Officers: John

Pickering, captain; Daniel S. Yeaton, A. Lawrence Hamilton, Eben H. Ellenwood, and Eugene J. Mason, lieutenants,—all of Lawrence.

Company K, "Washington Light Guard," Boston. Officers: Walter S. Sampson, captain; Ansell D. Wass, Moses J. Emery, Thomas Walwork, and John F. Dunning, lieutenants. This company was detached from the First Regiment to complete the Sixth. The company was drilling in its armory, on Eliot Street, Boston, on the evening of the 16th. About ten o'clock, the Adjutant-General brought to Captain Sampson, at the armory, an order from the Governor, attaching the company to the Sixth Regiment, to proceed the next morning to Washington. The order was received with nine cheers. Every man was ready and eager to go.

Company L, "Light Infantry," Stoneham. Officers: John H. Dike, captain; Leander F. Lynde, Darius N. Stevens, and John F. Rowe,—all of Stoneham,—and William B. Blaisdell, of Lynn, lieutenants.

This company was detached from the Seventh Regiment. The Adjutant-General, in his Report for 1861, says,—

"It was nine o'clock, in the evening of the 16th, before your Excellency decided to attach the commands of Captains Sampson and Dike to the Sixth Regiment. A messenger was despatched to Stoneham with orders for Captain Dike, who reported to me, at eight o'clock the next morning, that he found Captain Dike at his house in Stoneham, at two o'clock in the morning, and placed your Excellency's orders in his hands; that he read them, and said, 'Tell the Adjutant-General that I shall be at the State House, with my full command, by eleven o'clock to-day.' True to his word, he reported at the time; and that afternoon, attached to the Sixth, the company left for Washington. Two days afterwards, on the 19th of April, during that gallant march through Baltimore which is now a matter of history, Captain Dike was shot down while leading his company through the mob. He received a wound in the leg, which will render him a cripple for life."

The orders were promulgated at Stoneham immediately. The bells of the several meeting-houses were rung. The company and the inhabitants assembled. Immediate preparations to leave were made. The citizens made up a purse of five hundred dollars, and gave it to Captain Dike, for the service of himself and company.

At eleven o'clock in the forenoon of the 17th, the Sixth Regiment marched from Boylston Hall to the State House, where it received the new rifled muskets in exchange for smooth-bores. When in line in front of the State House, the Governor made a short and eloquent speech to the regiment, and presented it with a new set of colors. Colonel Jones received the colors, and pledged himself and the regiment that they should never be disgraced. At seven o'clock that evening, the Sixth marched to the depot of the Boston and Worcester Railroad, and embarked by the land route for New York. At the depot, and along the entire line of road, they received one continued ovation. At several places, the bells were rung, and salutes of artillery fired. At Worcester, an immense throng cheered them; at Springfield, the military and the fire department turned out to do them honor. The regiment reached New York at sunrise on the 18th, having been in the cars all night. The march down Broadway to the Astor House, where the officers and men breakfasted by invitation of the proprietor, General Charles Stetson, and from the Astor House down Cortland Street, to the Jersey-City Ferry, is described as one of the most grand and effective scenes ever witnessed. The wildest enthusiasm inspired all classes. Strong men wept like tenderly-nurtured women, and silently implored the blessings of Heaven upon the regiment, and the State which had placed it at the extreme right of the Union column. A gentleman who witnessed the scene wrote, "I was always proud of my native State; but never until now did I fully realize how grand she is." Another writer thus describes the scene:—

"Having breakfasted, they employed their time until eleven in conversation, smoking, and preparing for the march. All appeared determined to stand by the old flag under all hazards, and to punish those who would dare to insult it. Many of the men are exceedingly intelligent, and not a few came from families eminent in the history of the old Bay State. They spoke of the ability of Massachusetts to send thirty thousand men, and even more volunteers, to the support of the Government, if needed. At eleven o'clock, the various companies, having assembled at the Astor House, formed in Broadway. By this time, thousands of our citizens had gathered to bid the brave fellows God-speed. No language can describe the excitement of the vast concourse. Cheer followed cheer, until the welkin rung as with a sound of thunder. There were cheers for the star-spangled banner; for the dear old flag; for the red, white, and blue; for the Government; for the North; for Lincoln; for Major Anderson; for every thing the loyal heart could suggest. Old men, young men, and lads waved the American flag over their heads, pinned it to their hats and coats; cartmen displayed it on their horses; Barnum flings it from every window of the Museum. The guests of the Astor House shouted till they were hoarse; so did the visitors at the Museum; and when at last, at half-past eleven, the police taking the lead, the regiment took up their march for the Jersey-City Ferry, the enthusiasm was perfectly overwhelming. At every step, the roar of the multitude was increased; at every window, the flags were waved.

"Turning from Broadway into Cortland Street, the scene was such as has seldom, if ever, been seen in New York. The stores could hardly be seen for the flags, of which there must have been, on an average, one for every window in the stores. Every building was thronged with persons eager to see the regiment; while the sidewalks, awning-posts, and stoops were literally covered with a mass of excited humanity. There was one uninterrupted and unprecedented cheer from Broadway to the ferry. Those who have witnessed all the great demonstrations of the city for a half-century back, remember none so spontaneous and enthusiastic. As the regiment filed off to go upon the ferry-boat, which was gayly decorated with flags, as was the ferry-house, there were loud cries of 'God bless you!' 'God bless you!' and unbounded cheers for the Old Bay State."

On crossing the river, the troops were met by a dense crowd of Jersey men and women. Flags were waved by hundreds of fair hands, and miniature flags were distributed by them to the regiment before the train moved. There was delay in getting off; and the crowd continued to increase, and the enthusiasm to grow more intense. The passage across New Jersey was marked with similar scenes. At Newark, they were received with a salute of artillery, and also at Trenton, which was ordered by the Governor of the State. The reception at Philadelphia was a fitting climax to what had taken place elsewhere. A member of the regiment wrote, "So enthusiastic were our friends, that they rushed into our ranks, threw their arms about the necks of our soldiers, and, emptying their own pockets for our benefit, seemed fairly beside themselves with joy. I doubt if old Massachusetts ever, before or since, received such encomiums, or her sons such a generous welcome, as that night in the City of Brotherly Love." The regiment reached Philadelphia at seven o'clock in the evening, partook of a bountiful supper at the Continental Hotel, and were quartered for the night in the Girard House, where I shall leave them for the present.

The Eighth Regiment, which had arrived in Boston on the 16th, did not leave the city until the 18th. The field and staff officers were Timothy Monroe, of Lynn, colonel; Edward W. Hinks, of Lynn, lieutenant-colonel; Andrew Elwell, of Gloucester, major. Colonel Monroe resigned on the 12th of May: and, on the 16th of May, Edward W. Hinks was elected colonel; Andrew Elwell, lieutenant-colonel; and Ben. Perley Poore, of Newbury, major; George Creasey, of Newburyport, was appointed adjutant; E. Alfred Ingalls, of Lynn, quartermaster; Rowland G. Usher, of Lynn, paymaster; Bowman B. Breed, of Lynn, surgeon; Warren Tapley, of Lynn, assistant-surgeon; Gilbert Haven, Jr., of Malden, chaplain; John Goodwin, Jr., of Marblehead, sergeant-major; Horace E. Monroe, of Lynn, sergeant-major; and Samuel Roads, of Marblehead, drum-major.

Company A, "Cushing Guards," Newburyport. Officers: Albert W. Bartlett, of Newburyport, captain; George Barker, Gamaliel Hodges, Nathan W. Collins, all of Newburyport, and Edward L. Noyes, of Lawrence, lieutenants.

Company B, "Lafayette Guard," Marblehead. Officers: Richard Phillips, of Marblehead, captain; Abiel S. Roads, Jr., William S. Roads, and William Cash, all of Marblehead, lieutenants.

Company C, "Sutton Light Infantry," Marblehead. Officers: Knott V. Martin, of Marblehead, captain; Samuel C. Graves, Lorenzo F. Linnel, John H. Haskell, all of Marblehead, lieutenants.

Company D, "Light Infantry," Lynn. Officers: George T. Newhall, of Lynn, captain; Thomas H. Berry, E. Z. Saunderson, C. M. Merritt, all of Lynn, lieutenants.

Company E, "Light Infantry," Beverly. Officers: Francis E. Porter, of Beverly, captain; John W. Raymond, Eleazer Giles, Albert Wallis, and Moses S. Herrick, all of Beverly, lieutenants.

Company F, "City Guards," Lynn. Officers: James Hudson, Jr., of Lynn, captain; Edward A. Chandler, Henry Stone, Mathias N. Snow, all of Lynn, lieutenants.

Company G, "American Guard," Gloucester. Officers: Addison Center, of Gloucester, captain; David W. Lowe, Edward A. Story, Harry Clark, all of Gloucester, lieutenants.

Company H, "Glover Light Guard," Marblehead. Officers: Francis Boardman, of Marblehead, captain; Thomas Russell, Nicholas Bowden, and Joseph S. Caswell, all of Marblehead, lieutenants.

Company I, "Light Infantry," Salem. Officers: Arthur F. Devereux, of Salem, captain; George F. Austin, Ethan A. P. Brewster, and George D. Putnam, all of Salem, lieutenants.

This company belonged to the Seventh Regiment, but was ordered, on the evening of the 17th of April, to join the Eighth, and, at ten o'clock the next morning, reported at Faneuil Hall with full ranks. Before leaving Salem, it was addressed by the Mayor and other prominent citizens. A great crowd met it at the depot, and cheered it when it left. This company wore a Zouave uniform, and, in skirmish drill, was probably the most efficient in the State.

Company K, "Allen Guard," Pittsfield. Officers: Henry S. Briggs, of Pittsfield, captain; Henry H. Richardson and Robert Bache, both of Pittsfield, lieutenants. This company was detached to complete the organization of the Eighth. It was ordered to join the regiment at Springfield, when on the way to Washington. The captain was a son of Ex-Governor Briggs. Before the company left Pittsfield, each soldier was presented by the citizens with ten dollars.

On the 18th of April, the regiment marched to the State House, and was presented with a set of regimental colors by Governor Andrew, who also addressed it as follows: —

"Mr. Commander and Soldiers, — Yesterday you were citizens: to-day you are heroes. Summoned by the sudden call of your country, true to the fortunes of your flag, to the inspirations of your own hearts, and to the mighty example of your fathers, you have hurried from the thronged towns of Essex, and all along the shore from Boston to Cape Ann, famed through all Massachusetts for noble men, brave soldiers, and heroic women. You have come to be cradled anew, one night in Faneuil Hall, there breathing once more the inspiration of historic American liberty, and standing beneath the folds of the American banner. [Applause.] From the bottom of my heart of hearts, as the official representative of Massachusetts, I pay to you, soldiers, citizens, and heroes, the homage of my most profound gratitude; and the heart of all Massachusetts beats with full sympathy to every word I utter. There is but one pulsation beating through all this beautiful domain of liberty, from the shores of Cape Cod to the hills of Berkshire; and the mountain waves and mountain peaks answer to each other. Soldiers, go forth, bearing that flag; and, as our fathers fought, so, if need be, strike you the blow.

'Where breathes the foe but falls before us,
With freedom's soil beneath our feet,
And freedom's banner waving o'er us?'

We stay behind, to guard the hearthstones you have left; and, whatever may be the future, we will protect the wives and children you may leave, and, as you will be faithful to the country, so we will be faithful to them. I speak to you as citizens and soldiers, not of Massachusetts, but of the American Confederate Union. While we live, that Union shall last. [Applause.] And until these countless thousands, and all their posterity, have tasted death, the Union of the American people, the heritage of Washington, shall be eternal. [Applause.]

"Soldiers! go forth, bearing with you the blessing of your country, bearing the confidence of your fellow-citizens; and under the blessing of God, with stout hearts and stalwart frames, go forth to victory. On your shields be returned, or bring them with you. Yours it is to be among the advanced guard of Massachusetts soldiers. As such, I bid you God-speed, and fare-you-well."

At the close of the Governor's speech, Colonel Monroe received the colors, and said, "We shall do our duty." Three cheers were given for the regiments, and three for General Butler, who, being present, advanced, and said, —

"Soldiers, — We stand upon that spot to which the good pleasure of the Commander-in-chief, and our own dearest wishes, have assigned us. To lead the advance guard of freedom and constitutional liberty, and of perpetuity of the Union, is the honor we claim, and which, under God, we will maintain. [Applause.]

"Sons of Puritans, who believe in the providence of Almighty God! as he was with our fathers, so may he be with us in this strife for the right, for the good of all, for the great missionary country of liberty! [Applause.] And, if we prove recreant to our trust, may the God of battles prove our enemy in the hour of our utmost need!

"Soldiers! we march to-night; and let me say for you all to the good people of the Commonwealth, that we will not turn back, till we show those who have laid their hand upon the fabric of the Union, there is but one thought in the North, — the union of these States, now and for ever, one and inseparable."

The regiment left Boston at four o'clock that afternoon by Worcester and Springfield, and was greeted with the same unbounded enthusiasm the Sixth received. General Butler accompanied it as commander of the Massachusetts brigade. While the train stopped at Worcester, he spoke a few words to the crowd at the depot. "In this contest," he said, "we banish party differences. We are all Americans. We love our country and its flag; and it is only by the sword we can have peace, and only in the Union, liberty."

The regiment reached New York on the morning of the 19th, and marched down Broadway amid the congratulations of the vast multitude. This was the second Massachusetts regiment that had marched through that city in advance of all others, while two other regiments were on the seas for Fortress Monroe. After partaking of the generous hospitalities tendered them, the regiment crossed to Jersey City, and proceeded by railroad to Philadelphia, which it reached at six o'clock that evening, and first received positive information concerning the attack made upon the Sixth in Baltimore that day.

The field and staff officers of the Fifth Regiment were, Samuel C. Lawrence, of Medford, colonel; J. Durell Greene, of Cambridge, lieutenant-colonel; Hamlin W. Keyes, of Boston, major; Thomas O. Barri, of Cambridge, adjutant; Joseph E. Billings, of Boston, quartermaster; G. Foster Hodges, of

Roxbury, paymaster; Samuel H. Hurd, of Charlestown, surgeon; Henry H. Mitchell, of East Bridgewater, surgeon's mate; Benjamin F. De Costa, of Charlestown, chaplain; Henry A. Quincy, of Charlestown, sergeant-major; Charles Foster, of Charlestown, drum-major.

Several changes occurred while the regiment was in service. Colonel Greene, Major Keyes, and Adjutant Barri were appointed officers in the regular army. To fill these vacancies, Captain Pierson was elected lieutenant-colonel; Captain John T. Boyd, major; and Lieutenant John G. Chambers was appointed adjutant. The following is the roster of the companies: —

Company A, "Mechanic Light Infantry," Salem. George H. Pierson, of Salem, captain; Edward H. Staten and Lewis E. Wentworth, of Salem, lieutenants.

Company B, "Richardson Light Guard," South Reading. John W. Locke, of South Reading, captain; Henry D. Degen, Charles H. Shepard, James D. Draper, and George Abbott, all of South Reading, lieutenants.

Company C, "Charlestown Artillery," Charlestown. William R. Swan, of Chelsea, captain: Phineas H. Tibbetts, of Charlestown; John W. Rose, of South Boston; Hannibal D. Norton, of Chelsea; and George H. Marden, Jr., of Charlestown, lieutenants.

Company D, "Light Infantry," Haverhill. Officers: Carlos P. Messer, of Haverhill, captain; George J. Dean, Daniel F. Smith, Charles H. P. Palmer, and Thomas T. Salter, all of Haverhill, lieutenants.

Company E, "Lawrence Light Guard," Medford. Officers: John Hutchins, of Medford, captain; John G. Chambers and Perry Colman, of Medford, and William H. Pattee, of West Cambridge (Arlington), lieutenants.

Company F, "Wardwell Tigers," Boston. Officers: David K. Wardwell, Boston, captain: Jacob H. Sleeper, of Boston; George G. Stoddard, of Brookline; Horace P. Williams, of Brookline; and Horatio N. Holbrook, of Boston, lieutenants.

This was a new company, recruited, organized, uniformed, and equipped in two days.

Company G, "Concord Artillery," Concord. Officers: George L. Prescott, of Concord, captain; Joseph Derby, Jr., Humphrey H. Buttrick, and Charles Bowers, all of Concord, lieutenants.

Company H, "City Guards," Salem. Officers: Henry F. Danforth, of Salem, captain; Kirk Stark, William F. Sumner, George H. Wiley, and John E. Stone, all of South Danvers, lieutenants.

Company I, "Light Infantry," Somerville. Officers: George O. Brastow, of Somerville, captain; William E. Robinson and Frederick R. Kinsley, both of Somerville, lieutenants.

Company K, "City Guards," Charlestown. Officers: John T. Boyd, of Charlestown, captain; John B. Norton, Caleb Drew, and Walter Everett, all of Charlestown, lieutenants.

This regiment did not receive orders to report until Friday, April 19. It was in readiness to go forward the next day, but was detained until Sunday, with headquarters at Faneuil Hall. The line was formed on South Market Street, at five o'clock on Sunday morning, April 21; and the regiment marched to the Worcester Depot. Notwithstanding the early hour and the sabbath day, thousands were on the streets, and at the depot, to witness the departure. Kind greetings met this regiment everywhere on the route. To state what was said and done would be only a repetition of what has already been said in regard to regiments which had preceded. It reached New York safely on Sunday evening, at eight o'clock. After partaking of a hearty meal at the hotels, the regiment was put on board of two transports; four companies, under command of Major Keyes, going on board the "Ariel," and six, under command of Colonel Lawrence, on board the "De Soto." The Third Battalion of Massachusetts Rifles, under command of Major Devens, and Major Cook's Light Battery, were placed on board the same vessels; the former in the "De Soto," and the latter in the "Ariel."

The duties of the week had been incessant day and night at the State House. The attack upon the Sixth Regiment in Baltimore had added to the number of people who crowded in, and intensified the earnest feelings of every one. Late on

Friday night (the 19th), the Adjutant-General, wearied with the labors of the four preceding days, left the State House with Senator Wilson. They obtained lodging at Young's Coffee House. About four o'clock on Saturday morning, a messenger brought an order to him from Governor Andrew, that a telegram had just been received from General Butler, at Philadelphia, to send forward immediately Major Cook's Light Battery. The Governor's orders were to notify the officers at once, that the battery might be ready, and pushed forward that night. The Adjutant-General told the messenger to get a carriage, and he would be ready by the time he returned. Major Cook lived in Somerville, but in what part of it he did not know. The adjutant lived in Chester Square, Boston: he ordered the carriage to drive there. The city was asleep; not a human being was on the streets. The silence of the great city appeared more impressive and profound than that of a primeval forest. At Chester Square, he learned that the adjutant had sailed for Europe the week before. He then was driven to Cambridge Street, where the former commander of the battery, Major Nims, lived. He was aroused from a sound sleep, and informed of the purpose of the errand. He knew where Major Cook lived, and volunteered to carry the orders to him without delay. The orderly sergeant of the company boarded in McLean Place. The Adjutant-General found him also asleep; but soon aroused him, and ordered him to notify the company. The sergeant said he " knew where every man lived, and they all wanted to go." Early in the forenoon, the company reported with full ranks. The Quartermaster-General succeeding in purchasing horses, and providing ammunition. The field and staff were Asa M. Cook, of Somerville, major; Frederick A. Heath, of Boston, adjutant; Thomas J. Foss, of Boston, quartermaster; John P. Ordway, of Boston, surgeon; F. Le Baron Monroe, assistant-surgeon; Josiah Porter, of North Cambridge; William H. McCartney, of Boston; C. C. E. Mortimer, of Boston; and Robert L. Sawin, of Boston, lieutenants.

The company numbered one hundred and twenty men. The battery had six brass six-pounders. They took with them seventy horses, selected mainly from the stables of the Metropolitan Horse railroad Company, and ten tons of cartridges of shot and grape. They marched to the Worcester Railroad Depot, between one and two o'clock that afternoon, ready to start; but waited until the next morning for the Fifth Regiment. They went to New York in the same train with the Fifth, and to Annapolis in the transports with four of the companies of that regiment.

Orders were issued from the State House on Saturday, the 20th of April, for the Third Battalion to go forward to Washington. It consisted then of three companies, with headquarters in Worcester. They were in line, ready to proceed, at five o'clock that afternoon. The battalion was addressed by Hon. Isaac Davis, Mayor of Worcester, and by Major Devens, in command. A prayer by Rev. Dr. Hill closed the ceremony. At half-past ten that evening, they took the cars for New York, where they arrived early on the morning of the 21st. While there, they quartered in the armory of the New-York Seventh. During the day, they were visited by Hon. Charles Sumner, who made a short address. At eight o'clock, they embarked on board the transport "Ariel" for Annapolis, with a part of the Fifth Regiment, and arrived at Annapolis on the morning of the 24th, where they remained until the 2d of May, when they were ordered to Fort McHenry, in the harbor of Baltimore, which they reached by transport on the morning of the third.

The field and staff of the Third Battalion of Rifles were, Charles Devens, Jr., major; John M. Goodhue, adjutant; James E. Estabrook, quartermaster; Oramel Martin, surgeon; Nathaniel S. Liscomb, sergeant-major; George T. White, quartermaster-sergeant, — all of Worcester.

Company A, "City Guards," Worcester. Officers: Augustus R. B. Sprague, captain; Josiah Pickett, George C. Joslin, Orson Moulton, Elijah A. Harkness, lieutenants, — all of Worcester.

Company B, "Holden Rifles," Holden. Officers: Joseph H. Gleason, of Holden, captain; Phineas R. Newell, Holden; Edward F. Devens, Charlestown; Samuel F. Woods, Barre; George Bascom, Holden, lieutenants.

Company C, "Emmet Guards," Worcester. Officers: Michael P. McConville, captain; Michael O'Driscoll, Matthew J.

McCafferty, Thomas O'Neil, and Maurice Melvin, lieutenants, — all of Worcester.

Company D, Boston. Officers: Albert Dodd, captain; Charles Dodd, Cornelius G. Atwood, George A. Hicks, and Joseph Nason, lieutenants, — all of Boston.

Company D was raised in Boston on the morning of the 19th of April, by the gentlemen who were afterwards commissioned its officers. It was attached to the Third Battalion, and left Boston in the steamer "Cambridge" on the 2d of May for Fortress Monroe, and from thence by the Potomac River to Washington. The vessel sailed from Boston with sealed instructions, which were not opened until outside of Boston Light. In these instructions to Captain Dodd, the Adjutant-General says, "It is the earnest desire of His Excellency the Commander-in-chief, that the ship 'Cambridge' shall reach Washington, and demonstrate that a Massachusetts ship, manned with Massachusetts men, shall be the first ship to arrive by that route, as our Sixth Regiment was the first to arrive at Washington, through the hostile city of Baltimore." The "Cambridge" arrived safely with the company, and was the first that reached Washington by the Potomac River. After remaining in Washington twelve days, the command was sent to Fort McHenry, Baltimore harbor, and joined the Battalion.

The Third Battalion completed the number of three-months men called for by the Government, which consisted of five regiments, one battalion, and one battery.

By the constitution and laws of Massachusetts, company officers were elected by the men composing the company, regimental officers by the commissioned officers of companies, brigadier-generals by the regimental field-officers of the brigade, and major-generals by the Legislature. The General Statutes of the Commonwealth allowed four lieutenants to each infantry company. In the regular army, only two lieutenants were allowed to a company of infantry. The reader will have observed that some of the companies in the regiments forwarded to the front had two, some three, and some four lieutenants. This was permitted by our laws. The extra lieutenants belonging to the two regiments sent to Fortress Monroe were not mustered into the service, the mustering officers refusing to muster them. They had, therefore, either to return home, or join the ranks as enlisted men. In the regiments which were sent to Washington, the extra lieutenants were mustered in, and served with their companies to the end of their terms. The reason for this distinction has never been given.

The material of these commands was of the best. They were young men who had a taste for military duty. They were from the middle walks of life, and depended upon their health and hands for support. Most of them were mechanics, farmers' sons, and clerks in stores. They bought their own uniforms, and paid company assessments out of their own pockets. They were public-spirited, full of life, and knew their duty. Many of the companies had honorable records, running back to the war of 1812, of which they were proud. They had rivalries and jealousies. They demanded their right position in the regimental line, and would have it. They obeyed their officers because they were their officers, and held positions by their votes. They chose the color and style of their own uniforms. If a rival company wore blue, they would have gray or red. The uniforms in a regiment were variegated, like the colors of a rainbow. They were made more for show than use, as active service proved. Yet they cost much money. But it was no one's business but their own, as they paid the bills. They had their pet names, as well as the regimental letter, and they preferred being known by the name they had themselves chosen. Thus there were the N. E. G.'s and B. L. I.'s, the "Tigers," the "Savages," and the "Guards." Each had its friends and followers, and each its enemies and detractors. Yet beneath all these there was a substratum of genuine good feeling, and a soldierly pride. The very opposition they received from those who laughed or sneered at the militia cemented them in closer union, and made them more determined to be militia. Their armories were their own. There they could meet and drill, and talk back at the outside world, free from interruption, as in their own homes. These they adorned with pictures of old generals, photographs of former captains, and fac-similes of the Declaration of Independence. There they talked of bygone musters and sham fights, and of excursions to neighboring cities and States, and of receptions given in return. The dates of prominent events were fixed by the year of such a spring training or fall review. The politics of the members were not of the intense type. Their votes were generally given to men who were friendly to the military, and politicians sometimes made nominations with a view to catch their votes. On public affairs, they were simply friends of their country, with a strong leaning toward liberal legislation and popular rights. They were, of all the community, the least fanatical in religion, and the least dogmatic in politics. They took a broad view of their country and its institutions. They were stronger Union men than they could explain. If the Union was attacked, it was their duty to defend. This they knew, and were ready. There was no hatred in their hearts to any living man. If the mob in Baltimore had known the men they attacked and murdered on the 19th of April, they would have welcomed them with open hands, instead of with death. These were the men who saved Fortress Monroe and the city of Washington, as we shall now proceed to show.

We left the Third Regiment on board the transport, bound for Fortress Monroe. The following is its record:—

"At ten o'clock, A.M., April 18, weighed anchor, and steamed out of Boston harbor, bound for Fort Monroe. Arrived at Fort Monroe at eight, A.M., April 20, disembarked at eleven, A.M., and marched into the fort, every man for duty. Found the Fourth Regiment there, which had arrived two hours before, and seven companies of United-States artillery in garrison. Colonel Dimick, commanding post, asked Colonel Wardrop 'if he was a minute-man.' He answered, 'Yes.'—'How long will it take to get your regiment ready?'—'Fifteen minutes.'—'Get it.' In ten minutes, he received the following order:—

HEADQUARTERS, FORT MONROE, VA., April 19, 1861.
Order No. 55.
The Colonel of the Third Regiment of Massachusetts Volunteers will immediately report for orders to Commodore Paulding, United-States Navy.
By order of Colonel Dimick,
(Signed) T. J. HAINES, *Adjutant.*

"Colonel Wardrop requested to know the object, and was informed that it was to hold possession of Gosport Navy Yard. Colonel Wardrop reported to Captain Paulding, U.S.N., at four o'clock, P.M., and was ordered to embark on board of United-States steamer 'Pawnee,' which was done at once, without a single ration; Captain Paulding saying he could not wait, and that rations would be obtained at the yard. Left Fort Monroe at five, P.M. At dusk, reached the mouth of the Elizabeth River, and found the enemy had sunk five vessels in the channel to obstruct the passage. Between seven and eight, P.M., a river steamer, loaded with passengers, passed us, bound to Norfolk. Our men were kept out of sight. At nine, P.M., when within about two hundred yards of United-States frigate 'Cumberland,' were hailed by an officer from her. They did not appear to hear our answer, when the officer hailed us again. Same effect. Then we distinctly heard from the deck of the 'Cumberland' a voice, saying, 'Shall I fire, sir?' At the same moment, we saw six ports opened from United-States ship 'Pennsylvania.' She was lying broadside to us. It was an anxious moment. It seemed as if our friends were intending to do the enemy's work. Another hail from the 'Cumberland,' an answer from us, and the same voice, 'Shall I fire, sir?' A hundred voices yelled 'Pawnee,' and then cheer upon cheer broke from the 'Cumberland' and 'Pennsylvania,' and as heartily answered by us, who felt relieved from peril. The regiment immediately disembarked, and marched to a central position in the yard, and ordered to find quarters and rations; did not succeed in doing either. About eleven, P.M., Captain Paulding informed Colonel Wardrop that he had been ordered to send out the United-States vessels 'Merrimac,' 'Raritan,' 'Germantown,' and 'Cumberland,' and destroy all public property that he could not carry away; that he had intended to hold the yard, if possible; but, from Captain Pendergast's representation, he doubted if he could. Captain Pendergast had felt so sure of this, that he had commenced destroying property during the afternoon, and had scuttled the very ships that he had been ordered to take away. Colonel Wardrop thought the yard might be held, and begged that Captain Paulding would consider the great stake, and try by some means to save the place. Captain Paulding said he would consult again before deciding. Near midnight, Captain Paulding informed Colonel Wardrop, in presence of Captain Pendergast, that he could not hold the yard, but should destroy all the buildings and ships and other property. Colonel Wardrop remonstrated strongly; advising that the 'Cumberland' retain her position, while the 'Pawnee' ran up and down the river, preventing the enemy from sinking any more obstruction, or building batteries on the banks of the river, while his regiment manned the walls, and put the yard in the best state of defence possible. If we were attacked, to threaten a bombardment of the cities of Norfolk and Portsmouth; that we could not destroy all the large guns in the yard (variously estimated from one thousand to twenty-five hundred) that night; that together, in his opinion, the place could be held until sufficient reenforcements arrived; that the great importance of the place demanded that a great risk should be taken for its preservation. Captain Pendergast said the enemy was too strong for us, and that, if we did not get away with the two vessels that night, we never should; and that every moment lessened our chances; and that the 'Cumberland' ought to be saved at all hazards, being, in his opinion, more valuable than all else. The two captains then had a private consultation, from which Colonel Wardrop was quietly excluded. Shortly afterwards, Captain Paulding informed the colonel that he should withdraw the two ships, and abandon the yard; and then ordered him to furnish eighty men to assist in undermining the dry dock, another detail to assist in firing the buildings and vessels, and the balance were employed in rolling solid shot overboard. During this time, a mob broke into the yard, but were promptly driven out by the marines and our regiment. About three o'clock, A.M., of the 21st, the regiment embarked on board of the 'Pawnee,' and dropped down the river a short distance. At four, A.M., every thing was fired that would burn. We waited until five o'clock, A.M., before all the men returned by small boats, when we found that Captain H. G. Wright, United-States engineer, and Captain John Rodgers, United-States Navy, had been captured by the enemy. The ships were burned to the water's edge, excepting the 'United States;' and she was so old and rotten she would not burn. The public buildings were mostly destroyed. Some, however, were but slightly damaged. After all our trouble with the dry dock, the mine did not explode. We succeeded in knocking off the trunnions of *seven* guns: the others were useful to the rebels. When we arrived at the mouth of the Elizabeth River, we found the enemy had almost obstructed the channel. The 'Pawnee' passed through; the 'Cumberland' did not that afternoon, when they turned one of the sunken vessels, and passed through, and anchored off the fort. We disembarked from the 'Pawnee' a little after eight o'clock, A.M., and marched into the fort to our quarters, having eaten nothing since the day before. Thus ended the Norfolk expedition.

"April 22, the regiment became a part of the garrison of Fort Monroe. April 23, the regiment was properly mustered into the United-States service for three months. Companies I and M joined May 14.

Company I, Captain Chamberlain, was raised in Lynn, for three years' service; company M, Captain Tyler, was raised in Boston, for three years' service. Companies D and E joined the regiment May 22; Company D, Captain Chipman, raised at Sandwich; Company E, Captain Doten, raised at Plymouth, for three years' service. On this day, Major-General Butler assumed command of the Department of Virginia, North and South Carolina, headquarters at Fort Monroe. May 27, Company G, of Lowell, Captain P. A. Davis, was assigned to the regiment temporarily.

"July 1, the regiment and naval brigade left Fort Monroe early in the morning, crossed Hampton Creek, and occupied the town; had a slight skirmish with the enemy; took up quarters in the town, and established advanced posts on the outskirts. The Fourth Regiment was added to the command, and all placed under Brigadier-General Ebenezer W. Peirce. The duties on the outposts were arduous and harassing, as the enemy was hovering about the lines, firing upon the sentinels occasionally, and attempting to capture some of the most distant posts; but, by keeping out beyond our lines strong bodies of scouts and skirmishing parties, we soon drove them from our vicinity. July 4, at night, a strong body of the enemy, having artillery and cavalry, crossed New-Market Bridge, threatening Hampton. At two o'clock, on the morning of the 5th, Colonel Wardrop, with nine companies of the Third and seven companies of the naval brigade, with four pieces of artillery, marched out, and took up position at the forks of the road, two miles from Hampton. Remained there until an hour after sunrise, when the scouts brought the intelligence that the enemy had retired beyond the New-Market Bridge. Returned to quarters without firing a shot. Immediately sent out fresh scouts, who followed the enemy to Big Bethel. They saw a regiment march from there that night, and followed it to within five miles of Yorktown; then passed over to Lee's Mills, on the James River, crossed the Warwick River, and returned by way of Buck River, without losing a man. This party was commanded by Lieutenant Chamberlin, Company C, and consisted of thirty-five of his own men. They were absent a little over five days. Too much credit cannot be given for the skill, courage, and fidelity displayed by this scouting party. A remarkably correct report of the enemy's position and strength on the Peninsula was made by Lieutenant Chamberlin, which, ten months after, was verified. During all this time, the troops in Hampton were busily engaged in finishing the intrenchments, sending detachments on water expeditions, &c. It was a remarkable fact, that grumbling ceased among the men when the regiment marched out of Fort Monroe.

The harder the duties, the more contented they seemed to be, like men determined to perform the most disagreeable duties cheerfully, forgetting self in patriotic desire to benefit their country. On the 16th of July, the regiment, leaving Companies D, E, I, and M, who had enlisted for three years, behind, marched into Fort Monroe, where, by order of General Butler, they gave up their rifled muskets for old smoothbore muskets, and five rounds of ammunition and four days' rations, embarked on board of steamer 'Cambridge,' at four, P.M., and left for Boston about five, P.M.; arrived at Long Island, Boston harbor, about daylight. July 19, disembarked at Long Island about ten, A.M. Reported to the Adjutant-General of the State. Was mustered out of the service of the United States July 23, 1861."

The Fourth Regiment arrived at Fortress Monroe on the morning of April 20. The adjutant of the regiment writes, "At daybreak, the long low lines of the fort were visible. Anxiously the regiment watched as the boat lay off and on, until at sunrise they saw the old flag unfolding from the flagstaff. The men were quickly landed, and, amid the cheers of the little garrison, marched into the fort." This was the first loyal regiment in the war that landed upon the "sacred soil of Virginia." The adjutant continues, "Hardly was the regiment well in quarters before their labors commenced. The fort was found to be almost unarmed on the land side, and ill supplied with material of war. For several weeks the men were employed mounting heavy guns, unloading vessels, storing provisions, and keeping guard. General Butler arrived about the middle of May, and took command of the Department of Virginia." On the 27th of May, the Fourth Regiment, in conjunction with a New-York regiment under Colonel Bendix, and a Vermont regiment under Colonel Phelps, took possession of Newport News, and made an entrenched camp. Here the regiment remained, there doing the usual camp duty, until the 9th of June, when "five companies were detailed, with a portion of the Vermont and New-York regiments, to make up a detachment to join one from Hampton, to start at one o'clock the next morning to attack Big Bethel, a position held by the enemy about twelve miles from Newport News. Of the battle of Big Bethel it is needless to go into details. Its unfortunate result [says Adjutant Walker] was owing to a variety of causes; but if other troops had done their duty as well, and gone as far as those from Massachusetts and Vermont, the name of Big Bethel would not have headed a long list of federal repulses." Major Whittemore was the officer who reported to the commander of the fort. In a letter never published before, he says, —

"I was the first to step on shore, and the regiment was reported by myself to the Officer of the Day. I inquired of him who had possession of this fort, — the regulars or the rebels? He replied, United-States regulars. He was answered, 'Then the Fourth Regiment, Massachusetts Militia, has come to help you keep it.' On the 22d of April, we were mustered into the United-States service, and were, as I believe, the *first* troops mustered. We remained at the fort some two or three weeks, engaged in mounting guns, and on the work necessary to put the place in suitable condition for defence. Some time in May, General Butler arrived; and one of the first things he did was to send three regiments, of which the Fourth was one, about twelve miles up the river to Newport News. We set to work, as soon as we could obtain tools, at building entrenchments, and were engaged in this work all of the time until our departure in the latter part of June. While here, the affairs at Little Bethel and Great Bethel occurred, which might have had, and ought to have had, and would have had, a very different result.

"Five companies of the Fourth took part in this expedition, and were under my command, and we were all volunteers. The march was commenced at 12¼, A.M., and continued until daylight without interruption. Then, unfortunately, Colonel Townsend's regiment of Troy, N.Y., was mistaken for rebels, and a fire was opened between it and our rearguard, composed of a part of Colonel Bendix's New-York volunteers, which resulted in the killing and wounding of eleven men of Townsend's command. Further damage was prevented, and the affair ended, by the major of the Fourth Massachusetts riding out alone in front of his line, and discovering the New-York troops. This mishap made it evident that the object of our expedition, if it had any, had been frustrated; and it was the pretty general opinion, that the best thing to be done was to return to camp. It was decided, however, to go on; and we marched until within gunshot of Big Bethel, when the rebels opened fire with a rifled gun. The troops were immediately put in line for an attack; and the five Massachusetts companies were ordered to turn the enemy's left, in connection with five companies of the First Vermont. This they proceeded to do, and were gallantly and rapidly succeeding, some of my men being on the very brink of the works, when Colonel Townsend, of New York, peremptorily ordered a retreat. The Massachusetts men retired in good order, having had two men killed and one mortally wounded, and were drawn up on the same line they started from, where I soon reported to General Peirce, expecting to receive orders to go in again. I now learned that General Peirce — as brave a man as I have ever seen in battle * — had not ordered a retreat, nor did he intend to do so; but circumstances beyond his control compelled him to do so, and the five Massachusetts companies brought up the rear on the march back to camp, whither they returned in good order, and marched into Newport News with closed ranks and shouldered arms, feeling that they at least had done their duty, and with no reason to be ashamed of their part in this the first battle of the war.

"Thus the Fourth Massachusetts, under my command, were the first troops from Massachusetts in the first *battle* of the war. I have been in many actions since; but never have I seen a hotter fire than that at Great Bethel. After this, until our departure from Newport News, nothing of consequence occurred."

The Fourth remained at Newport News until the 3d of July, when it moved to the village of Hampton. Adjutant Walker writes, "On our arrival at Hampton, we found the quaint old town deserted. Hardly a score of its former white inhabitants remained, although many negroes, especially old and very young ones, were still there. The troops had quarters assigned them in the various houses, and remained there undisturbed until Wednesday, July 11, when we marched over to Fortress Monroe, preparatory to embarking for home." Previous to leaving, their Springfield rifled muskets were exchanged for old smoothbores. On the eve of departure, the regiment was addressed by General Butler and Colonel Dimick. On the 15th of July, it embarked on board the steamer "S. R. Spaulding," and in fifty-six hours arrived in Boston harbor, after an absence of three months. It was mustered out at Long Island, Boston harbor, on the 22d of July.

The Fifth Regiment arrived at Annapolis on the morning of

---

* Major Whittemore was afterwards major and lieutenant-colonel of the Thirtieth Regiment, Massachusetts Volunteers, and served three years.

כרך א'

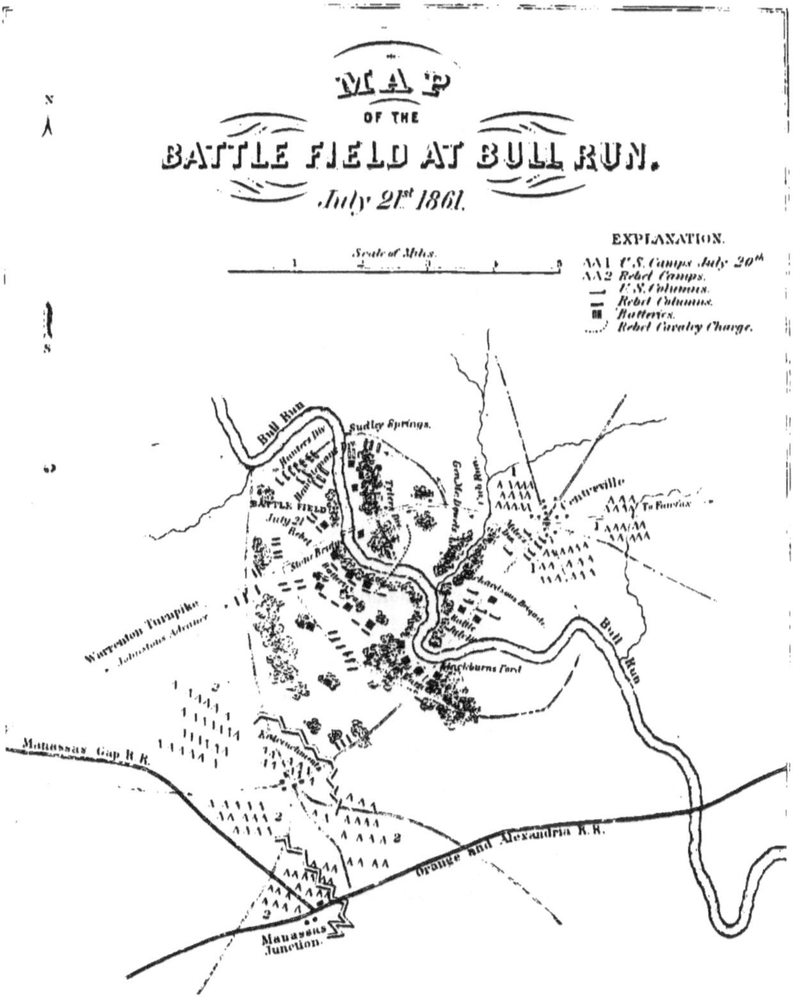
MAP
OF THE
BATTLE FIELD AT BULL RUN.
July 21st 1861.
N
S
Scale of Miles.
EXPLANATION.
1 U.S. Camps July 20th
2 Rebel Camps.
U.S. Columns.
Rebel Columns.
Batteries.
Rebel Cavalry Charge.
Bull Run
Sudley Springs.
Centreville
To Fairfax
BATTLE FIELD
July 21
Stone Bridge
Warrenton Turnpike
Johnstons Advance
Blackburns Ford
Manassas Gap R.R.
Orange and Alexandria R.R.
Manassas Junction.

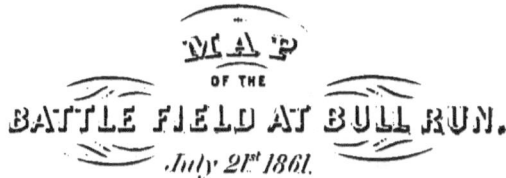

the 24th of April, and landed in the afternoon. The next day, the regiment was ordered to Washington. Only four companies could find car accommodation to the Annapolis Junction. The other six, under command of Lieutenant-Colonel Greene, marched to that point. The regiment arrived in Washington on the 26th, and was quartered in the Treasury building; and was mustered into the United-States service on the 1st of May. From that time to the 24th of May, the regiment was exercised in drill. On the 25th, it was ordered to Alexandria, and, marching across the Long Bridge, entered Virginia, and that evening encamped near Alexandria. The regiment had only brought with it the State colors. Several Massachusetts gentlemen in Washington presented it with a handsome national flag. On the 28th, they formed camp near Shuter's Hill, not far from Alexandria, and named it "Camp Andrew," in honor of the Governor of Massachusetts. Nothing of special interest occurred until the 25th of June, when Lieutenant-Colonel Greene, Major Keyes, and Adjutant Barri, having been appointed officers in the regular army, took leave of the regiment. This was a grievous loss; for the gentlemen named were among the very best officers in the volunteer service at that time. The regiment celebrated the Fourth of July in camp. The chaplain read the Declaration of Independence, Colonel Lawrence made a speech, and the "Star-spangled Banner" was sung. On the 16th of July, the regiment was put in General Franklin's brigade, and soon after advanced towards Bull Run. The Fifth bore an honored part in that disastrous battle, which was fought on the 21st of July, exactly three months from the day the regiment left Faneuil Hall. In this battle, Colonel Lawrence was slightly wounded. The regiment left Washington on the 28th of July, and arrived in Boston on the 30th, having been in service three months and seven days. Its reception in Boston was worthy of its military record.

The famous Sixth Regiment arrived at Philadelphia, as we have already stated, on the afternoon of the 18th of April. This regiment has the undisputed honor of having been the first to reach Washington, and the first to sacrifice life in the great war. Its passage through Baltimore, a city of two hundred thousand inhabitants, more than half of whom were rebels; the attack upon it by the mob; the death of four, and the wounding of thirty-six, of its members, on the memorable 19th of April, — sent a thrill through the heart of the nation, and aroused it like a giant to defend its life. This was the anniversary of the battle of Lexington, in which, on the soil of Massachusetts, the first blood was shed in the struggle for Independence in 1775. This regiment came from the county of Middlesex, in which are " Lexington, Concord, and Bunker Hill ; " and some of the men who were attacked in Baltimore were the direct descendants of the men who breasted the power of England in those memorable conflicts.

At midnight on the 18th, reports reached Philadelphia, that preparations were being made to dispute the passage of this regiment through Baltimore, and to attack Washington. The long roll was beat; and the men formed in column, and marched to the depot of the Philadelphia and Baltimore Railroad, and took their places in the cars. At one o'clock in the morning, the train started; Colonel Jones intending to have his command pass through Baltimore early in the morning, before a force could be gathered to impede its march. Mr. Felton, President of the railroad, says, —

"Before they left Philadelphia, I called the colonel and principal officers into my office, and told them of the dangers they would probably encounter, and advised that each soldier should load his musket before leaving, and be ready for any emergency. We had arranged a cipher, by which messages were sent and received every few moments along the whole road, and from the officers of the Baltimore and Ohio road; so that we were posted up constantly as to the exact condition of affairs. Just before the starting of the Sixth, I received a message that a part of a Pennsylvania regiment had arrived over the Northern Central road, and passed through Baltimore without any demonstrations of hostility, save a few hisses.* This fact I communicated to the Sixth, but, at the same time, advised that they should relax no vigilance on that account. The regiment started; and I stood at the telegraph instrument in Philadelphia, constantly receiving messages of its progress. Finally, it was announced from Baltimore that they were

---

* This was a regiment without arms.

in sight; next, that they were received at the station with cheers; then that ten car-loads had started for the Camden-street station, and all was right; then that the other four car-loads had started, and turned the corner on to Pratt Street all right; then, after a few moments, that the track was torn up in front of the last four cars, and they were attacked on Pratt Street. Then the reports subsided into mere rumors, and we could not tell whether the mob was to succeed, or the military was to be triumphant, as guns were being fired by both rioters and military, and the tide of battle was surging, now this way, and now that; then that the mob had turned upon an unarmed Pennsylvania regiment [Colonel Small's, which had left Philadelphia with the Sixth]; that the mob had mounted tops of the cars, and were breaking them in, and throwing down paving-stones and other missiles upon the heads of the volunteers, and chasing those who had left the cars through the streets of the city. The excitement, anxiety, and oppression that I felt at that moment may be better imagined than described. At this juncture, I received a message from the Mayor of Baltimore and the Police Commissioners as follows in substance: 'Withdraw the troops now in Baltimore, and send no more through Baltimore or Maryland.' An immediate answer was demanded. I, in order to get time to ascertain more exactly the condition of affairs before deciding what to do, telegraphed to the Mayor and Commissioners, that I had received such a message as the above, and asked, 'Is it genuine?' In the mean time, I ascertained that the bulk of the Sixth had got through Baltimore, and were on their way to Washington; and believing that the mob would murder the unarmed men under Colonel Small if I allowed them to remain where they were exposed to their violence and fury, and believing that our bridges would be at once destroyed, and that some other route must be adopted, I bethought myself of the Seaford and Annapolis scheme before communicated to General Scott, and at once telegraphed to the Mayor of Baltimore, 'I will withdraw the troops now in Baltimore, and send no more through the city till I first consult with you.' I made no allusion to sending any through Maryland; but so worded my message that they would rather conclude that no more troops would be sent, and thus be unprepared to throw any impediment in the way of the Annapolis route."

Persons who have not passed over the railroad from Philadelphia to Washington may not know that the cars from Philadelphia enter the depot in Baltimore on the north side of the city. Here the locomotive is detached, and the cars for

Washington are drawn by horses about two miles, across the lower part of the city, to the depot of the Baltimore and Washington Railroad, on the south side of the city, where the locomotive is again attached, and the train taken by steam-power to Washington. It is one hundred miles from Philadelphia to Baltimore, and about forty from that city to Washington.

Colonel Jones's account is dated "Capitol, Washington, April 22, 1861." He says, —

"After leaving Philadelphia, I received intimation that the passage through the city of Baltimore would be resisted.* I caused ammunition to be distributed and arms loaded, and went personally through the cars, and issued the following order; viz., —

"'The regiment will march through Baltimore in columns of sections, arms at will. You will undoubtedly be insulted, abused, and perhaps assaulted, to which you must pay no attention whatever, but march with your faces square to the front, and pay no attention to the mob, even if they throw stones, bricks, or other missiles; but if you are fired upon, and any one of you are hit, your officers will order you to fire. Do not fire into any promiscuous crowds, but select any man whom you may see aiming at you, and be sure you drop him.'

"Reaching Baltimore, horses were attached the instant that the locomotive was detached, and the cars were driven at a rapid pace across the city. After the cars containing seven companies had reached the Washington Depot, the track behind them was barricaded, and the cars containing band and the following companies; viz., Company C, of Lowell, Captain Follansbee; Company D, of Lowell, Captain Hart; Company I, of Lawrence, Captain Pickering; and Company L, of Stoneham, Captain Dike, — were vacated by the band; and they proceeded to march in accordance with orders, and had proceeded but a short distance before they were furiously attacked by a shower of missiles, which came faster as they advanced. They increased their step to double-quick, which seemed to infuriate the mob, as it evidently impressed the mob with the idea that the soldiers dared not fire or had no ammunition; and pistol-shots were numerously fired into the ranks, and one soldier fell dead. The order, 'Fire,' was given, and it was executed; in consequence, several of the mob fell, and the soldiers again advanced hastily. The Mayor of Baltimore placed himself at the head of the column, beside Captain Follansbee, and proceeded with

---

* This is an error. The information was received before the regiment left Philadelphia.

them a short distance, assuring him that he would protect them, and begging him not to let the men fire; but the Mayor's patience was soon exhausted, and he seized a musket from the hands of one of the men, and killed a man therewith; and a policeman, who was in advance of the column, also shot a man with a revolver.

"They at last reached the cars, and they started immediately for Washington. On going through the train, found there were about one hundred and thirty missing, including the band and field-music. Our baggage was seized, and we have not as yet been able to recover any of it. I have found it very difficult to get reliable information in regard to the killed and wounded, but believe there were only three killed."

Here follows a list of the killed and wounded, which was incomplete and incorrect.

"As the men went into the cars, I caused the blinds to the cars to be closed, and took every precaution to prevent any shadow of offence to the people of Baltimore; but still the stones flew thick and fast into the train, and it was with the utmost difficulty that I could prevent the troops from leaving the cars, and revenging the death of their comrades. After a volley of stones, some one of the soldiers fired, and killed a Mr. Davis, who, I ascertained by reliable witnesses, threw a stone into the car. Yet that did not justify the firing at him; but the men were infuriated beyond control. On reaching Washington, we were quartered at the Capitol, in the Senate Chamber, and all are in good health and spirits. I have made every effort to get possession of the bodies of our comrades, but have not yet succeeded. Should I succeed, I shall forward them to Boston, if practicable; otherwise, shall avail myself of a kind offer of George Woods, Esq., who has offered me a prominent lot in the Congressional Burying-ground for the purpose of interment. We were this day mustered into the United-States service, and will forward the rolls at first opportunity after verification."

It appears, that, on arriving at the Susquehanna, they overtook a Pennsylvania regiment, called "Small's Brigade," having about a thousand unarmed and ununiformed men, on their way to Washington. These made the train very heavy, and caused a change of the order in which the cars containing the Sixth were arranged when the regiment left Philadelphia. This was not known until afterwards; it interfered with previous orders, and accounts in a degree for the separation of the regiment in

Baltimore. Seven companies went safely through that city to the Washington Depot. Four others, with the band, were in the rear, and those were the companies which bore the brunt of the attack. They are designated in Colonel Jones's report. It was the expectation that the entire regiment would march through Baltimore to the Washington Depot, in conformity with previous orders. The companies in the forward cars were being drawn across the city while those in the rear cars were in the depot, waiting orders to file out. A writer and eye-witness says, —

"No orders came to file out; and, in a few minutes, all the cars forward of the one occupied by Captain Sampson's company disappeared. We knew nothing of the movements of the balance of the regiment, as no intimation had been transmitted to us of a change of the orders. Meanwhile the mob increased in numbers about the depot. Soon the car moved on. At the first turn of a street, it was thrown from the track. The men were ordered to remain in the car until it was put again on the track. The mob now began to throw stones and brickbats, some of which entered the car. On Pratt Street, the mob surrounded it; the car was made a complete wreck. Shots were fired by the mob, which were returned by the company, and was kept up with more or less spirit until the company reached the Washington Station, and joined the other seven."

Major Watson was with this company in its perilous passage, and exhibited much coolness and capacity. The other three companies, which had been separated from the rest of the command after crossing the Susquehanna, had not yet been heard from. These were the companies commanded by Captains Follansbee, Pickering, and Dike. Before they got from the Baltimore Depot, the rebels had barricaded the streets, and removed the rails from the track crossing the city, so the cars containing these companies could not move. They had, therefore, either to force their way through the city on foot, retreat, or surrender. They determined to go forward. In getting out of the cars, cheers were given by the mob for Jeff Davis and South Carolina. Secession flags were flaunted in the faces of the men; they were told to dig their graves; that thirty Southern men could whip the whole of the Yankee State of Massachusetts. Our men bore these affronts with silence. They were two hundred men against ten thousand, in a strange and hostile city. Under command of Captain Follansbee, they begun their march. The mob increased in numbers. Stones, bricks, oyster-shells, and other missiles were thrown at them. Random shots were fired. Shouts of derision and yells of savage hatred rent the air. Still the gallant band moved on. No one skulked; no one thought of looking back. Washington was their goal, and the streets of Baltimore the way to it. Several men were already wounded with pistol-shots; two were killed; the time had come for retaliation. They had suffered with closed lips insults and indignities hard for brave men to bear; but, when they saw their dead comrades, they brought their muskets to the shoulder, and fired. Their shots told. Several of the mob fell lifeless on the pavement, and a large number were wounded; and so for two miles these brave, devoted men fought their way, and joined their comrades at the Washington Depot.

The killed were Addison O. Whitney, Luther C. Ladd, and Charles A. Taylor, of Company D, Lowell, and Sumner H. Needham, Company I, of Lawrence. Thirty-six were wounded, three of whom were Captain Dike, and Leander F. Lynde and James F. Rowe, of the Stoneham company.

The mob howled like wolves around the Southern Depot, where the regiment now was, and threw stones at the cars after the men were seated. Several of the mob were shot by our men from the cars while waiting to start. The regiment reached Washington at five in the afternoon, and was received by the loyal people who surrounded the depot with the wildest enthusiasm. Soon after, it marched to the Capitol building, and was quartered in the Senate Chamber, and rooms connected with it. Thus, under the roof of the Capitol, were sheltered the men who first marched to save it, and in whose ranks the first blood had been shed, and the first lives sacrificed in its defence.

The regiment remained in Washington until the 5th of May, when it was ordered to the Relay House, — a railroad station about ten miles from Baltimore, — where it remained doing guard and picket duty until the 29th of July, when it broke camp and returned to Massachusetts, and arrived in Boston on the 31st of July, after a service of three months and a half.

Distinguished honors have been paid this regiment, as the historic regiment of the war. Distinguished ladies volunteered to nurse the sick and wounded. Poets sung its praises in heroic verse. The loyal ladies of Baltimore presented it with a national flag; and the citizens of Bergen Point, in New Jersey, with another, as a "slight acknowledgment of their appreciation of its moral and soldierly deportment, its gallantry at Baltimore, and timely rescue from danger of the capital of our common country." The United-States House of Representatives unanimously voted these soldiers the thanks of the House for their "prompt response to the call of duty," and "their patriotism and bravery in fighting their way through Baltimore to the defence of the capital;" and, in so doing, spoke the sentiments of the loyal men of the nation.

The Eighth Regiment reached Philadelphia, as we have before stated, on the evening of April 19. There they learned that the Sixth Regiment had been attacked in Baltimore, and compelled to fight its way through the city. This intelligence gave new energy and enthusiasm to the men, and made them more eager to press forward to Washington. They had expected to reach the capital by way of Baltimore; but that route was now closed, and a new one had to be opened, which served as the military highway to Washington for Eastern troops until sedition was suppressed in Baltimore, and that city assumed a loyal attitude. The new route was by the Susquehanna and Chesapeake Bay to Annapolis, the capital of Maryland. A branch railroad of seventeen miles connected Annapolis with the Baltimore and Washington Railroad. By this route, Washington could be reached without touching Baltimore. It was a flank movement; and the honor of suggesting and making it successful belongs to Samuel M. Felton, Esq. The honors due him for this service can only be measured by the important ends which it accomplished. General Butler was in Philadelphia with the Eighth. His orders were to march to Washington by way of Baltimore. That was now impossible. Mr. Parton, in his "Life of General Butler," says, —

"On this evening, at Philadelphia, there was telegraphing to the Governor of Massachusetts; there were consultations with Commodore Dupont, commandant of the navy yard; there were interviews with Mr. Felton, President of the Philadelphia and Baltimore Railroad,— a son of Massachusetts, full of patriotic zeal, and prompt with needful advice and help; there was poring over maps and gazetteers. Meanwhile, Colonel A. J. Butler was out in the streets buying pickaxes, shovels, tin-ware, provisions, and all that was necessary to enable troops to take the field, to subsist on army rations, to repair bridges and railroads, and throw up breastworks. All Maryland was supposed to be in arms; but the general was going through Maryland."

The same writer says, —

"Before evening was far advanced, he had determined his plan. His officers were summoned to meet him. On his table were thirteen revolvers. He explained his design to go by way of Annapolis, and took upon himself the sole responsibility. Taking up one of the revolvers, he invited every officer who was willing to accompany him to signify it by accepting a revolver. The pistols were all instantly appropriated."

A "Memorial of Plan and Reasons for Proceeding to Annapolis," written that evening by General Butler, was received by Governor Andrew, enclosed in a letter from Major P. Adams Ames, an officer of Major-General Andrews's staff of the Massachusetts Volunteer Militia, who happened to be in Philadelphia at the time. This paper was as follows: —

"I have detailed Captain Devereux and Captain Briggs, with their commands, supplied with one day's rations and twenty rounds of ammunition, to take possession of the ferry-boat at Havre-de-Grace for the benefit of this expedition. This I have done with the concurrence of the present master of transportation. The Eighth Regiment will remain at quarters, that they may get a little solid rest after their fatiguing march. I have sent to know if the Seventh (New York) Regiment will go with me. I propose to march myself at the hour of seven o'clock in the morning, to take the regular eight and a quarter o'clock train to Havre-de-Grace. The citizens of Baltimore, at a large meeting this evening, denounced the passage of Northern troops. They have exacted a promise from the President of the Baltimore and Ohio Railroad not to send troops over that road through Baltimore; so that any attempt to throw troops into Baltimore entails a march of forty miles, and an attack upon a city of two hundred thousand inhabitants at the beginning of the march. The only way, therefore, of getting communication with Washington for troops from the North is over the Baltimore and Ohio Railway, or marching from the west. Commodore Dupont, at the navy yard, has given me instructions of the fact in accordance with these general statements, upon which I rely. I have therefore thought I could rely upon these statements as to time it will take to proceed in marching from Havre-de-Grace to Washington. My proposition is to join with Colonel Lefferts, of the Seventh Regiment of New York. I propose to take the fifteen hundred troops to Annapolis, arriving there to-morrow about four o'clock, and occupy the capital of Maryland, and thus call the State to account for the death of Massachusetts men, my friends and neighbors. If Colonel Lefferts thinks it more in accordance with the tenor of his instructions to wait rather than go through Baltimore, I still propose to march with this regiment. I propose to occupy the town, and hold it open as a means of communication. I have then but to advance by a forced march of thirty miles to reach the capital, in accordance with the orders I at first received, but which subsequent events, in my judgment, vary in their execution, believing, from the telegraphs, that there will be others in great numbers to aid me. Being accompanied by officers of more experience, who will be able to direct the affair, I think it will be accomplished. We have no light batteries; I have therefore telegraphed to Governor Andrew to have the Boston Light Battery put on shipboard at once to-night to help me in marching on Washington. In pursuance of this plan, I have detailed Captains Devereux and Briggs, with their commands, to hold the boat at Havre-de-Grace.

Eleven, A.M. — Colonel Lefferts has refused to march with me. I go alone at three o'clock, P.M., to execute this imperfectly written plan. If I succeed, success will justify me. If I fail, purity of intention will excuse want of judgment or rashness.

B. F. BUTLER.

His Excellency Governor ANDREW.

This despatch of General Butler is inaccurate and obscure. When he speaks of Havre-de-Grace, he means Perryville, as Perryville is on the northern side of the Susquehanna, and Havre-de-Grace is on the southern side. When he says, "If Colonel Lefferts thinks it more in accordance with the tenor of his instructions to wait rather than go through Baltimore," he means rather than go through *Annapolis;* for Baltimore was the city to be avoided. Neither the despatch nor the biography gives just credit to Mr. Felton, who had suggested and fixed upon this route on the 19th, when the Mayor of Baltimore telegraphed him to send no more troops through that city, and he promised that no more would be sent. Mr. J. Edgar Thompson, President of the Pennsylvania Central Railroad, and Isaac Hazlehurst, Esq., of Philadelphia, were in his office when the despatch from the Mayor of Baltimore was received; and to them he suggested the Annapolis route, and they agreed that it was "the only thing to be done." He immediately telegraphed to Captain Galloway, of the ferry-boat "Maryland," at Perryville, to fill her up with coal, and to make her ready to go to Annapolis; and also to procure a pilot who knew Annapolis Harbor. These three gentlemen also conferred with the steamboat owners in Philadelphia about getting their boats ready to take troops from Perryville to Annapolis; and, in some cases, they became personally responsible for the pay of the officers of the boats. Some of the men declined absolutely to put their boats at the disposal of the Government; and they were seized by Governor Curtin, who arrived that evening from Harrisburg. A consultation was held that night at the house of General Patterson, in Philadelphia, at which Governor Curtin, Mr. Felton, Mr. Thompson, Mr. Hazlehurst, and Mr. Henry, Mayor of Philadelphia, were present. The exciting state of affairs was discussed, and Mr. Felton explained the route to Washington by way of Annapolis. "After considerable discussion, the Annapolis route was adopted by the military, and the programme of Mr. Felton and Mr. Thompson approved." I now quote from Mr. Felton's manuscript:—

"General Butler arrived in Philadelphia the same evening, with the Eighth Massachusetts Regiment; and I requested General Patterson to give me an order to take to General Butler, directing him to go to Washington by the Annapolis route. The general said he had no military authority over General Butler, and could not give the order; but that I might say to him that he most urgently advised that he should go to Annapolis. I then, in company with Admiral, then Commodore, Dupont, and my brother Frank, called upon General Butler at the Continental Hotel, and told him all I knew about the condition

of things in Baltimore, and of the impossibility of his going that way, as then they had the streets barricaded, and a large force under arms, with artillery, to resist his march through the city. I then advised his taking the Annapolis route, which he at first declined, saying his orders were to go to Baltimore, and he would go that way; and, if they fired upon him from any house, he would raze that house to the ground, by the help of God, or leave his bones and ashes in the streets of the city. We told him he could not get through that way; that our bridges would be burned that night, if they were not already; and we could not land him in the city: so the only route left was Annapolis. After some considerable discussion and hesitation, the general concluded to go by Annapolis, in our ferry-boat, from Perryville, with Captain Galloway, and the pilot whom I had engaged, in charge of the boat. I was to see Colonel Lefferts, of the New-York Seventh, then on its way to Philadelphia, and give him all the facts that I had come in possession of, and urge him to join General Butler. I then went to my office; and at about three, A.M., Colonel Lefferts arrived at the depot, but declined to go with General Butler, saying his orders were to go through Baltimore. Mr. Thompson and myself endeavored to persuade him to join General Butler. He finally concluded to embark on board the steamer 'Boston,' one of the steamers we had secured, and go up the Potomac. I earnestly advised him against this course, as I had heard that the rebels had erected batteries on the banks of the Potomac. I urged his going to Annapolis in the steamer 'Boston,' and then joining General Butler for a march to Washington, as the next best thing to going to Perryville, the Perryville route being quicker than the route down the Delaware and by sea. He finally gave up his Potomac route, and joined General Butler at Annapolis. At three o'clock the next day (Saturday), April 20, General Butler started from the Broad and Prince Streets Station, in the cars, to Perryville, and thence by steamer 'Maryland' to Annapolis. I watched his progress from station to station by telegraph with great anxiety, as our bridges had been burnt, as I had expected, the night before, between the Susquehanna and Baltimore, by J. R. Trimble, at the head of a military rebel force of about one hundred and fifty men; and he was threatening to come to the river, and take possession of our boat, which was then our chief dependence. I had, however, so arranged matters on board the boat as to make it impossible for him to capture it, if my orders were obeyed. We also found that our bridges would be destroyed on this side of the Susquehanna, unless we were better guarded than on the other side. Trimble did not succeed in reaching the river and capturing the ferry-boat, being frightened from his undertaking by one of our engine-men, who was on the engine that Trimble had seized, in order to take his force out to the river. This man told him, when he was within about eight miles of the river, that there were twenty-five hundred soldiers on board the ferry-boat, who would give him a very warm reception if he attempted to go to the river. Trimble thereupon concluded that discretion would be the better part of valor, and returned to Baltimore, burning the bridges after passing over them. At six, P.M., the telegraph announced that General Butler had arrived at Perryville. He embarked immediately on board the 'Maryland,' with his regiment, and started for Annapolis. After this, I went home completely worn out by anxiety, labor, and loss of sleep, having eaten only irregularly in my office, and having neither changed my linen, shaved, nor closed my eyes in sleep, for three days and two nights."

In making up the record of this gallant regiment from its departure from Philadelphia until its return, I am under especial obligations to the full and interesting narrative of Captain George T. Newhall, of Company D, Lynn Light Infantry. On arriving near Perryville, the cars stopped, and skirmishers were thrown forward. The main body followed closely. A crowd was at the ferry. The regiment moved by "double quick." Captain Newhall says, "The steamer, a very large ferry-boat, called the 'Maryland,' being in its slip, was instantly taken without firing a shot." It is evident from this, that neither the officers nor men of the regiment knew that the "Maryland" had been prepared, and was waiting to take them to Annapolis. After getting on board the luggage, the "Maryland" proceeded to Annapolis, where it arrived on Sunday morning, April 21, and anchored in the harbor, near the frigate "Constitution." The men suffered from fatigue. Seven hundred persons were on board. The United-States Naval Academy is at Annapolis. The frigate "Constitution" was the school-ship of the academy. It was the most famous ship in our naval annals; having, in the war of 1812, won the choicest laurels. It was supposed that she would be seized by the rebels: to save her from such a disgrace was the duty of the hour. Two companies of the Eighth were placed on board; the crew not being strong enough to defend her, if seriously attacked. Captain Rogers, U.S.N., who commanded her, was prepared to sink her, rather than strike his colors. Both the "Maryland" and the "Constitution" were aground; great efforts were made to float them, and tow the frigate over the bar. This was accomplished with the assistance of the steamer "Boston," which arrived in the harbor in the morning with the Seventh New-York Regiment. Company K, of Pittsfield, was sent by steamer to Fort McHenry, Baltimore Harbor, and did not join the regiment again for three weeks. The "Constitution" was taken safely from Annapolis to New York, having Captain Devereux's company, and a detail of Lynn, Gloucester, and Marblehead men on board under command of Lieutenant Berry, of Company D, Lynn, to assist in working her. They afterwards joined the regiment at Washington. The rest of the Eighth was kept on board the "Maryland" forty-eight hours, short of rations, and without water. Captain Newhall says the men were "supplied with pilot-bread from the 'Constitution,' stamped '1848,' the year it was made, and salt pork bearing the same brand, which the men were obliged to eat raw. Salt water only could be procured: this was eagerly drank by some, making them more thirsty than ever." The regiment was not landed until Tuesday morning. The Seventh New York, which arrived in the harbor a day after the Eighth, landed first. Several communications had passed between General Butler and the Governor of Maryland, the latter protesting against landing the troops, and also between the general and the commandant of the Naval Academy, who rendered him all the assistance in his power. On the day on which the troops landed, a report was brought to General Butler, that the slaves in the city and surrounding country were to rise against their masters, and assert their right to be free. General Butler immediately offered the services of himself and command to put down the insurrection. The offer was declined; there being no truth in the report, and the masters being able to maintain peace, and suppress a revolt of their slaves.

The railroad from Annapolis to the Junction, where it connects with the Baltimore and Washington Railroad, had, in part, been destroyed, and the engines and cars partially broken. After considerable delay, the track was relaid, and the engines and cars were put in order by the men of the Eighth. Many of them were mechanics, who had made locomotives and cars. On the 24th of April, the Eighth and the New-York Seventh marched twenty-two miles to the Junction. The heat was oppressive, and the men suffered for want of food. " On arriving at the Junction, they dropped asleep." On the afternoon of Friday, April 26, the regiment arrived in Washington, eight days after its departure from Boston. The National Intelligencer the next morning, speaking of the Eighth, said, " We doubt whether any other single regiment in the country could furnish such a ready contingent to reconstruct a steam-engine, lay a rail-track, and bend the sails of a man-of-war." General Butler remained behind at Annapolis in command of that important post.

The hard labor of laying the railroad track, and repairing the locomotives and cars, had worn out the men's uniforms. The fact being presented to the President by Colonel Monroe, he ordered them to be furnished with army trousers and blouses. On the 30th of April, the regiment was mustered into the United-States service. The regiment remained in Washington until the middle of May, when it was ordered to the Relay House to guard the railroad. It remained there, with changes of detail, until the 29th of July, when it received orders to return home. It arrived in Boston on the 1st of August, where it was honorably received, and addressed by the Mayor of the city.

These soldiers received the thanks of the United-States House of Representatives, " for the energy and patriotism displayed by them in surmounting obstacles upon sea and land, which traitors had interposed to impede their progress to the defence of the national capital." On the 4th of July, while at the Relay House, the regiment was presented with a new flag, made and forwarded by the ladies of Lynn. On the 12th of May, Colonel Monroe resigned his commission, and Lieutenant-Colonel Hinks was elected to fill the vacancy. In acknowledgment of the long and valuable services of Colonel Monroe in the militia of his State and country, Governor Andrew directed the Adjutant-General to address him the following letter : —

COMMONWEALTH OF MASSACHUSETTS.

ADJUTANT-GENERAL'S OFFICE, BOSTON, May 15, 1861.
Colonel MUNROE, M.V.M.

SIR, — I am directed by His Excellency the Commander-in-chief to inform you, that, in assenting to your discharge from the command of the Eighth Massachusetts Regiment, now in active service at Washington, to defend the Union, the Constitution, and the Government of the United States, he is impressed by your long and meritorious services in the militia of the Commonwealth; that you have earned long years ago an honorable discharge; but by your alacrity and patriotism so recently exhibited in answer to the order to march your command to Washington, where you have taken an honorable and prominent part in the defence of the country, you are doubly entitled to it.

His Excellency takes this occasion to assure you of his high appreciation of your services, and expresses a hope that you may live many years in the enjoyment of that peaceful Union to which your services have been devoted.

Major-General Sutton will transmit this letter to Colonel Monroe, together with his discharge.

By order of His Excellency John A. Andrew, Governor and Commander-in-chief.

WILLIAM SCHOULER, *Adjutant-General.*

To the Eighth Regiment will ever be the honor of having opened the route to Washington by way of Annapolis, and of having saved from possible loss the frigate "Constitution," the "Old Ironsides" of the war of 1812.

The Third Battalion of Rifles, by transport from New York, reached Annapolis April 24, and quartered in the Naval Academy, where it remained until the 2d of May, when it was ordered to Fort McHenry, where it continued until the end of its term of service. The battalion was drilled in the practice of heavy ordnance, and in infantry tactics. The men were always ready for duty, and by their good conduct and discipline received the confidence and praise of the garrison commanders. They were engaged in no battle; but the fort which it held saved Baltimore and Maryland from going with Virginia and other Southern States headlong into rebellion. They were thanked by General Dix, post commandant, for their patriotism and good behavior, and, at his request, remained on duty two weeks after their term of service had expired. This battalion was from Worcester, "the heart of the Commonwealth." Company C was originally a local organization, composed of men of Irish birth, who, on the call for troops, offered their services to the Governor, which were accepted, and the company was attached to the Third Battalion. It was the first Irish company to reach the seat of war, and be mustered into the United-States service; and Company D, of the same battalion, was the first to reach Washington by the Potomac River.

Major Cook's Light Battery, which left New York with the Fifth Regiment and Rifle Battalion, arrived at Annapolis on the 24th of April, and was quartered at the Naval Academy, where it remained until the 4th of May, when it was sent to the Relay House. On the 13th of June, it was ordered, with the Sixth Regiment, to Baltimore, to protect the polls on election day. It remained in that city until the 30th of July, four days beyond the term of its enlistment. Two detachments were stationed in Monument Square, and others at the Custom House. The battery arrived in Boston on the 3d of August, where it was cordially received by the Mayor of the city, and a large crowd of people. The First Battalion of Dragoons, the Second Battalion of Infantry, and the National Lancers honored the corps with an escort to their old quarters.

In the preceding pages, I have sketched the departure, the services, and the return of the first three-months men. They made an honorable record. Speaking of them, the Adjutant-General, in his annual report for 1861, says, —

"They were the first to respond to the call of the President; the first to march through Baltimore to the defence of the capital; the first to shed their blood for the maintenance of our Government; the first to open the new route to Washington by way of Annapolis; the first to land on the soil of Virginia, and hold possession of the most important fortress in the Union; the first to make the voyage of the Potomac, and approach the Federal city by water, as they had been the first to reach it by land. They upheld the good name of the State during their entire term of service, as well by their good conduct and gentlemanly bearing, as by their courage and devotion to duty in the hour of peril. They proved the sterling worth of our volunteer militia. Their record is one which will ever redound to the honor of Massachusetts, and will be prized among her richest historic treasures. These men have added new splendor to our revolutionary annals; and the brave sons who were shot down in the streets of Baltimore on the 19th of April, have rendered doubly sacred the day when the greensward of Lexington Common was drenched with the blood of their fathers."

The three-months service was a good preparatory experience. It educated officers to command three-years companies and regiments, which were then being raised in the State; several of whom came back, when the war was over, with distinguished fame, and with generals' stars upon their shoulders. Among these we name Hinks and Devens and Briggs and Martin and Devereux and McCartney. Others rose to high rank, who never came back, but who fell in distant battle-fields, by the side of their men, and beneath the shadow of the flag they carried, which symbolized their cause and the nation's. Of these we name Chambers and Pratt and Parker and Prescott and Keyes and Dodd.

While the events here enumerated were transpiring at a distance, others of great importance and interest were of daily occurrence at home, as will appear in the next chapter.

CHAPTER III.

The People of the Towns — The Press — The Pulpit — Edward Everett — Fletcher Webster offers to raise a Regiment — The Sunday Meeting in State Street — Mr. Webster's Speech — Meeting in the Music Hall — Speech of Wendell Phillips — Meeting in Chester Park — Speeches of Edward Everett and Benjamin F. Hallett — Meeting under the Washington Elm in Cambridge — Ex-Governor Banks, George S. Hillard, and others — Letters received by the Governor — Extracts — Reception of the Dead Bodies of the Killed in Baltimore — Mr. Crowninshield goes abroad to buy Arms — Ex-Governor Boutwell sent to Washington — Letter of John M. Forbes to Mr. Felton — Letter to General Wool — To Rev. Dr. Stearns — To Robert M. Mason — Offer of a Ship Load of Ice — Purchase of the Cambridge — Provisions sent to Fortress Monroe and Washington — Governor to President Lincoln — Attorney-General Foster — The Ladies of Cambridge — Call for Three Years' Volunteers — Letter of John M. Forbes — Letters received by the Adjutant-General — Extracts — Letters from Dr. Luther V. Bell and Richard H. Dana, Jr. — Ex-Governor Boutwell arrives at Washington — Letters to the Governor — State of Affairs at Washington — Letter from Mr. Foster — Cipher Telegram — Judge Hoar at Washington — Letters to the Governor — The War Department will accept no more Troops — Charles R. Lowell, Jr., Massachusetts Agent at Washington — His Instructions — Letter of Governor to Dr. Howe — Appointed to examine the Condition of the Regiments — His Report — Colonel Prescott — Letters of the Governor and General Butler — Slavery.

THE people of Massachusetts were deeply moved by the departure of the three months' men, and the attack made upon the Sixth Regiment at Baltimore. Meetings were held in city and town. Speeches were made by the most distinguished orators in the State. In some of the towns, the people were called together by the ringing of church-bells, and in others by the town-crier. The meetings generally were opened with prayer; and the oldest and most venerable of the inhabitants were seated on the platform. The veterans of the Revolution had passed away, and the seats which they would have filled were occupied by the surviving soldiers of the War of 1812. Addresses were made by clergymen, lawyers, and by young men, to whom the cause gave words of earnest eloquence. The UNION, one and inseparable, and how Massachusetts could best serve it, were the themes which inspired them all. Resolutions were passed, pledging life and fortune to the cause. Large sums of money were subscribed and paid. Historic memories were revived, and the sacrifices of the fathers in the War for Independence held up for imitation. The women formed aid societies to sew and knit and work for the absent soldiers and for their families at home. Young men formed military companies, and more companies were offered than the Government would receive; and more articles of clothing and stores of provisions than the men required.

The public journals of the Commonwealth spoke with one voice. Party spirit was allayed, political differences forgotten. The past was buried with the past. The Boston Morning Post, the leading Democratic paper in New England, gave to the cause its strong support. It had sustained the nomination of John C. Breckinridge for President the preceding year; but it did so without intent or thought of following him into rebellion. On the morning of April 16, the Post published a patriotic appeal to the people, from which we make the following extract: —

"Patriotic citizens! choose you which you will serve, the world's best hope, — our noble Republican Government. — or that bottomless pit, — social anarchy. Adjourn other issues until this self-preserving issue is settled. Hitherto a good Providence has smiled upon the American Union. This was the morning star that led on the men of the Revolution. It is precisely the truth to say, that when those sages and heroes labored they made UNION the vital condition of their labor. It was faith in Union that destroyed the tea, and thus nerved the resistance to British aggression. Without it, patriots felt they were nothing; and with it they felt equal to all things. The Union flag they transmitted to their posterity. To-day it waves over those who are rallying under the standard of the LAW; and God grant, that in the end, as it was with the old Mother Country, after wars between White and Red Roses and Roundheads and Cavaliers, so it may be with the daughter; that she may see PEACE in her borders, and all her children loving each other better than ever!"

The Boston Liberator, edited by William Lloyd Garrison,

the well-known and ably conducted organ of the extreme Abolition party, spoke with equal spirit in support of the Government. The religious press, without exception, invoked the blessings of Heaven upon our soldiers and the holy cause they had gone forth to uphold. Religious creeds, like political dogmas, were harmonized in the general current of opinion. Edward Everett, who in the preceding fall election was the Conservative candidate for Vice-President, threw himself, with all his powers of eloquence and culture, into the struggle. He was absent from the State when the call for troops was made, but returned to Boston on the 18th of April. He fully approved the measures taken by the Government, and thought the Administration ought to be cordially supported by all good citizens.

Among the first to raise a regiment for the service was Fletcher Webster, the sole surviving child of Daniel Webster. On Sunday morning, April 21, an immense meeting was held in State Street, in front of the Merchants' Exchange. It had been announced in the papers of the preceding day that Mr. Webster and other gentlemen would speak. There was much excitement and enthusiasm, notwithstanding it was the sabbath. Mr. Webster began his address from the steps of the Merchants' Exchange. The position was unfavorable; the crowd could not hear, and calls were made to adjourn to the rear of the Old State House. The adjournment was carried. The crowd remained in the street. Mr. Webster spoke from the rear balcony, facing State Street. He was received with great favor. He said he could see no better use to which the day could be put than to show our gratitude to Divine Providence for bestowing upon us the best Government in the world, and to pledge ourselves to stand by it and maintain it. He whose name he bore had the good fortune to defend the Union and the Constitution in the forum. This he could not do; but he was ready to defend them on the field. [Applause.] But this is no time for speeches; it is a time for action. He proposed to raise a regiment for active service; he called for volunteers. Mr. Webster then gave directions regarding the manner in which companies were to be raised, in order to comply with the laws of the State and the requirements of the War Department. He concluded by saying, —

"Time presses. The enemy is approaching the capital of the nation. It may be in their hands now. [Cries of 'Never; it never shall be.'] Promptness is needed. Let us show the world that the patriotism of '61 is not less than that of the heroes of '76; that the noble impulses of those patriot hearts have descended to us. Let us do our duty, and we shall yet see the nation united, and our old flag remain without a star dimmed or a stripe obliterated."

The report of the meeting in the Daily Advertiser says, —

"The remarks of Mr. Webster were received with great enthusiasm, and at the close of his speech he was loudly cheered. Loud calls were then made for General Schouler, who was seen upon the balcony. In response, he stepped forward, and thanked the vast assembly in an almost inaudible voice for their good feeling, and asked Mr. Webster to speak for him. Mr. Webster at once informed the audience that the General was utterly prostrated with the arduous labors during the past week, and that he had scarcely been in bed for fifty-four hours; that he must be excused, as he was utterly unable to address them. The crowd then gave three cheers for General Schouler."

The meeting was ably addressed by William Dehon, Edward Riddle, and Charles Levi Woodbury, who were received with great favor and satisfaction. Mr. Webster's appeal met with a prompt response. More companies were offered than he could accept; but, before the regiment was ready to leave the State, orders came from Washington that no more three months' regiments would be received. On the receipt of this information, Mr. Webster's regiment immediately volunteered to serve for three years: it was accepted, and during the war was known as the Twelfth Regiment of Massachusetts Infantry.

Wendell Phillips spoke in the afternoon of this memorable Sunday in the great Music Hall, which was crowded in every part; and thousands were unable to gain admission. Many feared that he would not be permitted to speak; and that, if he attempted to sustain the position which he assumed in his speech at New Bedford ten days before, a riot would occur. The first sentence uttered by Mr. Phillips, however, gave assurance that the events of the preceding week had not been without their effect upon his mind. The hall was profusely decorated with the stars and stripes; and the speaker stood upon the platform beneath an arch formed by the national colors. The speech was remarkable not only for its force and vigor, its patriotic and elevated sentiments, but for its strong contrast with the speech quoted in the first chapter. He began by saying, —

"I am here to retract not a single word of what I have ever said. Every act of my life has tended to make the welcome I give this war hearty and hot. Civil war is a momentous evil, and needs the soundest justification. I rejoice before God, that every word I have said has counselled peace; and I rejoice, for the first time in my anti-slavery life, I stand under the stars and stripes, and welcome the tread of Massachusetts men. [Great applause.] No matter what may have been done in the past. To-day the slave asks but a sight of this banner, and calls it the twilight of his redemption; to-day it represents sovereignty and justice. The only mistake I have ever made is in supposing Massachusetts wholly choked with cotton dust and caukered with gold. [Laughter.] The first cannon shot upon our forts has put the war-cry of the Revolution on her lips. I cannot acknowledge the sentiment, 'Our country, right or wrong.' In a moral light, it is knavish and atheistical; but it is sublime to see this rallying of a great people to the defence of the national honor; a noble and puissant nation, arising like a strong man from a sleep and shaking his locks. She is thus collecting her scattered elements and rousing her dormant thunder. How do we justify this last appeal to arms? I always cry for peace; and the anti-slavery banner has that name upon it. We have thought to set free the millions of slaves, and the North has responded. It is in the increasing education of our people, and in that moral sense which is fast gaining ground, that we are to accomplish this. No man can prevail against the North in the nineteenth century. It thinks. It can appreciate the argument. The South is the fourteenth century. Wat Tyler and Jack Cade loom up on the horizon. There the fagots still burn, and men are tortured for opinion. Baron and serf are names which form too flattering a picture. Sumner stamped them the barbarous States. The struggle now is, not of opinion, but of civilization. There can be but two things, — compromise or battle. The integrity of the North scorns the first; the general forbearance of nineteen States has preceded the other. The South opened with a cannon-shot, and Lincoln showed himself at the door. [Applause.] The war is not of aggression, but of self-defence; and Washington becomes the Thermopylæ of liberty and justice. Rather than surrender it, cover every foot of ground with a living man. Guard it with a million of men, and empty our bank-vaults to pay them. Proclaim that the North is under the stars and stripes, and no man is in chains."

He said the North is all right and the South all wrong; that for thirty years there has been no exhaustion of conciliation and compromise. "We must," he said, "acknowledge the right before you send Massachusetts through the streets of Baltimore, and carry Lexington and the 19th of April into the Southern States."—"During long and weary years we have waited. Massachusetts blood has consecrated the streets of Baltimore, which are now too sacred to be trodden by slaves."—"When the South cannonaded Sumter, the bones of Adams rattled in his coffin; and we might have heard him from his granite grave in Quincy say, 'Seize the thunderbolt, and annihilate what has troubled you for sixty years.'"—"There are four sections of people in this struggle: First, the ordinary masses, mingling mere enthusiasm in the battle; Second, those that have commercial interests,—the just-converted hunkerism; Third, the people,—the cordwainers of Lynn and the farmers of Worcester,—people who have no leisure for technicalities; Fourth, the Abolitionists, who thank God that he has let them see salvation before they die. Europe, and some of you, may think it a war of opinion; but years hence, when the smoke of the conflict shall have cleared away, we shall see all creeds, all tongues, all races one brotherhood; and on the banks of the Potomac the Genius of Liberty robed in light, with four and thirty stars in her diadem, broken chains under her feet, and the olive branch in her right hand."

Mr. Everett made his first speech in the war on Saturday the 27th of April, to a vast crowd of citizens in Chester Square, Boston. The people who lived in the south part of the city had erected a lofty flag-staff, and from its height the national banner was to be unfurled that afternoon. The ceremonies were opened with prayer by Rev. Mr. Hepworth, and national songs were sung by the school-children. Mr. Everett was received with loud applause; which he gracefully acknowledged, and said, —

"The great assemblage that I see around me; the simple but interesting ceremonial with which the flag of our country has been thrown to the breeze; the strains of inspiring music; the sweet concord of those youthful voices; the solemn supplication of the reverend clergyman, which still fills our ears, — all these proclaim the deep, patriotic sentiment of which the flag is the symbol and expression. Nay, more: it speaks for itself. Its mute eloquence needs no aid from my lips to interpret its significance. Fidelity to the Union blazes from its stars: allegiance to the Government under which we live is wrapped within its folds. We set up this standard, my friends, not as a matter of idle display, but as an expressive indication, that, in the mighty struggle which has been forced upon us, we are of one heart and one mind, — that the Government of the country must be sustained. We are a law-abiding, quiet-loving community. Our time, our thoughts, our energies are habitually devoted to the peaceful arts by which States grow and prosper; but, upon an issue in which the life of the country is involved, we rally as one man to its defence. All former differences of opinion are swept away. We forget that we ever had been partisans. We remember only that we are Americans, and that our country is in peril. . . . Why does it float as never before, not merely from arsenal and masthead, but from tower and steeple, from the public edifices, the temples of science, the private dwelling, in magnificent display or miniature presentment? Let Fort Sumter give the answer. When on this day fortnight, the 13th of April (a day for ever to be held in inauspicious remembrance, like the *Dies Alliensis* in the annals of Rome), the tidings spread through the land, that the standard of United America, the pledge of her union and the symbol of her power, which so many gallant hearts had poured out their life-blood on the ocean and the land to uphold, had, in the harbor of Charleston, been for a day and a half the target of eleven fratricidal batteries, one deep, unanimous, spontaneous feeling shot with the tidings through the bosoms of twenty millions of freemen, — that its outraged honor must be vindicated."

Mr. Everett then described the bombardment of Sumter, and paid a high tribute to Major Anderson and his gallant command. He also referred to his long and intimate acquaintance with the leading men of the South, from whom he had hoped never to have been separated by civil war. He closed with these words : —

"All hail to the flag of the Union! Courage to the heart and strength to the hand to which in all time it shall be intrusted! May it ever wave in unsullied honor over the dome of the Capitol, from the country's strongholds, on the tented field, upon the wave-rocked topmast. It was originally displayed on the 1st of January, 1776, from the headquarters of Washington, whose lines of circumvallation around beleaguered Boston traversed the fair spot where we now stand; and it was first given to the breeze within the limits of our beloved State: so may the last spot where it shall cease to float in honor and triumph be the soil of our own Massachusetts!"

The gentleman who succeeded Mr. Everett was Benjamin F. Hallett, who, for thirty years, had been a distinguished leader of the Democratic party. He had made its platforms, advocated its principles, and labored for its success. No Democrat in Massachusetts was better known than Mr. Hallett. He had never wavered in his love or faltered in his allegiance to his party. No one doubted his sincerity, no one questioned his ability. As a lawyer, he held a high rank. Notwithstanding his determined zeal and devotion to his party, his nature was kind and generous; and his private character was pure and spotless. Like Mr. Everett, he gave up party for his country. His speech in Chester Square was worthy of his talents and of the occasion which called it forth. Like Mr. Everett, he remained true to the Union; and, like him, he died ere the end was gained.

In the city of Cambridge, almost within the shadows of the halls of Harvard University, stands the "Washington Elm," where it has stood sentinel since the foundation of the college. They have grown old and venerable together. Beneath the branches of the tree, Washington first took command of the American army, in 1775, which was drawn up in line on the Common in front. On this historic spot, on the same day that Mr. Everett and Mr. Hallett spoke in Chester Square, the people of Cambridge held a meeting. John Sargent, the mayor of the city, presided. Among the vice-presidents were Jared Sparks, Henry W. Longfellow, Joel Parker, Emory Washburn, Isaac Livermore, and Theophilus Parsons. A preamble and resolutions were read by John G. Palfrey. One of the resolutions was in these words: —

"*Resolved* by us, citizens of Cambridge, convened under the shadow of the Washington Elm, that animated, we trust, by the spirit of him who, in the clouded dawn of the Revolution which created our nation, drew his sacred sword on this memorable spot, we desire to consecrate ourselves to the services of freedom and our country."

The meeting was addressed by John C. Park, ex-Governor Banks, George S. Hillard, and Thomas H. Russell in speeches filled with patriotic sentiments and earnest appeals to the judgment and conscience of the people.

We now return to the State House, where the work of fitting out regiments, organizing new departments, listening to various propositions, answering innumerable questions, receiving and writing letters, pressed upon the Governor and his personal staff, the Adjutant-General and his assistants, the Quartermaster-General and his clerks, from early morning until midnight. An abstract of a portion only of the correspondence will show the nature and extent of a part of the labor performed.

April 18. — The Governor writes to Miss A. J. Gill, also to Miss Anna M. Clarke, also to Mary A. G. Robinson, who have offered themselves to be nurses; to Robert B. Forbes, acknowledging the receipt of his "Address to the Merchants and Seamen of Massachusetts to organize a Coast Guard;" to Dr. Winslow Lewis, who offered to give medical advice and attendance to soldiers' families free of charge. Thanks Leopold Morse, of Boston, for a gift of one hundred pairs of ready-made pants for soldiers. To Secretary Cameron, asking for more muskets.

April 19. — Governor telegraphs to the Secretary of War, "Would you like another regiment composed of Irishmen enlisted specially?" Writes to Arthur Hanley, who had inquired "if unnaturalized persons would be accepted in the militia," to "go ahead." Acknowledges "with gratitude the devoted and benevolent offer of Mrs. Harriet M. Gibson;" also a letter from Miss Hannah E. Stevenson, who offered her services as a nurse. Telegraphs to Secretary Cameron that "the steamer 'State of Maine,' with the Fourth Regiment on board, is detained at New York; depends on his providing a convoy from the capes of Virginia, if necessary. Writes to William Gray, accepting the offer made by ladies through him "to supply under-clothing for the soldiers." Thanks James M. Stone "for his valuable aid as assistant quartermaster in getting off the regiments. Acknowledges the receipt of a beautiful fire-arm from Dr. Henry G. Clark, "to be given to the surgeon of the forces of Massachusetts who shall best perform his duty in the exercise of his profession towards the brave men who have taken up arms in behalf of liberty and the country." Telegraphs, seven o'clock, P.M., to General Butler, "When did you reach Philadelphia? When will you leave? Is the way open? Can you communicate by telegraph with Washington? Has Jones reached Washington?"

April 20. — Writes to Dr. H. H. Fuller that "surgeons are appointed under the militia law by colonels of regiments, and not by the Governor." Acknowledges receipt from Captain Edward Ingersoll, Springfield Armory, of "two hundred and fifty rifled muskets." Thanks Miss Laura A. Phillips, of Great Falls, N.H., for her offer to nurse our wounded men in Baltimore; also Miss Laura B. Forbes, of Cambridgeport, for the same offer. Telegraphs Hon. Hannibal Hamlin, Vice-President, Hampden, Me., "I advise you to come forward without delay, in view of possible events at Washington." Telegraphs Governor Washburn, of Maine, "One advance regiment [the Sixth] has reached Washington: No other yet beyond Philadelphia." Directs the Adjutant-General "to grant all applications for organizing new companies when he has confidence in the parties. When doubts exist, consult the Governor." Directs the Adjutant-General "to get off Cook's Light Battery by steamer before midnight; also the left wing of the Fifth Regiment, under Lieutenant-Colonel Greene, and the right wing, under Colonel Lawrence, by railroad during the night." This arrangement could not be made; and the Governor telegraphed to Simeon Draper, New York, to "engage steamers for twelve hundred troops, six cannon, caissons, and seventy-two horses, from New York to Annapolis, to leave New York Sunday morning." Telegraphs Major Ladd, "Senator Wilson will be in New York to-morrow morning, and will inform you fully what our wants are for the troops on their march." Telegraphs

Major P. Adams Ames, Philadelphia, "We will send horses, artillery, and infantry to New York by rail, thence by steamer to Annapolis." Telegraphs the Mayor of Baltimore, "I pray you to cause the bodies of our Massachusetts soldiers dead in Baltimore to be immediately laid out, preserved with ice, and tenderly sent forward by express to me. All expenses will be paid by this Commonwealth." Telegraphs Simeon Draper, New York, "Procure, to be delivered to Colonel Lawrence, of our Fifth Regiment, to-morrow morning, eight hundred knapsacks suitable for service, or else slings for carrying blankets." Thanks Mrs. William Ward for her offer "to aid in any manner in her power, our departing troops, and to cheer those whom they leave behind." Telegraphs to Mayor Sargent, of Lowell, "We have no official information of the names of the dead. A despatch from the Mayor of Baltimore says the bodies cannot be sent on at present, as communication by land and sea is stopped. But they have been carefully cared for, and will be put in Greenwood Cemetery till they can be sent to Massachusetts." Informs A. B. Ely, of Boston, that "we are taking *most active* measures for procuring a supply of efficient arms." Thanks Rev. Eli A. Smith "for his patriotic and Christian offer" of assistance; also Dr. Coale, of Boston, for offer of professional services, and Miss Hazard and Miss Burns, who offer themselves as nurses. Notifies Mr. Crowninshield that the Executive Council have "approved of his suggestion, and he has appointed him to proceed to Europe in the next steamer to purchase arms." Telegraphs George William Brown, Mayor of Baltimore: "Dear Sir,—I appreciate your kind attention to our wounded and our dead, and trust that at the earliest moment the remains of the fallen will return to us. I am overwhelmed with surprise, that a peaceful march of American citizens over the highway, to the defence of our common capital, should be deemed aggressive to Baltimoreans. Through New York the march was triumphal." To Adams & Co.'s Express, Boston: "Can't you get the bodies of our dead through Baltimore? The Mayor telegraphs the railroad is interrupted." Major Ladd, who is referred to above, was an officer on the staff of Major-General Sutton; and Major Ames, also mentioned, was an officer on the staff of Major-General Andrews, of the Massachusetts Volunteer Militia. They had been detailed on special duty at New York and Philadelphia.

April 22. — The Governor telegraphs to the Superintendent of the Springfield Armory, "Can you send me to-night a first-rate armorer, who is a judge of arms, ready to go where he may be wanted for six weeks?" A first-rate armorer, Charles McFarland, was procured, who went abroad with Mr. Crowninshield, two days after, to purchase arms. Governor acknowledges receipt of a check for five hundred dollars from George Draper, "to be appropriated for the relief of the families of those who have fallen or may fall in obeying the call of their country." Gives a letter to Rev. N. Shepard, pastor of the Tremont-Street Baptist Church, who said he should "start for Washington this evening, if he had to walk all the way." Acknowledges the receipt from William Dehon of eighty-eight flannel shirts "for the soldiers of Massachusetts who may be unprovided for in the present emergency." Requests S. G. Ward, of Boston, banker, "to issue a letter of credit in favor of F. B. Crowninshield for fifty thousand pounds sterling." Telegraphs Simeon Draper, New York, that Mr. Crowninshield "will be at Fifth Avenue Hotel to-night, to take steamer 'Persia' for Liverpool on Wednesday." Writes to General Butler, that "the citizens of Salem have appointed Dr. Lincoln R. Stone to attend to the wants of the companies that have marched from that city, and that he would see that the funds raised by subscription for that purpose may be properly expended." Writes to President Lincoln, that "Ex-Governor Boutwell has been appointed the agent of the Commonwealth to proceed to Washington to confer with him in regard to the forts in Massachusetts and the militia." Governor Boutwell was also to see General Wool in New York. Instructs Mr. Crowninshield "that he is to procure twenty-five thousand stand of arms, of the best style and patterns, and to have them conform as nigh as possible to those now in use in the army." He was to co-operate with agents from other loyal States, and to look out if agents of disloyal States were abroad on a similar errand. Writes to Secretary Cameron, that Ex-Governor Boutwell will confer with him in regard to garrisoning our forts with militia; also recommends that a guard be placed at the United-States Arsenal at Springfield. "Two thousand men could be thus employed, who would enlist for one or two years, be drilled as soldiers, and sent forward when required." Telegraphs to Secretary of War for "one or two thousand smooth-bore muskets, of which there are one hundred thousand at the Springfield Arsenal." Acknowledges with thanks the offer of the Empire Association of Lynn to "give to the new volunteer company raised in that city sixty-six military frock-coats." Thanks "Mr. Tilson, and the ladies of the Baptist Church and Society of Hingham, for the tender of their services to make clothing and sew for the soldiers."

April 23. — The Governor writes a letter to Major-General Wool, introducing William L. Burt, of Boston, who was instructed to "get authority to garrison the forts in Boston harbor with militia." John M. Forbes, by direction of the Governor, writes to Samuel M. Felton, of Philadelphia: "Your information about matters at Annapolis received. The expedition which left New York yesterday will take care of Annapolis; but we shall continue our preparations, including armed ships. Look out for Port Deposite. Keep us posted." Governor writes to Mrs. Harriot C. Gould and Mrs. Harriot A. Jaquith, who had offered to furnish the 'soldiers with the New Testament, and informs them "that each soldier of the Fifth Regiment, which left Boston on Sunday, had been furnished with a Bible; and there is an abundant supply to furnish those who are expected to leave." Writes to Henry A. J. Williams that "colored men cannot be enrolled in the militia. It cannot be done by law, which limits the militia to white male citizens. Personally, he knows no distinction of class or color, in his regard for his fellow-citizens, nor in their regard for our common country." Writes to Mrs. Devereux, wife of Captain Devereux, of the Eighth Regiment, who had offered her services as a nurse, "that he would be reluctant to call into the field another member of a family which has already contributed so many of its children to the country." Two brothers of Captain Devereux were also in the service.

April 24. — The Governor writes to Governor Washburn, of Maine, that "the understanding is, that Mr. Crowninshield is to purchase three thousand rifled muskets, of the most approved pattern, for Maine, and Maine is to bear her proportion of the expenses of the agent." Also to Governor Goodwin, of New Hampshire, that Mr. Crowninshield is to purchase two thousand muskets for that State, with the same understanding in regard to sharing expenses.

April 25. — The Governor writes to the Trustees of the State Nautical-School Ship, inclosing an order passed by the Executive Council, "to place guns on board the ship, and to have the boys drilled in their use for the defence of the coast. The guns are to be four bronze six-pounders." Writes to the Secretary of War a letter introducing Wilder Dwight and George L. Andrews, who were going to Washington to get authority to raise a regiment of volunteers for the war. He had written to the Secretary on the 17th on the subject, but had received no answer. He fully indorses the scheme, and "hopes it may receive such assistance and co-operation from the United States as can with propriety be offered. Major Gordon, who will command the regiment, is a gentleman of careful military education and large executive ability; and it will be officered by such gentlemen as Mr. Andrews and Mr. Dwight, gentlemen of the best standing in Massachusetts." Writes to the Commander of the Charlestown Navy Yard, "Allow me to advise and urge you to hold at the navy yard, or under your control, all naval officers who will not swear allegiance to the United-States Government, until instruction can be got from Washington." Writes to the Secretary of War, "In addition to raising Gordon's regiment, we can send you four thousand more troops within a very short time after receipt of a requisition for them. Do you wish us to send men as we may get them ready, without waiting requisitions? What shall we do, or what do you wish us to do, about provisioning our men? Is Fortress Monroe supplied with provisions? Will you authorize the enlistment here, and mustering into the United-States service, Irish, Germans, and *other tough men, to be drilled and prepared here for service?* We have men enough of such description, eager to be employed, sufficient to make three regiments. Finally, will you direct some general instructions and suggestions to be sent to me as to any thing, no matter what or how much, you may wish from Massachusetts, and procure General Scott also to do so? and we will try and meet, so far as may be, every wish of the Government up to the very limit of our resources and power. Will you put the six thousand rifles, now at the United-States Arsenal at Watertown, at our disposal for our men, and send *immediately* orders for that purpose? We shall be able to replace them at an early day, if it shall be necessary." Acknowledges the receipt of a letter from George T. Curtis, of New York, who had written "to express his sincere appreciation of, and thanks for, his co-operation in all actions taken by the Commonwealth, and by himself as its chief magistrate, to maintain the integrity and supremacy of the Federal Union."

April 26. — Governor writes to Commodore Hudson, Navy Yard, Charlestown, "John M. Forbes is acting as agent for the Commonwealth in fitting up and preparing the 'Cambridge' as an armed steamer for coast defence, and for the benefit of the common cause. Will you be good enough to oblige us with furnishing him with guns, armament, and ammunition he may need from the navy yard? Any aid you may give will serve the great object nearest the hearts of us all, and receive my lasting gratitude." To George S. Boutwell, Groton, Mass.: "We need your information, influence, and acquaintance with the Cabinet, and knowledge of Eastern public sentiment, to leave immediately for Washington. Hope you will proceed at once, and open and preserve communication between you and myself." To Montgomery Blair, Postmaster-General: "Hon. Dwight Foster, our Attorney-General, will hand you this note, with my full commendations. Mr. Foster is a gentleman with whom you can take counsel, finding him full of the fire and hard-working zeal of Massachusetts. How long, O Lord! how long will they delay our people?" To George Ashmun, Springfield, Mass.: "A Mr. T. Jones Lyman, of Montreal, Canada West, informs me that there are two hundred thousand percussion muskets at the armories, either at Quebec or Montreal. Will you ascertain if there is any way in which they can be bought?" Governor to General John E. Wool, commanding Department of the East, New York: "I have garrisoned Fort Independence, on Castle Island, in Boston harbor, with a battalion of infantry of one hundred and fifty men; and shall have another battalion of the same strength in Fort Warren, on George's Island, on Monday morning. I have a third battalion, which I can station at Fort Winthrop; and there are from two to three thousand volunteers, whom I wish to place under drill and discipline, in these forts. In Fort Independence, there are none of the casemate guns mounted, and no barbette guns on the face which vessels entering the harbor approach. In Forts Warren and Winthrop there are no guns. This important harbor, therefore, seems to be almost entirely undefended. I would therefore request you to order Captain Rodman [Watertown Arsenal] to supply these forts with the guns and carriages necessary for their defence, and detail an officer of engineers to put the works in proper condition. If an officer of artillery could also be detailed to give the necessary instruction, the garrison would soon be able to use the guns with effect. Please give us the order for the guns and carriages at once." Governor to Governor Washburn, of Maine (telegram): "New York urges that Maine would hurry forward her men. We have parted with certain equipments to Mr. Blaine, the agent of your adjutant." Governor to Governor Fairbanks, of Vermont (telegram): "New York wants Vermont to hurry. The case is urgent. Your adjutant said that the three hundred muskets we let him have would finish equipment."

April 27. — By direction of the Governor, Colonel Sargent, aide-de-camp, writes to Secretary Cameron, asking "to have the Irish Brigade, so called, sent to the forts to help man them and place the guns." Governor to General Wool, "Cannot you send us an officer of the United States army, with authority to superintend the military operations, and to give us some advice, from time to time, on military questions?" By direction of the Governor, Colonel Browne, private secretary, writes to the Mayor of Boston, in reply to a letter of the day before, "Concerning the action of the city of Boston in reference to the subsistence of troops detailed to garrison the forts in the harbor, His Excellency directs me to say, that at the earliest practical moment, probably during the first days of the coming week, he shall place troops in the forts, to whom the bounty of the city will apply; and the Adjutant-General is instructed to superintend and arrange all the details of the operation." Governor to John M. Forbes, "Buy the 'Pembroke' on the best terms possible, letting the merchants or coast-guard company put in such part of the cost as you can arrange. She must be armed and fitted with all reasonable speed, and be prepared to carry stores. She must only be used as coast-guard, when we can spare her from transportation. Let the alterations be as few as possible, so as to keep her cost down to the lowest point compatible with efficiency as an armed storeship." Governor to James M. Stone, who had given valuable aid as assistant-quartermaster: "I received your account last Saturday, with your admirable, full, and accurate report. The whole forms a model statement. I will have the account passed to-day by the Council." The Council approved Mr. Stone's account, and voted to pay him seventy-five dollars for his services, which he declined to receive, as he intended his services to be gratuitous.

April 29. — Governor to Rev. Dr. Stearns, President of Amherst College : " I have the honor to acknowledge the receipt of your letter concerning the three young gentlemen, students of Amherst College, — *Mr. James A. Rhea* and *Mr. Joseph B. Rhea*, of Blountville, Tenn., and *Mr. William A. Staymaker*, of Alexandria, Va., — who, you assure me, are loyal to their Government, and who, on account of the perils of the times, are summoned by their friends to return to their homes. No persons who are loyal to their Government need any 'passport or testimonial,' from me or from any other person, to travel freely throughout this Commonwealth; and I feel confident, that the travel of such persons throughout the United States will be obstructed nowhere, unless by traitors and rebels, or as a military necessity by troops acting against traitors and rebels." Governor to George Dwight, Superintendent of the Springfield Armory, introducing Mr. Blaine, agent of the State of Maine, who wished to get three thousand muskets for that State. Governor to Robert M. Mason, of Boston : " I hold a check for ten thousand dollars, payable to my order, being the gift of William Gray, Esq., for the benefit and relief of the families of the Massachusetts privates and non-commissioned officers called into active service. It was tendered to me before the formation of the 'Committee of One Hundred;' and I now, with Mr. Gray's consent, at your convenience, desire to place it in your hands, as the treasurer of the committee, for appropriate distribution according to the methods and rules of that organization. I cannot perform this pleasing task without adding a feeble expression of the deep sensibility with which I received this noble and characteristic munificence, and of the honor I feel in being made the instrument of its transmission." Also, a similar letter to Mr. Mason, transmitting a check of Mrs. Hannah F. Lee for one thousand dollars. To Governor Buckingham, of Connecticut, " We cannot furnish you with muskets, as we have exhausted our store. Will you co-operate with us, and have some bought by our agent in England?" To Dr. William J. Dale, "Express to Mrs. Tyler, and other citizens of Baltimore, my thanks for the care they have taken of our wounded men in that city."

These extracts show the variety of topics which, in the first two weeks of the war, engaged the Governor's attention. The letters on file in the Adjutant-General's office, embracing the same period, also disclose much that is of interest, though in a more limited and local sense. They are chiefly confined to answering inquiries made by selectmen of towns, and applications made by young men to raise new companies, many of whom were afterwards officers in the volunteer service, and rose to high commands. On the 25th of April, the Adjutant-General received a letter from Addison Gage & Co., of Boston, tendering to the Massachusetts soldiers a ship-load of ice. The letter says, —

" The Massachusetts troops who have so nobly responded to the call of our Government for the defence of the capital, being, for the most part, in the habit of using ice, and now called to a warm climate, where it is more a necessity than a luxury, we shall be happy to contribute a cargo for their use, the time to be at your disposal, whenever you deem it expedient to send it. In case there is no suitable place to receive the cargo, it can be packed in the vessel, and kept for months, with proper care."

The offer was accepted, and a vessel was chartered to take the ice to Fortress Monroe. The occupants of Quincy Market, of whom Hiscock & Winslow and Harrison Bird were a committee, contributed a large quantity of fresh provisions, which were preserved on the ice, and sent in the ship.

On the 1st of May, the bodies of Luther C. Ladd, Addison O. Whitney, and Sumner H. Needham, who were killed in Baltimore on the 19th of April, reached Boston. Even then the names of the dead were not positively known. The bodies were properly received, and placed in the receiving-vault at King's Chapel. That same afternoon, the Governor wrote to Colonel Jones, of the Sixth Regiment,—

"Mr. Merrill S. Wright arrived at Boston this afternoon in charge of the bodies of three Massachusetts soldiers who fell at Baltimore. They were received by me at the depot, and were conveyed, under an appropriate escort, to the King's Chapel, where they are deposited until they can be finally interred with appropriate funeral honors. Whenever you can obtain the finite and absolutely certain information concerning the names of the three dead, I desire you to inform me. I understand them to be James Keenan, of Stoneham; Edward Coburn, of Lowell; and S. Henry Needham, of Lawrence: but I desire to obtain final and official information as to the correctness of my present understanding."

He also wrote to Mr. Sargent, Mayor of Lowell,—

"I met these relics of our brave and patriotic soldiers at the Worcester Railroad Depot, accompanied by my military staff and the Executive Council, where we took them in charge, and, under the escort of the corps of 'Independent Cadets,' bore them through our streets, thronged by sympathizing citizens, and placed them in the 'Vassall' tomb, beneath the ancient King's Chapel, at the corner of Tremont and School Streets. There they remain, subject to the orders of those friends who have the right to decide their final disposition. But it would be most grateful to the Executive Department, in co-operation with those nearest to the lamented dead, to assist in the last funeral honors to their memory; and I should be pleased to meet you, and the Mayor of Lawrence, and the Selectmen of Stoneham, as soon as you may convene them, at the State House, to consider the arrangements suitable to this occasion."

On the 2d of May, Colonel Sargent, of the Governor's staff, wrote to Mrs. Mary E. Whitney: —

"I promised to write to you if I learned any thing of interest to you. There are no marks of any description whatever on the arms of the man whom you saw this afternoon. I had a careful examination made. There is no doubt whatever that this man and your husband are two entirely different persons. There is no reason to think that any harm has come to your husband. I have no doubt he is alive and well, and doing his duty like a good citizen and brave soldier."

James Keenan and Edward Coburn were wounded in Baltimore, but neither of them fatally. Of the four who were killed, Charles Taylor was buried in Baltimore. No trace of his family or friends has ever been discovered. Needham was buried in Lawrence; Whitney and Ladd, in Lowell. The funeral services at Lawrence and Lowell, over the bodies of these first martyrs of the great Rebellion, were grand and imposing. In each city, monuments of enduring granite have been raised to commemorate their deaths, and to be their sepulchres.

On the 2d of May, Governor Andrew wrote to Simeon Draper, of New York, that he had "about four thousand troops already in the field, as many more ready at brief notice; probably ten thousand drilling, hoping for an opportunity. Why don't the Government call faster? We sent a steamer with supplies to-day." The steamer here referred to was the "Cambridge," which had been fitted out by the State, and had sailed, laden with supplies of clothing and provisions for the Massachusetts troops, on the 1st of May. She had also some recruits for the Third Regiment, and a company for the Rifle Battalion. After taking out certain supplies and men at Fortress Monroe, she was to go by the Potomac to Washington, if it were safe to do so. Governor Andrew wrote to General Scott a detailed statement of the expedition. He said, —

"1st. I desire our Massachusetts troops to receive and have the first benefit of our supplies, but, if need be, that others should share them.

"2d. That, if you see any objection to the 'Cambridge' going up the Potomac, you would give orders to Captain Matthews, her commander, who is instructed to receive your directions."

The vessel cleared for Annapolis; but her real destination was Washington, and she was the first ship that arrived there with troops and supplies of clothing and provisions. On arriving at Washington, Captain Matthews was ordered to report to General Scott, and, if he needed the steamer for the public service, to obey his commands; if not, to return immediately to Boston. His sealed orders were to report " first to the senior Massachusetts officer at Fortress Monroe, and deliver to him such supplies and special packages as shall be designated for that port.

"Second, if at Fortress Monroe he should hear from General Butler that the passage up the Potomac was dangerous, he was to wait twenty-four hours for orders from General Scott; and, if he received orders from him not to proceed up the Potomac, he was to proceed forthwith to Annapolis, land Captain Dodd's company, and turn over the stores to the senior Massachusetts officer in command. He was to bring back 'such sick or duly discharged soldiers' as he might be requested to take and could accommodate." If at any time he should be attacked, he was to resist, and, if possible, to take or sink the attacking vessel. He was to preserve strict discipline, and to practise, at suitable times, with his guns. He was to offer to every Massachusetts command he fell in with to bring home any letters or packages they might wish to send home to friends.

The following is a list of reserved stores sent to Fortress Monroe, purchased and shipped by John M. Forbes, under orders from the Governor: —

60 beef barrels mess beef, at $10 per bbl.	$600.00
30 beef barrels prime pork, at $14 per bbl.	420.00
5,000 lbs. hams, about, at 10 cents per lb.	500.00
20 kegs lard, about 850 lbs., at 12 cents per lb.	102.00
1,000 lbs. butter, about, at 23 cents per lb.	230.00
2,000 lbs. cheese, about, at 11 cents per lb.	220.00
2,000 lbs. of sugar, about, at 8 cents per lb.	160.00
500 lbs. Oolong tea, about, at 35 cents per lb.	175.00
1,000 lbs. coffee, about, at 13 cents per lb.	130.00
10,000 lbs. pilot bread, about, at 4 cents per lb.	400.00
5 beef bbls. pickles, about, at 1s. per gall.	33.33
Lot meats in canisters, for officers, valued at	100.00
	$3,070.33

On the 3d of May, Governor Andrew addressed the following letter to President Lincoln: —

" I hand you copy of a letter addressed to the Commissary-General, explaining the action they (the agents I have appointed) have taken to provide subsistence for our Massachusetts troops.

" Cut off as we were from connection with you, I took the responsibility of providing and forwarding such things as could be bought advantageously here, believing they will be found useful to the army and navy.

" I hope that you will direct the proper department to take charge of such of their supplies as are suitable to their use, and pay for the same, as suggested. We have, further, under the pressure of the exigency, taken the responsibility of joining the underwriters and merchants of Boston in buying, fitting out, and, with the help of Captain Hudson, arming two propellers, for the combined purpose of coast-guard and transports for troops and supplies.

" Neither of the vessels is exactly what is wanted; but they are strong, useful, nearly new, and are bought at prices but little above their commercial value in peaceful times, and can hardly fail to be useful to the public service in the impending struggle. *If you approve our action*, will you be pleased to direct the proper departments, either to receive the vessels at their cost, as if bought for the United-States Government, or, if that is impossible, to give them employment in carrying stores and troops, at the highest prices which are paid to individuals, with the assurance that the vessels will be always at the disposition of Government, and will meantime be used to guard our coasts, and allay the apprehension of our people regarding the threatened piratical proceedings of the secessionists? A description of these vessels is annexed.

" I beg leave to add, that, immediately upon receiving your proclamation, we took up the war, and have carried on our part of it in the spirit in which we believe the Administration and the American people intend to act; namely, as if there was not an inch of red tape in the world.

" We have now enough additional men to furnish you with six more regiments to serve for the war, unless sooner discharged.

" We think the efficiency of any further levies will be much greater if you will muster them, and put them into camps at once for some drilling here. The men we offer, besides fighting, can do any other things for which there may be occasion, from digging clams up to making piano-fortes.

"Fervently devotional to the cause of our country and to the great interests of our country and of the great interests of posterity as well as our own time, and cordially in earnest in the support of the honor and success of your Administration, the people of Massachusetts are ready for the amplest and promptest obedience to your commands."

The above letter was inclosed in one to Mr. Foster, the Attorney-General of the State, who was in Washington. He was requested to call upon the President and deliver it to him, and to exert his power and influence to have matters properly adjusted and permanently settled.

A number of ladies of Cambridge formed a society to work for the soldiers. They requested Professor Washburn, of the Law School, to communicate their purpose to the Governor, who wrote, May 3, in acknowledgment of the offer as follows: —

"In glancing over the list of their names, I realize most completely how deep a hold the cause, in behalf of which those troops are mustered, has upon every social class in our community; that there are no hands in Massachusetts too delicate to contribute something to the work. Almost the next letter which I opened, after breaking the seal of yours, was from a poor needle-woman, saying she had but little, but desiring to give something from that little in the same behalf; and surely a cause which so appeals both to the garret and the drawing-room cannot be other than *national* and *just*."

May 4, Governor writes to J. Amory Davis, President of the Suffolk Bank, —

"Please read the within. We shall have an extra session of our Legislature on Tuesday, May 14. Will the banks of Massachusetts take $5,000,000 of United-States loan at par? If not, — supposing that the Legislature of Massachusetts should authorize a loan of $5,000,000 to the United States, — would the banks lend that amount to this Commonwealth? They have already offered it more than $6,000,000. Will you confer on this subject with the gentlemen upon State Street? I should like to see you, and any others who will take an interest in this subject, at your first convenience."

This brings the correspondence of the Governor to the day when orders were issued by the War Department, that no more three months' regiments would be accepted. On the 3d of

May, 1861, the President called for thirty-nine regiments of infantry and one regiment of cavalry, to serve for three years, or during the war, making an aggregate of officers and enlisted men of 42,034 volunteers. On the 4th of May, General Order No. 15 was issued by the Secretary of War, in which directions were given respecting the organization of the volunteers, but nothing was said regarding the number of regiments which each State was to furnish; and it was not until the 22d of May, eighteen days after the call had been made, that the quota which Massachusetts was to furnish was received from Washington. During this interval, companies in all parts of the State were offering their services, and pressing to be accepted. These companies comprised in the aggregate at least 10,000 effective men. After much solicitation on the part of the Governor, by letter, telegram, and gentlemen appointed by him to visit Washington, leave was given to furnish six regiments of infantry. But, before entering upon a narration of the three years' regiments, other matters claim attention.

Reference has already been made to the valuable services rendered by John M. Forbes at the outbreak of the war. His labors ceased only with the war. In a letter of recent date, written by Mr. Forbes, he says: —

"When the war fairly broke out, on the Monday after Fort Sumter fell, 14th or 15th of April, I *first* remember taking part in the transport question. In common with all Massachusetts, I then offered my services to the Governor, and was authorized to make preliminary arrangements for securing transportation. I accordingly got posted up, with the help of George B. Upton, Esq., of Boston, and Colonel Borden, of Fall River, as to the available steamers at both places, and was accordingly prepared to act, when, about five, P.M., of Tuesday, the 16th [?] of April, Colonel Harry Lee, of His Excellency's staff, conveyed to me an order to go ahead with vessels; the despatch having arrived to start two regiments for Fortress Monroe, besides those which it was arranged to send by land. I remember well the electric shock which this order gave me. I felt that it would the whole country. A north-east storm was blowing; and a glance at the window was enough to enable me to tell the colonel, 'Too late for to-night.' But, with the help of the friends above referred to, you will remember, that, the following night (Wednesday), we got off one regiment by the 'Spaulding,' one by the 'State of Maine,' in company with the Sixth, which was sent by railway to New York, Baltimore, and Washington. In this connection, it may be worth while to recall the circumstances under which Governor Andrew disobeyed (fortunately) the order of the War Department to send his troops to Fortress Monroe *via* Baltimore by rail. I had heard two months earlier from S. M. Felton, not only the plot to attack Mr. Lincoln in Baltimore, but also the plan which he had discovered of burning the bridges on his road between Perryville and Baltimore; and this suggested still more strongly than the mere arguments of convenience the importance of re-enforcing Fortress Monroe *by sea*. I accordingly took a chart of the coast up to the State House, and pointed out to the Governor the ease and certainty with which he could place the troops at the fortress by water, with the additional advantage of having any or all of them taken directly up to Annapolis or Washington, in case they were needed for the defence of the capital. The Governor looked at his orders from General Scott, which were to send the whole by rail, then scrutinized the chart carefully, and, after a short delay, replied, 'It's a clear case; be ready to send the two regiments by water.' This was, I think, on Monday, the glorious day when our Massachusetts men were rallying from their fields, workshops, and homes to defend the flag. If you will take the trouble to look at the charters of the 'Spaulding' and the 'State of Maine,' you will find a clause allowing the Governor to order the ships either to Annapolis or Washington; and in the telegraphic letter-book at the State House you will find a telegram, dated, I think, Wednesday, to General Scott, informing him when, these two regiments would be due at Fortress Monroe, and also that the charters of the vessels provided for taking them up to either place. This, you will notice, was before the burning of the bridges or the fight of 19th of April in Baltimore; and it is due to Samuel M. Felton, that the historian should award to him the credit of calling General Butler's attention to the Annapolis route, as the best means of reaching Washington."

While Mr. Forbes, Mr. Upton, and Colonel Borden were active in securing transports to forward troops, other gentlemen were interesting themselves with the subject. William F. Durfee, of Fall River, wrote to the Adjutant-General, April 15, —

"Governor Sprague, of Rhode Island, has been trying to charter steamers of Colonel Borden, of Fall River, to take a Rhode Island regiment to Washington. I think they may succeed in getting the

'Empire State.' The 'Metropolis' is laid up, and will not be ready for two or three days. Application has also been made from New York. I write for the purpose of posting you in regard to the operations of our neighboring States. The gentleman stated that Governor Sprague intended to have the Rhode-Island troops in Washington in advance of any other State in New England; and I have an ambition to see the Massachusetts men there as soon as 'Little Rhody's,' — sooner, if possible. If they can get the 'Empire State,' they intend to leave Providence Thursday, at twelve o'clock."

The "Empire State" was chartered by Governor Sprague, but the Rhode-Island troops did not get to Washington first. The following extracts from letters received by the Adjutant-General show in part the patriotic feeling which inspired the people: —

April 15. — Charles Bowers, of Concord, writes, "Believing most fervently in the doctrine vindicated at 'the Old North Bridge' in 1775, that resistance to tyrants is obedience to God, in this hour of our country's peril I offer my poor services in her defence. If you can assign me to any position, however humble, where I can do any thing for freedom and the right, I will hasten to the post in your command." The writer went out lieutenant in the Concord company attached to the Fifth Regiments. He was afterwards captain in the Thirty-second Regiment, and served through the war. Rev. B. F. De Costa writes, "I hereby tender my services as chaplain for any of the forces now called into service by the State. I should be glad to accompany any regiment to the capital or elsewhere, and cheerfully endure with them the hardships of the campaign." Mr. De Costa was appointed and commissioned chaplain of the Fifth Regiment. A. A. Marsh, of Cincinnati, Ohio, telegraphs, "I wish you would let me know if you can buy ten six-pounder rifled field-pieces ready for use, and at what price, and when we can get them. We want them for use here, for the protection of this city. Telegraph the price." General George H. Devereux, of Salem, writes, "I earnestly hope that the General Government will go into this contest with the olive branch frankly and cordially displayed in one hand, offering every reasonable opportunity to avoid the dreadful alternative of a civil war with our own countrymen. But, if war must come, all sound policy and even humanity requires that it be vigorously sustained, and that we show ourselves capable of maintaining the honor, dignity, and safety of our country." General Devereux had three sons officers in the war, one of whom was brevetted a general.

April 16.—General Nettleton, of Chicopee, writes, "I hereby tender to His Excellency the Governor, and through him to the President, my personal services to any appointed post in the gift of either. I cannot, by reason of age, be admitted to the ranks by enlistment; yet I am hearty and hale, and not older than my grandsire was when following the lead of Washington." General Nettleton's son raised a company for the Thirtieth Regiment, of which he went out captain, and came home colonel of the regiment.

April 17.—Edward Kinsley, of Cambridge, writes, "The patriotic ladies of Cambridge are making bandages and preparing lint for our troops who have been ordered out of the State. A box will be ready to-morrow morning. Please tell the bearer where you will have it sent." Colonel Borden, of Fall River, writes, "The 'Empire State' will be let at a thousand dollars a day; the 'State of Maine,' for eight hundred." George B. Upton, of Boston, writes that he had made a "contract with the agents of the 'S. R. Spaulding' to take troops to Fortress Monroe at twelve dollars each. The vessel will be ready in eight hours after notice is received."

April 18.—E. C. Peirce, of Weymouth, writes, "If the services of an active horse and rider as courier are required for any distance, great or small, let me know." Daniel Denny, of Boston, writes, "I have three spacious lofts, No. 142, Fulton Street, quite light and airy, which I freely offer for the use of the military. Being considerably more than forty-five years old, I fear my personal services would not be accepted if offered." Captain Peard, of Milford, writes, "I offer my company, the 'Davis Guards,' all of whom are adopted citizens, for the service." This company was accepted, and formed part of the Ninth Regiment, of which Captain Peard was commissioned major. He died in the service.

The following letter is from one of the most noble and highly cultivated men whom Massachusetts sent to the war, and who sacrificed his life for the cause: —

MONUMENT SQUARE, CHARLESTOWN, April 19, 1861.

ADJUTANT-GENERAL SCHOULER, — We are at that point where every man who can devote himself to his country's service should come forward. I beg that you would put on file this my application for any position in the medical service of the Commonwealth in which I could be useful. I am aware of the law under which surgeons are appointed, and of course understand that you have no direct control of this matter. But there may be exigencies from deaths, resignations, unusual demands, or unforeseen circumstances, when you may be called upon to advise or suggest. If such a call is made, be pleased to remember this application of your old personal and political friend. I may be allowed to say, should this communication ever be brought up for consideration, that, while I am known mainly in another specialty, I was educated in the New-York hospitals for a surgeon; and for some years, in a wide field, I was much engaged in that capacity. Inquiry in New Hampshire would show, that there are but few of the greater operations of surgery which I have not performed. I am a little above fifty; in health so good as not to have been confined to my house a day in the past three years; and, entirely removed from all cares by easy personal circumstances, of course am ready at the shortest notice for any duty. As this application is for use, not show, may I beg of you, that it may not reach the press, which, in its avidity for paragraphs, might be ready to put me unnecessarily before the public?

Truly yours, LUTHER V. BELL.

Dr. Bell's offer was accepted. He was appointed surgeon of the Eleventh Regiment Massachusetts Volunteers, was commissioned June 13, 1861, and immediately entered upon his duties. His family was one of the oldest and most distinguished in New Hampshire; his father, John Bell, having been Governor of the State and a member of the United-States Senate. Dr. Bell for many years had charge of the McLean Asylum for the Insane, in Somerville, and was at the head of his profession in that branch of medical science. His figure was tall and commanding; his face was eminently handsome and pleasant. On the 3d of August, 1861, while with his regiment at the front, he was appointed brigade-surgeon by President Lincoln, and was placed on the staff of General Joseph Hooker. About four o'clock, on the wintry morning of February 5, under his canvas shelter at Camp Baker, two miles from Budd's Ferry, on the Potomac, Dr. Bell was taken suddenly ill; and about nine o'clock, on the evening of the 11th, he passed peacefully away for ever. We shall have occasion to refer again to this distinguished person in the next chapter.

April 19. — General John S. Tyler, commanding the "Ancient and Honorable Artillery Company," "tenders, by vote of the corps, their services for coast defence." The Massachusetts Bible Society " offers a supply of Bibles and Testaments for the soldiers."

April 21. — Mrs. Julia R. Seavy, Jamaica Plain, writes, " I am anxious to contribute in some way to the comfort of our brave volunteers. Would twenty flannel shirts be acceptable? If so, I will have them made and forwarded to you for distribution. Our country, right or wrong."

April 23. — Edward Greenmon, or Greenmast, of Mendon, writes, " Will you accept the service of a Dartmoor prisoner in the war of 1812, and near seven years on board of a British ship-of-war? Impressed at the age of twelve years, when the war was declared, I was most cruelly flogged and threatened to be hung, because I would not fight against my country. I am ready now to fight the traitors of my country, and battle for freedom." Edward S. Waters, of Salem, suggests " the organization of an engineer corps, to repair the bridges between Philadelphia and Washington." George Gregg, of Boston, informs the Adjutant-General, that " certain British subjects in Boston and vicinity have formed themselves into a rifle company, and offer their services for duty anywhere within thirty miles of Boston, to be drilled, armed, and clothed at private expense."

April 27. — Colonel Newell A. Thompson, of Boston, reports, " Have fulfilled the duty for which I have been detailed, — to remove certain arms and ammunition from the United-States Arsenal at Watertown, to the State Arsenal at Cambridge." Rev. George D. Wilde, of Salem, sends a roll of forty men for " field-hospital corps, to be sent to the front; and each pledges himself to submit to all the requirements of military life."

April 28. — James L. Merrill, of Athol, volunteers himself and three "of my seven sons, with eight or ten other good, faithful, and temperate men, to go to the front, and act as scouts, to be armed with rifles and side-arms." John Waters, of West Sutton, writes, "I and several citizens of this town, being well acquainted with the use of the rifle, are anxious to form a company of sharpshooters." Captain Rand, First Regiment of Infantry, writes, "At a meeting of my company, held last evening, it was unanimously voted to adopt the following as a company name, 'Schouler Volunteers,' with many thanks to you for your numerous kindnesses." This company was Company I, First Regiment Massachusetts Volunteers. Captain Rand was killed at Chancellorsville. Captain Peirson, of Byfield, "volunteers his whole command (Company B, First Battalion of Rifles) for the war."

May 1. — Samuel Fowler, of Westfield, writes, "This town has appropriated ten thousand dollars for the equipment and outfit of a company of volunteers, and to drill them until called for. God save the Commonwealth of Massachusetts."

Richard H. Dana, Jr., of Cambridge, writes, —

"The topi I left with you yesterday is the result of fifty years' experience of the British in the East. It is now universally used by the British military in India, China, and Indian Islands. I wore that topi in China, India, and Egypt some six months, including June, July, and August. It is the best thing possible. It gives air between the head and the outer case all round. This is the best safeguard against sunstroke or congestion. It is a mistake to wear any thing thin or light like straw. The desiderata are (1) a thick wall between the head and the sun's rays, and (2) air between the wall and the head. The weight on the head, when adjusted around the side, and not on the top, is of little consequence, as all men experienced in Eastern life and travel will tell you. The rim to this protects the eyes, and back of the head and neck. In the East, the back of the head and back of the neck are considered specially sensitive to the sun. The topi may be made either of felt (as mine is) or of pith. I prefer the felt."

The topi spoken of was a most excellent protection to the head from the heat of the sun, but was never adopted, either by the State or the Federal authorities.

May 6. — President Felton, of Harvard University, informs the Adjutant-General that "between three and four hundred students have entered their names for a drill-club; and between one and two hundred have brought their fathers' certificates, that they consent to the watch. In a day or two, I shall probably be able to furnish you a complete list of both." The "watch" here spoken of was in reference to a guard of students to watch the State Arsenal at Cambridge.

May 10. — Colonel Newell A. Thompson presented "a roll of one hundred past members of the 'Boston City Guards,' who have voluntarily placed themselves under my command, and authorized me to tender their services as a Home Guard."

The foregoing extracts, from letters received by the Adjutant-General in the first days of the war, serve to show in a degree the patriotic spirit of the people. They are selected from a great mass of letters received by him in those early days of the war; all of which bear more or less on the same subject, and are imbued with the same spirit and determination.

From the time the three months' troops left the State until a call was made for three years' volunteers, May 3, communication with the departments at Washington was dilatory and unsatisfactory; which caused the Governor to request Ex-Governor Boutwell, Attorney-General Foster, Judge Hoar, and William L. Burt to go forward, and endeavor to keep up a line of communication with him. This will explain some of the letters and telegrams given in preceding pages. One great point to be gained was authority from the War Department to garrison and man the forts in Boston Harbor, the defenceless condition of which exposed the city to attack, and caused much uneasiness among the merchants, underwriters, and other citizens of Boston. After the attack upon the Sixth Regiment in Baltimore, on the 19th of April, inquiry was made by the Governor in regard to establishing hospital accommodations for the sick and wounded who may return to the State. The matter was referred to Dr. William J. Dale, who, on the 21st of April, reported, "I have conversed with Mr. Rogers, chairman of the Trustees of the Massachusetts General Hospital, and the institution will be open for soldiers in the service; and, at short notice, they can put up a large temporary building in the hospital yard for the accommodation of the sick and wounded." This excellent institution, during the whole war, gave all the accommodation and assistance within its power to the sick and wounded soldiers.

Ex-Governor Boutwell left Boston for Washington on the 23d of April. In New York, he had an interview with Major-General Wool, commanding the Department of the East, and with Vice-President Hamlin, whom he met there. On the 24th he wrote to the Governor, " General Wool and Vice-President Hamlin are in favor of your taking the responsibility of sending two regiments to take charge of the forts, and to furnish and arm three vessels for the protection of the coast. You can exercise the power, under the circumstances, better than any one else." On the same day on which this letter was written, an order passed the Executive Council, that the Governor send a force of militia to garrison the forts, and one company to each of the arsenals at Cambridge and Watertown, the whole not to exceed seven hundred men; the Adjutant-General to furnish subsistence, and the Quartermaster-General transportation. On the same day, Mr. Boutwell telegraphed from New York to Governor Andrew, "Send without delay a steamer, with provisions, for General Butler's command at Annapolis. She must be armed. Mr. Burt returns by eleven-o'clock train with orders from General Wool."

On the 25th of April, Mr. Crowninshield, who was in New York to take the steamer for Europe to purchase arms, writes to the Governor, " I am detained till this forenoon for despatches from the British minister. I learn that he has telegraphed to Halifax for a fleet to go to Washington to protect him and save the archives of their Government. I believe it."

Before leaving New York, Mr. Boutwell succeeded in obtaining an order from General Wool upon the ordnance officer at the United-States Arsenal at Watertown, for four thousand stand of arms. These arms were what were known as the " Windsor rifle," and had the sword bayonet. Upon the receipt of Mr. Boutwell's telegram to forward provisions to General Butler at Annapolis by armed steamer, Governor Andrew consulted John

M. Forbes, and put the matter in his charge. On the afternoon of the same day, he addressed the following letter to Governor Andrew: —

BOSTON, April 25, 1861.

To His Excellency Governor ANDREW.

SIR, — Having reference to the letter of Hon. George S. Boutwell, I beg leave to say, that, after you showed it me this morning, I found that the only really suitable vessel in port for the purpose indicated was on the point of being sold for $75,000. Just before the war, her owners asked $70,000 for her, which I thought a little too high. Under the circumstances, however, she seemed to me cheap; and I took the responsibility of buying her, intending to offer her to you or to the General Government.

I have since applied to the underwriters and merchants to take and own half of the ship, if the State will take the other half, with the understanding that she is to be managed as an armed transport, used to convey troops and stores, at the prices·current for other transports; and, when not so used, to act as coast-guard or despatch vessel, under the management of a Government agent or agents.

It is hoped, upon this basis, to make her pay her way, with little or no loss, besides doing good service, and keeping up the confidence of our citizens and the fears of our enemies.

If you approve the plan, I should like to have you own such part of her as I cannot get readily taken by the underwriters; also, proportion of her outfit, which I estimate at under $10,000.

She can at once load coal and the stores ordered, get on board the guns, which the Navy Yard will lend us temporarily, and be ready for troops or other service.

I have inquired also about other vessels. The only suitable propeller is a small vessel of about three hundred tons, nearly new, due here to-night, which can be bought for a trifle under $30,000. She would make a good temporary gunboat; could carry her crew, a good load of stores upon a pinch, and a few troops, not many.

If you are disposed to have another vessel, she is the most available, and is not dear. I think, if you wish it, the merchants and underwriters would take part of her, — probably half. She would be well adapted to the coast-guard now being raised.

In addition to these, I have found a side-wheel ship of about one thousand tons, older than the others, and having the single advantage of light draught of water, — a good serviceable ship. She can be bought on reasonable terms to-day, — *not cheap*, not very dear, — but, in my opinion, not so desirable as either of the others, unless some new arrangement arises.

I should strongly recommend some prompt action as to the first two vessels, if you knew the emergency as I do, and are willing to take the responsibility.

The money for the "Cambridge" ought to be appropriated immediately, and orders given as to the name in which she shall stand registered, — perhaps two trustees, one to represent the State, and one the individual subscribers.

With much respect, your obedient servant,   J. M. FORBES.

N.B. — I do not think the merchants ready, at this moment, to share in the third vessel, — *the side-wheel steamer.*

On the same day, the letter was referred by the Governor to a committee of the Executive Council, who reported that "the Committee authorize the Governor to procure, on the basis of the letter, two steam-vessels, the State to take one half and the underwriters the other, to be managed as armed transports to convey troops and stores, and, when not so used, as a coast-guard or despatch vessels." These vessels were immediately purchased, — the "Cambridge" at a cost of $75,000, and the "Pembroke" at $30,000. The outfit of the "Cambridge" cost $10,000. The Council also ordered, "that the Governor, with the advice of the Council, employ John M. Forbes, Esq., to procure proper rations for the supply of four thousand men in service for thirty days, to be furnished immediately."

Mr. Boutwell arrived at Washington on the 28th of April, and, on the evening of that day, wrote the following interesting letter to Governor Andrew, which was the first satisfactory communication he had received from Washington since the regiments had left the State: —

WASHINGTON, April 28, 1861.

To His Excellency Governor ANDREW.

SIR, — I arrived in Washington to-day, after a journey of forty-eight hours from Philadelphia by Annapolis. There have been no mails from the North for a week; and you may easily understand, that the mighty public sentiment of the Free States is not yet fully appreciated here.

The President and Cabinet are gaining confidence; and the measures of the Administration will no longer be limited to the defence of the capital. Secretary Welles has already sent orders to Captain Hudson to purchase six steamers, with instructions to consult you in regard to the matter. I regret that the Secretary was not ready to put the matter into the hands of commissioners, who would have acted efficiently and promptly.

Mr. Welles will accept, as part of the quota, such vessels as may have been purchased by Mr. Forbes.

Senator Grimes, of Iowa, will probably give Mr. Crowninshield an order for arms. The United-States Government may do the same; but no definite action has yet been taken.

Martial law will be proclaimed here to-morrow. Colonel Mansfield will be appointed general, and assigned to this district. He is one of the most efficient officers in the country.

Baltimore is to be closed in from Havre-de-Grace, from the Relay House, from the Carlisle line, and by an efficient naval force. She will be reduced to unconditional submission. The passage of the troops through Maryland has had a great moral effect. The people are changing rapidly in the country-places. Many instances of a popular revolution, in towns through which troops have passed or been stationed, have come to my knowledge. I came to Washington with the Twelfth New-York Regiment; and from Annapolis Junction there were cheers from three-fourths of the houses by the wayside.

Every thing appears well at Annapolis, where General Butler commands in person. There is a large body of troops, the people are gradually gaining confidence in the army and the Government, and the regulations seem to be effective. General Butler is popular with the officers whom I met. He has taken command of the highlands that command the town and the encampment. All sorts of rumors are spread among the troops concerning an attack upon the Annapolis Station; but the place can be defended under any conceivable circumstances. I am sorry to say, that every thing is in confusion at Annapolis Junction; and a moderate force might, in a single night, break off the connection of this city with the North. It is at present a military station without a permanent head. Each colonel, as he moves towards Washington, commands for twelve or twenty-four hours. My own belief, however, is, that Maryland will never see two thousand men together as a military organization in opposition to the Government.

I presume that your Excellency has means of obtaining information concerning the condition of Massachusetts men, morally and physically; but, as I am here, I shall try to obtain and transmit any information that seems important. I may say now, that the Eighth Regiment is quartered in the rotunda of the Capitol; and a military man, not of

Massachusetts, says, that they are already suffering from the cold and dampness of the place. He advises tents and out-door encampment.

I repeat what is every hour said in my hearing, that Massachusetts has taken her place at the head of the column in support of the Government; and our regiments are everywhere esteemed as noble examples of citizen-soldiers. I, for one, feel anxious that every thing that is proper should be done.

I have written this communication in great haste; and I have only time to subscribe myself your Excellency's obedient servant,

GEORGE S. BOUTWELL.

On the 30th of April, Governor Andrew received from Attorney-General Foster a telegram from Washington, saying, "Arrived last night. All well at Annapolis and here." Mr. Foster had followed on the heels of Mr. Boutwell. While at New York, on his way to Washington, he wrote to Governor Andrew as follows: —

NEW YORK, April 27, 1861.

I have spent to-day in trying to find the utmost known in this city; but there is no reliable intelligence not known to you. New York has sent up to this time five thousand four hundred troops, and by Tuesday next will send four thousand more.

Three regiments from Connecticut are nearly ready, — two thousand four hundred. New Jersey claims to have four regiments nearly ready, — three thousand two hundred. Notwithstanding all this, it seems to be the strong desire of every one here, that more men should go from Massachusetts, without waiting for a requisition. General Wool says, if you telegraph to him whether you shall send two more regiments, he will answer, "Yes." I have seen him, and he appears well, but very much overworked and worn out. For the occasion, the committee of merchants are working very hard, and comprise many of their best men. I did not feel it was a sufficiently clear case in favor of sending more men to telegraph to that effect. But I would do it unless you get later advices adverse. The present feeling here is, that Washington is safe, but that more troops are greatly needed; and the universal cry is, that the Government is far behind the people. I am going to Washington to-night *via* Annapolis, and no doubt shall find the way open and safe. There are a number of bills here for transportation by steamer, and for subsistence furnished our men; and I am very confident, that a faithful, sensible man, with a small office in this city, to act as agent for Massachusetts, and to whom alone you should refer all bills, &c., would save a great deal of money and time. There will be men going and returning, and a great variety of wants, large and small, until the end is reached; and we shall have undesirable men claiming to represent the State, and intermeddling in many ways, unless there is some one agent on the spot all the time.

The praise of the Old Bay State is in every mouth; and the repetition of the half said of her Governor to you would be flattery.

Very respectfully and truly yours,

DWIGHT FOSTER.

Mr. Boutwell remained in Washington until the 1st of May, when he left for Boston. At Perryville, he telegraphed to "Mr. Forbes & Co., — Two lots of stocks additional ordered by Cabot." This was in the cipher arranged by Mr. Forbes, and meant, "Two regiments of troops additional ordered by Cameron." Mr. Boutwell arrived at New York on the 2d of May, and wrote to Governor Andrew that evening: —

I arrived here this afternoon, and I hope to report to you in person Saturday. I had free conversation with the President, General Scott, Mr. Seward, Mr. Chase, General Cameron, and Mr. Blair, upon public affairs. The impression I received from all, except perhaps Mr. Seward, was favorable to a vigorous prosecution of the war. Mr. Seward repeated his words of December and February, "The crisis is over." It is, however, understood at Washington, that Mr. Seward favors vigorous measures. Mr. Chase says, that the policy of the Administration is vigorous and comprehensive, as sure to succeed in controlling the Rebellion, and preserving the whole territory of the Union. I will only say now, that I left Washington with a more favorable impression of the policy of the Government than I entertained when I left Boston.

General Cameron agreed to authorize Massachusetts to raise two regiments in addition to that of Dwight's. The papers were all made, and only a Cabinet meeting prevented their completion on Tuesday. I did not wish to remain another day, and I left the papers with the chief clerk; and I also received the assurance of Colonel Ripley, that he would give personal and prompt attention to transmitting them to Boston. I shall expect them on Saturday.

Colonel Ripley issued an order on Tuesday for rifling cannon. Mr. Forbes's letter aided very much.

I am very truly your most obedient servant,

GEORGE S. BOUTWELL.

The "Cambridge" had arrived in Washington from Boston, with troops and military stores. Judge Hoar was in the city. There appears to have been no one to act for the Government to take charge of the stores, or to superintend their distribution. The following letter from E. Rockwood Hoar, one of the justices of the Supreme Court, to the Governor, relates to this matter, and to the hardships borne by the Fifth Regiment, from the time it left Boston until it arrived in Washington, which, in part, were occasioned by haste and bad management in loading the transports at New York, by which the rations and the bales of blankets, which were to have been distributed to the men, were covered with other merchandise, and could not be got at, so that the men suffered for want of food and blankets: —

WASHINGTON, May 6, 1861.
To His Excellency Governor ANDREW.

DEAR SIR, — Mr. Foster, I learn, has gone with General Butler, and cannot be communicated with. Dr. Howe has not arrived. The "Cambridge" arrived yesterday afternoon. I have therefore, as I wrote to you yesterday, "taken the responsibility," which I trust will meet your approbation, as there is nobody here to attend to the business; and, unless instant attention be paid to it, in the present extreme confusion of affairs here, there would be even great delay in getting their private packages to our troops. I saw the President this morning the instant he left the breakfast table, presented your letter to him, and explained to him the whole business. I also saw General Cameron, and he has agreed to take the stores, with the exception of such as we may retain for hospital use, and for the reasonable comfort of our men, at the invoice price, with the freight added at the price you named. The President sent for Mr. Seward; and I had a conference with them jointly as to the purchase or employment of the steamers, and also with General Cameron. The strong inclination of the Government is to purchase rather than charter vessels; and I think the arrangement can be made to sell them. But to-morrow they are to have a detailed report of the number of vessels already engaged, and I am promised a definite answer on Wednesday.

I took Senator Wilson with me, and consulted Colonel Lawrence, the senior officer in command of the Massachusetts men, and Colonel Monroe, and the quartermaster of the Sixth Regiment, as to the supplies and stores which should be retained for the hospital service and the comfort of the troops, and we have examined the invoice and made the selection; and I have the promise that by one o'clock the business shall be put through the proper department.

The Sixth Massachusetts Regiment left Washington yesterday, under General Butler's orders, for the Relay House, between Annapolis Junction and Baltimore. Their future destination is not certain; but, if there should be a march for the occupation of Baltimore, it is felt that *poetical justice* requires that regiment to have the first place.

I have the honor, further, to submit a matter which I venture to press upon your immediate attention.

The Fifth Regiment left Boston, by their own choice, partially equipped, on Sunday morning, April 21, rather than wait another day to have their equipments completed. They had to sleep in Faneuil Hall, in the confusion and bustle of the two preceding nights. They went to New York on that Sunday, marched the whole length of that city in the evening, hardly able to stand from fatigue and sleeplessness. They were crowded on board the steamer, and sent fresh from their country homes and habits to the sickness and misery of the sea voyage, with only the deck to lie down on, and not room enough for all to do that. They landed at Annapolis at night, were kept standing in line, waiting for orders, four or five hours, and at eleven, P.M., required to march on foot to Annapolis Junction, twenty miles. Their blankets and clothing were done up into bales and boxes on the steamer, and had only been partially landed when they started. Colonel Lawrence wanted to wait for it; but the danger and necessity of their immediate presence at the junction made their march imperative. He left forty men detailed to take charge of and forward the baggage; but, after the regiment had gone, General Butler ordered them off to serve as a guard on the line of the railroad. The regiment reached the Junction, and took their first substantial sleep on the ground, without shelter or blankets. Our Concord company had nothing but their guns, and what they left home in and their great-coats; and a number had not even the coats — left behind at Annapolis. The baggage, left without charge, got mixed with general United-States stores, and got distributed to Pennsylvania and other troops promiscuously. It is gone past redemption. Thirty men of the Concord company have not yet got a blanket, and sleep on a hard floor. They had not a shirt in the company till last Friday, two weeks from home, except those they wore from home, nor a pair of drawers or stockings till Saturday, and then not enough to go round. There is no complaint. Health generally good, and spirits and patriotism as high and cheerful as yours or mine, — the heroes! The United States have no blankets here; and all attempts possible have been made, here and at Annapolis, to supply them. Colonel

the selection; and I have the promise that by one o'clock the business shall be put through the proper department.

The Sixth Massachusetts Regiment left Washington yesterday, under General Butler's orders, for the Relay House, between Annapolis Junction and Baltimore. Their future destination is not certain; but, if there should be a march for the occupation of Baltimore, it is felt that *poetical justice* requires that regiment to have the first place.

I have the honor, further, to submit a matter which I venture to press upon your immediate attention.

The Fifth Regiment left Boston, by their own choice, partially equipped, on Sunday morning, April 21, rather than wait another day to have their equipments completed. They had to sleep in Faneuil Hall, in the confusion and bustle of the two preceding nights. They went to New York on that Sunday, marched the whole length of that city in the evening, hardly able to stand from fatigue and sleeplessness. They were crowded on board the steamer, and sent fresh from their country homes and habits to the sickness and misery of the sea voyage, with only the deck to lie down on, and not room enough for all to do that. They landed at Annapolis at night, were kept standing in line, waiting for orders, four or five hours, and at eleven, P.M., required to march on foot to Annapolis Junction, twenty miles. Their blankets and clothing were done up into bales and boxes on the steamer, and had only been partially landed when they started. Colonel Lawrence wanted to wait for it; but the danger and necessity of their immediate presence at the junction made their march imperative. He left forty men detailed to take charge of and forward the baggage; but, after the regiment had gone, General Butler ordered them off to serve as a guard on the line of the railroad. The regiment reached the Junction, and took their first substantial sleep on the ground, without shelter or blankets. Our Concord company had nothing but their guns, and what they left home in and their great-coats; and a number had not even the coats — left behind at Annapolis. The baggage, left without charge, got mixed with general United-States stores, and got distributed to Pennsylvania and other troops promiscuously. It is gone past redemption. Thirty men of the Concord company have not yet got a blanket, and sleep on a hard floor. They had not a shirt in the company till last Friday, two weeks from home, except those they wore from home, nor a pair of drawers or stockings till Saturday, and then not enough to go round. There is no complaint. Health generally good, and spirits and patriotism as high and cheerful as yours or mine, — the heroes! The United States have no blankets here; and all attempts possible have been made, here and at Annapolis, to supply them. Colonel

Lawrence is doing, and has done, all in his power, and is entitled to great credit for his services. But they want what the enclosed list states, — instantly. I know you will send them if you can. If the State cannot pay for them, send the bill for the Concord company to Concord, and it shall be paid as soon as I get there. I will write again this evening.

The commissary says Government is very short of money. Treasury-notes are but partially serviceable, because they are used to pay dues to the Government, and so must cut off revenue; in fact, substantially amount only to an anticipation of revenue.

The matter of the loan, on which we addressed you last week, is therefore of the highest importance.

I learned on my arrival, that the orders for Massachusetts regiments to be enlisted, mustered, and drilled at Boston had been forwarded. If they have not come to hand, telegraph me or Wilson, and duplicates will be sent.

Faithfully your Excellency's friend, and the servant of the committee and the cause, E. R. HOAR.

With the following letter from Judge Hoar to the Governor, we close this part of the correspondence relating to matters connected with the three months' troops, and the disposition of the War Department neither to accept more troops, purchase transports, nor to take charge of commissary stores which had been forwarded by Massachusetts : —

WASHINGTON, May 8, 1861.
To His Excellency Governor ANDREW.

DEAR SIR, — The " Cambridge " arrived this morning, having been detained between two and three days at Fort Monroe to bring on some heavy guns and shells. Dr. Howe arrived this morning, having been detained on the way by illness.

Mr. Cameron told me this morning, that his department would not purchase, or agree to employ, the steamers; and, in answer to my urgent representations about the six Massachusetts regiments for the war, said that none could be received at present, and that he could give no promise or encouragement for the future. I asked Mr. Chase if he could help us, and he said he was afraid he could not, as he had been trying to get Cameron to receive ten regiments from Ohio, and had succeeded in getting him to accept only three.

In regard to the steamers, I have made a very strong application to the Secretary of the Navy, which I think has produced some impression; and he has promised to have the naval inspectors examine the "Cambridge" to-morrow, and to see if he can take her. I put the matter upon all the public grounds I could urge, and upon the claim which our State has for consideration from what she has done and what she is doing; and I am sure Mr. Welles feels personally friendly to our purpose. The "Pembroke" I do not believe you can sell to either department, and think you had better put her freight charge, and make your plans for her future employment upon that supposition.

I have the promise, that the duplicate orders for our troops to be mustered into service in Boston shall be immediately transmitted. I received your telegram too late to have it done to-day. I must leave Washington to-morrow morning, and shall leave Mr. Lowell in charge of the affairs of the "Cambridge" until he is superseded by some one else. I trust he may receive express and direct authority, addressed to him personally from you, or by your order, which I think will facilitate his action and communication with the authorities.

Dr. Howe prefers he should go on with the business, as he understands and has begun it; and it requires a great deal of running about and personal hard work. I think it will be done to your satisfaction. The captain of the "Cambridge" thoughtlessly omitted to make any bargain for the transmission of the guns and shells from Fortress Monroe, and that will make some trouble, but will be carefully looked after. Senator Wilson will do all he can to forward the sale of the vessel; and he and Dr. Howe will advise with Mr. Lowell.

Faithfully your Excellency's obedient servant, E. R. HOAR.

The letters of Mr. Boutwell and Judge Hoar describe the duties with which they were charged by the Governor. They were to consult with the President and his Cabinet and with General Scott respecting the exigencies of the occasion, and keep up a communication with the authorities of the State. They had also charge of the provisions, clothing, and munitions of war, forwarded from the State to the Massachusetts soldiers. Judge Hoar, who was in Washington about the time when the proclamation of the President was issued for regiments of three years' volunteers, made, by direction of the Governor, urgent efforts to induce the Government to accept of all the regiments which Massachusetts was prepared to furnish. On the 8th of May, a proposition was made by him in writing, to the Secretary of War, offering, on behalf of the State, to "furnish six regiments for three years, or for the war, *perfectly equipped*, in addition to the quota which Massachusetts might be called upon to furnish under the first call of the President; and, on the same day, it was refused by the Secretary. He also, in co-operation with Mr. Foster, the Attorney-General, and Senator Wilson, by direction of the Governor, offered such aid as Massachusetts could furnish to the pecuniary credit of the Government.

Judge Hoar left Washington on or about the 15th of May, to return home; and his duties and responsibilities were assumed by Charles R. Lowell, Jr., who had been appointed by the Governor as the agent of Massachusetts in Washington. Before leaving Washington, Judge Hoar addressed a letter to Mr. Lowell, in which the duties he was expected to perform were carefully and concisely stated. He was to communicate with the departments in relation to stores sold, or troops carried on the Massachusetts transports. He was to communicate with the officers commanding Massachusetts regiments; and every thing wanting by them was to be received and distributed through him. He was to keep an account of his expenses, and report as nearly daily as practicable of all his doings to the Governor. He was empowered to buy a copying-press, and "to employ a clerk, if necessary."—"The object of the whole arrangement is," says Judge Hoar, "to have some *one* responsible, competent agent, who will know all that is done and sent from Massachusetts, and all that is wanted and received at Washington, or by the troops, wherever stationed; to take care of property, take vouchers, prevent waste, and to be the sole channel of communication between supply and demand."

This letter of Judge Hoar to Mr. Lowell brings up pleasant and sad memories of one of the best and bravest of men. Mr. Lowell was born in Boston, Jan. 2, 1835. He was the son of Charles R. Lowell, and the grandson of Rev. Charles Lowell. The best blood of Massachusetts flowed in his veins. He graduated at Harvard University at the head of his class in 1853. When the Rebellion broke out, he was in Cumberland, Md. He had charge of the Mt. Savage Iron Works at that place. On the 20th of April, 1861, hearing of the attack upon the Sixth Regiment in Baltimore, he abandoned his position, and set out for Washington. In what manner he made the journey is not clearly known; but he reached the capital on Monday, April 22. On the 24th, he wrote to his mother, "I was fortunate enough to be in Baltimore last Sunday, and to be here at present. How Jim and Henry will envy me! I shall come to see you if I find there is nothing to be done here. So have the blue-room ready." Mr. Lowell remained at his post as the agent of Massachusetts in Washington until the 14th of May, when he was appointed by the President a captain in the Sixth United-States Cavalry. On the 15th of April, 1863, he was commissioned by Governor Andrew colonel of the Second Regiment of Massachusetts Cavalry, a regiment which was recruited by him in this State. It was while raising and organizing this regiment that we became acquainted with him. On the 19th of October, 1864, he was made a brigadier-general of volunteers by President Lincoln. On the same day, he fell from his horse, from wounds received at the battle of Cedar Creek, and died on the day following, October 20. The writer was in Washington when the battle was fought in which Colonel Lowell was killed. The following is an extract from a letter addressed by me to Governor Andrew, and which is printed in the Adjutant-General's Report for 1864: —

"On arriving at my hotel in Washington, I had the honor of an introduction to Brigadier-General Custar, of General Sheridan's army. He had arrived in Washington that afternoon (Oct. 22) from the Shenandoah Valley, having in his custody twelve battle-flags, which had been captured from the enemy the Wednesday preceding. He was to present them the next day to the Secretary of War, and he was pleased to give me an invitation to be present. From him I first learned that Colonel Lowell, of the Second Massachusetts Cavalry, had been killed, gallantly leading the regiment in the front of battle. This news saddened my heart. Colonel Lowell was my *beau idéal* of an officer and a gentleman. I had seen much of him while he was in Massachusetts, raising and organizing his regiment, and had become warmly attached to him. He was one of our best and bravest. General Custar informed me that Colonel Lowell was severely wounded in the early part of the engagement, and was advised to retire to the rear. He thought, however, he could stand the fatigues of the day, and stoutly held to his command; in a few hours afterwards, he fell, mortally wounded. It was pleasant to listen to the words of praise which General Custar bestowed upon his fallen comrade."

Mr. Lowell was succeeded as agent for Massachusetts in Washington by Charles H. Dalton, of Boston, who was commissioned assistant quartermaster-general, with the rank of colonel, May 23, 1861. Of his services we shall speak hereafter.

On the 2d of May, Governor Andrew addressed the following letter to Dr. Samuel G. Howe: —

EXECUTIVE DEPARTMENT, BOSTON, May 2, 1861.

To Dr. SAMUEL G. HOWE, Boston.

MY DEAR SIR, — The Massachusetts Volunteer Militia now in the field demand and deserve our anxious care, as well in respect to their sanitary condition (including their medical and surgical supplies and attendance, their nursing and comfort in sickness), as also in respect to the departments of the commissary and the quartermaster.

I desire to avail myself of your experience, and good judgment, and energy, to procure a speedy and exhaustive survey of the condition, in those respects, of our men pertaining to General Butler's brigade, wherever they may be, and an early and minute report thereon.

We wish to know what they have received, so as to learn whether what we pay for reaches them, whether it is distributed, and, if so, how carefully and skilfully, and whether it is properly husbanded.

I desire especially also to ascertain how it happens that we hear so much complaint from Colonel Lawrence's regiment about being stinted for food on the voyage from New-York City to Annapolis, when we are advised that Major Ladd obtained *fifteen* days' rations in New York for the whole command, and shipped them on board the steamers "Ariel" and "De Soto," on which the troops sailed.

Major Charles Devens, major of the Rifle Battalion of Worcester, will be found, among others, a most intelligent person with whom to consult.

Learn and report, if possible, what aid, if any, is needed in the commissary and quartermaster's departments and on the medical staff.

I desire you particularly to attend to the proper distribution of the stores shipped on the steamer "Cambridge," which will be due at Washington, probably on Saturday next. Please advise with Brigadier-General Butler and with Lieutenant-General Scott on this subject.

I annex invoices of the stores belonging to the Commonwealth, which were shipped on board of her.

In all these matters which I commit to your care for inspection and supervision, it must be left to your discretion to obtain the fullest and most accurate information possible, in order to direct your course of action. In all your operations, I do not doubt that you will receive the most cordial assistance and co-operation from General Butler, to whose kind attention I commend you, and with whom I desire you shall constantly advise and consult. What I desire to obtain is, a thorough comprehension of the position and condition of our troops, in all respects, so as to remedy existing deficiencies and provide against future evils.

It is impossible to convey any such thorough idea to me through written despatches so speedily as I wish to obtain it; and therefore, inasmuch as in the absence of a Lieutenant-Governor I cannot conveniently leave Massachusetts in person for that purpose, I desire you to act in a species of representative capacity for observation in my behalf.

Your expenses will be paid by the Commonwealth; and I congratulate the service that I have been able to induce you to undertake this duty.

With great regard, your friend and servant,

JOHN A. ANDREW, *Governor.*

Dr. Howe immediately entered upon his duties. Upon his return, he made a report of the condition of the regiments. He went by way of Annapolis to Washington. His first impression was at the changed appearance of the men. But yesterday they were citizens; to-day they are soldiers, five hundred miles from their homes, and ready to go a thousand more. On looking at the actual condition of the regiments, he was surprised to find how abundant had been the provision made for their comfort and efficiency. There were some complaints and grumblings about exposure and sleeping on the ground by night, and about hard fare and disgusting food by day; but on one who had found relish in boiled sorrel, and a luxury in raw snails, these complaints made but little impression. It was evident, as a general thing, there had been an abundant outfit, and a superabundance of what are usually considered luxuries at home. The breaking-in of a soldier to campaign life seems a rough and hard process; but it is not a killing one, especially to New-Englanders. In a while, the boys would laugh at what they have complained of. There is a vein of humor and sarcasm running through the report of Dr. Howe, such as might have been expected from a gentleman of his peculiar temperament, knowledge, and practical experience in the rough usage of active military life; and yet it is full of kind words and wise suggestions. He says, " The invoice of articles sent by the 'Cambridge' and other vessels for our troops, contains articles hardly dreamed of even by general officers in actual war. Hundreds of chests of Oolong teas, tons of white crushed sugar, and then a whole cargo of ice!" Besides these regular supplies, a vast variety of articles of use and luxury had been sent by the families of the soldiers and the town committees. "Their principal value (and that is priceless) is as a testimony of the patriotism, zeal, and generosity of the men and women, who felt that they must do something for the cause, which seemed to them, not only of their country, but of humanity." He speaks of the reports of cruelty practised in one of the regiments (not named), which are so frequent that they made a powerful impression on him. He found only about one per cent on the sick-list, and only two cases of dangerous illness. As to the matter of suffering, he says, " Some soldiers do indeed complain that they have undergone needless exposures, privations, and hardships, through the indifference of officers. It is hoped that the most flagrant cases of the kind arose from over-sanguine temper, which made the officers overlook the great liability to storms, when leading out troops unprovided with tents, and that longer experience will correct this." But, he says, —

" There will be many captains like one whom I could name in the Massachusetts Fifth, — the stalwart man, every inch of whose six feet is of soldier stamp; the captain who eschews hotel dinners, and takes every meal with his men, eating only what they eat; who is their resolute and rigid commander when on duty, but their kind and faithful companion and friend when off duty; who lies down with them upon the bare ground or floor, and, if there are not blankets enough for all, refuses to use one himself; who often gets up in the night, and draws the blankets over any half-covered sleeper, and carries water to any one who may be feverish and thirsty; the man who is like a father as well as a captain of his soldiers. He is the man who administered that stern rebuke the other day to the upstart West-Point cadet, sent to drill the company. The first day, the cadet interlarded the orders with oaths, — his commands with curses. The men complained to their captain. 'I'll stop that to-morrow,' says he. The next day's drill begins, and the cadet begins to swear at the soldiers. 'Please not swear at my men, sir,' says the captain. 'What do you know about the drill?' says the cadet; 'and what can you do about my swearing?' 'Sir,' says the captain sternly, 'I know this, and you ought to know it, — swearing is forbidden by the army regulation; and, if you continue to break the rule, I'll order my men to march off the ground, and they'll obey me, and leave you to swear alone.' The cadet took the rebuke, and swore no more at that company. There are many officers of this stamp; and then there is among the soldiers enough of the old Puritan leaven to lighten the lump."

"The stalwart man, every inch of whose six feet is of soldier stamp," was undoubtedly Captain Prescott, who commanded the Concord company in the Fifth Regiment, as the story is told of him in nearly the same words by Ralph Waldo Emerson, in his address, delivered a few months ago on the occasion of the dedication of the soldiers' monument, erected in Concord in honor of the soldiers of that town who fell in the war. On that monument is the name of George L. Prescott, who, as colonel of the Massachusetts Thirty-second Regiment, fell in front of Petersburg, mortally wounded, on the 18th of June, 1864, while leading his men in a charge upon the enemy, and who died on the field. A brave and generous gentleman!

Dr. Howe's report is too long to quote entire. It contains many wise suggestions in regard to cleanliness and cooking rations, and concludes with this pithy sentence: "If a tithe of the science, skill, and care which are so liberally given to improving all the means of killing the soldiers of other armies were devoted to the means of keeping our own soldiers in health, the present fearful mortality of war would be greatly lessened."

We have stated in the preceding chapter, that, when General Butler landed with the Eighth Regiment at Annapolis, a rumor reached him that the slaves in that vicinity were on the eve of rising in rebellion against their masters; and that he offered to Governor Hicks the Eighth Regiment to suppress it, which offer was declined peremptorily by the Governor of Maryland. The rumor had no foundation upon which to rest. Governor Andrew was informed that such an offer had been made, by a despatch from General Butler, written at Annapolis. He regarded it with disfavor, and immediately wrote to the General, expressing his approval of all that he had thus far done, with the exception of this offer to use Massachusetts troops for such a purpose, especially as their first duty was to get to Washington, and protect the national capital from threatened attack. Governor Andrew said, —

"I think that the matter of servile insurrection among a community in arms against the Federal Union is no longer to be regarded by our troops in a political, but solely in a military point of view; and is to be contemplated as one of the inherent weaknesses of the enemy, from the disastrous operations of which we are under no obligations of a military character to guard them, in order that they may be enabled to improve the security which our arms would afford, so as to prosecute with more energy their traitorous attacks upon the Federal Government and capital. The mode in which outbreaks are to be considered should depend entirely upon the loyalty or disloyalty of the community in which they occur; and, in the vicinity of Annapolis, I can on this occasion perceive no reason of military policy why a force, summoned to the defence of the Federal Government, at this moment of all others, should be offered to be diverted from its immediate duty, to help rebels, who stand with arms in their hands, obstructing its progress towards the city of Washington. I entertain no doubt, that, whenever we shall have an opportunity to interchange our views personally on this subject, we shall arrive at entire concurrence of opinion."

General Butler, on the 9th of May, wrote a long letter to Governor Andrew, in which he defended his action in offering the Eighth Regiment to suppress a slave insurrection. He began by apologizing for delay in writing; his active official duties pressing him for time, and a slight attack of illness, being his excuses. He acknowledges "the more than usual accuracy" of the despatch received by Governor Andrew, and then proceeds to defend his course. He said, "I landed on the soil of Maryland against the formal protest of the Governor and the corporate authorities of Annapolis, but without armed opposition on their part." He informed Governor Hicks that the soldiers of his command were armed only against insurgents and disturbers of the peace of Maryland and of the United States. He received from the Governor and Mayor assurances of the loyalty of the State to the Union. He told the Governor and Mayor, that, supported by the authorities of the State and city, he should repress all hostile demonstrations against the laws of Maryland and the United States; and would protect both himself and the city of Annapolis from any disorderly persons whatever. Therefore, when he was subsequently informed of the probable insurrection, he could do nothing less than make the offer he did, as it came within the pledge he had given. He proceeds, "The question seemed to me to be neither military nor political, and was not to be so treated. It was simply a question of good faith and honesty of purpose." He then speaks of "the benign effect" which his offer had upon the people of Annapolis. The people had returned to their homes, and peace and order everywhere prevailed. "Confidence took the place of distrust, friendship of enmity, brotherly kindness of sectional hate; and I believe to-day there is no city in the Union more loyal than the city of Annapolis. I think, therefore, I may safely point to the results for my justification." He also says, — the "neighboring county of Washington" had a few days before elected a Union delegate to the Legislature by a vote of four thousand out of five thousand ballots, — This vote "is among the many fruits of firmness of purpose, efficiency of action, and integrity of mission." But, as he may have to act hereafter "in an enemy's country, among a servile population, when the question may arise as it has not yet arisen, as well in a moral and Christian as in a political and military point of view, what shall I do?" The remainder of the letter we give entire: —

"I appreciate fully your Excellency's suggestion as to the inherent weakness of the rebels, arising from the preponderance of the servile population. The question, then, is, in what manner shall we take advantage of that weakness? By allowing, and of course causing, that population to rise upon the defenceless women and children of the country, carrying rapine, arson, and murder — all the horrors of San Domingo a million of times magnified — among those whom we hope to re-unite with us as brethren, many of whom are already so, and all who are worth preserving will be, when this horrible madness shall have passed away or be threshed out of them? Would your Excellency advise the troops under my command to make war in person upon defenceless women and children, of any part of the Union, accompanied with brutalities too horrible to be named? You will say, God forbid! If we may not do so in person, shall we arm others so to do, over whom we can have no restraint, exercise no control, and who, when once they have tasted blood, may turn the very arms in their hands against ourselves as a part of the oppressing white race? The reading of history, so familiar to your Excellency, will tell you, the bitterest cause of complaint which our fathers had against Great Britain, in the war of the Revolution, was the arming by the British Ministry of the red man with the tomahawk and the scalping-knife against the women and children of the colonies; so that the phrase, 'May we not use all the means which God and nature have put in our hands to subjugate the colonies?' has passed into a legend of infamy against the leader of that ministry who used it in Parliament. Shall history teach us in vain? Could we justify ourselves to ourselves, although with arms in our hands, amid the savage wildness of camp and field, we may have blunted many of the finer moral sensibilities, in letting loose four millions of worse than savages upon the homes and hearths of the South? Can we be justified to the Christian community of Massachusetts? Would such a course be consonant with the teachings of our holy religion? I have a very decided opinion upon the subject; and if any one desires — as I know your Excellency does not — this unhappy contest to be prosecuted in that manner, some instrument other than myself must be found to carry it on. I may not discuss the political bearings of this subject. When I went from under the shadow of my roof-tree, I left all politics behind me, to be resumed only when every part of the Union is loyal to the flag, and the potency of the Government through the ballot-box is established.

"Passing the moral and Christian view, let us examine the subject as a military question. Is not that State already subjugated which requires the bayonets of those armed in opposition to its rulers to preserve it from the horrors of a servile war? As the least experienced of military men, I would have no doubt of the entire subjugation of a State brought to that condition. When, therefore, — unless I am better advised, — any community in the United States who have met me in an honorable warfare, or even in the prosecution of a rebellious war in an honorable manner, shall call upon me for protection against the nameless horrors of a servile insurrection, they shall have it; and from the moment that call is obeyed, I have no doubt we shall be friends, and not enemies.

"The possibility that dishonorable means of defence are to be taken by the rebels against the Government I do not now contemplate. If, as has been done in a single instance, my men are to be attacked by poison, or, as in another, stricken down by the assassin's knife, and thus murdered, the community using such weapons may be required to be taught, that it holds within its own border a more potent means for deadly purposes and indiscriminate slaughter than any which it can administer to us.

"Trusting that these views may meet your Excellency's approval, I have the honor to be, very respectfully, your obedient servant,

"BENJ. F. BUTLER."

The letter of Governor Andrew was not written for publication: whether the reply of General Butler was written for that purpose, the reader can judge for himself. To the surprise of the Governor, both letters appeared in the public prints shortly after the reply of General Butler was received by him. General Butler gave as one reason for the publication, that the Boston correspondent of the New-York Tribune had referred to the correspondence in one of his letters to that paper; and stated that the correspondent had received information concerning them from the Governor's private secretary, Colonel A. G. Browne. This charge was emphatically denied by the secretary, in a letter addressed to General Butler, and he also obtained from the Tribune correspondent a letter denying, in the fullest and broadest sense, that he had given him the information. Copies of these letters are on file in the executive department in the State House.

The letters of Governor Andrew and General Butler are interesting and important as an exhibition of the sentiments of the two gentlemen respecting the proper course to pursue in regard to the slave population in a rebellious State, and also as to what was the proper course to pursue in the exigency which then existed. The Government had called for troops to proceed without delay to Washington, which was threatened by rebel forces from Virginia and Maryland. The troops had been called from their homes and workshops, and sent from the State to perform this duty, not to put down a negro insurrection in Maryland. They had not volunteered for that purpose. They were to go to Washington with all possible despatch, and report to the United-States officers in command of that post. The capital of the nation was in imminent peril. They were to defend it against the enemy. Thus Governor Andrew remonstrated against their being diverted, in violation of express orders, from the purpose for which they had been called into action.

General Butler, in his reply, does not touch this point, which was the strong point in Governor Andrew's letter. The General goes into a long argument upon the question of slave insurrections, illustrating his meaning by references to the atrocities of San Domingo, and the barbarities committed by the Indian allies of Great Britain in the war of the Revolution. It is not our intention, however, to pursue this subject further. The correspondence makes an interesting episode in the war record of Massachusetts, and therefore could not properly be passed over without remark. Nor is it necessary now to criticise the argument used by General Butler, to show how utterly, at that time, he misunderstood and wrongly appreciated the character of the colored race in the Southern States.

The only notice which Governor Andrew took of General Butler's letter was in a letter addressed to him, dated May 21, 1861, from which we extract as follows: —

"Your note of the 16th instant is before me. While I have no objection to your publishing your views on military, political, and moral questions in the character of a private controversialist (for of that it is your own supreme right to judge as a gentleman and a citizen), yet I cannot engage in the controversy, however agreeable to me it might be to do so under other circumstances, since a great and noble cause ought not to be disturbed or imperilled by personal complications. And therefore, although your paper, by its discussions of questions not logically arising out of that to which it is in professed reply, has the tendency to mislead the reader injuriously to myself, yet I cannot persuade my own judgment that I should do otherwise than wrong, considering our mutual and public relations, were I to join issue, and go to trial before the popular tribunal of newspaper readers. On this ground you will excuse my silence and non-appearance in the arena of debate."

It is proper to state, that the offer made by General Butler to Governor Hicks was not known to the colonel of the Eighth Regiment, who informed the writer that he was not aware that such an offer was ever made, or that a correspondence had passed between General Butler and Governor Andrew on such a subject.

We now close the record of the three months' troops. A call for volunteers to serve for three years or the war had been issued by the President. An extra session of the Legislature had been called by the Governor of Massachusetts. The war began to assume a giant form, that increased in stature and in power, and cast its shadow to the ends of the civilized world.

CHAPTER IV.

Companies sent to the Forts — Officers appointed to command — Militia Battalions — First Call for Three Years' Troops — Delays at Washington — Letter to Montgomery Blair — Letter of Secretary of War — General Order No. 12 — Six Regiments allowed — Governor anxious to send more — Letter of General Walbridge — Governor to Senator Wilson — More Delay — Extra Session of the Legislature — Address of the Governor — Proceedings of the Legislature — War Measures adopted — Debate on Colored Troops — Bills passed by the Legislature — Sinking Fund — Government Securities — Pay of Troops — Established Camps — Seven Millions of Dollars — State Aid to Families of Soldiers — The Six Regiments of Three Years' Men — Ten more Regiments called for — Their Organization — Additional Staff Officers appointed — Surgeon-General's Department organized — Letter of Governor to Dr. Lyman — Board of Medical Examiners — Promotion of the Surgeon-General — Letter of the Governor to Colonel Frank E. Howe — New-England Rooms, New York — Letter of Colonel Lee to Charles R. Lowell — Letters of the Governor to Different Parties — Circular of the Secretary of War — Colonel Browne to Colonel Howe — Abstract of Correspondence — Colonel Sargent to General Scott — Cobb's Battery — Letter to Colonel Webster — Letter to the President — Irish Regiments — Flag-raising at Bunker-Hill Monument — Speech of Governor Andrew — Speech of Colonel Webster — Interesting Ceremonies — Conclusion.

THE defenceless condition of the forts in Boston Harbor, in the early part of the war, was a cause of much labor and anxiety to the Governor, and to the merchants and underwriters, whose vessels at anchor in the harbor, or lying at the wharves, were greatly exposed. Frequent representations of the insecure condition of Boston were made by the Governor to the Secretary of War, which, for a considerable time, failed to elicit attention. To allay, in some degree, the general feeling of insecurity, the Governor, on the 24th of April, ordered the Fourth Battalion of Infantry, under command of Major Thomas G. Stevenson, to garrison Fort Independence, where it remained until the 21st of May. On the 29th of April, the Second Battalion of Infantry, under command of Major Ralph W. Newton, was ordered to garrison Fort Warren, where it remained until the 1st of June.

Major-General Samuel Andrews, of Boston, was ordered to take command of both forts, which position he held from the 1st of May until the 1st of June, when he was relieved. The command of Fort Warren was given to Brigadier-General Ebenezer W. Peirce, on the 13th of May. He was relieved on the 27th of the same month, having been appointed to take command of the Massachusetts troops at the front, and to fill the vacancy occasioned by the promotion of General Butler to be a major-general of volunteers. General Peirce was succeeded in command of Fort Warren by Brigadier-General Joseph Andrews, who remained on duty there, and at Camp Cameron, in Cambridge, until Nov. 18, 1861.

On the 21st of May, the Fourth Battalion of Rifles, Major Samuel H. Leonard, was ordered to Fort Independence, where it was recruited to a regiment of three years' volunteers, afterwards known as the Thirteenth Regiment. A camp was also formed on Long Island, in Boston Harbor, to which a number of companies, composed of men of Irish birth, were ordered. These companies were to form two regiments of three years' men, to be known as the Thirteenth and Fourteenth Regiments. They were afterwards consolidated into one, and known as the Ninth. Of this camp, on the 11th of May, Brigadier-General William W. Bullock was placed in command. He remained on duty until the 12th of June, when the Ninth was ordered to Washington, and the camp was broken up.

The battalions first ordered to the forts performed much labor in removing rubbish, old shanties, piles of bricks, and lumber; filling up excavations; erecting chimneys and cook-houses; arranging hospital accommodations, and preparing them, as well as the limited means would permit, for defensive operations. These labors have never been properly acknowledged by the General Government; on the contrary, a captious and unjust report of the condition of the forts was made, in June, 1861, by an army officer, a copy of which was sent to Governor Andrew by Major-General Wool. This report sets forth that the forts had been greatly injured by the two battalions; that nails had been driven into the walls of the casemates, drains obstructed, filth accumulated, and chimneys so erected that large guns could not be properly manned and worked. That these statements had a slight foundation upon which to rest, we shall not deny; but if the officer had made a survey of the forts, and especially of Fort Warren, before the two battalions had taken possession, his report would have been of a different tenor, and he would have accorded to the soldiers praise instead of censure. They certainly deserved it: they saved the Government time and money in making the forts habitable, and by putting them in a condition to defend the harbor, and maintain garrisons.

The Governor, on the 25th of April, appointed the three major-generals of militia, — Messrs. Sutton, Morse, and Andrews, — with a portion of their respective staff, an examining board to pass upon the qualification of persons elected officers of new companies. This board remained in service until the 24th of May, when it was relieved from further duties. The number of persons examined by the board was six hundred and forty-one men, thirty-nine of whom were rejected.

On the 2d of May, Lieutenant-Colonel C. C. Holmes, of the First Company of Cadets, was placed in command of a guard at the State Arsenal at Cambridge, and the powder magazine at Captain's Island. The guard was composed of members of the cadets and students of Harvard University, who volunteered their services. They were relieved on the 30th of May, and received the thanks of the Governor.

We have already stated, that the President issued a proclamation, on the 3d of May, for volunteers to serve for three years, or during the war. On the 4th of May, Secretary Cameron issued General Order No. 15, setting forth the number of regiments to be raised, and the manner in which they were to be organized. There were to be thirty-nine regiments of infantry, and one regiment of cavalry. Nothing was said or intimated in the Secretary's order about the proportion of men or regiments which each State was to furnish. At this time, there were, in Massachusetts, upwards of ten thousand men organized into companies. They had enlisted as militia: they now pressed forward to the State authorities to be accepted and organized as volunteers for three years. The Governor could not accept them; could not muster them; could not encourage them, further than with kind words, until answers were received from Washington to messages which he had sent, asking that they might be accepted. Days passed on: no requisitions came. The companies held to their organizations; paraded the streets, partly for drill, but chiefly to pass the time, until information should come from Washington, that their services would be accepted. No orders came; delay and disappointment marked the hour; men could not understand why the Government would not accept their services. They pressed daily to the State House; the Governor wrote and telegraphed again and again to Washington, beseeching the Secretary to accept the services of men anxious to serve their country. No answer came for more than a fortnight after the President's call had been issued. A letter from Secretary Cameron was received by Governor Andrew, on the 22d of May. As a favor, Massachusetts was allowed to furnish six regiments of three years' men.

From among a number of letters written at this time, and upon this subject, we select the following, to Montgomery Blair, Postmaster-General: —

May 6, 1861.
Hon. MONTGOMERY BLAIR, Washington, D.C.

MY DEAR FRIEND, — Your last letter, in which was mentioned a possible plan for retaking Sumter, reached me in the midst of cares and toil, which have left no opportunity to pursue the subject.

I do not know what may be your opinion, or that of the Administration, as to operating at that point.

The whole matter has now assumed the broadest proportions, and we in Massachusetts are only anxious to be up to our whole duty; and it is my strong desire to receive from you every friendly and prompting hint, and to endeavor to follow it. At the same time, I wish your aid in affording Massachusetts those full opportunities which become her services and her character.

I have not the honor of personally knowing the Secretary of War, nor do I know how far he may share your sympathy with Massachusetts in her present attitude. At all events, I cannot address him on paper in the earnest and familiar manner I wish, and which, indeed, I might adopt if face to face.

Massachusetts, first in the field, hurrying thither but half prepared, eager, at any risk, to save the capital, and, if possible, clinch by a blow the national resolve, and, by some gallant act or exhibition, revive the flagging pulsations of the public heart, by reason of her promptness of action; of the blood which, flowing from her veins, has once more rendered the 19th of April an historic day; by the good conduct of her Old Colony Regiment, in the affair of Norfolk Navy Yard; of Butler's whole command at Annapolis, in holding the post, saving "Old Ironsides," cutting out a ship-of-war at Baltimore, rebuilding railroads, and reconstructing locomotives, — may possibly be looked upon, even though useful to the country, as too forward in earning renown.

But, my dear Blair, I can trust you, that you both believe and know of Massachusetts, that we fight from no love of vulgar glory, no desire to conquer what is not ours, but that from the quiet industry of their peaceful callings, all unused to arms, and with no thirst for war, our men have drawn their swords, simply because their country called, and justice, patriotism, and honor summoned them to the field.

Trusting that no shameful concessions of the Government will ever purchase the cherished blessings of peace for a price incompatible with the undoubted, eternal, and confirmed establishment and restoration of natural rights, and the cause of liberty and democratic constitutional government, we relent at no sacrifice appropriate to a patriotic and devoted people. In that spirit we began, and are continuing to prepare soldiers and material.

We are enlisted for the war; we have put ourselves, or rather keep ourselves, where we belong, under the national lead of the President and his Cabinet, under the folds of the flag our fathers helped to raise. But we wish to go *onward*, not to *stand still*.

"From the blood of the slain, from the fat of the mighty, let the bow of Jonathan turn not back, and his shield return not empty."

I pray you now, as my personal friend, who may speak for me and my people to the President and in the Cabinet, — I pray you claim and secure to us the right, as ours was the first military force to encounter the shock of arms (namely, the Sixth Regiment of the Massachusetts line), — the right to furnish six regiments in number, and to march with the advancing column over the very streets where our brothers poured out their blood. The number of our citizens ready to go, the strength of their convictions, their willingness to support the Government, the variety of useful capacity which characterizes our people, certainly leave them behind no others. Moreover, we believe, since we have a war on hand, in making it a short one, by making it an *active* one; and, as we have it to carry on, we desire to "pay attention to it," finish it up, suppress speedily the rebellion, and then restore the waste places of Zion.

Tell Mr. Chase I have begun inquiries and efforts, in the hope that Massachusetts may take five millions of his loan. It ought all to be taken at *par*, on six per cent interest.

I am, ever faithfully,   JOHN A. ANDREW.

P.S. — I understand that matters at our navy yard, in Charlestown, are not as expeditious as they would be if some old incumbents were away. The blacksmith is especially complained about. We do need men in sympathy with the great work; and I hope Mr. Welles will refer to Mr. Greene, of the Ordnance Department, and Mr. Roulstone, of the same carriage department, and see if, with their suggestions, he cannot inspire some new life, with new blood, into certain branches of the work.

The letter of Secretary Cameron, permitting Massachusetts to furnish six regiments of volunteers, as before stated, was not received until the 22d of May. It was not calculated to inspire either spirit or enthusiasm. We copy it entire.

                                     WAR DEPARTMENT, WASHINGTON, May 15, 1861.
Governor JOHN A. ANDREW, Boston.

DEAR SIR, — I have the honor to forward you enclosed herewith the plan of organization of the volunteers for three years, or during the war. *Six* regiments are assigned to your State; making, in addition to the *two regiments* of three months' militia already called for, eight regiments.

It is important to reduce rather than to enlarge this number, and in no event to exceed it. Let me earnestly recommend to you, therefore, to call for no more than eight regiments, of which six only are to serve for three years, or during the war, and, if more are already called for, to reduce the number by discharge. In making up the quota of three years' men, you will please act in concert with the mustering officers sent to your State, who will represent this Department.

                  I am, sir, respectfully,
                        SIMON CAMERON, *Secretary of War.*

On the receipt of this letter, General Order No. 12 was issued by direction of the Governor, which gave notice that the quota of Massachusetts was "fixed at six regiments of infantry, to be organized as prescribed in General Order No. 15 from the War Department." The plan for the organization of the regiments was substantially the same as in the regular army. Each regiment was to be composed of ten companies, each company to have a captain, two lieutenants, and ninety-eight enlisted men. The field and staff officers of a regiment were to consist of a colonel, lieutenant-colonel, major, adjutant, quartermaster, assistant-surgeon, sergeant-major, quartermaster-sergeant, commissary-sergeant, hospital-steward, two principal musicians, and a band of twenty-four musicians. This system of regimental organization was observed during the whole of the war, with the exception that an additional surgeon was allowed, and regimental bands were discontinued.

The six regiments selected to complete the requisition of the Secretary of War, were, the *First*, which was ordered to "Camp Cameron," in North Cambridge. The regiment left the State on the 15th of June, for Washington, and marched through Baltimore on the 17th, the anniversary of the battle of Bunker Hill. It was the first three years' regiment that reached Washington in the war. The *Second*, which was recruited at "Camp Andrew," in West Roxbury, left the State on the 8th of July, for the front. The *Seventh*, which was recruited at "Camp Old Colony,"·in Taunton, left for Washington on the 11th of July. The *Ninth*, which was reëcruited and organized on Long Island, in Boston Harbor, left the State in the steamer "Ben De Ford," on the 24th of June, for Washington. The *Tenth*, which was recruited in the western part of the State, remained in camp near Springfield, until completely organized. Before leaving the State, the regiment was ordered to Medford, and was there until the 25th of July, when it was sent forward to Washington. The *Eleventh*, which was quartered in Fort Warren, left for Washington on the 24th of June. These six regiments were organized, armed, equipped, clothed, and sent forward, within four weeks after orders were received that they would be accepted. Several others were in a state of formation, some of them in camp with full complement of men, and could have been sent to the front with little delay if the Secretary had given his consent. This could not be obtained. His letter of the 15th of May cast no ray of hope that more regiments would be accepted from Massachusetts: on the contrary, "it was important to reduce rather than to enlarge this number." The Governor, nevertheless, continued to urge upon the President and the Secretary the acceptance of more regiments.

Among the men who sympathized with the Governor in his desire to have more troops accepted was General Hiram Walbridge, of New York. He was earnest to have the war carried on with vigor. At the request of Governor Andrew, General Walbridge brought the subject to the attention of the President. His efforts were successful. He wrote to the Governor from Washington, June 17th, —

"I am gratified to enclose you herewith a copy of a letter addressed to me by the Secretary of War, with the sanction of the President, in response to my application in favor of taking additional forces, authorizing me to notify you that ten additional regiments will be called from the loyal and patriotic State of Massachusetts, in accordance with the terms stated in your letter to me of the 12th inst."

This permission to send forward ten more regiments gave great satisfaction, and relieved the Governor from much anxiety and care, with which, at this particular period, he was sorely pressed.

Immediate orders were issued to organize and send forward the regiments. The correspondence of the Executive Department reveals some of the embarrassing questions which pressed upon it at this time. On the 8th of May, Senator Wilson who was in Washington, wrote to the Governor, that "the condition of the uniforms and equipments of the Massachusetts three months' troops was bad, as compared with those of other States." On the receipt of this letter, the Governor wrote to the Senator a long and able reply. The letter is dated May 10th; and in it he said, "he has sent and is sending forward large supplies both of provisions and of clothing; but as he is not gifted by the Lord with omniscience, and as in no single instance has he received any report from any of the regiments in and about Washington of what they need, he is sorry he is unable to satisfy everybody, and still more sorry that Massachusetts troops should be permitted to suffer. Although a month has now elapsed since they left the State, the muster-rolls of the Eighth Regiment are the only ones which have as yet been received." He then recites the facts concerning the blankets which were put on board of the transport at New York for the Fifth Regiment, which were stowed away so that the regiment could not get them, and were finally taken at Annapolis, and distributed among Pennsylvania troops.

He also speaks of the neglect of officers to report to him what they need fully and frequently, in order that he may know what to furnish. In no single instance had authentic information been received of any needs, without measures being taken instantaneously to supply them. "We have not less than fifty thousand dollars' worth of under-garments and other clothing now on hand. We are now having manufactured no less than six thousand summer uniforms; and we have spent not less than fifty thousand dollars in merely supplying subsistence to our troops on their way and in the field." He had, when the call was first made for troops, informed the Secretary of War that the troops needed some articles of equipment, who replied in substance, "No matter: only hurry them forward, we will look out for all that, and will remedy all such needs when they are arrived here: it is essential to us that they should be sent at once." Notwithstanding, from that day to this he had not been advised in any manner what supplies he has furnished or expects to furnish. Notwithstanding repeated requests, no United-States officer had been detailed here to muster troops or to advise with the Governor concerning military affairs, as has been done in the instance of New York and other States. Notwithstanding he had frequently called attention to the defenceless state of Boston Harbor, it remains undefended by a single gun. His requests meet either with silence, or with positive refusal. He is even denied by the Secretary of War permission to *clean* Fort Warren at the expense of the State, so as to render it healthy and comfortable for the volunteer troops to be placed there. The Governor suggests "that the influence of all the agents of Massachusetts at Washington is needed, and may be profitably exerted to *extort* from the national Government, if it cannot be done by persuasion, at least some approach to the courtesy and attention which have evidently been extended to other States in these respects, and which is pre-eminently due to Massachusetts, by reason of her constant loyalty, her prompt movement to the defence of the nation, her children dead at Baltimore, and the sacrifice of money and of men which she expects, and is willing, to make for the common cause."

The delay at Washington in calling for more troops, and the apparent neglect with which the Governor's letters were treated, did not change his purpose nor daunt his spirit. He never doubted that a change of policy would soon be adopted at Washington, and that the war would be carried on with might and vigor. Foreseeing that it would be a long war, he determined that the State should be placed in a condition to sustain her part with all the resources of men and money at her command. Accordingly, he called an extra session of the Legislature, which met at the State House on Tuesday, the 14th of May.

Mr. Claflin, in calling the Senate to order, referred to the extraordinary events which had transpired since the adjournment, and urged upon the Senate the importance of meeting them in a proper spirit. "To this end, let us act our part faithfully, that those who placed in our hands these great trusts may not be disappointed, and we, in coming time, may have the proud consciousness of having done our duty."

Speaker Goodwin congratulated the House that the Old Bay State had so nobly sustained her heroic fame. He referred to the absence of some of the members who were with their regiments in the field, and concluded by saying, "I know you will all join in a most ardent aspiration, that an honorable peace may soon be won by our army, and the arts of peace once more become the engrossing topic of the Legislature of the Commonwealth."

The two branches met in convention, and Governor Andrew delivered his address.

"The occasion," he said, "demands *action*, and it shall not be delayed by *speech;* nor do either the people or their representatives need or require to be stimulated by appeals or convinced by arguments. A grand era has dawned, inaugurated by the present great and critical exigency of the nation, through which it will providentially and triumphantly pass, and soon, emerging from apparent gloom, will breathe a freer inspiration in the assured consciousness of vitality and power. Confident of our ultimate future; confident in the principles and ideas of democratic republican government, in the capacity, conviction, and manly purpose of the American people, wherever liberty exists, and republican government is administered under the purifying and instructing power of free opinion and free debate, — I perceive nothing now about us which ought to discourage the good or to alarm the brave."

The Governor then spoke of the nature of the war. "This is no war of sections, no war of North and South. It is waged to avenge no former wrongs, nor to perpetuate ancient griefs or memories of conflict. It is the struggle of the people to vindicate their own rights, to retain and invigorate the institutions of their fathers." He then recapitulated the services of the Massachusetts troops, — their prompt response to the call of the President; the march through Baltimore; the garrisoning of Fortress Monroe; the advance by way of Annapolis and the Potomac River; the saving of "*Old Ironsides;*" the activity of General Butler and of the State officers; the cost of equipping and provisioning the regiments, which, up to that time, amounted to $267,645.18, exclusive of the fifty thousand pounds sterling drawn in favor of Mr. Crowninshield, for the purchase of arms in Europe, and of contracts made, which, when fulfilled, would amount to $100,000 more.

Up to that time, one hundred and twenty-nine new companies had been organized. The Governor recommended the formation of a State camp for military instruction, under proper rules and regulations, but which encampment "should be confined to those enlisting themselves for an extended term of actual service, and should not include the ordinary militia." He was opposed to towns' paying bounties to men enlisting in local companies, and to all costly and inefficient modes of organizing and disciplining troops. His recommendations to the Legislature met with unanimous approval, as the patriotic and judicious acts passed at this brief session abundantly prove. Near the close of his address, the Governor paid the following merited tribute to the services and worth of the then commanding General of the United-States army : —

"For myself, I entertain a most cordial trust in the ardor and patriotism of the President of the United States and his Cabinet, and of the venerable head of the American army, whose long and eminent career has given him a place second to no living captain of our time. True to his allegiance to his country and to himself, may he long be spared to serve his countrymen, and to enjoy their gratitude! and though white the marble, and tall the aspiring shaft, which posterity will rear to record his fame, his proudest monument will be their affectionate memory of a life grand in the service of peace, not less than of war, preserving in their hearts for ever the name of WINFIELD SCOTT."

He spoke also in fitting words of the generous sympathy and munificent gifts of the entire people for the soldiers and their cause, which came "from every department of social, business, and religious life; from every age, sex, and condition of our community; by gifts, by toil, by skill, and handwork; out of the basket and the store, and out of the full hearts of the community, — they have poured through countless channels of benevolence."

In concluding, he asks, —

"But how shall I record the great and sublime uprising of the people, devoting themselves, their lives, their all? No creative art has ever woven into song a story more tender in its pathos, or more stirring to the martial blood, than the scenes just enacted, passing before our eyes in the villages and towns of our dear old Commonwealth. Henceforth be silent, ye cavillers at NEW-ENGLAND thrift, economy, and peaceful toil! Henceforth let no one dare accuse our Northern sky, our icy winters, or our granite hills! ' *Oh, what a glorious morning!* ' was the exulting cry of SAMUEL ADAMS, as he, excluded from royal grace, heard the sharp musketry, which, on the dawn of the 19th of April, 1775, announced the beginning of the war of Independence. The yeomanry who in 1775, on Lexington Common, and on the banks of CONCORD RIVER first made that day immortal in our annals, have found their lineal representatives in the historic regiment, which, on the 19th of April, 1861, in the streets of Baltimore, baptized our flag anew in heroic blood, when Massachusetts marched once more '*in the sacred cause of liberty and the rights of mankind.*'"

Before passing from the consideration of this remarkable address, we would refer to the following paragraph, which illustrates so well the liberal and just mind of the author, — we mean his defence of the right of citizens to freely discuss the acts of public men and the policy of government: —

"Let us never," he said, "under any conceivable circumstances of provocation or indignation, forget that the right of free discussion of all public questions is guaranteed to every individual on Massachusetts soil, by the settled convictions of her people, by the habits of her successive generations, and by express provisions of her Constitution. And let us therefore never seek to repress the criticism of a minority, however small, upon the character and conduct of any administration, whether State or national."

It is probable that the occurrence spoken of in the following letter of Colonel Lee caused the Governor to incorporate in his address the paragraph quoted: —

BOSTON, May 13.

Messrs. CARTES, HESCOCK, BIRD, and others, Quincy Market.

DEAR SIRS, — The Sunday papers report the extortion of one hundred dollars from a produce-dealer named Walker, who seriously and jestingly expressed sympathy with the secessionists, and hoped that our troops would starve. The receipt of this money casts a slur upon the reputation of our State, and upon the sincerity of all the generous men who freely contributed. It must be returned at once, or we are disgraced: our cause is too good to be injured with illegal violence. While we fight for liberty and the law, let us respect them ourselves. I feel sure, upon reflection, you will agree with the Governor on the subject.

Yours truly,   HENRY LEE, *A. D. C.*

When the Governor concluded his address, the Senate returned to its chamber, and the two branches entered at once upon the business of the session.

In the Senate, on the same day, on motion of Mr. Stone, of Essex, it was voted, that a committee of seven on the part of the Senate, and fifteen on the part of the House, be appointed, to whom the address of the Governor, and the accompanying documents, should be referred. The motion was adopted: and the committee appointed on the part of the Senate were Messrs. Stone of Essex, Bonney of Middlesex, Northend of Essex, Rogers of Suffolk, Davis of Bristol, Walker of Middlesex, and Cole of Berkshire; on the part of the House, Messrs. Bullock of Worcester, Calhoun of Springfield, Branning of Lee, Davis of Greenfield, Tyler of Boston, Coffin of Newburyport, Peirce of Dorchester, Peirce of New Bedford, Jewell of Boston, Gifford of Provincetown, Clark of Lowell, Kimball of Lynn, Merriam of Fitchburg, Bamfield of West Roxbury, and Hyde of Newton.

Mr. Northend, of Essex, introduced a bill of eighteen sections, entitled "a bill to provide for the disciplining and instruction of a military force."

Petitions were presented of James W. White, and eighty others of Grafton, and of the commissioned officers of the Twelfth Regiment of Infantry (Colonel Webster), severally for an act to legalize the appropriations of cities and towns in behalf of the volunteer militia, and for other purposes.

Referred to the Committee on the Judiciary.

May 15. *In the Senate.* — Petition of Robert Morris and seventy-one others, for a law authorizing colored men to form military companies; of John Wells and others, of Chicopee, for a law to allow cities and towns to raise money for the support of volunteers and their families.

On motion of Mr. Carter, of Hampden, a joint committee was appointed to consider the expediency of tendering the service of members of the Legislature free of expense.

Mr. Stone, of Essex, reported a bill regulating drill companies, also in favor of the bill for the establishment of a home guard. On motion of Mr. Boynton, of Worcester, it was voted, that the joint special committee on the Governor's address consider the expediency of providing by law for the expense of improving and drilling the volunteer companies, and also of re-imbursing such expenditure of money as towns and military companies have incurred for such purposes.

Mr. Northend, of Essex, reported his bill from the joint committee to provide for the discipline and instruction of a military force.

The same gentleman, from the same committee, introduced a bill "in aid of the families of volunteers." Mr. Stone, of Essex, from the same committee, reported a bill to enable banks to purchase government securities.

In the House, Mr. Bullock, of Worcester, from the same committee, reported a bill "to provide for the maintenance of the Union and Constitution."

Also a bill to repeal the act of the previous session "to authorize the Treasurer and Receiver-General to indorse the notes of the United States."

And, under a suspension of the rules, these bills passed to a third reading.

May 16. *In the Senate.* — The Senate discussed the bill in aid of the families of volunteers. Several amendments were offered, after which it was recommitted. The bill for the organization of a home guard was passed to be engrossed.

A bill to regulate drill companies was opposed by Mr. Rogers, of Suffolk, and Mr. Battles, of Worcester, and rejected.

The bill to enable banks to purchase Government securities, under a suspension of the rules, was passed to be enacted. Mr. Whiting, of Plymouth, moved an amendment to limit the purchase to fifteen per cent of their capital stock. Lost.

The bill to provide for the discipline and instruction of a military force was amended, on motion of Mr. Schouler, of Middlesex, to limit the force to five thousand men, instead of three thousand. The bill and the amendment were then recommitted.

In the Senate. Afternoon Session. — On motion of Mr. Hardy, of Norfolk, the act to provide for the maintenance of the Union and the Constitution was taken up. An amendment was proposed by Mr. Clark, of Middlesex, to strike out the clause ratifying the acts done by the Governor and Council in any way connected with the disbursements made by them, &c. Mr. Whiting, of Plymouth, favored the amendment; but it was rejected, — yeas 10, nays 11. The bill was then passed to be engrossed.

The bill authorizing the issue of State scrip to the amount of seven millions of dollars was passed unanimously, by a yea and nay vote.

The bill for the discipline and instruction of a military force was reported, providing for five regiments of infantry and one battery of artillery, to be sent to camp; and, in this form, it passed to be engrossed.

The Special Committee reported, that the petitions of J. Sella Martin, and Robert Morris and others, to strike out the word "white" in the militia laws, be referred to the next General Court.

In the House. — A petition of John T. Hilton and twenty-two others, colored citizens of Massachusetts, that the word "white" be stricken from the militia laws, was laid on the table.

The Senate report referring the petitions of J. Sella Martin and Robert Morris and others, to the next General Court, was opposed by Mr. Slack, of Boston, who spoke in favor of striking out the word "white" from the militia laws. He said the colored men were anxious to serve their country, and that no law should be enacted to prevent them.

Mr. Hammond, of Nahant, spoke in favor of accepting the report.

On motion of Mr. Albee, of Marlborough, the question on receiving the report was taken by yeas and nays. The report was accepted, — yeas 119, nays 81.

The Senate bill to enable banks to purchase Government securities was passed to be engrossed, under a suspension of the rules.

The Senate bill for the organization of a home guard was passed to be engrossed, without opposition.

May 17. *In the Senate.* — Mr. Whiting, of Plymouth, moved a reconsideration of the vote whereby the petition of J. Sella Martin, Robert Morris, and others, was referred to the next General Court. Placed in the orders of the day.

In the House. — A petition was presented by B. C. Sargent, Mayor of Lowell, and a committee of the City Council of Lowell, for State aid in the erection of a monument to Luther C. Ladd and Addison O. Whitney, who fell at Baltimore, April 19. Referred.

Mr. Jewell, of Boston, from the Special Committee, reported a bill "to provide for a sinking fund."

May 18. *In the Senate.* — The motion to reconsider the

vote referring the petition of J. Sella Martin, Robert Morris, and others, to the next General Court, was advocated by Mr. Whiting, of Plymouth, who said this was not a time to make invidious distinctions between the different classes of citizens.

Mr. Cole, of Berkshire, spoke in opposition.

The vote stood, for reconsideration, 11; against it, 22.

In the House. — Mr. Stebbins, of Boston, asked and obtained leave to introduce a bill, "withholding certain aid from the people in the so-called seceded States," which was referred to the Special Committee.

Mr. Drew, of Dorchester, asked leave to introduce a bill to strike out the word "white" from the militia laws. Leave was refused, — yeas 56, nays 139.

May 20. *In the Senate.* — Almost the entire day was occupied in debating the bill "in aid of the families of volunteers." A number of amendments were proposed, some of which were adopted, others rejected. The bill, as amended, was ordered to a third reading. Laid on the table, and ordered to be printed.

In the House. — Mr. Bullock, of Worcester, from the Joint Special Committee, reported "resolves concerning the present crisis" (five in number).

A debate arose upon ordering them to be printed, in the course of which Mr. Durfee, of New Bedford, said the resolves could not be fairly understood by the House from merely hearing them read. He wished to see them in print.

Mr. Drew, of Dorchester, spoke at length. In the course of his speech, he attacked General Butler, for offering, to the Governor of Maryland, Massachusetts soldiers to put down a slave rebellion. He said the war was a means of emancipation, and complained of the Legislature for retaining the word "white" in the militia laws, which forbids a portion of our people from taking part in the struggle.

Mr. Stevens, of Boston, could not see any thing objectionable in the resolutions, and was in favor of their immediate passage.

The resolves were ordered to be printed.

May 21. *In the Senate.* — The whole of the forenoon session was taken up in discussing and amending the bill "in aid of the families of volunteers." It finally passed to be engrossed, — yeas 27, nays 7.

The resolves from the House, "concerning the present crisis," were discussed in the Senate a great part of the afternoon session, but, before taking the question, were laid on the table, to allow a committee to be appointed to wait upon the Governor, and request him to return the bill "for the organization of a home guard."

The committee subsequently reported, that they had returned with the bill; when, on motion of Mr. Stone, of Essex, the vote whereby the bill was passed, was reconsidered; and on motion of Mr. Boynton, of Worcester, it was referred to the Committee on the Judiciary.

In the House. — Mr. Jewell, of Boston, from the Joint Special Committee, reported "a bill in addition to an act for the maintenance of the Union and the Constitution," which was passed to be engrossed, under a suspension of the rules.

Mr. Branning, of Lee, from the same committee, reported that the bill offered by Mr. Stebbins, "withholding certain aid from the people of the so-called seceded States," ought not to pass.

The resolves concerning the present crisis were taken up, discussed, and ordered to be engrossed.

Mr. Pierce, of Dorchester, introduced a bill authorizing the Governor to pay the company of Cadets of Boston for guard duty at the State Arsenal at Cambridge, and at Captain's Island; also, the Second Battalion, for garrison duty at Fort Warren, and the Fourth Battalion, for garrison duty at Fort Independence, one dollar a day, including rations to each man while in service; which was referred to Special Committee on Governor's Address.

The bill withholding certain aid from the people of the so-called seceded States was taken up, and, after being amended, was passed to be engrossed.

The bill giving aid to the families of volunteers was discussed, amended, and passed to a third reading.

Wednesday, May 22. *In the Senate.* — On motion of Mr. Northend, of Essex, the bill to provide for the discipline and instruction of a militia force was taken from the table, — the question being on passing it to be enacted.

Mr. Bonney, of Middlesex, opposed the bill. He said that it authorized the Governor to order into camp a military force of not less than six thousand men. It provided for nothing less than a standing army, for an unlimited period. It conferred upon the Governor a power which the sovereigns of England and France did not possess over their troops.

Mr. Northend spoke briefly in support of the bill, after which, no amendment being in order, the bill was passed to be enacted, — yeas 27, nays 2.

Mr. Northend then moved to take from the table the resolves concerning the present crisis, which motion was rejected, — yeas 10, nays 24.

The House bill, entitled an act "withholding certain aid from the people of the so-called seceded States," was rejected.

Mr. Stone, of Essex, from the Committee on the Judiciary, reported, in a new draft, "a bill to provide for a home guard," which, under a suspension of the rules, was ordered to be engrossed.

In the afternoon session, Mr. Whiting, of Plymouth, moved a reconsideration of the vote by which the bill "withholding certain aid from the people in the so-called seceded States" was rejected, which was placed in the orders of the day.

In the House. — The bill for aid to the families of volunteers was discussed in the morning session, until adjournment; without taking the question, several amendments were offered.

In the afternoon, a petition was received from Robert Morris and sixty-three other colored citizens, for leave to form a home guard. Referred to the Committee on the Militia.

Mr. Pierce, of Dorchester, reported that the bill to pay for the services of the Cadets, and other militia organizations, for services, ought not to pass, as payment had been provided in another bill.

The bill giving aid to the families of volunteers was passed to be engrossed.

Also, the Senate bill to organize a home guard.

May 23. *In the Senate.* — Mr. Davis, of Bristol, introduced a series of resolutions "on the national crisis;" but as they were opposed by Messrs. Northend of Essex, Bonney of Middlesex, Battles of Worcester, Cole of Berkshire, Carter of Hampden, and Boynton of Worcester, Mr. Davis reluctantly withdrew them.

The resolves which had been rejected in the House, "in regard to the rights of citizens," elicited a warm debate. Mr. Schouler, of Middlesex, spoke in favor of the resolves. He could not see the objection to this act of simple justice to the colored man.

Mr. Northend asked what good the passage of these resolutions would do in the present crisis. Would it strengthen the hands of the Administration? No: no one believed that it would. It would embarrass them.

Mr. Bonney, of Middlesex, was not opposed to the sentiments of the resolves; but he did not believe it was expedient to instruct our Senators and Representatives in Congress at this time.

Mr. Davis, of Bristol, said it was always safe to do right. He should vote for the resolves.

Mr. Schouler said we were afraid all the time of doing something that would hurt the feelings of the South. The resolves were then passed to a third reading, — yeas 18, nays 12.

On their passage to be engrossed, Mr. Cole, of Berkshire, and Mr. Hardy, of Norfolk, spoke in opposition. They were then passed to be engrossed, — yeas 17, nays 13, — and were sent back to the House.

In the House. — Mr. Durfee, of New Bedford, from the Committee on the Militia, reported that the petition of Robert Morris and others be referred to the Joint Special Committee.

On motion of Mr. Slocum, the report and accompanying papers were laid on the table.

Mr. Durfee, of New Bedford, introduced resolutions in relation to the rights of colored citizens, which were referred to the Special Committee. Subsequently, Mr. Davis, of Greenfield, from the committee, reported, that, in view of the exigencies of public affairs, and the near approach of the close of the session, the resolves ought not to pass. He deemed it unwise to legislate on a minor point of the controversy, when the fact is, the battle for the black man is being fought every day, and will be fought on battle-fields yet unknown.

Mr. Albee, of Marlborough, spoke in favor of the resolves.

Mr. Slack, of Boston, recurred to the days of the Revolution, when the deeds of the colored citizens were the subject of the highest marks of approval.

Mr. Pierce, of Dorchester, advocated the passage of the resolve, and read the words of General Andrew Jackson in commendation of the bravery of the colored battalions at New Orleans, in the war of 1812.

Mr. Branning, of Lee, had always been, and was now, in favor of the rights of colored men; but he did not think it was wise to pass these resolves at the present time.

The vote to accept the report that the resolves ought not to pass was then taken, — yeas 78, nays 69.

The following was the principal resolution : —

"*Resolved*, That our Senators in Congress be instructed, and our Representatives requested, to use their utmost efforts to secure the repeal of any and all laws which deprive any class of loyal subjects of the Government from bearing arms for the common defence."

On assembling in the afternoon, a committee of the two branches was appointed to inform the Governor that the Houses were ready to be prorogued.

The House then took a recess of an hour. On re-assembling, at three o'clock, the resolves in relation to the rights of colored citizens came down from the Senate, adopted.

Mr. Pierce, of Dorchester, moved a suspension of the rules, that they might be considered at once.

Mr. Bullock, of Worcester, made an earnest argument against suspending the rules, and against passing the resolves. He avowed his willingness to remove every vestige of disability from the colored citizens, and, in a proper time, he hoped to see it.

This was not the time. Twenty-three sovereign States are a unit in this conflict. He who would now cast a firebrand among the ranks of the united North and West and the Border States, will initiate a calamity, the extent of which will be appalling and inconceivable. Let us cultivate unity and union. Let us frown upon every element of distraction and weakness and discord. "I am therefore willing," said he, "to place my name in the negative upon an imperishable record, believing that I am doing a service to my beloved and imperilled country."

After further remarks by Mr. Pierce, of Dorchester, the previous question was moved; and the House refused to suspend the rules, by a yea and nay vote of 74 to 69. Two-thirds not voting for suspension, the motion was lost. The resolves then went into the orders of the day.

Mr. Slack, of Boston, moved that a committee be appointed to wait upon the Governor, and request him to postpone, for the present, the prorogation of the Legislature.

During his remarks, the Secretary of State was announced, with a message from the Governor, that his Excellency had prorogued the Legislature, according to request.

The Legislature was then prorogued, and the resolves were left among the unfinished business in the orders of the day.

We have given prominence to the debate upon these resolves, as it reflects the opinions of members at that period in regard to the rights of colored men. This was undoubtedly the first debate in the war touching the right of colored men to bear arms, and the expediency of employing them as soldiers to put down the rebellion. The resolutions passed the Senate; and, if the vote in the House to suspend the rules was a test of the opinions of the members, the resolutions would have also passed the House, had it remained another day in session.

The following is an abstract of the laws which bear upon our subject, passed in this session: —

First. An act to provide a sinking fund. The Treasurer is to report, on Jan. 1, 1863, the amount of all scrip, or certificates of debt, of the United States, which shall have been received by this Commonwealth from the United States, under provisions of acts of the Legislature, and the actual market-price of the same at the date of such report; and the same shall be pledged and held as part of the sinking fund hereby created, the same to be applied for the redemption of the debt. It also provides, that there shall be raised, by tax, twice in each year, commencing Jan. 1, 1863, a sum equal to one-tenth part of the difference found by the report of the Treasurer, as above provided, to exist between the amount of scrip, or certificates of debt, issued under said acts, and the actual market-value of the scrip or certificates, and to be held as a sinking fund to pay the same. Approved May 21, 1866.

Second. An act to enable banks to purchase Government securities provided that loans directly made by any bank to the Commonwealth or to the United States, and notes or scrip of the Commonwealth or United States, held by any bank, and directly purchased by such bank from the Commonwealth or United States, shall not be deemed debts due within the meaning of the twenty-fifth section of the fifty-seventh chapter of the General Statutes.

Third. An act to provide for the maintenance of the Union and the Constitution confirmed and ratified all that the Governor, Executive Council, or any other person, with his or their sanction, had done in furnishing and forwarding troops for the service of the Government. It vested the Governor, with the advice of the Council, with full power and authority, as he might deem best, to provide for additional troops, and also to appoint and commission all needful officers and agents, and to fix their rank and pay; also, to investigate, adjust, and settle all accounts and matters between the State and the General Government, which might arise under the provisions of this act; also, to pay, out of the fund created by this act, any of the troops of this Commonwealth which had been or might be mustered into the service of the United States, during the whole or a part of the time of such service, and to settle the same with the United States: also, created a fund, to be called the Union Fund, of three millions of dollars, to be raised by the issue of scrip. The scrip to bear interest of six per cent, to be redeemable in not less than ten, nor more than twenty, years from the first of July, 1861; and not more than five hundred thousand dollars shall be redeemable in any one year.

Fourth. An act entitled an act in addition to the act for the maintenance of the Union and the Constitution, gave the Governor, with the advice of the Council, power to issue scrip or certificates in the name and in the behalf of the Commonwealth, for sums not exceeding, in the aggregate, seven millions of dollars.

Fifth. An act further in addition thereto authorized the Governor, with the advice of the Council, to pay from the Union Fund any of the troops of the Commonwealth, mustered into the service of the United States from the time that they reported themselves for service until they were mustered into the service of the United States.

Sixth. An act to provide for the discipline and instruction of a military force empowered the Governor, with the consent of the Council, to establish one or more camps in suitable places within the Commonwealth, for the instruction and discipline of a military force, not to exceed five regiments of infantry, and one battery of six pieces of artillery, at any one time; for which tents, camp-equipage, and other necessary articles, were to be furnished by the State.

The Governor was also empowered to rent land for such camp purposes.

No companies or regiments were to be placed in such camps until all the members should agree to be mustered into the United-States service, on such terms as the President should direct in his calls for volunteers. The entire formation, organization, drill, and discipline of these forces was to conform as near as possible to the regular army, and be subject to the rules and articles for governing militia in actual service.

Each camp was to be under the command of a suitable officer appointed by the Governor, and subordinate only to him. He had the power to recommend, and the Governor to commission, such subordinate camp officers as might be proper; the pay and rank of such officers to be fixed by the Governor. The authority of the officers commanding these camps might be extended by the Governor one-fourth of a mile beyond the limits of the camp; and certain rules and regulations were to be made for the admission of visitors.

The privates, when in camp, were to receive the same pay as privates in the regular service; and the officers were to receive such pay as the Governor and Council might determine, provided that the pay of no officer should exceed that of a captain in the regular army. The officers and men to be paid once a month.

The Governor, with the consent of the Council, could appoint and fix the pay of a suitable person for paymaster, to pay the men in the camps, he giving bonds and securities for the proper discharge of his duties.

The regimental and line officers were to be chosen and commissioned as provided for by the militia laws of the Commonwealth.

Seventh. "An act in aid of the families of volunteers, and for other purposes," contained eight sections, and was one of the most humane and admirable passed during the war. It provided, —

1st, That any town or city might raise money by taxation, and apply the same for aid of the wife, and of the children under sixteen years of age, of any volunteer mustered into the service of the United States to the credit of Massachusetts, and for each parent, brother, sister, or child, who, at the time of his enlistment, was dependent on him for support.

2d, The sum so paid or applied should be annually re-imbursed from the State treasury to such city and town, provided it did not exceed one dollar a week for the wife, and one dollar for each child or parent of such soldier; provided that the whole sum for the family and parents of each soldier did not in the aggregate exceed twelve dollars a month.

The act also provided, that any town or city might raise money by taxation to defray any expense already incurred, or to carry out any contracts heretofore made with any of its inhabitants who might have enlisted in the volunteer service, or who may have been or might be called into the service of the United States; but all other contracts in the militia should terminate in ninety days.

The act also provided, that any city or town, "when danger from attack from the sea is apprehended, is authorized to organize an armed police to guard against such an attack, and may provide by taxation to maintain the same." Such police might act in any part of the county within which city or town might be situated.

The act provided for the "discipline and instruction of the military forces," and gave the Governor the power to appoint such staff officers as he might consider necessary, which power continued in force until the end of the war.

After the six regiments first called for by the Secretary of War for three years' service had left the State, and ten more had been accepted, a constant demand was made upon the State until the close of the Rebellion, for all the troops that could be raised, which were sent forward to the front as they were organized. Therefore the establishment of a State camp, as contemplated by the act of the Legislature, for drill and organization, was never established; but, instead thereof, temporary camps were formed in different parts of the State to accommodate the local demand. Thus it was, that the First Regiment, Colonel Cowdin, which was recruited in Boston and its immediate vicinity, was sent to "Camp Cameron" in North Cambridge, where it remained until June 15, when it was ordered to Washington. The Second Regiment, which was recruited by Colonel Gordon, and officers under his command, established a camp in West Roxbury, which was called "Camp Andrew," in honor of the Governor.

Governor Andrew determined that the regimental number should not be duplicated; hence it was, that the Third, Fourth, Fifth, and Sixth Regiments should retain their own designations, and should not be confounded with the three years' regiments. Therefore the next three years' regiment which was recruited by Colonel Couch at "Camp Old Colony," near Taunton, was called the Seventh Regiment. The Eighth Regiment, being a three months' regiment, retained its original number; and the next three years' regiment was called the Ninth Regiment, which was composed of men of Irish birth, and their immediate descendants, and was recruited and organized under the superintendence of Colonel Thomas Cass, at Long Island, in Boston

Harbor. The Tenth Regiment was recruited in the five western counties, and had its camp near the city of Springfield, until it was fully organized. The Eleventh Regiment was recruited in Boston and vicinity by Colonel Clark, and was placed at Fort Warren, where it was recruited to the full standard, and mustered into the service. These regiments completed the quota under the first requisition of the Secretary of War. When leave was given to send forward ten more regiments spoken of in the letter of General Walbridge to Governor Andrew, measures were taken immediately to consolidate the companies in different parts of the State into regiments. The first of these was the Twelfth Regiment, which was always familiarly known as the Webster Regiment, because it was recruited and organized by Colonel Fletcher Webster, who held command of it until he was killed at the second battle of Bull Run, Aug. 30, 1862. He fell gallantly at the head of his regiment, for "Liberty and Union, now and for ever, one and inseparable." The Twelfth Regiment was recruited and organized at Fort Warren. It left Boston for Washington, July 23, 1861.

The Thirteenth Regiment was recruited at Fort Independence. The Fourth Battalion of Rifles formed the nucleus of this regiment. It had been ordered, on the 25th of June, to garrison the fort; and, while upon that duty, it was recruited to a full regiment of three years' volunteers. Major Samuel H. Leonard commanded the Fourth Battalion; and he was commissioned the colonel of the Thirteenth, the regiment having been recruited by him. It left the State for the front on the 30th day of July, 1861, and was stationed during the year on the line of the Potomac in Maryland.

The Fourteenth Regiment was recruited by Colonel William B. Greene, a graduate of West Point, at Fort Warren. He was in Paris with his family when the Rebellion broke out, and immediately returned to his native State, and tendered his services to the Governor. On the 25th of June, he was placed in command of the regiment at Fort Warren, and left Boston with his command on the 7th of August, 1861, for Washington. This regiment was afterwards changed to heavy artillery, and during the war was known as the First Regiment Massachusetts Heavy Artillery.

ORGANIZATION OF TEN NEW REGIMENTS. 189

The Fifteenth Regiment was recruited in the county of Worcester, at "Camp Lincoln," in the city of Worcester. Major Charles Devens, Jr., who commanded the Second Battalion of Rifles in the three months' service, was appointed colonel. It left the State on the 8th of August, 1861: it bore a prominent part in the battle of Ball's Bluff of that year, which made it one of the marked regiments of Massachusetts.

The Sixteenth Regiment was raised in Middlesex County. It was ordered to "Camp Cameron," Cambridge, June 25, 1861, and left the State, August 17, 1861, for Washington. Colonel Powell T. Wyman, who commanded it, was a graduate of West Point, and had served with distinction in the regular army. He was in Europe when Fort Sumter was fired upon. When the news reached him, he wrote by the next steamer to the Adjutant-General, tendering his services to the Governor in any military capacity in which he might be placed. Without waiting for an answer, he came home, and reported in person to the Governor. His offer was accepted; and he was commissioned colonel of the Sixteenth, which was recruited at "Camp Cameron," Cambridge, and left the State for the seat of war on the 17th of August, 1861. Colonel Wyman was killed in battle near Richmond, June 30, 1862; having in this short time achieved a reputation for military capacity and bravery not surpassed by any.

The Seventeenth Regiment was recruited at "Camp Schouler," Lynnfield, of which eight companies belonged to the county of Essex, one to Middlesex, and one to Suffolk. Captain Thomas J. C. Amory, of the United-States Army, a graduate of West Point, was commissioned colonel. He belonged to one of the oldest and best families of Massachusetts. He died in North Carolina, while in command of the regiment. The Seventeenth left Massachusetts for the front on the 23d of August, 1861.

The Eighteenth Regiment was recruited at "Camp Brigham," Readville, and was composed of men from Norfolk, Bristol, and Plymouth Counties. The camp was named in honor of Colonel Elijah D. Brigham, Commissary-General of Massachusetts. James Barnes, of Springfield, a graduate of West Point, and a veteran officer, was commissioned colonel. The regiment left the State for Washington, on the 24th of August, 1861. Colonel Barnes graduated at West Point in the same class with Jeff Davis. He was commissioned by President Lincoln brigadier-general of volunteers.

The Nineteenth Regiment was organized and recruited at "Camp Schouler," Lynnfield. It was composed of Essex-County men. Colonel Edward W. Hinks, of Lynn, who had command of the Eighth Regiment in the three months' service, was appointed colonel. This regiment left for Washington on the 28th of August, 1861. Captain Arthur F. Devereux, of Salem, who commanded a company in the Eighth Regiment in the three months' service, was commissioned lieutenant-colonel; and Major Henry J. How, of Haverhill, a graduate of Harvard College, class of 1859, who was killed in battle June 30, 1862, was commissioned major.

The Twentieth Regiment was recruited at "Camp Massasoit," Readville, and left the State for Washington on the 4th of September, 1861. William Raymond Lee, of Roxbury, a graduate of West Point; Francis W. Palfrey, of Boston, son of Hon. John G. Palfrey; and Paul J. Revere, of Boston, — were chiefly instrumental in raising the regiment: and they were commissioned, severally, colonel, lieutenant-colonel, and major. The roster of this regiment contains the names most distinguished in the history of Massachusetts. The Twentieth bore a prominent part in the disastrous Battle of Ball's Bluff, Oct. 21, 1861. Many of the officers were killed and wounded. Colonel Lee, Major Revere, and Adjutant Charles L. Peirson, of Salem, were taken prisoners, and confined in a cell as hostages at Richmond. We shall have occasion to speak of these gentlemen in subsequent chapters.

The Twenty-first Regiment was recruited at "Camp Lincoln," at Worcester. The men belonged to the central and western portions of the Commonwealth. This was one of the five regiments recruited in Massachusetts for special service, designed originally to be commanded by General Thomas W. Sherman, but which command was afterwards given to General Burnside; but of which more in the next chapter. Augustus Morse, of Leominster, one of the three major-generals of militia of the

Commonwealth, was commissioned colonel. A. C. Maggi, of New Bedford, who had volunteered as quartermaster-sergeant in the Third Regiment of the three months' militia, was commissioned lieutenant-colonel. He was an Italian by birth, a citizen by choice, and a thoroughly educated officer. William S. Clarke, a professor of Amherst College, was commissioned as major. The regiment left the State for Annapolis, Maryland, on the 22d of August, 1861.

The Twenty-second Regiment, known as Senator Wilson's regiment, because it was recruited by him, under special permission of the Secretary of War if agreeable to the Governor, was organized at "Camp Schouler," Lynnfield. It left the State, on the 8th of October, 1861, for Washington. To this regiment were attached the Second Company of Sharpshooters, Captain Wentworth, and the Third Light Battery, Captain Dexter H. Follett. Shortly after the arrival of the Twenty-second at Washington, Colonel Wilson, whose duties as Senator precluded the possibility of retaining command, resigned; and Colonel Jesse A. Gove, of Concord, New Hampshire, a regular-army officer, was commissioned colonel. Colonel Gove was killed in battle before Richmond, July 27, 1862. This regiment was attached to the army of the Potomac during the war. The lieutenant-colonel was Charles E. Griswold, of Boston, who was afterwards colonel of the Fifty-sixth Regiment, and was killed in the Battle of the Wilderness, May 6, 1864. The major was William S. Tilton, of Boston, who afterwards became colonel, and, for brave and meritorious services in the field, was commissioned by the President brigadier-general of volunteers.

The Twenty-third Regiment was recruited at Lynnfield, and left the State for Annapolis, on the 11th of November, 1861. The Twenty-third was one of the five regiments of General Burnside's special command. The field officers were Colonel John Kurtz, of Boston, who commanded a company in the Thirteenth Regiment. The lieutenant-colonel was Henry Merritt, of Salem, who was killed in battle in North Carolina, March 14, 1862. The major was Andrew Elwell, of Gloucester, who was afterwards commissioned colonel.

The Twenty-fourth Regiment was known as the New-England

Guards Regiment. It was recruited by Colonel Thomas G. Stevenson, at "Camp Massasoit," Readville, and left the State for Annapolis on the 9th of December, 1861, and formed part of General Burnside's command. The Twenty-fourth was one of the best regiments ever recruited in Massachusetts. Colonel Stevenson, its first commander, was a gentleman of intelligence, high character, and sterling worth. For his bravery and efficiency, he was appointed by the President, Dec. 27, 1862, brigadier-general of volunteers, and was killed in the Battle of Spottsylvania, Va., May 10, 1864. The lieutenant-colonel, Francis A. Osborne, also rose to the rank of brigadier-general, and served with distinction during the war. Major Robert H. Stevenson, after the promotion of his superiors, was commissioned lieutenant-colonel, and served in that capacity until after the death of his brother, General Stevenson, when from wounds received he resigned his command, and returned home.

The Twenty-fifth Regiment was raised in Worcester County, and was organized at "Camp Lincoln," near the city of Worcester. It left the State for Annapolis, on the 31st day of October, 1861, and formed a part of General Burnside's division. The field officers were Edward Upton, of Fitchburg, colonel; Augustus B. R. Sprague, of Worcester, lieutenant-colonel; and Matthew J. McCafferty, of Worcester, as major. These gentlemen had held commissions in the volunteer militia, and were possessed of considerable military knowledge. Lieutenant-Colonel Sprague commanded a company in the Rifle Battalion in the three months' service, and, before the close of the war, was commissioned lieutenant-colonel in the Third Regiment Heavy Artillery.

The Twenty-sixth Regiment was recruited at "Camp Chase," Lowell, and was attached to Major-General Butler's division, designed to attack New Orleans. Many of the officers and men of this regiment belonged to the Sixth Regiment in the three months' service, which was attacked in Baltimore, on the 19th of April, 1861. The Twenty-sixth left Boston in the transport steamer "Constitution," on the 21st day of November, 1861, for Ship Island, Mississippi. This was the first loyal volunteer regiment that reached the Department of the Gulf. Its field officers were Edward F. Jones, of Pepperell, colonel; Alpha B. Farr, of Lowell, lieutenant-colonel; and Josiah A. Sawtelle, of Lowell, major, — all of whom were officers in the Sixth Regiment in the three months' service.

The Twenty-seventh Regiment was recruited at "Camp Reed," Springfield, from the four western counties in the State. It left the Commonwealth for Annapolis on the 2d day of November, 1861, and formed a part of General Burnside's command. The field officers were Horace C. Lee, of Springfield, colonel, who afterwards rose to the rank of brigadier-general; Luke Wyman, of Northampton, lieutenant-colonel; and Walter G. Bartholomew, of Springfield, major, — both of whom were made full colonels before the close of the war.

The Twenty-eighth Regiment was recruited at "Camp Cameron," Cambridge. Its officers and men were chiefly of Irish birth or descent. It did not leave the State until January, 1862. Its field officers were William Monteith, of New York, colonel; Maclelland Moore, of Boston, lieutenant-colonel; George W. Cartwright, of New York, major. The colonel and major had served in one of the New-York regiments in the three months' service. The lieutenant-colonel had been for many years connected with the militia of Massachusetts, and commanded a company in the Eleventh Massachusetts Regiment, three years' volunteers, from which he was discharged for promotion in the Twenty-eighth.

The Twenty-ninth Regiment was composed of seven companies originally raised as militia in the three months' service, but which volunteered for three years, and were sent by detachments to Fortress Monroe, while the Third and Fourth three months' regiments were still there: on the return of the three months' regiments, these seven companies remained at the fortress, and were formed into a battalion, under the command of Captain Joseph H. Barnes. Permission was given by the Secretary of War to recruit the battalion to a regiment, by the addition of three new companies. The field officers of the regiment were Ebenezer W. Peirce, of Freetown, colonel; Joseph H. Barnes, of Boston, lieutenant-colonel; and Charles Chipman, of Sandwich, major. Colonel Peirce, on the breaking-out of the war, was brigadier-general of the Second Brigade, First Division, Massachusetts Militia, and succeeded General B. F. Butler, after his promotion to major-general of volunteers, to the command of the Massachusetts three months' men at Fortress Monroe. General Peirce had command of the expedition against Big Bethel, in May, 1861. On the return of the three months' men, he was mustered out of service, and remained without command until he was commissioned colonel of the Twenty-ninth by Governor Andrew, Dec. 13, 1861. He lost his right arm in the battle before Richmond at "White Oak Swamp," in 1862.

The seven original companies of this command were among the first three years' volunteers raised in Massachusetts, that were mustered into the United-States service.

While these infantry regiments were being organized and forwarded to the front, a battalion of infantry for three years' service was organized, and sent to Fort Warren for garrison duty. It was composed of five companies, of which Francis J. Parker, of Boston, was commissioned major. It was on duty at Fort Warren, at the close of the year 1861.

Two companies of sharpshooters, with telescopic rifles, were recruited at Lynnfield. The first company, under command of John Saunders, of Salem, was not attached to any regiment. It left the State for Washington on the 3d day of December, 1861, and was ordered to report to General Frederick W. Lander, who commanded a brigade near Maryland Heights, on the Upper Potomac. The second company was attached to the Twenty-second Regiment, and left the State with it. In these two companies were many of the best marksmen in the Commonwealth.

The first regiment of cavalry was ordered to be raised on the third day of September, 1861; and Colonel Robert Williams, of Virginia, one of the most accomplished cavalry officers in the regular army, was detailed to accept the command. Horace Binney Sargent, of West Roxbury, senior aide-de-camp to the Governor, was commissioned lieutenant-colonel; Greely S. Curtis, of Boston, and John H. Edson, of Boston, were commissioned majors. The regiment was recruited at "Camp Brigham," Readville, and left for the seat of war in detachments, — the first being sent forward Dec. 25; the second, Dec. 27; and the third, on Sunday, December 29, 1861. The regiment was ordered to Annapolis; and Colonel Williams was to await orders from the Adjutant-General of the United States. The regiment remained at Annapolis until the close of the year.

The First Light Battery was recruited at "Camp Cameron," Cambridge, by Captain Josiah Porter, assisted by William H. McCartney, Jacob H. Sleeper, Jacob Federlien, and Robert L. Sawin, of Boston, who were severally commissioned lieutenants. The battery left the State on the 3d of October, 1861, for Washington.

The Second Battery was recruited at "Camp Wollaston," Quincy, and left for Washington, on the eighth day of August, 1861. Its officers were Ormond F. Nims, Boston, captain; John W. Wolcott, Roxbury, first lieutenant; George G. Trull of Boston, Richard B. Hall of Boston, second lieutenants.

The Third Battery was recruited at Lynnfield, by Captain Dexter H. Follett, and was temporarily attached to the Twenty-second Regiment, and left the State on the seventh day of October, 1861. Its officers were Dexter H. Follett, Boston, captain: Augustus P. Martin, Boston, and Caleb C. E. Mortimer, Charlestown, first lieutenants: Valentine M. Dunn and Philip H. Tyler, Charlestown, second lieutenants.

Soon after the battery reached Washington, Captain Follett resigned his commission, and Lieutenant Martin was appointed to fill the vacancy.

The Fourth Light Battery was recruited at "Camp Chase," Lowell, and formed part of Major-General Butler's command to invade Louisiana. The nucleus of this battery was a section of light artillery in the Second Division of Militia at Salem, commanded by Captain Charles H. Manning. When recruited to a full battery, it left Boston in the steam-transport "Constitution," Nov. 21, 1861. Its officers were Charles H. Manning, of Salem, captain: Frederick W. Reinhardt, Boston, and Joseph R. Salla, Boston, first lieutenants: Henry Davidson and George W. Taylor, of Salem, second lieutenants.

The Fifth Light Battery was recruited at Lynnfield, and at "Camp Massasoit," Readville, and left the State for Washington, with orders to report to Major-General McClellan. Its officers were Max Eppendorff, of New Bedford, captain: George D. Allen, Malden, and John B. Hyde, New Bedford, first lieutenants; Robert A. Dillingham, New Bedford, and Charles A. Phillips, Salem, second lieutenants.

This battery was the only one which left the State in 1861 without a complete equipment. Every thing was furnished except horses, which Quartermaster-General Meigs, U.S.A., preferred to have supplied at Washington.

These regiments and batteries of three years' volunteers comprised, in the aggregate, twenty-seven thousand officers and enlisted men. They had been organized, officered, equipped, and sent to the front, within six months. Including the three months' men, the number of soldiers furnished by Massachusetts, from the sixteenth day of April to the thirty-first day of December, 1861, in the aggregate was thirty thousand seven hundred and thirty-six officers and enlisted men. This is exclusive of six companies, raised in Newburyport, West Cambridge, Milford, Lawrence, Boston, and Cambridgeport, which went to New York in May, and joined what was called the Mozart Regiment, and Sickles's brigade; nor does it include two regiments which were recruited by Major-General Butler at Pittsfield and Lowell, and which were originally known as the Western Bay State and the Eastern Bay State Regiments, of which we shall speak in the next chapter; nor does it include three hundred men who were recruited in Massachusetts for a military organization at Fortress Monroe, known as the Union Coast Guard, and commanded by Colonel Wardrop, of the Third Regiment Massachusetts Militia, in the three months' service. Including these enlistments, the total number of officers and soldiers, furnished by Massachusetts in 1861, would be thirty-three thousand six hundred and thirty-six, or more than twice the number of the entire army of the United States at the commencement of the war. But, in addition to this large number of men furnished by this Commonwealth for the military defence of the nation, it appears, by the enlistment-record of the receiving-ship at the navy yard in Charlestown, that seven thousand six hundred and fifty-eight Massachusetts men entered the navy to maintain our rights, and defend the flag upon the ocean. Add these to the men furnished for the army, and the aggregate is forty-one thousand two hundred and ninety-four.

To avoid confusion, we have given, in consecutive form, the organizing and getting off the regiments during the year 1861, which required great attention and much labor, and rendered necessary the appointment of additional staff officers, and the creation of new military departments. On the twenty-fifth day of May, 1861, General Ebenezer W. Stone was appointed master of ordnance, with the rank of colonel, which position he held until the third day of October of the same year. Albert G. Browne, Jr., of Salem, was appointed, on the twenty-seventh day of May, 1861, military secretary to the Governor, with the rank of lieutenant-colonel, which position he held until the close of Governor Andrew's administration in 1865. On the thirteenth day of June, 1861, Dr. William J. Dale, of Boston, was appointed Surgeon-General of Massachusetts, with the rank of colonel. Dr. Dale and Dr. George H. Lyman had given their time and professional services in a medical supervision of the troops, and the selection of proper persons for surgeons to the regiments, from the commencement of the Rebellion. Dr. Dale, in a letter addressed to me, says, —

"Whatever of success attended the preparation of the troops, prior to my commission, is attributable to Dr. Lyman, who showed great energy and good judgment. He was constantly in consultation with the Governor; while I attended to the routine of office duties, and gave such help to Dr. Lyman as my limited knowledge of such matters allowed. He is an accomplished man, an able surgeon, and stood high in his profession. He was considered one of the most energetic and thorough officers on the medical staff in the United-States army, until honorably mustered out at the expiration of the Rebellion."

The following letter of the Governor to Dr. Lyman shows how well he appreciated the services rendered by him: —

June 14, 1861.

MY DEAR SIR, — I wish to render you my sincere thanks, both personally and in behalf of the Commonwealth, for the constant and valuable services which you have so kindly rendered in our medical service, and of the faithfulness of which, I beg to assure you, I am deeply sensible.

I shall esteem it an especial favor, if you will retain your connection with the medical department for the present, in order to co-operate with Dr. Dale in the work respecting ambulances, hospital outfits, &c., on which you are now engaged, and if you will also henceforth act as a member of the Board of Medical Examiners, to which I beg you to consider this letter as an appointment.

I shall always remember with gratitude — almost beyond any other service I have ever received — the friendly co-operation of those who came to the assistance of the Commonwealth during the anxious and hurried days of April, when, destitute as we were of any efficient military organization, we were enabled, as individuals working in a common spirit, to effect a result which was creditable to Massachusetts.

   Yours faithfully and respectfully,   JOHN A. ANDREW.
To Dr. G. H. LYMAN.

At the beginning of the war, a memorial was addressed to the Governor, signed by Drs. James Jackson, George Hayward, and S. D. Townsend, asking that none but well-qualified and competent surgeons should receive medical appointments. The memorial was favorably regarded by the Governor; and he appointed Drs. Hayward, Townsend, John Ware, Samuel G. Howe, J. Mason Warren, S. Cabot, Jr., R. M. Hodges, George H. Lyman, and William J. Dale, as a medical commission. Drs. George H. Gay, Samuel L. Abbott, John C. Dalton, and R. W. Hooper were subsequently appointed to fill vacancies caused by death or resignation. This board was charged with the responsibility of examining candidates for the medical staff, and also acted as a board of consultation in sanitary matters, when called upon by the Surgeon-General. Their valuable services were in constant requisition during the war; and, being composed of men distinguished and humane, their opinions had great weight. Their services were entirely voluntary, and continued during the war.

The Surgeon-General established hospitals, received and cared for the sick and wounded who returned; and his labors in the reception and care of these men continued until the establishment of general hospitals by the Government, and were exceedingly laborious, and of great usefulness.

Soon after the commencement of the war, as there was no army-surgeon in Boston, the Medical Bureau at Washington appointed Surgeon-General Dale acting assistant surgeon in the United-States army, for the purpose of giving him official responsibility in matters pertaining to the sanitary welfare of the troops. Under these joint commissions, he furnished medical supplies, organized hospitals, received and cared for the sick and wounded, and remained acting medical director in the United-States army, until relieved, in July, 1862, by Surgeon McLaren, of the regular service.

The admirable manner in which General Dale organized his department, and discharged his duties, his humane and tender care of the sick and wounded, will ever be regarded with gratitude by our people; in acknowledgment of which, he was appointed to the rank of brigadier-general by Governor Andrew, by General Order No. 24, dated — .

HEADQUARTERS, BOSTON, Oct. 7, 1863.

In view of the considerate, able, and unwearied services rendered the past two years by Colonel William J. Dale, as Surgeon-General of the Commonwealth, his Excellency the Governor directs that he hereafter take rank as brigadier-general, and that he be obeyed and respected accordingly. WILLIAM SCHOULER,
Adjutant-General.

Elijah D. Brigham, of Boston, on the thirteenth day of June, 1861, was commissioned Commissary-General of Massachusetts, with the rank of colonel, which rank he held until May 14, 1864, when he was promoted by the Governor to the rank of brigadier-general.

Charles H. Dalton was appointed assistant quartermaster-general, on the twenty-third day of May, 1861, with the rank of colonel. Colonel Dalton did very acceptable services at Washington, as the agent of the Governor, in the early part of the war, which were given gratuitously.

William P. Lee and Waldo Adams, of Boston, were appointed assistant quartermaster-generals, with the rank of first lieutenant, June 14, 1861. The services rendered by these gentlemen were given gratuitously.

Frank E. Howe, of New York, was appointed assistant

quartermaster-general Aug. 23, 1861, with the rank of lieutenant-colonel. Colonel Howe was a native of Massachusetts, doing business in New York. In the month of May, he had written to Governor Andrew, tendering the use of rooms in his store, and his own personal services, to take charge of the sick and wounded Massachusetts soldiers who might pass through New York on their return from the front. On the twentieth day of May, Governor Andrew wrote him the following letter in reply: —

FRANK E. HOWE, Esq., 203, Broadway.   May 20, 1861.

SIR, — I have received, with great pleasure, the liberal and patriotic tender of the services of yourself and employees, and the use of your premises on Broadway, for the benefit of the Massachusetts troops, and the general advancement of the interests of this Commonwealth in its relations to the present war.

Expressing to you my thanks, I accept your generous offer. It will be of great advantage to our soldiers to make your premises their headquarters, so far as convenient, while in New York; and you may expect, from time to time, to be intrusted with the performance of various offices for their benefit.

Should you fall in with any sick or wounded Massachusetts officers or soldiers, you will please to relieve them at the expense of the State, and take measures for forwarding them to their homes.

With regard to the sundry other duties that we may ask of you to perform, you will, so far as possible, receive specific instructions as they arise.

You will please to make a weekly return of the expenses to be defrayed by the State to this department.

       Yours faithfully,   JOHN A. ANDREW.

This was the origin of what was familiarly known as the New-England Rooms in New York, of which Colonel Howe had charge during the entire war. It became a home and hospital for the sick and wounded of New-England soldiers, both in going to, and returning from, the front. Other New-England States, following the lead of Massachusetts, appointed Colonel Howe their agent to take care of their soldiers. These rooms were supported, by voluntary subscriptions, by patriotic and liberal men in the city of New York. We shall have occasion to speak again of this admirable institution and Colonel Howe in a subsequent chapter.

Charles Amory, of Boston, who, in the early part of the war, had tendered to the Governor his services, free of charge, in any position where he could be of use, was appointed master of ordnance, upon the discharge of General Stone, on the seventh day of October, 1861, with the rank of colonel. Colonel Amory performed the duties of the office until Jan. 9, 1863, when he resigned, there being no further necessity for his services. He received the thanks of the Governor, in General Orders No. 2, series of 1863.

William Brown, of Boston, who was chief clerk in the office of the Adjutant-General when the war broke out, and for several years previous thereto, was commissioned Assistant Adjutant-General, with the rank of colonel, on the twenty-ninth day of October, 1861, which position he held until removed by death, Feb. 16, 1863. He was a faithful and intelligent officer, and died at his post.

These were all the staff commissions issued in 1861.

We now return to the correspondence of the Executive Department.

A large amount of valuable stores for our troops had been forwarded to Fortress Monroe, in the steamer "Pembroke," early in the month of May, 1861. The following letter, written by Colonel Lee by direction of the Governor, has reference to these stores: —

May 20, 1861.

DEAR SIR, — The captain of the steamer "Pembroke," just returned from Fort Monroe, reports, that several boxes and bales, put ashore for the Fifth and Eighth Regiments, remained as long as the "Pembroke" lay at the fort, exposed to mud and the weather; and that, although he applied successively to the quartermasters of the Third and Fourth Regiments, and to the colonels, then to the quartermaster of the regulars, and, lastly, to Colonel ——, he did not succeed in interesting any one to receive and store these goods, or to engage to forward them to the regiments in Washington, or elsewhere.

Governor Andrew would like to have the whereabouts of these goods discovered; and, if they have not been delivered, would like to have them sent to the regiments to whom they are addressed. Commodore Stringham very kindly promised to send them by the first opportunity, but that may not have come.

The Governor would also express his great surprise at the indifference — almost surliness — exhibited by United-States officers, when applied to as to the reception and care of these comforts for Massachusetts troops; also, his astonishment that room could not be found in Fort Monroe for their storage.

As you are obliged to leave Washington, the Governor has commissioned for the time, as Massachusetts agent, Mr. Charles H. Dalton, a gentleman of perfect integrity, and great business experience and ability, and he leaves Boston for Washington, this evening; and any business you have in hand, when obliged to leave, you will give to his charge.

Your obedient servant,

HENRY LEE, JR., *Aide-de-camp.*

CHARLES R. LOWELL, JR., Esq., Washington, D.C.

May 23, 1861. — The Governor telegraphs to Hon. Charles Sumner, at Washington, "Why can't I send a brigadier in Butler's place? It is my wish, and is only just to General Peirce. Butler recommends him. He is sound, faithful, and ardent. Answer immediately." Permission was given, and General Peirce was appointed. On the same day, the Governor writes to Professor Rogers, thanking him for eight hundred military hats, contributed by the "Thursday Evening Club;" also, to Mrs. Jared Sparks, Cambridge, and the ladies with whom she is associated, for presents of needle-books and handkerchiefs for the soldiers.

May 24, 1861. — Governor writes to Lieutenant Amory, U.S.A., mustering officer at Boston, "Whatever rations, clothing, &c., you may want for the soldiers, after they are mustered in, will be furnished upon proper requisitions." The same day, he writes to A. W. Campbell, of Wheeling, Va., inclosing an order passed by the Executive Council, loaning that city two thousand muskets. He writes to William Robinson, of Baltimore, Md., —

"I have gratefully received, and desire cordially to acknowledge your very kind letter, concerning the fate and last days of poor Needham, of Lawrence, Mass. Allow me also to render to you my thanks in behalf of those most nearly related to the young man, as well as in behalf of all my people, for your Christian, brotherly conduct towards the strangers who fell in your way, rendering the offices of a good Samaritan. I have sent a copy of your letter to the Mayor of Lawrence, who will send it to the Needham family.

"I beg leave to add the assurances of my personal respect, and the hope that I may yet see you in Boston."

He writes to Salmon P. Chase, Secretary of the Treasury: —

"I have consulted with the representatives of many of our principal banking institutions, and with our leading private capitalists; and I feel confident, that, if *necessary or desirable*, $5,000,000 *of the* $14,000,000 *of the next loan can be taken in this Commonwealth.*

"If the United-States bonds to that amount should be guaranteed by the Commonwealth of Massachusetts, they would command a premium probably, and could certainly be readily negotiated at par. Will you advise me what would be the wishes of the national Administration in this respect?"

He writes again to the Secretary of War, calling his attention to the defenceless condition of the forts in Boston Harbor; also to General Stetson, of the Astor House, thanking him for his kindness and liberality to our soldiers in passing through New York; also thanks Daniel Lombard, Esq., of Boston, who offers to clear "a cargo of rice, free of expense, for the use of our troops."

He writes to Colonel Dalton, at Washington, inclosing him an extract from a letter written by F. A. B. Simkins, to the effect that a soldier of the Fifth Regiment had told him that the quartermaster of the regiment had neglected his duty. "Mattresses that came with the regiment had since lain in a cellar, while the men have slept on stone floors; tons of cheese from Boston had been there more than a week, before the men could get a mouthful of it; canteens had also been there, for a considerable time, and had not been distributed, — thinks something wrong." He also incloses another letter from a gentleman in Washington, giving an entirely different account of the condition of the regiment. Colonel Dalton is asked to look into the matter, and report.

May 28, 1861. — Governor writes to Jacob F. Kent, Esq., Providence, R.I., that "Massachusetts is allowed six regiments, and would be glad to send twenty, if they would let her."

He writes to Governor Washburn, of Maine, —

"If I have a chance to make an appointment of a good man as officer, I make no question as to his age, unless he comes somewhere near Methuselah. I hold that I am not bound to take judicial notice of a man's age, or to enter into any particular investigation on the subject, provided I feel that I have got the *right man*. Both of us know some people at fifty who are younger than some at twenty-five; yet, on the whole, I like the suggestion of the War Department; and, if they err in favor of young men, why, that is so uncommon an error now-a-days among Government officials, that I regard it with great charity, as a hopeful symptom."

This letter undoubtedly has reference to a circular letter addressed to the Governors of the loyal States by the Secretary of War, in which the following suggestions are made in respect to the appointment of officers in the volunteer service: —

"1. To commission no one of doubtful morals or patriotism, and not of sound health.

"2. To appoint no one to a lieutenancy (second or first) who has passed the age of twenty-two years, or to a captaincy over thirty years; and to appoint no field officers (major, lieutenant-colonel, or colonel), unless a graduate of the United-States Military Academy, or known to possess military knowledge and experience, who have passed the respective ages of thirty-five, forty, forty-five years.

"This department feels assured, that it will not be deemed offensive to your Excellency to add yet this general counsel, that the higher the moral character and general intelligence of the officers so appointed, the greater the efficiency of the troops, and the resulting glory to their respective States."

May 28. — The Governor telegraphs to Governor Dennison, of Ohio, "If you wish us to buy or contract for any equipments for you, can get two hundred a day made, suitable, if you wish."

He telegraphs to the Secretary of War, "The First Regiment

has been mustered in. I want to know whether they shall be sent to Fortress Monroe, as General Butler wants them to be, or what I shall do with them. They are ready to start at twenty-four hours' notice."

May 29. — He telegraphs to Colonel Dalton, Washington, "Urge Government to let me have guns from ordnance yard, and mount them in harbor forts. Merchants here constantly pressing me to obtain them."

He writes to M. C. Pratt, Holyoke, "I have no orders for cavalry. Nothing would give me greater pleasure than to furnish more infantry and cavalry, but cannot do it."

He writes to Colonel Jonas H. French, Boston, declining to accept his offer to raise a regiment, "as there are troops now under arms in the State sufficient to fill double the quota assigned to Massachusetts. Nothing would give me greater pleasure than to have liberty to send more troops."

In the early weeks of the war, several debts were contracted in the name of the Commonwealth, by officers and others, for supplies for the immediate use of troops on their way to Washington. The commissary and quartermaster's departments had yet to be organized, and a proper system of expenditure and personal accountability established. Many of the bills which were forwarded from New York and other places to the State authorities for payment contained items which were not recognized in "the regulations," and the prices charged were extravagantly high. The files of the Governor contain a number of letters relating to these matters. One of these letters states that in "almost all the New-York bills for supplies bought at that time for the troops, the charges average very much more than Boston prices for similar articles." One of the committee of the Governor's Council, to whom these bills were referred for settlement, remarked that "the purchasers, whoever they were, seemed to have looked for persons who sold at retail prices, and to have succeeded admirably in finding what they were looking for." These bills were, however, paid; and the appointment of Colonel Frank E. Howe as the agent of the Commonwealth to look after the wants of our soldiers in New York put an end to these early attempts to peculate upon the liberality of Massachusetts. The Executive Council also kept a close watch upon expenditures, and scrutinized all bills presented for payment, which relieved the Governor and heads of departments from much of the drudgery of examining and ascertaining the accuracy of this description of accounts.

May 30. — The Governor writes to Colonel Dalton, at Washington, asking him to urge again upon the Government the *necessity of arming our forts.* "There are plenty of guns at the navy yard, at Watertown, and Springfield, which could easily be put into position. The necessity is urgent."

He acknowledges the receipt of the letter of Powell T. Wyman, from Europe, forwarded to him by the Adjutant-General, offering his services in any military capacity.

May 31. — The Governor telegraphs to Henry Ward Beecher, New York, "The Milford company will arrive by the Norwich boat, to-morrow morning; the Newburyport company, by the Stonington boat; the West-Cambridge company, by the land train, leaving here at eight o'clock, this evening. Prepare to receive them: they are consigned to you." These three companies were impatient to enter the service. They could not be placed in any regiment here, as the quota assigned to this State was full, and the Secretary of War would accept no more. They were induced, by representations made, to go to New York, and complete a regiment said to be forming in Brooklyn, and to be known as the "Beecher Regiment." Upon arriving at New York, they were sadly disappointed in their expectations. No such regiment as had been represented was in readiness to receive them, and they were utterly neglected. Those by whom they were encouraged to come to New York gave them no support or assistance; and they telegraphed to the Governor for transportation to return home again. They came back, and again went to New York, and entered the Mozart Regiment, so called.

June 3. — In regard to these companies, the Governor telegraphed to Frank E. Howe, "Brooklyn must prepare to return our three companies. We have incurred expense, raised hopes; and Brooklyn has cruelly misled, disappointed, and mortified us." Colonel Sargent, by direction of the Governor, writes to

Henry Ward Beecher, asking if Brooklyn people will send the companies back. If not, Massachusetts will pay the expense. Also, writes a letter of introduction for William E. Parmenter, Esq., of West Cambridge, to Colonel Howe. Mr. Parmenter went on to see about the West-Cambridge company.

The Governor telegraphs to Colonel Dalton, at Washington, "Urge desperately for one more regiment from Massachusetts. It is next to impossible for us to get along without at least one more."

June 4. — Governor telegraphs to Colonel Dalton, at Washington, "Can regiments be received without tents and wagons? Hearing that the Government can't supply them, we contracted, and expect some in a few days, and can forward regiments soon as mustered, and wagons and tents received. Will forward the regiments, and send things afterwards, if permitted."

June 5. — Governor writes a long letter in answer to one received from Colonel Hinks, of the Eighth Regiment, then in Maryland, who had asked that the regiment might be detained in the service as one of the six regiments asked for the three years' service. The Governor declines to entertain the proposition. "As the men have a right to come home at the end of three months, and the officers cannot speak for them, they must speak for themselves."

June 10, 1861

To Lieutenant-General WINFIELD SCOTT.

GENERAL, — His Excellency the Governor of Massachusetts orders me to make a detailed statement to you in regard to Cobb's Flying Artillery. Major Cobb raised, drilled, and commanded Cook's Battery, now in service under General Butler; and *understands himself*.

He has one hundred and fifty picked men, *most carefully selected;* six pieces rifled and throwing twelve-pound shot and nine-pound shell (concussion), intended to burst on striking a column of men. The principle is beautiful.

Captain Van Brunt, of the "Minnesota," saw a trial of these guns with shot, and expressed surprise and delight. The trials with shell are pronounced by competent judges to be even more satisfactory, with equal precision, *at three and a half degrees* elevation, one thousand three hundred and fifty yards' distance, one and a half pounds powder, time four and a half seconds. The shot, weighing with patch twelve pounds, were thrown from these rifled *six-pounders* with precision enough to strike a section nearly every time; and most of them were thrown within four feet lateral deviations, towards the latter part of the trial. The guns are bronze, of course.

At twelve degrees elevation, chronometer measurement over water indicated a flight of two and a half miles before ricochet. At twenty degrees, ricochet was lost.

The shells burst beautifully. There is no lead to strip off over the heads of men, and they are very safe to handle or drop. The charge fits so loosely, expanding after ignition of the powder, that a child can ram the shot home. Major Cobb can fire one hundred rounds from his battery in six minutes.

Every thing — horses, wagons, and all — is ready for your call.

I have the honor to be sir, your most respectful and obedient servant, HORACE BINNEY SARGENT, *Aide-de-camp.*

June 10. — The Governor writes to Governor Buckingham, of Connecticut, "I have your letter of the 7th, inclosing duplicate letter of credit for £10,000 on George Peabody, which you state will be sent to Mr. Crowninshield. That gentleman has already received orders to execute your orders; and I trust that he will be able to do so."

On the same day, the Governor gave written instructions to Colonel Ritchie, of his personal staff, to visit our regiments at the front, and confer with General Scott as regards future movements, and to report. The Governor writes to General Scott, asking the discharge of Captain Henry S. Briggs, of the Eighth Regiment, M.V.M., three months' regiment, that he may commission him colonel of the Tenth Regiment, three years' service. Captain Briggs was discharged, and commissioned colonel of the Tenth, June 21, 1861. He served gallantly through the war, and was appointed brigadier-general of volunteers by President Lincoln, for brave and meritorious services in the field. He was wounded in the seven days' fight before Richmond, in 1862, but remained in service to the end of the war. He is a son of the late Hon. George N. Briggs, formerly Governor of Massachusetts, and he is now Auditor of State, having been elected three times to that responsible position.

June 14. — Governor telegraphs to the Secretary of War,

"Lieutenant Amory, U.S.A., mustering officer in Boston, thinks we ought to furnish thirty wagons, instead of fifteen, for every thousand men. If so, we will send wagons additional to fifteen." The Executive Council passed an order to have the Twelfth Regiment (Colonel Webster) go to Fort Warren, preparatory to being mustered into the service.

On the same day, the Governor's military secretary addressed the following letter to Colonel Webster: —

To Colonel WEBSTER.

DEAR SIR, — His Excellency the Governor, having accepted an invitation to assist in raising an American flag on the summit of the monument at Bunker Hill, will take pleasure, if you will join his military staff on that occasion, — the 17th of June.

The staff will meet at the private room of the Governor, at the State House, on the morning of that day, in season to take carriages for Charlestown at eight o'clock.

It is desired that there may be no delay as to the time of starting for Charlestown; for, according to the programme of the managers of the celebration, it is expected that the Governor and staff shall be present at the house of Mr. Warren, President of the Monument Association, at half-past eight o'clock.

Very truly, your obedient servant,
A. G. BROWNE,
Military Secretary to Commander-in-chief.

June 15. — The Governor addressed the following letter to the President of the United States, which was given to Mr. William Everett, and taken by him to Washington, and delivered to Mr. Lincoln: —

His Excellency A. LINCOLN, President United States.

SIR, — I beg to present Mr. Everett, of Boston, a son of the Hon. Edward Everett, and through him to present to your notice a copy, —

1. Of a letter from Bishop Fitzpatrick to yourself.
2. Copy of your Excellency's endorsement thereon.
3. Copy of endorsement of the Secretary of War.
4. A letter from myself to Mr. H. A. Pierce, the agent of the regiment referred to.
5. A copy of my general order, under which our six regiments were designated, and encamped regiments provided for.

I do this for the purpose of showing the system in which I have proceeded in regard to the three years' men, the effect of progress made and making, and what we are willing and desire to do; and also what is the truth as to the Fourteenth[*] (Irish regiment), which I am as willing to forward as any other, but not to the cost or injustice to others by deranging the scheme. If the United-States Government will designate any special regiment, without leaving any responsibility of selection on me, I will, however, proceed with the utmost zeal and alacrity to execute its order, whether it agrees with my scheme or not.

Again I wish to urge attention to our splendid new battery of light artillery, specially prepared for service; and to add, that, if the want of a United-States army officer is in the way, I should be very glad to have one detailed, and allowed to take its command.

I am, with great respect, your obedient servant,

JOHN A. ANDREW.

The above letter requires explanation. The Fourteenth Regiment referred to was composed, in great part, of men of Irish birth. At the beginning of the war, Colonel Thomas Cass, of Boston, proposed to raise an Irish regiment for the three months' service. He had been long and favorably connected with the volunteer militia of Massachusetts. His request was granted, and the regiment was raised; but, before its organization could be completed, information was received from Washington that no more three months' regiments would be accepted. Coincident with the request made by Colonel Cass, an offer was made by Dr. Smith and others, of Boston, to raise a second Irish regiment, which they were pleased to designate "the Irish Brigade." This regiment was to be commanded by a person by the name of Rice, who was not a citizen of Massachusetts, although he was here at the time, and, so far as the writer knew, of no military experience whatever. This regiment was also raised, but was not accepted, for the same reasons that Colonel Cass's regiment was not. When the call was made for three years' troops, a very large proportion of the men composing the two regiments agreed to enlist for three years; and both were sent to Long Island, Boston Harbor, until their organizations could be completed, and the regiments accepted by the Government. The

---

[*] The disbanded old Fourteenth Regiment.

long delay, by the Secretary of War, in fixing the quota of Massachusetts under the first call of the President for three years' men, and his persistent refusal, for a still longer time, to accept more than six regiments from this State, and the uncertainty which existed whether they would be accepted at all, had a demoralizing and pernicious effect upon both commands. When, however, orders were received on the twenty-second day of May, that Massachusetts was to furnish six regiments, the Governor determined that one of the six should be an Irish regiment. At this time, neither of the Irish regiments were full. They were designated the Thirteenth and Fourteenth Regiments. Until a regiment was full, — that is, with ten companies, and each company with ninety-eight enlisted men and three commissioned officers, — it could not be mustered into the United-States service, and consequently could not receive United-States pay. Colonel Cass's regiment lacked about two hundred men to complete it to the maximum. These men were to be obtained at once; and the Governor decided that these men should be taken from the Fourteenth Regiment, which numbered only about six hundred men.

The Adjutant-General was ordered by the Governor to effect this consolidation. He proceeded the same day to Long Island with the Governor's orders, which he read to the officers of the Fourteenth, and requested their assistance to fill up the regiment of Colonel Cass. It appeared that the intention of the Governor had been known at the camp before the Adjutant-General arrived; and a meeting of the officers had been held, at which resolutions had passed condemnatory of the orders of the Governor, which resolutions were to appear in the Boston papers the next morning. The resolutions which were passed were shown to the Adjutant-General upon his arrival at Long Island. He read them with surprise, and told Mr. Rice and the officers, that, if they were made public, he thought the Governor would order the organization to be disbanded at once. The resolutions were suppressed. After considerable difficulty, and a good deal of forbearance, a sufficient number of men agreed to join Colonel Cass's regiment to fill it up; and, in a few days afterwards, it was mustered into the service of the United States as the Ninth Regiment, Massachusetts Volunteers. The remaining men of the Fourteenth, through heeding advice given them by disappointed aspirants for commissions, became dissatisfied, and left the island. As they had not signed the enlistment paper, and had not been mustered into the United-States service, they could not be held to service. Nothing was further from the desire of the Governor or the Adjutant-General than to break up or disband this nucleus of a regiment. But bad counsels prevailed, and unjust complaints were made, which demoralized the men, and rendered it necessary in the end to disband the organization. Many of the men went to New York, and joined regiments there. Some returned to their homes, and others entered regiments which were being organized in other parts of the State. The letter of Bishop Fitzpatrick, mentioned in the Governor's letter to the President, we have no doubt was an earnest request that the President would allow more regiments to be furnished by Massachusetts, and that the so-called Fourteenth Regiment should be one of them.

One of the most interesting and imposing ceremonies of the year was the flag-raising from the summit of Bunker-Hill Monument on the seventeenth day of June, the anniversary of the battle. The day was warm and pleasant, and a large concourse of people were assembled. At the base of the monument a stage was erected, on which were the officers of the Association, the school children, the city authorities of Charlestown, Governor Andrew and his staff, Colonel Fletcher Webster, of the Twelfth Regiment, and many other prominent citizens of the State. A fine band of music played national airs. The services were opened by prayer by the Rev. James B. Miles; and a short and eloquent address was made by Hon. G. Washington Warren, introducing Governor Andrew, who was received with hearty cheers by those present. The Governor's address was brief, fervent, eloquent, and patriotic. After referring to the men of the Revolution who had sacrificed their lives for independence, and made moist the soil of Bunker Hill with their blood, he said, —

"It is one of the hallowed omens of the controversy of our time, that the men of Middlesex, the men of Charlestown, the men of Concord, of Lexington, of Acton, are all in the field in this contest.

This day, this hour, reconsecrated by their deeds, are adding additional leaves to the beautiful chaplet which adorns the fair honor of good old Massachusetts. Not unto me, not unto us, let any praise be given. Let no tongue dare speak a eulogy for us; but reserve all the love and gratitude that language can express for the patriotic sons of Massachusetts who are bearing our country's flag on the field of contest. . . .

"Obedient, therefore, to the request of this Association, and to the impulse of my own heart, I spread aloft the ensign of the republic, testifying for ever, to the last generation of men, of the rights of mankind, and to constitutional liberty and law. Let it rise until it shall surmount the capital of the column, let it float on every wind, to every sea and every shore, from every hill-top let it wave, down every river let it run. Respected it shall be in Charlestown, Massachusetts, and in Charleston, South Carolina, on the Mississippi as on the Penobscot, in New Orleans as in Cincinnati, in the Gulf of Mexico as on Lake Superior, and by France and England, now and for ever. Catch it, ye breezes, as it swings aloft; fan it, every wind that blows; clasp it in your arms, and let it float for ever, as the starry sign of Liberty and Union, now and for ever, one and inseparable."

The flag had been at the summit of the staff, rolled up as the signal-flags are on board of a man-of-war. As Governor Andrew concluded, he pulled the rope, the knot was loosened, and the flag floated out on the breeze, amid the shouts of the assembled thousands, and the playing of the Star-spangled Banner by Gilmore's band. The words of the Star-spangled Banner were then sung by F. A. Hall, Esq., of Charlestown; and the whole assemblage joined in the chorus, the ladies taking part with peculiar zest.

The Governor then called for nine cheers to the glorious Star-spangled Banner, which were given with great heart, the ladies waving their handkerchiefs.

When the excitement had somewhat subsided, the Governor came forward, and, in a few complimentary remarks, introduced to the audience Colonel Webster. The speech of this gentleman was brief and appropriate. His father had made the oration when the corner-stone of the monument was laid, and again when the monument was completed. Colonel Webster said he well remembered the preliminary meetings of the committee selected to decide upon the size, character, design, and site of this monument. They met frequently at his father's house. He could remember the appearance of most of them,— Colonel Thomas H. Perkins, William Sullivan, and Gilbert Stuart, the great painter, whose enormous block-tin snuff-box attracted his youthful attention.

"As a boy, I was present at the laying of the corner-stone of this great obelisk under whose shadow we now are. La Fayette laid the stone with appropriate and imposing masonic ceremonies. The vast procession, impatient of unavoidable delay, broke the line of march, and in a tumultuous crowd rushed towards the orator's platform; and I was saved from being trampled under foot, by the strong arm of Mr. George Sullivan, who lifted me on his shoulders, shouting, 'Don't kill the orator's son!' and bore me through the crowd, and placed me on the staging at my father's feet. I felt something embarrassed at that notice, as I now do at this unforeseen notice by His Excellency; but I had no occasion to make an acknowledgment of it." He had also noticed the ceremonies of the completion of the monument in the presence of many distinguished persons from all parts of the country, "some of whom," said Colonel Webster, "I regret to say would hardly like to renew that visit, or recall that scene.

"Within a few days after this, I sailed for China; and I watched, while light and eyesight lasted, till its lofty summit faded at last from view. I now stand again at its base, and renew once more, on this national altar, vows, not for the first time made, of devotion to my country, its Constitution and Union."

He concluded as follows:—

" From this spot I take my departure, like the mariner commencing his voyage; and, wherever my eyes close, they will be turned hitherward toward this North; and, in whatever event, grateful will be the reflection that this monument still stands,— still, still is gilded by the earliest beams of the rising sun, and that still departing day lingers and plays on its summit for ever."

The services concluded by a benediction by the venerable Father Taylor. The flag thus raised, floated from its serene height during the entire war, until it was respected in Charleston, South Carolina, as in Charlestown, Massachusetts. Few men who knew Colonel Webster, can read the words uttered by him on this occasion, without recalling many pleasant memories connected with his name. It was his last utterance in public; for, before the close of the next year, he fell in Virginia, at the head of his regiment, in a desperate battle. His body was brought home to Massachusetts, and lay in state at Faneuil Hall a day, when it was taken to Marshfield, and buried by the side of his illustrious father, "and there it will remain for ever."

CHAPTER V.

Death of Governor Andrew — The Great Loss — Mission of Mr. Crowninshield to Europe — The Purchase of Arms — Colonel Lucius B. Marsh — Vote of Thanks by the Council — The Policy of the Governor in making Military Appointments — Letter to General Butler in regard to our Soldiers — Neglect of Officers — Letter to Colonel Couch, of the Seventh — Sends Two Thousand Muskets to Wheeling, Va. — General Lander — Governor Stevens, of Oregon — General Sherman comes to Boston to confer with the Governor — The War Department and Appointments — Governor makes an Address to the People — Mission to Washington — Writes to Governor Curtin, of Pennsylvania — Blockade-runners at Halifax — Governor saves the Life of a Private Soldier — His Letter to Patrick Donahoe — Religious Toleration — To the Editor of the Boston Post — Massachusetts Companies in New-York Regiments — General Sherman's Command — Liberality of the People — Battle of Ball's Bluff — The Massachusetts Dead — A Noble Letter — Exchange of Prisoners — Governor's Letter to President Lincoln — Scheme to invade Texas — Suggests that Congress offer Bounties — Controversy about making Massachusetts Soldiers catch Fugitive Slaves — Letter to General McClellan — Another Letter to the President, about Exchange of Prisoners — Our Men in Richmond Jail — San Francisco sends Two Thousand Dollars for Soldiers' Families — The Maryland Legislature — Liberal Action — The Republican State Convention — Interesting Debate — Democratic Convention — Thanksgiving Proclamation — Thanksgiving in the Massachusetts Camps — Major Wilder Dwight — The Second Regiment at Harper's Ferry — Full Account of the Controversy between Governor Andrew and Major-General Butler about recruiting and raising Regiments in Massachusetts.

THE last chapter was finished on the thirtieth day of October, when an event occurred which brought sorrow to every true heart in the nation: John A. Andrew died on that day. The preceding pages of this work have exhibited, in an imperfect and feeble manner, a portion of the services which he rendered to his State and country in the hour of its greatest peril, — we say imperfect and feeble, because much which he did was never put in writing, and many of his best thoughts and wisest suggestions were the inspiration of the moment, and conveyed to his friends and subordinates in colloquial conversation. We had known him long and well; and, during the five years of his administration as Governor of this Commonwealth, our connection was official and confidential. We saw him every day, and had occasion to consult him upon nearly every matter in relation to the part which Massachusetts took in the war. He was one of the few men whom we have known, upon whom public life worked no detriment to the simplicity, honesty, and kindness of their character. No man ever appeared in his presence to make a dishonest proposition. If any one approached him for such a purpose, he would not have had the hardihood to make it. His mind was active, and labor appeared to give him strength, rather than weakness. It was the wonder of us all, how he could stand so much bodily and mental labor. When not absent from the city upon business connected with the war, at Washington, he was in his room at the State House, like a skilful and steady pilot at the helm, guiding the Ship of State.

We all felt his loss when he was absent, and felt relieved when he returned. In the darkest hours of the war, — after the first Bull Run battle, the disastrous affair at Ball's Bluff in 1861, after the retreat of McClellan from before Richmond, and many of the stoutest hearts were despondent, and the peril of the nation oppressed the minds of men, — Governor Andrew never lost faith or hope in the ultimate success of our arms, and the favorable termination of the conflict. It was in these days of depression, these hours of sadness, that he shone forth with the brightness of the sun.

Never despair of the republic, was his motto, and guide of life. He infused hope into minds bordering almost on despair, and his acts corresponded with the promptings of his heart. We well remember one night, when the news of McClellan's retreat reached Boston; the papers were filled with accounts of the terrible disaster; the names of the dead and wounded of Massachusetts' bravest and best were arrayed in the ghastly bulletins transmitted from the front. That very night, the Governor said, "We must issue a new order, call for more men, incite recruiting, inspire hope, dispel gloom; this is the time which requires boldness, firmness, and every personal sacrifice." The order was issued; it aroused the latent energies of the people; young men, who had not before thought of volunteering, offered themselves as recruits, eager to press forward to fill the gaps which disaster and death had made in our ranks: and so it was all through the war. He always had a kind word for the soldiers and their families, and he felt every word he spoke. It was no lip-service; it was no honeyed phrase; it was no politician's flattery. It was earnest talk, kind talk. Every one felt it, and were wiser men and truer patriots because of it.

This is not the time, nor this the place, to speak his eulogy. No one but Pericles could fitly pronounce the honors of the Athenian dead; and no one less gifted than the great orator of Greece can speak the eulogy of him whom we have lost.

It was fitting that the heart of Massachusetts should sigh when John A. Andrew died. It was fitting that his remains should be borne to the grave by those who knew him best, and loved him most, — the funeral cortege, as it wound its solemn way from the church in Arlington Street around the Common, past the State House, over the broad avenue leading from the city; the march of the Cadets, with reversed arms, keeping step to the funeral dirge; that the sidewalks should be crowded with well-dressed men and women, who bowed their heads, or raised their hats, as the coffin moved before them to its resting-place in Mount Auburn.

He was a private citizen when he died; he held no office; he had no honors to bestow: but his was a name beloved and cherished in all loyal hearts, and his was a death that moved them to the inmost core. He died when his manhood was in its prime; when the fruits of his wisdom and knowledge were ripening, and the future was holding out, with favoring hand, the highest honors of the republic; but —

> "He has gone on the mountain,
> He is lost to the forest,
> Like a summer-dried fountain,
> *When our need was the sorest.*"

We pass from the contemplation of the character and merits of the dead to the consideration of his services while living.

We have already stated, that Francis B. Crowninshield, of

Boston, was appointed, in April, to proceed to England to purchase arms. Mr. Crowninshield discharged the important trust confided to him with great fidelity, and to the satisfaction of the Governor. It may be interesting to learn, from so intelligent a party, the state of feeling in England towards this country in the beginning of the war.

Mr. Crowninshield arrived in London on Sunday morning, the sixth day of May. He found, on his arrival, that there were a very few rifles for sale in England. The "Persia," the steamer in which he was a passenger, had taken out many orders to purchase. He found an agent there from South Carolina, to purchase arms for that State. New York had also sent out an agent in the same ship with him; but he did not know the fact until after his arrival in England. There were also several private speculators in the ship for the purchase of arms. Many telegrams were sent from Queenstown to England, on the arrival of the "Persia" at that port. The London Times, the morning on which Mr. Crowninshield arrived in that city, contained the announcement that agents had come over to purchase rifles, which caused great excitement in the trade.

On arriving at Liverpool, Mr. McFarland, who had been employed to go with Mr. Crowninshield, was despatched to Birmingham, and directed to act promptly in the purchase of arms, if he found any there suitable for our purpose. John B. Goodman, the chairman of the gun trade in Birmingham, had the control of about twenty-five thousand Enfield rifles, of excellent quality, which could be delivered in a very short time. The current price for these arms was sixty shillings sterling each; a party stood ready to give one hundred shillings each for the lot to go South. The preference of purchase was given to Mr. Crowninshield, and he purchased two thousand of them at that price. One thousand of them were to be sent in the "Persia," on her return voyage. In London, he purchased two thousand eight hundred, at seventy shillings each; he also purchased two hundred from the London Armory, at sixty-five shillings each.

The New-York agent purchased about the same number, and contracted for about fifteen thousand more; he also contracted for five thousand second-hand rifles, used in the Crimea. The first lot of guns were ready to be sent over; but the "Persia" would not take them, which delayed their arrival here.

In a letter to the Governor, Mr. Crowninshield says, "I have not ventured to approach the British Government about guns, at the strong recommendation of Mr. Baring; but one of the gun trade, who has the means to do so, has promised to sound them about buying some from them on his own account. I have but little hope of success. Colonel Fremont, who is here, assured me that he was confident I could do nothing in France, but has written for information, which he will give me. The Government seems inclined to favor the South, so far as the question of cotton is concerned, — I think no further. I have a credit of one hundred thousand dollars from Ohio, with authority to buy to that extent. It does not seem to me, under the emergency, that we ought to haggle too much about the price: to save ten thousand dollars might be to lose every thing."

Before Mr. Crowninshield's return, he had bought and contracted for Massachusetts, and forwarded part of them home, 19,380 Enfield rifles, and 10,000 sets of equipments, with which several of our regiments were provided, and rendered much service in the war.

Among the gentlemen who were very active in procuring arms and equipments in the States, and indefatigable and untiring in their exertions to serve the Commonwealth and the cause, was Lucius B. Marsh, whose services were rendered gratuitously. In recognition of them, the following order was passed by the Executive Council: —

Ordered, That the thanks of the executive branch of the Government of Massachusetts be tendered to Lucius B. Marsh, for his very valuable services to the State in the procurement of arms and military equipments. These services were rendered as a patriotic duty to the country, and wholly without compensation, and entitle him to the gratitude of the State, and to that of every loyal citizen; and it is further ordered, that the generous act of Mr. Marsh be recorded upon the books of the Council, and that a copy of the record be transmitted to him.

Mr. Marsh was chiefly instrumental, in the succeeding year, in raising and organizing the Forty-seventh Regiment, — nine months' troops, — of which he was commissioned colonel. The regiment was sent to the Department of the Gulf, and served out the time of its enlistment in the defences at New Orleans.

On the twenty-second day of July, 1861, Congress, in extra session, passed an act authorizing the President to accept the services of five hundred thousand volunteers; in which it was provided, that "the President shall, from time to time, issue his proclamation, stating the number desired, and the States from which they are to be furnished, having reference in any such requisition to the number then in service from the several States, and to the exigencies of the service at the time, and equalizing, as far as practicable, the number furnished by the several States, according to the federal population." This act also provided, that the volunteer regiments and companies should be recruited and organized, and the officers commissioned, by the Governors of the several States. Under this authority given by Congress, requisitions continued to be made upon Massachusetts, as upon other States, during the year 1861, and regiments were organized, formed, and sent to the front, in the order stated in the preceding chapter. It was the desire of the Governor to have the regiments commanded by the best educated and most experienced officers he could find. In the selection of company officers, the same care was taken. Political influences to obtain appointments had no effect upon him'; as he frequently declared, that the lives of the soldiers, their health and discipline, depended in a great degree upon the officers who commanded them, and that mere political opinions, and the mere political services of applicants for commissions, properly had no connection with these matters. It was his desire to have as many of the three months' men enlist in the three years' regiments as possible; and, as an encouragement to this end, he telegraphed, on the twenty-second day of June, to Colonel Ritchie, who was then in Washington, "Wouldn't it be expedient for the Massachusetts militia-men now in the service to be discharged, who will enlist in our new volunteer regiments? Many of the Eighth Regiment, I am told, would enlist, if this opportunity were given."

He also telegraphed to the Secretary of War, asking that

Lieutenant Palfrey, of the regular army, stationed at Fortress Monroe, and Lieutenant Paine, of the regular army, stationed at Fort Schuyler, New York, both of whom were Massachusetts men, might be furloughed to accept colonelcies in Massachusetts volunteer regiments. He also telegraphed to Senator Sumner, requesting him to urge Joseph Hooker, afterwards major-general of volunteers, then in Washington without a command, to accept the commission of colonel in one of our regiments. Neither of these requests were granted.

June 24. — Lieutenant William P. Lee, assistant quartermaster-general, was directed to accompany the steamers "Cambridge" and "Pembroke," to Fortress Monroe, as the agent of the Commonwealth, with authority to sell, charter, or make any disposition of the "Pembroke" as he should think best.

On the same day, the Governor wrote a long letter to General Butler, at Fortress Monroe, concerning the Massachusetts troops at that post, under his command; it having been represented to him by Colonel Ritchie, of his staff, who had made a tour of inspection, that the men were suffering for the want of canteens, shoes, and other necessary articles. The letter fills eight pages, and expresses with great freedom the Governor's profound regret that no requisitions had been made, either upon the General Government or upon the State, for articles necessary to the comfort and health of the troops. 'He informs General Butler that he has that day forwarded eight hundred canteens to supply the Massachusetts troops at Fortress Monroe, although no requisition had been made for them by any one, nor proper information received that they were in need of them. He had also been informed by Colonel Ritchie that the men were in want of shoes; but no intimation of the kind had reached him from the officers at Fortress Monroe. It would have been absurd to "have launched out canteens, shoes, or any other articles, upon mere unauthorized rumors of need for them." At the same time, "no properly authenticated requisitions have ever reached me which have not been promptly and amply answered." "In the complicated and unprecedented relation in which this State stands to the Federal Government with regard to supplies," he thought "application for every thing should in the first place be made to the United States." The men were mustered into the United-States service, and were United-States soldiers. When the men were forwarded upon the requisition of the President, the Governor represented that they were deficient in certain necessary equipments: the answer was, "No matter for any deficiencies: only hurry on the men, and any and all deficiencies will be supplied here."

He considered, therefore, that the Federal Government had pledged itself to see our troops properly supplied. He had also received a despatch from General Butler, dated May 20, which said, "The Massachusetts troops are now supplied with all provisions and clothing necessary for their term of service." However, in view of their present wants, the Governor asked him to impress upon the officers, "that if their men need any necessary equipments or provisions whatever, and fail to obtain them from the United States, the State will furnish them."

Colonel Ritchie had also informed the Governor, that there were, at Fortress Monroe, several hundred pairs of thin trousers, which had been condemned as unfit for service, and had not been issued to the soldiers. These were part of a lot of thin clothing sent forward in April, and which were designed to be used during the warm weather. The Governor hoped General Butler would issue them to the troops, as they would serve them during the brief remainder of their term. "Let them," he says, "get what comfort out of them they can. If the United States will not accept the pecuniary responsibility for the cost, then this Commonwealth must defray it. The question who shall pay for them afterwards, is of secondary importance, if our troops need clothes." The Governor also represented that no report had reached him, from any source, of the disposition of the Massachusetts stores sent to our troops at Fortress Monroe, and particularly of the cargo sent by the bark "Aura." He hoped, as a Massachusetts man, having a common interest in the comfort and reputation of Massachusetts soldiers, the General would interest himself in these matters.

On the eighth day of July, the Governor telegraphed to Colonel Dalton, at Washington, that he might sell the steamer "Cambridge" for $80,000, exclusive of her armament.

July 16.— He wrote a long letter to General Butler, protesting against his taking "from the three months' regiments under his command, when about to leave for home, on the expiration of their time of service, the Springfield rifled muskets, which they carried with them, and giving them poor smooth-bores in exchange. The muskets belonged to Massachusetts, and were wanted to arm our three-years' volunteers." The rifled muskets were retained, however, and the men came home with the smooth-bores.

On the same day, he wrote to the Secretary of the Navy in regard to Southern privateers capturing our commerce on the seas, and of the anxiety felt in the mercantile community about them. He urges that stronger measures be taken to seal up the Southern ports, and again offers him the privilege of buying the steamers "Cambridge" and "Pembroke."

The Governor was unable to visit the camp at Taunton, and witness the departure of the Seventh Regiment from the State. He wrote an excuse to Colonel Couch, in which he expressed warmly and sincerely his regrets that business required his presence at the capital. "I am reluctant," he says, "to permit any regiment to depart from Massachusetts without a chance to bid it God-speed, that I was even inclined to delay you for a day or two in order to secure such an opportunity; but, on reflection, it seemed to me unwise to postpone for a mere sentiment your call to active duty. We shall watch your career, and rejoice in your successes with no less eager interest than that with which we followed those regiments which preceded you, and those which are to tread in your footsteps. And to you, personally, I wish to express my thanks for your quiet, considerate, and judicious conduct; and I beg you never to hesitate to call upon Massachusetts, whenever you need, for sympathy and aid."

About the beginning of June, an agent of the loyal people in the city of Wheeling, Va., came to Boston, and represented that they were greatly in need of two thousand muskets, which they could not obtain from the Government, nor from any of the other States. Governor Andrew, aware of the importance of Wheeling as a military point, agreed at once to furnish them, and, on the 19th day of July, telegraphed to Hon. John S. Carlisle, of Wheeling, that they had been forwarded, consigned to Thomas Hemlock, collector of the customs at that place.

July 25. — The Governor telegraphed to Colonel Dalton, at Washington, to find out whether a "company of sharpshooters, for one year or the war, would be accepted, — to be raised in four divisions of twenty-five men each, with four lieutenants and four sergeants. They should have twenty-five dollars a month. Their rifles will cost one hundred dollars each: will the Government pay for them?"

July 27. — The Governor telegraphed to Colonel Dalton, "See Frederick W. Lander, who is reported to be with McClellan; offer him the command of the Seventeenth Regiment, encamped at Lynnfield. Definite and final answer immediately desired."

July 30. — The Governor telegraphed to General Wilson, United States Senate, "I will give Governor S. an Essex regiment, if you are sure of your man. If you say that you are sure, telegraph reply and send him on immediately." This had reference to Governor Stevens, who was a Senator in Congress from Oregon, a man of Massachusetts birth, and an experienced officer. The doubt expressed by Governor Andrew in the despatch arose from the fact that Governor Stevens had supported John C. Breckenridge in the presidential election. From some cause unknown to the writer, Governor Stevens was not commissioned at this time. He was afterwards commissioned colonel of the Seventy-ninth Regiment, New-York Volunteers, and was killed in the second battle of Bull Run.

Aug. 1. — The Governor writes to General Ripley, chief of Ordnance Bureau, that the Massachusetts regiments, armed with the Enfield rifles, want an additional supply of ammunition; and he wishes to know whether the Government "does not intend to supply suitable ammunition; if not, what arrangements it is desirable for Massachusetts to make?"

Aug. 2. — The Governor telegraphs to Senator Wilson, at Washington, "Has any provision been made for half-pay to soldiers' families? Such an arrangement would prevent much suffering this winter."

Aug. 3. — The Governor telegraphs to Senators Sumner and Wilson, "Can it be intended by Congress, that volunteers in the field shall fill vacancies by election? Where is to be the source of discipline, when every candidate is seeking personal favor of the men?"

Aug. 14. — The Governor telegraphs to Governor Washburn, of Maine, "General Sherman left here, this afternoon, for Concord, N.H., intending to proceed thence to Augusta. His business is of importance, which justifies your waiting for him there."

General Sherman came to Boston to confer privately with the Governor, in regard to an expedition contemplated by the Government to the coast of North Carolina. Massachusetts was to furnish three regiments for it; New Hampshire and Maine were also to furnish regiments. General Sherman had commanded a brigade at the first battle of Bull Run, and had distinguished himself as a commanding officer. His subsequent career in the war is known and appreciated by all. The Governor entered warmly into the proposed scheme, and promised him the support he required. Out of this promise grew the subsequent controversy between the Governor and General Butler, to which we shall hereafter refer.

Up to this time, no definite instructions, pointing out the manner of filling vacancies in volunteer regiments after they had left the State, had been received from the War Department. The act of Congress of July 22 appeared to be clear enough, that the vacancies should be filled by appointments made by the Governors of the States; but the action of the War Department for a time appeared to contravene this mode of action. The Governor had written to our Senators in Congress in regard to the subject, but had received no satisfactory reply. Accordingly, on the 16th of August, he wrote to the Adjutant-General of the United States army, at Washington, upon the subject; stating that he was continually embarrassed, from want of information and direction from the military authorities of the

United States upon this important point. He therefore requested minute information. He says, —

"As I understand it, at present, I can appoint to no vacancy which is not officially certified to me by the United States Adjutant-General, from headquarters, at Washington. *But in no single instance has any such vacancy been so certified to me;* and yet I am aware that many such vacancies exist, and I am continually entreated by Massachusetts commanders to make appointments to fill them. Within the past week, I have received notices from Major-General Butler, from Fort Monroe; from Colonels Couch, Cowdin, and Cass, and Lieutenant-Colonel Blaisdell, at Washington; and from Colonel Gordon and Major-General Banks, at Harper's Ferry, — of vacancies existing among the officers of their respective commands, and I am anxious to fill them, if I have the power to do so: for delay in filling them is prejudicial in various ways, which I need not mention."

The letter had the desired effect; and from that time, when a vacancy occurred, the Governor was immediately notified of the fact by the Adjutant-General of the United States, and an appointment made to fill it.

Aug. 17. — The Governor telegraphs to the Secretary of War, "I have unofficial information, that General Fremont is wanting muskets and equipments in Missouri. Massachusetts can and will send him from five to ten thousand, if the Government says so, and will take them at cost price."

On the 20th of August, the Governor published a short and stirring address to "the citizen-soldiers of Massachusetts," calling upon them to fill up the regiments recruiting in the several camps in the State, and to fill the ranks of those in the front which had suffered loss at the battle of Bull Run, a few weeks before. The address closed in these words : "Citizen-soldiers of Massachusetts ! Duty, honor, the clearest sentiments of patriotic love and devotion, call for your hearts and unconquerable arms."

Aug. 30. — The Governor sent General Reed, Quartermaster-General, and Colonel Browne, his private secretary, to Washington, with instructions to arrange for the settlement of Massachusetts claims against the Government for money and stores furnished by the State. Among the results of this mission was the payment in cash, by the Government, of seven hundred and seventy-five thousand dollars. An elaborate and carefully matured system was also devised for the adoption and payment, by the Federal Government, of future contracts for military stores. These gentlemen were furnished with letters by the Governor to the President and members of the Cabinet.

Aug. 31. — Governor telegraphs Colonel Frank E. Howe, New York, "Find George S. Greene, late of the United-States Engineer Corps, and see if he will take command of a Massachusetts regiment." On the same day, the Governor wrote a letter to the Secretary of War, in regard to the high prices paid for provisions by the Government here, and concerning dishonest practices in the purchase of shoes; and, at his request, Senator Wilson, who was at the State House, sent the following telegram to the Secretary: "Pay especial attention to a letter you will receive from Governor Andrew and the Commissary-General of Massachusetts (Colonel Brigham), relative to the cost of rations here to the United-States troops. The Government is paying much more than the State does for the same article. It is reported here, on good authority, that army shoes condemned by inspectors in New York are sold again to contractors, who are permitted to fill their contracts with them. A competent inspector should be appointed here, to see that comdemned shoes are not sold again."

Sept. 2. — Governor wrote to Governor Curtin, of Pennsylvania, —

"I have read, with great interest and pleasure, the copy of your communication of the 21st ult. to the President of the United States, which you were kind enough to send me, and in which you have so thoroughly exposed the evils resulting from the interference of the War Department with the regular, legal mode of organizing regiments of volunteers.

"In common with Pennsylvania, Massachusetts has suffered much loss of enthusiasm, and great inconvenience, from those irregularities of which you so justly complain: but I trust we may congratulate ourselves, that this source of trouble is to be dried up at the fountain-head; as I have received the most positive assurance from the Secretary of War, that, in future, no outside interference with the regularly constituted authorities of the State will be permitted, and that persons holding commissions from the War Department, authorizing them to raise regiments of volunteers, will be required to report to, and take orders from, the executive departments of the States.

"Hopeful and confident, in these eventful days, that all will yet be well with the republic, I have the honor to remain your obedient servant."

When we come to speak of recruiting in Massachusetts by General Butler, which began about this time, we shall find that the confident hope expressed by the Governor, that the State authorities should not again be interfered with, proved wholly delusive.

On the 26th of August, the Adjutant-General wrote to Mr. Seward, Secretary of State, that he had reliable information, that five schooners had arrived at Halifax, N.S., — having run the blockade in North Carolina, — and had landed fourteen hundred barrels of turpentine. They were loading again with merchandise, intending to run the blockade on their return home. The names of the vessels were given, and two of them were captured on their return voyage. The following telegram, dated Sept. 3, we copy from the Governor's files: Senator Wilson to Mr. Seward, — "Is your consul at Halifax thoroughly loyal? Four vessels from North Carolina have recently arrived there, loaded with naval stores, and are now loading with contraband goods." Same day, Governor writes to General Lander, "Will you please look out for the welfare of Captain Sanders's company of sharpshooters, which will this day march almost from under the shadow of your own roof-tree, in the county of Essex?" This splendid company was recruited at "Camp Schouler," Lynnfield. Captain Sanders was killed in battle, Sept. 17, 1862.

Sept. 10. — Governor writes to the selectmen of Wellfleet, acknowledging the receipt of five hundred dollars, raised in that town for the benefit of the families of soldiers.

Sept. 11. — Governor writes to Major-General John A. Dix, commanding at Baltimore, "Pray do not execute private Stephen C. Scott, of our Sixteenth Regiment, until you have given his friends an opportunity to be heard; for I have every reason to believe the man has been for a long time crazy. Besides, Colonel Wyman promised his friends the case should be delayed until all the evidence on either side can be collected." The man was crazy. He was sentenced to be hung for killing a comrade: he was pardoned and discharged from the service.

It was represented to the Governor by Patrick Donahoe, Esq., of Boston, that the religious opinions of some of the Catholic soldiers in one of our regiments had been interfered with by the officers. The Governor wrote to Mr. Donahoe, saying, "I am utterly surprised by the intimation you make. I will cause our Adjutant-General to pursue a strict inquiry into this subject immediately." After expressing his views of religious toleration, he says, "Those who serve God according to their convictions, are not likely to fear man, or offend against the rights of others."

A paragraph appeared in the Boston Morning Post, reflecting upon a part of the Governor's personal staff, which caused him to address a private letter, on the 16th of September, to the editors of that paper, showing how unjust it was, and how laborious and useful their gratuitous services had been.

"In all these," he said, "my staff *help* me, — not deciding nor establishing any thing, but investigating, arranging, reporting and sometimes executing, — always modest, loyal, disinterested, respectful to others, and most capable and efficient.

"And the least duty *I* can do is to ask that *they* may not be rewarded by sarcasm or unkind remark.

"*Whatever is rightly done may be credited to any one; but whatever is deemed worthy of blame, charge it to me, not to them.* I am in truth responsible, acting often against their opinions and advice, and feeling at all times perfectly willing to meet whatever may fall thereon, — conscious of no merit of any sort, save a good intent. Excuse this note, — one I should not have written, but to gentlemen of urbanity who will appreciate the feelings of a gentleman in others."

Sept. 17. — The Governor wrote to the Secretary of War, calling his attention to the delay on his request for the transfer of three Massachusetts companies in the New-York Mozart Regiment, to be sent to Fortress Monroe, to be attached to the seven Massachusetts companies there, and the ten to form a regiment. It was a matter that ought to have been immediately attended to; for while the companies remained in the New-York regiment, and were credited to the quota of that State, the families of the men were deprived of the benefits of the Massachusetts State-aid law, which would amount to them, in the aggregate, to one hundred and forty-four thousand dollars a year. The subject was presented with much force by the Governor; but the transfer never was made, and the families were deprived of the State-aid until the following winter, when the Legislature amended the State-aid act, so as to include them in its provisions.

Sept. 18. — The Governor wrote to General Stetson, of the Astor House, acknowledging the receipt of fragments of the flag taken by Colonel Ellsworth, at Alexandria, and of that which waved over Fort Pickens, while commanded by Lieutenant Slemmer, U.S.A. These were placed among the military relics and trophies, side by side with mementoes of Lexington, Bunker Hill, and Bennington.

Sept. 19. — The Governor telegraphed to Governor Dennison, of Ohio, "Five thousand infantry equipments sent forward to day, as directed."

Sept. 20. — He received the following telegram from Joshua R. Giddings, American Consul, at Montreal, Canada.

"John Bateman, a major in the rebel army, bearer of despatches to Europe, and now returning, will be at the Revere House this evening. He is five feet nine or ten inches in height, dark complexion, dark hair, wears a moustache, and has the evidence of guilt on his person. I have also telegraphed Mr. Seward."

This was placed in the hands of John S. Keyes, United-States Marshal for this district. Major Bateman, however, did not come to Boston, but went by another route to Nova Scotia, and sailed in the steamer from Halifax to England. Marshal Keyes writes, "This was only one of the thousand instances of Governor Andrew's active efforts in the good cause."

Sept. 21. — The Governor telegraphs to Secretary Seward, "Large quantities of shoes are shipped from this city to

Louisville, Ky., and Baltimore, Md., intended for the rebel army. Cannot a stop be put to it?"

Sept. 28. — The Governor writes to Senator Wilson to "recommend James Magner as a first lieutenant in the Twenty-second Regiment, that he might be commissioned, and detailed on the staff of General Sherman." This was not done; but Magner was afterwards commissioned a lieutenant in the Twenty-eighth Regiment, and was killed in battle, May 18, 1864.

Oct. 1. — The Governor writes to Colonel Frank E. Howe. New York, "What has become of General Sherman? I have not heard from him for some days. Does he wish Wilson's regiment to go with him? The regiment is expected to leave on the 3d." On the same day, he writes to General Scott, —

"It is my desire that the regiment under Colonel Wilson shall form a part of the force of General Sherman, but I am not advised whether the battery attached to the regiment is desired for that especial service; and, as I have no positive recent information of the present location of General Sherman's camp, I await orders from you.

"There seems to be no diminution of the zeal or the patriotism of the people of Massachusetts; and I am happy in being able to report to you that all our regiments are in a fair way to be speedily filled to the maximum standard."

Oct. 3. — The Governor telegraphs to the proprietors of the Stevens House, New York, "Is General Sherman in New York? if so, ask him if he wants the Massachusetts battery that will arrive there to-morrow."

Oct. 7. — The Governor issues another address to the people of Massachusetts, urging them to assist, with all their power, recruiting for our regiments in the Commonwealth, and asking the citizens to forward to Boston, without delay, such blankets and underclothing, for our soldiers at the seat of war, as their means will admit of. Quartermaster-General Reed also addressed a letter to the Presidents of the Massachusetts railroads, inquiring if they would pass over their several roads without charge, during the next two weeks, such contributions as might be received. An immense quantity of blankets and underclothing was received in response to the call, and forwarded without delay to the front.

The Governor telegraphs to the Secretary of War, "Shall Wilson's regiment go to Old Point Comfort by sea from New York, as General Sherman requests by telegram just received?"

The same day, he telegraphs to General Scott, "A sufficient guard shall be placed at Fort Warren at any moment we are directed. If a force specially organized shall not be ready at that time, the Cadets, who constitute the Governor's body-guard, will act in the mean while."

The same day, he telegraphs to General Sherman, at New York, "Wilson's regiment starts to-morrow for Washington. He is directed to see you in New York, and take such other orders as may be given."

A sworn statement having been forwarded to the Governor, making serious charges against the quartermaster of the Fifteenth Regiment, the Governor sent it to Colonel Devens, with directions to make an investigation of the charges. In the letter, he says, "I am determined that no dishonest officer shall hold a commission for any length of time, after the full proof is furnished to me which establishes his guilt; and I feel quite sure, that, in this view of my official duties, I shall have your hearty support and co-operation." The charges were not sustained.

The Governor, at this time, visited Washington, where he had gone to arrange about the payment of Massachusetts claims, and did not return until the twenty-second day of October. He was successful in making arrangements for payment.

Oct. 23. — The Governor writes to Hon. David Sears, of Boston, thanking him for his offer to place the large hall in Liberty-tree Block at the disposal of the Executive, as a place of deposit for articles for the soldiers.

The battle of Ball's Bluff was fought Oct. 21. The Fifteenth and Twentieth Massachusetts Regiments were engaged in it. They behaved with great gallantry, and suffered severely, especially the Twentieth. On the 25th, Lieutenant-Colonel Palfrey telegraphed, "Colonel Lee, Major Revere, Adjutant Peirson, Dr. Revere, and Lieutenant Perry, prisoners; Lieutenants

Babo and Wesselhœft, probably drowned; Lieutenant S. W. Putnam, killed; Captains Dreher, Schmitt, Putnam, Lieutenants Lowell and Holmes, wounded, — not fatally. All other officers safe, including myself. Captains Dreher and Schmitt, badly wounded, — probably not fatally. Captain Putnam's right arm gone, — doing well. Lowell and Holmes doing very well."

This disastrous battle carried grief into many of our Massachusetts families, and depressed the buoyant and patriotic spirit of our people for a time. Its effect upon the country was also unfavorable. Nothing had occurred, since the battle of Bull Run, in July, which so disappointed the expectations and saddened the hearts of loyal people. A distrust was felt of the loyalty and military capacity of some of the high army officers. In many quarters, the Administration was blamed for our ill luck, and want of success. It was at this trying hour that the Governor wrote this splendid letter: —

BOSTON, Oct. 30, 1861.

HON. J. D. ANDREWS, Washington, D.C.

MY DEAR SIR, — I trust you will attribute my non-reply to your letters before this moment to the pressure of employment, and not to inadvertence or neglect.

I fear and feel sometimes in the spirit of your own state of mind, as given in your correspondence; but still I prefer not to lose faith in any one, much less in those in whom I have heartily confided, and to whom belongs the wielding of the national power. I see great proofs of energy and of skill. I also see tokens of slowness, both of sight and of insight. States falter, which should be firm. Counsels cross each other, which should combine, and bear up together.

O God! for a Cameronian battle-cry; for a grand, inspiring, electric shout, coming from the high priests themselves, from the very Jerusalem of our cause! I wait to hear it, and believe it will yet burst forth, and ring in all our ears. This people must be *welded* together with the fire itself, both of the spirit and the flesh. They must turn their backs upon the possibility of compromise; devote themselves to the labor and pains of this grand conflict of Western civilization; combine heartily in the industries, economics, and enterprises of public and social material life, and in the devoted and daring efforts of war. Every drop of blood shed by our braves will be avenged, not by the cruelty of savage warriors, but by the stern resolve of Christians, patriots, and philanthropists, who soon will understand the barbarism of our foes, and will know what price to ask for the lives of those who fall.

How many of our noblest and bravest shall give their blood for the ransom of a subject race, the redemption of their country's peace, and the final security of her honor and integrity?

Yours always, J. A. ANDREW.

Captain Schmitt, who is mentioned as having been wounded, was an instructor at Harvard College. We well remember the day he came to the Adjutant-General's office, accompanied by two young gentlemen, — Mr. Putnam and Mr. Lowell, one of whom was killed at Ball's Bluff, and the other wounded, — for leave to raise a company for the Twentieth Regiment. Leave was granted, the company was raised, and the three gentlemen were commissioned officers of it. Putnam and Lowell were cousins, and belonged to distinguished families. Lieutenant Putnam, we thought then, and think now, was, in style, manner, and features, a youth of rare beauty. The writer little thought then, that, in a few short months, he would attend his funeral ceremonies, which were performed in the old church on Cambridge Street, of which his grandfather, Dr. Charles Lowell, had been the pastor for half a century. But the paths of glory lead but to the grave. As an evidence among the thousand which might be given of Governor Andrew's kind regard for the soldiers and their relatives, we copy the following letter, written to the father of Captain Schmitt, while the son was lying wounded in hospital, near the banks of the Potomac: —

Oct. 29, 1861.

To Mr. MICHAEL SCHMITT, teacher at Versback, near Würzburg, Bavaria.

MY DEAR SIR, — The Twentieth Regiment of Massachusetts Volunteers, in which your son is a captain, formed part of a detachment of Federal troops, which, on the 21st inst., crossed the Potomac, some thirty miles above Washington, and had an engagement with the enemy. The latter, being far superior in numbers, and having a more favorable position, compelled our troops to retreat, after they had fought with a bravery unsurpassed by that of the best troops of either hemisphere. Your son was severely, but not mortally, wounded; and from one of my aides-de-camp, whom I have sent to the spot to see that no duty or care is neglected towards the wounded of our regiments, I received, last Sunday, a despatch, stating that your son, with some of his wounded fellow-officers, is cheerful, and doing well, and is expected soon to recover.

While I take occasion to communicate to you this afflicting information, I, at the same time, have pleasure in congratulating you upon the bravery of your son, which has enrolled his name upon the list of American heroes.

I remain truly your friend, JOHN A. ANDREW,
Governor of the Commonwealth of Massachusetts.

Oct. 31.

The news received concerning the condition of your son, up to this day, continues to be equally favorable to his sure recovery.

J. A. A.

Nov. 5. — The Governor writes to A. H. Bullock, at Worcester, forwarding to him a check from A. D. and J. G. Smith & Co., Providence, R.I., for one hundred dollars, payable to his order; fifty dollars to be expended for the soldiers of the Fifteenth, and fifty dollars for the soldiers of the Twentieth Regiment, — the two which had been engaged in the battle of Ball's Bluff.

Nov. 6. — The Governor writes to Surgeon Galloupe, of the Seventeenth Regiment, acknowledging the receipt of one of Ross Winans's pikes, made by him at Baltimore for the rebels, and says, "It will find a place among the other *souvenirs* of the war in Massachusetts. At present, it finds a place over the portrait in the Council Chamber of Rev. Mr. Higginson, one of the earliest clergymen of Salem, whose ghost must be astonished at the strange incongruity." On the same day, he writes to Colonel Palfrey, of the Twentieth, "Please write to me at once the facts concerning the young man now under arrest for sleeping on his post, as you understand them. I believe that he has always been subject to turns of fainting, and losing his consciousness, when suffering from fatigue, excitement, and exposure. Please see that he suffers no harm, until I can procure and forward the evidence."

No one in the Massachusetts regiments was too high or too humble to elude the vigilance, the watchful care and sympathy, of Governor Andrew. This was plainly visible throughout his entire official life. On the 25th of November, he wrote to the President of the United States, recalling to his mind an interview he had with him, when in Washington a few weeks before, in which he had advocated the policy of an exchange of prisoners. No action having been taken by the Government on the question, he wrote about it to the President. He was confident of the justice and expediency of making an exchange : it would be both convenient and humane. The letter concludes, "I earnestly hope that immediate measures may be taken to effect exchanges, and that the hearts of the people may not be sickened by hope deferred."

About this time, a private conference was held in this city, by some of our most practical, experienced, and influential business men, favoring an armed expedition to Texas. The Governor entered warmly into the scheme, and, on the 27th of November, wrote to Captain G. V. Fox, Assistant Secretary of the Navy, calling his attention to the subject, and drawing an outline of the objects to be gained. A demonstration was to be made on the coast of Texas. The force, when landed, was to proclaim martial law, and, when the proper time arrived, to free all the slaves, "compensating loyal owners if necessary." The results would be, first, we flank the entire rebellion ; second, we open a way for cotton ; third, we cut off future annexations in the interests of rebels, and demonstrate to foreign nations that this war is to stop the spread of slavery ; fourth, it would prevent loyal men from leaving Texas, and would encourage foreign emigration, and would demonstrate that cotton can be raised without slaves ; finally, it would "leave the question of slavery in the cotton States for philosophical treatment, unless it becomes necessary to settle it under the war power before the present war is ended." The letter concludes as follows : —

"These points are urged, not in the interests of abolitionists, but by leading commercial men and capitalists, as fairly coming under the necessities and rules of war. Martial law proclaimed, events will no doubt educate the people and the next Congress to a wise solution of all the questions which may afterwards arise in connection with slaves and slavery, in an exceptional State or dependency like Texas.

By such seizure and treatment of Texas as is briefly indicated above, it is urged, that we shall have, at the end of the war, material guaranties that will prevent any such compromise or settlement as to make a renewal of the struggle for ascendency, or another rebellion, possible."

A copy of the letter was sent to some friends of the Governor in New York and Washington, including the Postmaster-General, Montgomery Blair, to whom the Governor wrote, "I believe that the subject will be of interest to you, and that you will be pleased to say the right word at the proper time, in furtherance of some such measure as I have indicated." Of all the Cabinet officers, Mr. Blair appears to have been the one on whose judgment, influence, and activity he relied the most to advance his views of policy upon the Administration.

On the same day, the Governor wrote to Senator Wilson, suggesting that Congress offer a bounty of twenty-five dollars to raw recruits in new regiments, and double that sum to soldiers who will serve in regiments in the field.

On the 2d of December, he acknowledged, with thanks, the receipt of twenty-seven hundred and eighty-seven dollars, raised by voluntary subscription among the mechanics employed in the Charlestown Navy Yard. Commodore Hudson and Charles Field paid the money to the Governor. It was to be used "for the relief of poor and dependent families of volunteers in the military service of the United States."

During the month of December, information reached the Governor, that an order had been issued by Brigadier-General Stone, U.S.A., in command near Pottsville, Md., giving a description of two fugitive slaves, and directing, should they appear in camp, that they be arrested and returned to their owners. On Sunday morning, as usual, several negroes came into the camp of our Twentieth Regiment to sell cakes and fruits to the soldiers. Among the negroes who visited the camp were two who answered the description of the fugitives named in General Stone's order. They were immediately arrested. "A file of soldiers, under a sergeant, with loaded muskets, was sent to escort them to their supposed owners, and deliver them up." That Massachusetts soldiers should be employed to catch and return fugitive slaves, sorely vexed the Governor, who immediately wrote to Lieutenant-Colonel Palfrey against Massachusetts men being employed in such duty. He also wrote a long letter to Secretary Cameron, protesting against the practice. He said, "I invoke your interposition, not only now, but for the future, for the issue of such orders as will secure the soldiers of this Commonwealth from being participators in such dirty and despotic work." This letter he enclosed in another to Senator Sumner, with a request that he would read it, and hand it to the Secretary of War, and that he, Mr. Sumner, " would co-operate with him in his efforts to protect the soldiers of Massachusetts from being made the bloodhounds of slavery in obedience to the iniquitous and illegal orders of brigadier-generals, and others in the interest of the slave power." The War Department took no immediate action upon this particular case. Mr. Sumner brought it before the Senate, and denounced in strong language the order of General Stone, which drew from that officer a letter equally denunciatory of the Senator, and an implied challenge to a duel. Mr. Sumner took no notice of either. But the matter did not end here. On the thirtieth day of December, the Governor wrote a long letter to Major-General McClellan, in reply to a letter from Brigadier-General Stone, which had been forwarded and apparently approved by General McClellan, in which the order issued by General Stone, directing the arrest of the fugitives, is defended, and an attempt is made to belittle the State of Massachusetts, and in which he speaks of the "usurpations of these ambitious State authorities." It also speaks of the *soldiers* of the Twentieth Regiment being "enlisted in the service of the United States, in the State of which the Governor referred to is the respected chief magistrate; but this gives him no right to assume control of the internal discipline of the regiment." The Governor gives the General to understand that the regiment was recruited in Massachusetts, that the soldiers were Massachusetts men, that they were provided with every kind of equipment, including Enfield rifles, every thing "down to shoestrings and tent-pins," all of which was furnished by the State, and paid for by the State, that the officers were commissioned by him, "the colonel of the regiment was Colonel William Raymond Lee, an army officer, and graduate of West Point, now a prisoner in a felon's cell at Richmond. I would to Heaven he were back now, or that the Army of the Potomac were hammering at his prison-door with both hands, and neither hand averted to protect the institution which is the cause of all this woe." The Governor disclaimed any intention to "assume control of the interior discipline of the regiment." His purpose was to prevent Massachusetts soldiers from being used, contrary to law, to catch and return fugitive slaves. He was sorry "to perceive in the conduct of Brigadier-General Stone a levity of mind which does not appreciate the responsibility of the grave duties with which the power of appointment charges the officer in whom it is vested." This appears to have been the end of the correspondence. General Stone was afterwards imprisoned in Fort Lafayette, by order of the Secretary of War, Mr. Stanton; but the charges upon which the arrest was made have never been made public.

The inhuman treatment by the rebel authorities of the Massachusetts officers and soldiers taken prisoners at Ball's Bluff, caused the Governor, on the 16th of December, to write another letter to the President, upon the necessity of organizing a *system* for the mutual exchange of prisoners. A large portion of the prisoners in the hands of the rebels belonged to this State; and he urged upon the President to interpose for their immediate relief. He contrasts the cruel treatment of our men at Richmond with the humane treatment of rebel prisoners in Fort Warren.

"I am informed, from trustworthy sources, that our soldiers who are prisoners of war at Richmond are neither well fed nor well clothed, and they are subjected to the most rigid military surveillance, and occasionally exposed to the insulting language and demeanor of the populace of that city. Some of their number — among whom I may mention Colonel Lee and Major Revere, of the Massachusetts Twentieth Infantry, and Captains Bowman and Rockwood, of the Massachusetts Fifteenth (all of them gentlemen and soldiers, who have no superiors, in any sphere of human life, in all those qualities which ought to command respectful treatment) — are imprisoned in felon's cells, fed on felon's fare, in a common jail; huddled together in a space so narrow that there is not air enough for health or comfort; allowed, for exercise, to promenade half an hour each day on a narrow pathway surrounding their prison; and especially exposed to disease, by the fact, that some of their companions, who are grievously sick, are not removed to hospitals, but are left to share the same privations, and breathe the same foul air, with those whose physical vigor is not yet broken.

"In contrast, allow me to state, that the prisoners at Fort Warren are allowed certainly equal fare with the garrison, which consists of five companies of loyal Massachusetts troops, and are permitted all liberties consistent with retaining them upon the island; and that traitors, like Mr. Mason, of Virginia, and Mr. Slidell, of Louisiana, whose hands are red with the best blood of Massachusetts, are treated with *certainly equal* consideration (as to quarters, fare, and attendance, and all privileges consistent with retaining them in custody) with the officers of that loyal battalion. These facts and this contrast, sir, are sickening to many of our people, and are especially painful to those who are closely related, by friendship or blood, to our prisoners in the hands, and at the mercy, of the rebels. I submit to you, with the utmost respect, whether it is just or decent, that the contrast should continue. I urge no inhumanity towards even traitors. If we are at war with cannibals, that is no reason why we should eat human flesh ourselves; but it is a reason why we should spare no effort to rescue our brothers from the hands of such savages, lest they become their victims."

We now turn from these unpleasant subjects to others of a more agreeable character, which close the general correspondence of the Executive for the year 1861.

On the twenty-sixth day of December, the Governor received a letter from the Executive Committee of the Soldiers' Relief Society of San Francisco, Cal., dated Nov. 30, enclosing a draft for two thousand dollars upon Messrs. Duncan, Sherman, & Co., New York, the proceeds of which were to be distributed "among the wives, the children, the sisters and brothers, of the patriotic citizen-soldiers of Massachusetts." In acknowledgment of which, the Governor wrote a grateful and patriotic answer, which concludes by saying, that the "Hon. Francis B. Fay, the present Mayor of Chelsea, and George W. Bond, Esq., an eminent merchant of this city, — both gentlemen of the highest integrity, large experience, and humane sympathies, — will co-operate with me in the proper bestowal of the bounty of your association, in connection with the bestowal of a similar fund received for like purposes from other sources." The names of the San Francisco Executive Committee were Messrs. Frank B. Austin & Co., Moses Ellis, James P. Hunt, Aaron Holmes, William V. Welles, C. H. Sherman, William B. Swayne, and F. B. Folger.

Another pleasant and gratifying event, which closed this remarkable year in the history of Massachusetts, was the liberal and humane action of the Legislature of Maryland, which is best explained by publishing the correspondence entire: —

LEGISLATURE OF MARYLAND, HOUSE OF DELEGATES,
ANNAPOLIS, December, 1861.

His Excellency JOHN A. ANDREW, Governor of Massachusetts.

DEAR SIR, — The Committee on Militia have instructed me, as their chairman, to carry out an order passed by the House, a few days since, and referred to them, — to confer with you, and learn the condition of the widows and orphans, or any dependants on those patriots who were so brutally murdered in the riot of the 19th of April.

In obedience to that order, it gives me great pleasure to state, that the loyal people of Maryland, and especially of the city of Baltimore, after long suffering, are at length able, through a Union Legislature, to put themselves in a proper relation to the Government and the country.

In effecting the latter, they feel their first duty is to Massachusetts. They are anxious to wipe out the foul blot of the Baltimore riot, as far as it can be wiped out, and as soon as possible.

You will do us a great favor, therefore, by instituting an immediate inquiry into the condition of those who were dependent for support upon the services of those unfortunates, and by informing me, at your earliest convenience, of the result of your inquiry. I should be obliged to you, also, if you would designate what, in your opinion, would be the best manner of applying an appropriation to be made for that purpose.

Any suggestions you may make will be kindly received, and meet with proper consideration.

With many prayers, which I know I offer in common with you, that this unrighteous rebellion may be brought to a speedy close, I am

Your Excellency's obedient servant,

JOHN F. L. FINDLEY.

This letter was received by the Governor on the twenty-second day of December, the anniversary of the landing of the Pilgrims at Plymouth, which is referred to in the text.

Dec. 22, 1861.

To Hon. John F. L. Findley, Chairman of a Committee on Militia of the House of Delegates of the State of Maryland.

My dear Sir, — It is with feelings which I will not attempt to express that I have received, on this anniversary day, your letter, addressed to me from Annapolis.

I immediately addressed the Mayors of the cities of Lowell and Lawrence on the subject of your inquiries, and hope to be able to transmit their answers at an early day.

The past cannot be forgotten; but it can be and will be forgiven; and, in the good providence of God, I believe that the day is not distant, when the blood that was shed at Baltimore, by those martyrs to a cause as holy as any for which sword was ever drawn, shall be known to have cemented, in an eternal union of sympathy, affection, and nationality, the sister States of Maryland and Massachusetts.

With sincere regard, I have the honor to be, faithfully and respectfully, yours, JOHN A. ANDREW.

By direction of the Governor, a list of the killed and wounded on the 19th of April was prepared, and inquiries made in regard to the families and relatives of the men by the Adjutant-General, which information was subsequently transmitted to the Governor, and by him to Mr. Findley.

The Legislature of Maryland made an appropriation of seven thousand dollars, and transmitted it to the Governor, and, by him and the Executive Council, it was distributed among the families of the fallen, and to the wounded who survived. This was a most gracious act, and did much to remove the bitterness and ill feeling entertained by the people of the Commonwealth towards the city of Baltimore and the State of Maryland, for the blood of Massachusetts men, shed on their soil.

The people in the State were a unit in support of the war. The officers and enlisted men of the regiments were composed of all parties. In the selection of men to be commissioned, politics were never regarded. It was the desire of a large portion of the Republican party, that, in the nomination of a State ticket in the election in November, representative men of both the Republican and Democratic parties should be placed upon it. The Republican Convention met at Worcester, on the first day of October, of which Hon. Henry L. Dawes was chosen President. On taking the chair, he made an eloquent speech, in which he recommended that a liberal policy be pursued in making nominations, and carrying on the war. He paid a well-deserved tribute to the Boston Morning Post, the leading Democratic paper in the New-England States, for its patriotic course in sustaining the Government, and said, —

"It was fitting, therefore, as it was patriotic, for the organ of that party in this Commonwealth to summon, as it has, to this council the representatives of all her 'citizens who are in favor of union for the support of the Government, and for a vigorous prosecution of the war against wicked and unprovoked rebellion; and who are determined, in good faith and without reservation, to support the constituted authorities in all attempts to restore the sway of the Constitution and laws over every portion of our country.' [Applause.] . . . We are here, in the presence of the public peril, ready to sink, more than hitherto, the partisan in the patriot: counting it honor, as well as duty, to lock arms with such glorious patriots as the noble Holt [applause], working at the pumps, whoever is at the helm; the bold and unflinching Johnson [applause], nailing his flag to the mast; and the peerless Everett [applause], sounding the clarion-notes of his stirring eloquence along the ranks of the army of the Union, from the ocean to the perilous front of the war, on the dark and bloody ground of Kentucky or the battle-fields of Missouri."

This speech was the key-note to the convention. When Mr. Dawes concluded his speech, John A. Andrew was nominated by acclamation, and without opposition, for re-election. A motion was then made to have a ballot for Lieutenant-Governor. Thomas Russell, Esq., of Boston, moved to amend the motion, that a committee of two from each congressional district be appointed to report nominations for the other officers to the convention. He said, "We have come here to lock arms with Holt and Dickinson and Butler and Frothingham and Greene, and we have got to do it in some practical way." This amendment was carried, and a committee appointed, which subsequently reported, for Lieutenant-Governor, Edward Dickinson, of Amherst; for Secretary of State, Richard Frothingham, of Charlestown; for Treasurer, Henry K. Oliver, of Salem;

for Auditor, Levi Reed, of Abington; and for Attorney-General, Dwight Foster, of Worcester. Mr. Dickinson had been, in former years, a Whig; in later years, he was what was called a Conservative. He never had joined the Republican party. Mr. Frothingham had always been a Democrat, of the straightest sect; and was, at this time, one of the editors of the Boston Post. Mr. Oliver, Mr. Reed, and Mr. Foster were Republicans, and incumbents of the offices for which they had been renominated. On taking the vote upon the report of the committee, Mr. Frothingham failed of a nomination; the incumbent of the office, Oliver Warner, being the choice of the convention. The opposition to Mr. Frothingham was led by Mr. Moses Kimball, of Boston, who quoted part of an article from the Boston Post, of that morning, asking the convention "to drop such extreme men as Governor Andrew, and some of his associates, in the executive departments," in making up a new State ticket. The authorship of the article was attributed by Mr. Kimball to Mr. Frothingham. The effect on the convention answered the purpose of the gentleman who made use of it. Before the vote was taken upon the report, Richard H. Dana, Jr., of Cambridge, replied to Mr. Kimball. He said, "We are engaged in a struggle which the world has never seen equalled, either in its importance or its results; we have got beyond Wilmot Provisos and Dred Scott decisions; we have got to fight for the existence of the country. Let us rise above all personal prejudices, and nominate a ticket as men determined to serve the country; we are met here to send throughout the Union, and to the enemies of our institutions abroad, that the pattern Commonwealth is taking the lead in this crisis."

A motion was then made by Mr. Russell, of Boston, to substitute the name of Hon. Josiah G. Abbott, of Lowell, for Attorney-General, in place of Mr. Foster's name. This motion was sustained by the mover, and by Mr. Usher, of Medford; and opposed by Mr. A. H. Bullock, of Worcester. Mr. Dana, of Cambridge, said "he could not see his duty in any other way than by placing a Democrat upon the ticket. The rejection of Mr. Frothingham involved a reconstruction of the ticket." He paid a high compliment to Mr. Foster; but, for public reasons, would vote for Mr. Abbott. Mr. Abbott was nominated, by a vote of 286 to 239. This created much excitement and ill feeling in the convention, which, however, was soon allayed by Mr. Foster himself, who arose, amid great applause, and said, "it would give him great satisfaction to have placed upon the ticket any distinguished gentleman of his profession, like Judge Abbott, of different politics from himself, if, in the least degree, the harmony of the people of Massachusetts can be promoted, and if the national Administration can be sustained in the vigorous prosecution of the war. He hoped, therefore, his friends would join with him in the hope that the nomination of Judge Abbott would be made unanimous." [Cheers.]

The convention adjourned, having placed on the State ticket a "Conservative" for Lieutenant-Governor, and a Democrat for Attorney-General. Subsequently, both declined to be candidates; and their places were filled with John Nesmith, of Lowell, for Lieutenant-Governor, and Dwight Foster for Attorney-General.

The marked feature of the convention, however, was the speech of Hon. Charles Sumner, which, at the time, gave much offence to the convention, and to the Republican majority in the State. The offence was caused by his open advocacy of proclaiming freedom to the slaves, and using colored men as soldiers in the armies of the Union. He said, —

"Look at the war as you will, and you will always see slavery. Never were the words of the Roman orator more applicable, — *Nullum facinus exstitit nisi per te; nullum flagitium sine te.* ' No guilt, unless through thee; no crime without thee.' Slavery is its inspiration, its motive power, its end and aim, its be-all and end-all. It is often said, the war will make an end of slavery. This is probable; but it is surer still, that the overthrow of slavery will at once make an end of the war.

"If I am correct in this statement, which I believe is beyond question, then do justice, reason, and policy all unite that the war must be brought to bear directly on the grand conspirator and omnipresent enemy, which is slavery. Not to do this is to take upon ourselves, in the present contest, all the weakness of slavery, while we leave to the rebels its boasted resources of military strength. Not to do this is to squander life and treasure on a vain masquerade of battle, which can reach no practical result. Believe me, fellow-citizens, I know all the imagined difficulties and unquestioned responsibilities of the suggestion. But, if you are in earnest, the difficulties will at once disappear, and the responsibilities are such as you will gladly bear. This is not the first time that a knot hard to untie has been cut by the sword, and we all know that danger flies before the brave man. Believe that you can, and you can. The will only is needed. Courage now is the highest prudence. It is not necessary even, according to a familiar phrase, to carry the war into Africa: it will be enough if we carry Africa into the war, in any form, any quantity, any way. The moment this is done, rebellion will begin its bad luck, and the Union will be secure for ever."

The speech further elaborated these points. The resolutions which were reported to the convention made no mention, even remotely, of slavery, either as the cause of the war, or of its overthrow as a means of ending it. The only idea advanced in them was, that the purpose we had was to "put down armed rebellion," that "no rights secured by the Constitution to loyal citizens or States of the Union in any section ought to be infringed, and that rebels in arms against the Government can have no rights inconsistent with those of loyal citizens, which that Government is bound to respect." The whole tenor and purpose of the resolutions were to ignore the question of slavery, and to bring about a political union of men of all parties in the State. Such being the views of the convention, the speech of Mr. Sumner was regarded with disfavor. Rev. James Freeman Clarke, a delegate from Boston, offered two resolutions, which had a bearing towards sustaining the position taken by Mr. Sumner; but they failed to receive the approval of the convention. The first expressed confidence "in the wisdom of the national Administration," and that Massachusetts was ready to give of its blood and treasure to answer its calls; "yet, believing that slavery is the root and cause of this Rebellion, they will rejoice when the time shall come, in the wisdom of the Government, to remove this radical source of our present evils." The second declared, that, "when the proper time shall arrive, the people of Massachusetts will welcome any act, under the war power of the commander-in-chief, which shall declare all the slaves within the lines of our armies to be free, and accept their services in defence of the Union, compensating all loyal owners for slaves thus emancipated, and thus carrying liberty for all human beings wherever the stars and stripes shall float."

It is plain, that the Republican party of Massachusetts at this time, so far as its opinions were foreshadowed by the convention, did not favor the abolition of or interference with slavery. When charged with favoring such doctrines by the press of the opposition, the Boston Daily Advertiser of Oct. 4, three days after the convention was held, utterly disclaimed them. In its leading editorial it said, —

"The convention certainly disavowed any intention of indorsing the fatal doctrines announced by Mr. Sumner, with a distinctness that can be hardly flattering to that gentleman's conception of his own influence in Massachusetts. The resolutions offered by Rev. Mr. Clarke, as a crucial test of the readiness of the convention to adopt open abolitionism as its creed, went to the table, and were buried, never to rise."

Further on, it says, —

"It may not appear so to Mr. Sumner and his supporters, and it may be forgotten by some who oppose him; but we hold it for an incontestable truth, that neither men nor money will be forthcoming for this war, if once the people are impressed with the belief, that the abolition of slavery, and not the defence of the Union, is its object, or that its original purpose is converted into a cloak for some new design of seizing this opportunity for the destruction of the social system of the South. The people are heart and soul with their Government in support of any constitutional undertaking. We do not believe that they will follow it, if they are made to suspect that they are being decoyed into the support of any unconstitutional and revolutionary designs."

It would be easy to add similar extracts from the Republican papers in the Commonwealth; but they would only add weight to an accepted truth. At this time, the importance of saving the border slave States from being engulfed in the current of rebellion was immediate and paramount. The Union men of those States excited our sympathy and admiration. They had bearded the lion of Rebellion in its den. They knew its strong and weak points. They asked Massachusetts and other anti-slavery States to take no aggressive stand against slavery, as it would weaken them, and strengthen the enemy. Massachusetts was one of many States battling for the nation: it was not therefore deemed wise for her alone to attempt to change the issue from a war to preserve the Constitution and the Union, into one for the abolition of slavery. The calm judgment of the people accepted this argument; and hence they could not affirm the policy advanced by Mr. Sumner, because they did not believe it wise then to adopt it. The time might come, they argued, when it would be the highest wisdom to take such a stand; and that time came, and the nation was saved.

The Democratic convention was held in Worcester, Sept. 18, and nominated Isaac Davis, of Worcester, for Governor; Edwin C. Bailey, of Boston, Lieutenant-Governor; Charles Thompson, of Charlestown, Secretary of State; Moses Bates, of Plymouth, Treasurer; and Edward Avery, of Braintree, Attorney-General. These gentlemen were war Democrats.

Moses Bates was elected president of the convention, and, on taking the chair, made a long speech, which, so far as it related to the great national issue, was decided in favor of a vigorous prosecution of the war. Speeches were made by Oliver Stevens, of Boston; E. A. Alger, of Lowell; and Edwin C. Bailey, of Boston, — all of whom condemned the Rebellion, and favored "conquering a peace." The resolutions reported by A. R. Brown, of Lowell, and adopted by the convention, were of the same stamp.

It appears clear, therefore, that upon this great and vital question, which filled all minds, and overtopped all other issues, the two great political parties were a unit; and but for the habit of making separate nominations, and of rallying under different party names, a union would have been made, and the ticket, with John A. Andrew's name at the head, would have been elected by a vote approaching unanimity. A union of this sort was not required to insure the election of the Republican candidates. They were certain to be elected by majorities of thousands. Every one knew that. Therefore no political advantage could be gained by them in receiving Democratic support. The advantage would have been moral, not political; of effect abroad, not here. It would have shown, that in Massachusetts at least, among her people at home as in her regiments in the field, there was but one party, one thought, one impulse, while the Union was imperilled, and armed Rebellion reared its hated crest.

The annual election was held on Tuesday, Nov. 5. The aggregate vote was comparatively small, owing chiefly to the large number of men absent from the State in the army and navy. Governor Andrew received 65,261 votes; Isaac Davis, 31,264; scattering, 796; majority for Andrew, 33,201. The Legislature was unanimous for a vigorous prosecution of the war. The position of Massachusetts was thus clearly defined, and admitted of no doubt. The course taken by the Governor and the Legislature to sustain the Union and the Government, received the approving voice of the Commonwealth.

It is hardly possible even to name the vast number of letters received and answered by the Governor, the Adjutant-General, the Surgeon-General, and other department officers, during the years of this Rebellion: they fill more than three hundred volumes. Many of the letters received from officers contain matters of great interest, especially those received immediately after the battle of Bull Run, in July, and of Ball's Bluff, in October. Among these is a letter written by Dr. Luther V. Bell, surgeon of the Eleventh Regiment, to Surgeon-General Dale, which gives a graphic description of the advance of the army to Bull Run; his services to the wounded assisted by Dr. Josiah Carter and Dr. Foye. Dr. Bell improvised a hospital in a small stone church near the battle-field, in which seventy-five wounded men were brought, before the rout of the Union army brought the church within the rebel lines, and forced a retreat. The Massachusetts regiments engaged in this battle were the First, Colonel Cowdin, the Eleventh, Colonel Clark, three years' volunteers; and the Fifth, Colonel Lawrence, three months' regiment. The reports of these officers, and the testimony of others, show that the regiments behaved with great bravery, and that no part of the defeat can properly be attributed to them. We could fill many pages with extracts from these reports; but they would present no facts of special interest, which have not already been made public.

None of the officers of our regiments wrote with more ease and elegance than Major Wilder Dwight, of the Second Regiment. In one of his letters to the Governor, written in July, at Harper's Ferry, where the Second was encamped to protect the Ferry and hold the town, he says, —

"It is perhaps worthy of remark, that the guard-house occupied by the town-guard is the engine-house which John Brown held so long, and which is one of the few buildings left standing amid the general ruins of the Government property. Directly opposite to it, from the flag-staff, which lately bore the secession flag, our own banner now floats. Several unavailing attempts were made to raise it, when Sergeant Hill, of Company B, volunteered to climb the tall pole, and adjust the halyards. This he did amid the wildest enthusiasm of the people. There has been a reign of terror here; and to-day, for the first time, Union men dare to show themselves, and return to their homes. The protection of the flag is indicated everywhere, and many Virginian men and women have said with quivering lip they were glad to see the old flag again. Throughout our march, in every village, and by almost every house, we have made the hills echo again our national airs."

In the Governor's proclamation for Thanksgiving, this year, it may well be supposed the soldiers in the field were not forgotten. It was read in every Massachusetts camp, and the day was celebrated by the regiments with great spirit and cheerfulness. Major Dwight writes, "I had the honor and pleasure to receive the Governor's proclamation for Thanksgiving. I give a short record of the day's celebration. Military duty was, by authority of General Banks, suspended. At ten, A.M., we had the proclamation read, and religious service by the chaplain. The men afterwards sat down to dinner, which may be summed up as follows: turkeys 95, weight 997½ pounds; geese 76, weight 666 pounds; chickens 73, weight 165 pounds; plum-puddings 95, weight 1,179 pounds. If you state the weight in tons, the whole dinner amounts to one and a half, in round numbers. The men had games and dancing in the evening. It should perhaps be added, that they are in fine health this morning."

This gallant and accomplished officer was a graduate of Harvard College, in the class of 1853. He was promoted lieutenant-colonel of the Second, June 13, 1862, and was mortally wounded in the battle of Antietam, and died two days after, Sept. 19, 1862. His body was brought home to his father's house in Brookline, and was buried from St. Paul's Church, in that town. The Forty-fourth Regiment, Colonel Frank Lee, then in camp at Readville, volunteered as military escort. The Governor and staff were present at the funeral, and the people of the village followed, with the mourning relatives, his body to the grave, where it rests quietly from the noise of civil life and the conflict of battle.

We turn from these grand but solemn memories to the controversy between the Governor and Major-General Butler, which stands in Massachusetts' great record of the war as the only event in which the fulfilment of official duty grew into a protracted personal controversy.

The correspondence would make nearly one hundred pages of this volume. The causes which led to it we shall state as briefly as we can. Massachusetts had forwarded to the front sixteen regiments of infantry to serve for three years; and in August, 1861, was recruiting, in the various camps in the Commonwealth, six additional regiments of infantry, one regiment of cavalry, four companies of light artillery, and one company of sharpshooters. Two other regiments, to be composed of Irishmen, were also soon to be recruited. It was the intention of the Governor to have these regiments and batteries recruited to the maximum as speedily as possible; and, until they were filled, no recruiting, except for them and for regiments already in the field, would be permitted in the Commonwealth. Some of these regiments had been promised and designated as part of an expeditionary corps, to be commanded by Brigadier-General Thomas W. Sherman, U.S.A.

General Sherman arrived in Boston about the first of September, bringing with him a letter to Governor Andrew from Hon. Simon Cameron, Secretary of War, dated Washington, Aug. 27, in which he renews a previous request, that "you," the Governor, "will put three regiments, as soon as they can be prepared for service, under the orders of General Sherman, who will indicate the place of rendezvous." The place of rendezvous was somewhere in Long Island, N.Y. On the next day after this letter was written, — namely, on the 28th of August, — " Colonel " David K. Wardwell, who had commanded a company in the Fifth Regiment, three months militia, received authority from Secretary Cameron to raise a regiment of volunteers in this State. He was instructed " to report to His Excellency the Governor of Massachusetts, from whom you will receive instructions and orders in reference to the regiment which this department has authorized you to raise." Governor Andrew was very justly opposed to having these special permissions given to favored parties to recruit regiments in this Commonwealth, without his knowledge or consent. It interfered with previous arrangements, delayed the completion of regiments already partly recruited, detracted from the authority of the Governor, and violated the act of Congress under which volunteer regiments were authorized to be raised, which provided, section fourth, "That the Governors of the States, furnishing volunteers under this act, shall commission the field, staff, and company officers, requisite for said volunteers; and in cases where the State authorities refuse or omit to furnish volunteers at the call, or on the proclamation, of the President, and volunteers from such States offer their services under such call or proclamation, the President shall have power to accept such services, and to commission the proper field, staff, and company officers." It is clear from this, that the recruiting of regiments, and the commissioning of officers, in the loyal States, was intended to be under the exclusive control of the Governors of those States. Neither the President, nor the Secretary of War, nor any State or Federal officer, civil or military, had any right either, to authorize persons to recruit or to commission officers of volunteers, in States which had loyal Governors, who were ready and anxious to do whatever was demanded of them by the President and the laws of Congress. It was only in States having disloyal Governors, who would refuse to organize regiments and commission officers for the

Union service, that the President could act. Massachusetts was not a disloyal State, and John A. Andrew was not a disloyal Governor.

Captain Wardwell's authority to raise a regiment in Massachusetts was not recognized by the Governor. He was granted permission to raise a company for the Twenty-second Regiment, and he was afterwards commissioned captain in that regiment. Having protested to the authorities in Washington against this pernicious and illegal system of granting special permits to raise regiments in this State, on the 28th of August — the very day on which Wardwell had been given authority to recruit a regiment, — the Governor received a telegram from the Secretary of War, that "he would not sanction for the future any such irregularities;" and Quartermaster-General John H. Reed, who was then in Washington, was requested by Governor Andrew to call upon Mr. Cameron, and to "express the pleasure" which the information had given him. Innumerable difficulties had arisen in New York from similar practices, which led to the issuing by the War Department of General Order No. 71, which directed "all persons having received authority to raise volunteer regiments, batteries, or companies in the State of New York to report immediately to Governor Morgan." They and their commands were placed under his orders, who would organize them "in the manner he might judge the most advantageous." In a letter dated Washington, Sept. 6, written jointly by General John H. Reed and Colonel A. G. Browne, Jr., to Governor Andrew, they state that they had held interviews with the President and the Secretary of War the day before; and both had promised that no more special permits should be given, and that General Order No. 71 should be made to apply to Massachusetts the same as to New York. These preliminary details are necessary in order to have a correct understanding of the controversy which grew up between the Governor and General Butler.

On the seventh of September, the Governor received a telegram from President Lincoln, urging him to forward troops as speedily as possible to General Sherman's headquarters; to which he replied on the same day, "I have written General

Sherman about it during the past week. We are raising five new regiments, *all of which I mean Sherman shall have if you will get an order from the War Department to send them to him.*" This letter was returned to the Governor with the following indorsements: "Respectfully submitted to the War Department. A. Lincoln."—"Let this be done. Simon Cameron, Secretary of War."—"I send you the order you desire. William H. Seward." On the 9th of September, General Sherman writes from New York to the Governor, "The public interest requires that the remaining troops for this expedition assemble here at the very earliest day practicable." To which the Governor answered on the eleventh, "The new regiments are going forward towards completion very rapidly. General Wilson has about nine hundred men in camp to-day." The other regiments were rapidly filling up; two would be completed by the twentieth, "and three more in a good state of forwardness by that time."

So matters stood on the 11th of September. The Governor, every one connected officially with him, the city and town authorities, were actively at work, and lending all their energies to complete these regiments for General Sherman. It was a great surprise, then, that, after the promises made by the authorities at Washington, and the urgent necessity which existed of completing the organization of these regiments, the Secretary of War should, on the tenth of this very month, give authority to Major-General Butler to raise six new regiments in New England, and to arm, uniform, and equip them. The first intelligence Governor Andrew had that such authority had been given, was by a telegram dated Washington, Sept. 11, and jointly signed, "A. Lincoln, *President*," and "Simon Cameron, *Secretary of War*," stating that "General Butler proposes raising in New England six regiments, to be recruited and commanded by himself, and to go on special service: we shall be glad if you, as Governor of Massachusetts, will answer by telegraph that you consent." On receipt of this despatch, the Governor immediately answered, "Authorize *State* to raise whatever regiments you wish additional. We will first fulfil engagements with General Sherman, ordered by Secretary of War; then add others fast as possible; will help General Butler to the utmost." On the 12th (next day), Mr. Cameron telegraphed to the Governor, "Despatch of yesterday received. Massachusetts has done so well in all she has promised, that she shall not be disappointed in any thing she requires from the General Government." This was complimentary, but it was not an answer. A few hours before the Governor received this despatch from Mr. Cameron, he received the following, dated New York, Sept. 11, from General Sherman: "The object of my telegram of the 10th was to ascertain if there existed any *possibility of being disappointed in the time when the troops would be prepared*." Thus when General Sherman was anxiously waiting in New York for the five regiments authorized to be raised for him in Massachusetts, and when every possible effort was being made to complete them, the Secretary of War wrote the following paper. We do not know what to call it: it is not a letter, because it is addressed to no one; it is not an order, because it is not so designated, and bears no number.

WAR DEPARTMENT, Sept. 12, 1861.

Major-General Butler is authorized to fit out and prepare such troops in New England as he may judge fit for the purpose, to make an expedition along the eastern shore of Virginia, *via* the railroad from Wilmington, Del., to Salisbury, and thence through a portion of Maryland, Accomac, and Northampton Counties of Virginia, to Cape Charles. SIMON CAMERON, *Secretary of War*.

This document, in effect, gave General Butler authority over every new regiment raised, or to be raised, in New England. He was to have as many troops as he might "judge fit" for his purpose; and what that purpose was no one except himself and Mr. Cameron knew. The document wholly ignored the Governors of the New-England States, the act of Congress already quoted, and, so far as this State was interested, the promise made to General Sherman that he should have three of the Massachusetts regiments then in course of formation. This was not all — indeed, it was only a small part — of the complicated, contradictory, and painfully embarrassing position under which this new state of things placed the Governor of Massachusetts. He had been ordered to furnish five new regiments for General Sherman, he had promised the General he should have them, he had nearly completed a part of them, when, without consultation or previous knowledge, this paper, prepared in the War Office at Washington, and signed by the Secretary, was issued, placing all the troops in New England under the command of Major-General Butler, and as many more as he might "judge fit" for his purpose. Four days after Mr. Cameron had written the paper just quoted, Special Order No. 78 was issued from the War Department.

> WAR DEPARTMENT, ADJUTANT-GENERAL'S OFFICE,
> WASHINGTON, Sept. 16, 1861.
>
> All persons having received authority from the War Department to raise volunteer regiments, batteries, or companies, in the loyal States, are, with their commands, hereby placed under the orders of the Governors of those States, to whom they will immediately report the present condition of their respective organizations. These troops will be organized or re-organized, and prepared for service, by the Governors of their respective States, in the manner they may judge most advantageous to the interests of the Federal Government.
>
> By order, L. THOMAS, *Adjutant-General*.

This order was easy of comprehension, and in strict accordance with the acts of Congress; but it was in direct conflict with the paper signed by Mr. Cameron four days before. Upon its receipt, Governor Andrew directed the Adjutant-General of the Commonwealth to issue General Order No. 23, which enumerated the regiments and batteries then being recruited in the State, and the camps at which they were stationed. It also said, that "*until they were filled, no recruiting, except for these regiments and batteries, is authorized, or can be encouraged, by the Commander-in-chief.*" After quoting the preceding order of the War Department, signed by General Thomas, it proceeds to say, "*The Commander-in-chief directs that no new regiments or companies be formed, or ordered into camp, nor any already in camp change their location, without orders from these headquarters.*"

Although the order restricted recruiting for new regiments except those designated, it allowed and encouraged recruiting for regiments already in the field. It also gave notice that two new regiments, to be composed of men of Irish birth, were soon to be placed in camp, one of which, the Twenty-eighth, "to form a part of the command of Major-General Butler, whose headquarters is at Lowell."

On the 23d of September, Mr. Cameron telegraphed to the Governor, "Will the three regiments for General Sherman be ready this week? He must be supplied in advance of all other applications for same service. Please reply immediately." To which the Governor answered the same day, and requested the Secretary not to issue an order detailing particular regiments to General Butler, but to leave all such details to him: he could provide for him otherwise and sufficiently. To which Mr. Cameron answered, "Select the regiments yourself for Sherman, and supply him first." Same day, Colonel Browne, military secretary to the Governor, by order of His Excellency, addressed a note to General Butler, in which he proposed to assign to his command an Irish regiment, in the raising of which Patrick Donahoe, Esq., of Boston, took much interest. This was afterwards known as the Twenty-eighth Regiment. The receipt of this letter was acknowledged by Major Haggerty, of General Butler's staff, on the 24th, and information given that General Butler had gone to Portland, Me., and that his attention would be called to it as soon as he returned, which would be "to-morrow evening."

A letter was sent to General Sherman on the 23d by the Governor, requesting him to exert his personal efforts to secure for his command the regiments promised him, and prevent them from "being diverted to General Butler or any other officer." The regiments designed for him were the Twenty-second and Twenty-third, in camp at Lynnfield, and known as General Wilson's, and the Twenty-fifth, encamped at Worcester. The letter further stated that the Governor proposed "to assign to General Butler the Twenty-sixth Regiment, being raised by Colonel Jones at Lowell," and an Irish regiment. To this General Sherman replied, on the 27th, that he had immediately called the attention of the Secretary of War to it; that "five regiments are yet waited for, — three from Massachusetts, one from Maine, one from New Hampshire; and it is hoped that they will all be pressed forward at the earliest day." While this correspondence was going on, and Sherman waiting for his regiments in New York, the Secretary of War sent orders direct to General Wilson, which he received on the 24th, "to report to General Butler, and form a component part of his proposed expedition." The Governor then wrote to Secretary Cameron, "I have been much perplexed and embarrassed during the last few days by contradictory orders and assurances, issuing from your department." To avoid which, he said the regiments in this State should be organized *through*, and not *outside* of, its Governor. He also says, "General Butler, it is evident to me, desires naturally to secure to his own command, with or without consultation with me, according as best he may, all the force he can, even to the prejudice of what General Sherman has a positive right to expect from Massachusetts." Mr. Cameron replied on the 27th, that General Sherman was to be supplied first, afterwards General Butler. "It is the intention of this department," he says, "to leave to your Excellency all questions concerning the organization of troops in your State, and the orders to which you refer were designed to be subject to the approval and control of the Executive of Massachusetts. It will be my endeavor to act strictly in accordance with your suggestions." This extract is underscored in the original.

This appears explicit enough; and yet the same system of cross purposes was kept up for some time after at Washington, to the insufferable annoyance of the Governor, complicating and retarding recruiting, and delaying the completion of the regiments. On the 1st of October, General Order No. 86 was issued by the Adjutant-General of the army, forming the six New-England States a military department, the headquarters at Boston, and providing that "Major-General B. F. Butler, United States Volunteer Service, while engaged in recruiting his division, will command." In connection with this, the Secretary directed the Paymaster-General to detail an assistant to pay the men enlisted, and to be enlisted, by General Butler, a month's pay from date of muster in, which was a very proper order if it had been of general application; but it was very improper, to be applied only to General Butler's command, and denied to General Sherman's.

On the 2d of October, the Secretary telegraphs to the Governor, "Send three regiments for General Sherman to Hampstead Camp, on Long Island, by Monday morning at the latest, earlier if possible." On the 3d, next day, the Secretary telegraphs again to the Governor, "Send the Wilson Regiment to Washington direct. Give Sherman the next one, as soon as possible."

The name of General Sherman henceforth ceases to appear in the correspondence. He was assigned to another department. The command of the special expedition was given to General Burnside, and five Massachusetts regiments composed a part of it. These were the Twenty-first, Twenty-third, Twenty-fourth, Twenty-fifth, and Twenty-seventh. The camp of rendezvous was at Annapolis, and the point of attack was North Carolina, by way of Roanoke Island and Newbern. The expedition was successful.

Major-General Butler, having assumed command of the Department of New England, and established his headquarters at Boston, on the 5th of October issued his first general order, announcing his staff, and directing "all officers in command of troops mustered in the service of the United States to report, either in person or by letter, to his headquarters." An official copy of this order was forwarded to Governor Andrew.

On the 5th of October, General Butler addressed a long letter to the Governor, informing him that he had been authorized by the President to raise men for "a special purpose," to which, he stated, "your assent was given." He then says, —

"Acting upon that assent, I called upon you, and you desired that I should wait a week, when the regiment of Colonel Wilson, then being recruited, would be full, before I took any action upon that subject. To this I assented, and have been only looking out for officers for recruiting purposes, and have made no public announcement, and allowed no one who had a special corps to make advertisement, which I thought would be fully within the understanding.

"I then shew you an order to take regiments already raised, and not assigned to other officers, for another purpose, and you offered to assign me Colonel Jones' regiment. You also said, that an Irish regiment, now being raised, you would like to be assigned to me; to that I assented, and left for the purpose of organizing recruiting in Maine, and from thence to Washington. On my return, I find that recruiting officers have been making publications injurious to me and the recruiting service; so it becomes necessary to know exactly what is understood between us."

He then proceeds, "I desire, therefore, the simple announcement, by general order, that I have authority to enlist men for a regiment, to be numbered as you please, also a squadron of mounted men; these troops to be a part of the volunteer force of the State; these to be in addition to those already assigned by you." He also says he will make no objections, if the Irish regiment is withheld. These requests granted, he adds, "I see no difficulty in the way of filling up all these regiments at once, save this one," which was the practice here of "recruiting officers offering private bounties for men, of five and seven dollars." This he regarded as vicious, and as "the sale of men," and mentions other objections.

The Governor replied to the letter of General Butler the same evening, after his return from the cavalry camp at Readville. The letter is of considerable length. In the beginning, he says, —

"I beg leave to say at once, in reply to your remark relating to some supposed promise of mine, that I did not at any time say, that, while we were already raising so many regiments in Massachusetts, I could consent to an embarrassment of the service by additional competition for recruits. But while I assured you of my willingness, so far as it lay in my power, to assign to you, out of regiments in progress, our fair proportion, or more than that, of the six regiments you told me you wished to raise in New England, I have constantly declared that I could not concur in a policy, which, by crowding the competition of regiments, would be fatal, or very dangerous, to successful recruiting."

The Governor thought that we were overdoing recruiting; and, until the regiments already ordered were filled, recruiting for new regiments should not be undertaken. Having given his own opinion, however, he asks the General to forward a roster of company officers for the regiment he wishes to raise, and "he would authorize a new regiment to begin in a week from Monday next, under Captain Henry L. Abbott (of Massachusetts), of the United States Topographical Engineers, for colonel; and Charles Everett, late colonel of District of Columbia Volunteers, formerly serving in Mexico, or Major Francis Brinley, for lieutenant-colonel; the major to be seasonably selected."

The Governor disclaims any knowledge of recruiting officers offering private bounties, and asks that the names of such persons may be sent to him, "that the more speedy and vigilant measures for suppression and rebuke may be instituted." In the matter of recruiting and organizing regiments, the Governor says, "We have pursued a system, carefully, watchfully, faithfully, and zealously, in which, by the intelligent aid and loyal co-operation of all officers, of the State and of the Union, who have had any connection with such matters here, we have found reason to trust. In fact, almost any system is better than none." After stating that Massachusetts had already forwarded sixteen regiments of infantry, and other troops, to the front, he continues, —

"We are, at this very moment, doing half as much more, and doing it with the utmost of our ability; and we have thus far escaped the confusion and uncertainty of movement which have embarrassed some other States, and from which, with much effort, their Governors have only just now escaped. Now, with the utmost respect for the Department of War, and for yourself personally, and with the most loyal sentiments of obedience, I mean to continue to do just what I have, from the first, persistently done: and that is, to hold, with an iron hand and unswerving purpose, all the powers which, by the laws, pertain to me officially, in my own grasp, — yielding the most implicit obedience, in all things, to those having the right to direct me, but, at the same time, remembering that true subordination requires every officer to perform his own duties and fulfil his own functions himself, as well as to submit himself loyally to his superiors."

He then refers to the laws of Congress and the orders of the department, which give to the Governors of States the exclusive control of raising regiments in their own States: "Nor is it permitted by law, even to the President himself, even were he so disposed, to interfere in the premises." He also informs the General, that he has the assurance of the Secretary of War, "that he had issued no orders, and would issue none, tending to interfere with the State authorities."

He concludes this able letter by saying, —

"I shall do exactly by you as I have done by General Sherman and General Burnside, — that is to say, I shall use every exertion to furnish troops for the service you propose, in our full proportion; but it must be done by pursuing such methods and plans as we have found necessary for the general advantage of the service. Nor can I permit, so far as it lies with me, to decide *any officers of the United States* to raise troops as Massachusetts volunteers within this Commonwealth, except for the recruitment of existing regiments, or subject to the conditions indicated; while any advice or friendly assistance will be gratefully received from any quarter, much more from a gentleman of your capacity to advise, and your hearty zeal in the cause we are both anxious to serve."

The Governor had telegraphed, on the morning of the 5th, to the Secretary of War, to know if he "would pay our soldiers, as fast as mustered in, half a month's pay, detailing paymasters therefor. Do not authorize this for any, unless for all. What is General Butler's power and position here?" To which he received, as an answer, "We cannot pay in advance. General Butler has authority to concentrate a brigade for special service, all of which is to be organized under the several Governors of the Eastern States. We gave General Butler authority with regard to advance pay." The Governor also wrote a letter to Mr. Cameron in regard to matters. It would appear, that, some time on the seventh of the month, General Butler requested a personal interview with the Governor, and called at the State House; but, the Governor being engaged in the Council Chamber, the interview did not take place.

It does not appear that the letter of the Governor of Oct. 5 changed in the least degree the determination of General Butler to enlist men. He opened a camp in Pittsfield, and another in Lowell, and commenced recruiting two regiments of infantry,

— one designated the Western Bay-State Regiment, the other the Eastern Bay-State Regiment; also, a battery of light artillery, and three companies of cavalry.

The only reply made to the letter of the 5th is the following, which is given entire: —

HEADQUARTERS DEPARTMENT OF NEW ENGLAND,
BOSTON, Oct. 12, 1861.

Will "His Excellency Governor Andrew" assign to General Butler the recruitment of a regiment of Massachusetts volunteers, and a squadron of mounted men, to be armed and equipped by him, under the authority of the President; the officers to be selected by General Butler, but commissioned by "His Excellency," with, of course, a veto power upon what may be deemed an improper selection. As these officers are to go with General Butler upon duty, would "His Excellency" think it improper he should exercise the power of recommendation?

To the telegram of the President, asking consent that the authorization should be given to General Butler to raise troops, "His Excellency" telegraphed, in reply, that he would "aid" General Butler to the utmost.

General Butler knows no way in which "His Excellency" can aid him so effectually as in the manner proposed.

The selection by "His Excellency" in advance, without consultation, of a colonel and lieutenant-colonel of an unformed regiment, not a soldier of which has been recruited by the State, and both these gentlemen, to whom the General, at present, knows no personal objection, being absent from the State on other duty, seems to him very objectionable.

It is not certain that Lieutenant Abbott, of the Topographical Engineers, will be permitted to leave his corps. Colonel Everett has not lived in the State for many years, and has not such interest identified with the State, or the men of Massachusetts whom he would command, as to render his appointment desirable.

General Butler has had and can have the aid of neither in his regiments; and he believes that those who do the work, other things being equal, should have the offices. General Butler would have been happy to have conferred with "His Excellency" upon these and other points; but "His Excellency" did not seem to desire it.

General Butler has proceeded upon this thesis in his recruitment, to say to all patriotic young men who seemed proper persons, and who have desired to enter the service as officers, If you have the confidence of your neighbors, so that you can recruit a given number of men, then by giving evidence of your energy and capacity thus far, if you are found fit in other respects, on examination, I will recommend you for a commission to command the number of men you shall raise.

This is believed to be a course much better calculated to find officers than to hunt for them by the uncertain light of petitions and recommendations.

General Butler desires to make good his word to these young gentlemen. "His Excellency" will perceive the impossibility of at once furnishing a roster under such circumstances, as requested, for "His Excellency's" perusal.

"His Excellency's" attention is called to the fact that no reply has been received to General Butler's request, as to a squadron of mounted men.

General Butler is informed, by the returns of those who have recruited for him, that he has already a number of men equal to two regiments in such progress that they can be organized, being the most prompt recruitment ever done in this State, — these besides the Twenty-sixth and Twenty-eighth Regiments, assigned to him by general order.

General Butler trusts that "His Excellency" will not, without the utmost necessity for it, throw any obstacles in the way of his recruitment, as General Butler is most anxious to get his division organized, so as to start upon an expedition already planned, in the service of his country.

General Butler hopes that these views will meet "His Excellency's" concurrence and co-operation.

Most respectfully "His Excellency's" obedient servant,
BENJAMIN F. BUTLER.

The Governor being absent from Boston, the receipt of the letter was acknowledged by Colonel Browne on the 14th, and was by him forwarded to the Governor.

It does not appear that the Governor took any immediate official notice of this letter.

We pass over much that was written, but which were but eddies in the tide of this correspondence, to bring it to a fair and intelligent close. We will only state the fact, that, on the 11th of November, we received a letter from Colonel Ritchie, senior, directing the Adjutant-General to issue Order No. 570, which was, in substance, that General Butler, having sent an order to Colonel Stevenson, Twenty-fourth Regiment Massachusetts Volunteers, to deliver up to him certain soldiers mustered into said regiment, who had deserted from one of General Butler's regiments, that Colonel Stevenson was not to obey the order, as General Butler had no authority to enlist volunteers in Massachusetts, except for the Twenty-sixth and Twenty-eighth Regiments. Colonel Stevenson, at that time, had a part of his command at Fort Warren, on duty, although his headquarters were at Readville; and he was ordered, that, "if he cannot protect and hold his men at Fort Warren, he shall remove them immediately to 'Camp Massasoit,' at Readville, and hold them until otherwise ordered."

The Governor had been written to by Mr. Sargent, the Mayor of Lowell, and many other city and town authorities, asking him whether the families of the men who had enlisted under General Butler were entitled to the "State aid," which communications were referred to the Attorney-General, Hon. Dwight Foster, who returned, as an opinion, that all volunteers who are inhabitants of this State, and enlist here under the authority of the Governor, and the officers of the regiments are commissioned by him, their families are entitled to the aid; and, if General Butler's brigade is to be so raised and commissioned, then the families of the men enlisted should receive it. He concludes by saying, —

"I suppose this will be the case, and the men enlisted by him will be entitled to the usual aid; and I only state my opinion in this guarded form, because of the possible and highly improbable contingency of volunteers being enlisted in full regiments in Massachusetts, without the sanction of its Executive, the officers of which he might decline to commission or recognize."

This opinion was, in effect, against allowing the State aid to the families of the men who had been enlisted by General Butler. The "highly improbable contingency" already existed. State aid was not paid by the cities and towns to the families of enlisted men, until the authorities of the places to which the men belonged had received a certificate, signed by the Adjutant-General of the State, that the men were mustered in, and the muster-rolls had been deposited in his office. No muster-rolls had been received by the Adjutant-General from the corps said to have been recruited by General Butler. No assurance had been received from Washington, that the men had been mustered in, and credited to the contingent of the State.

On the 27th of November, Major Strong, chief of staff to General Butler, forwarded to the Adjutant-General of the State a list of officers which had been adopted by General Butler for "a company known as the Salem Light Artillery," with a request that they be commissioned by the Governor.

On the 17th of December, General Butler wrote to the Governor, calling his attention to the letter of Major Strong, with a request that he might be favored "with a reply whether he will or will not commission the officers therein named." General Butler also claimed, that the company "was raised under the authority of the State, and with His Excellency's approval."

By direction of the Governor, Colonel Browne replied on the same day to this communication, that it was the intention of the Governor "at a proper time to appoint and commission suitable officers for the battery; but that he was not advised of their intended removal from the Commonwealth, nor was any request made for such appointments, either from the company or from the acting officers, or from any source, until eight days after the whole company had been removed from Massachusetts, when the Governor was requested by Major Strong to commission certain persons, on the ground that they had been elected by the company, as it was said. But the company was gone. None of its rolls having been deposited in the office of the Adjutant-General, there was no means of identifying its men."

The letter further states, that the responsibility of appointing suitable officers rests with the Governor, and that, as regards one of the persons recommended, "the information received by the Governor is, that his character is such as to render him unfit for appointment."

The Governor further stated, that he was desirous of commissioning officers for the battery, "and would be glad to receive the testimonials of any on which their claims are founded."

On the 18th (next day), this letter was returned to Colonel Browne by Major Strong, with the following note: —

"SIR, — Major-General Butler, commanding the Department of New England, directs that the enclosed communication be respectfully returned to His Excellency Governor Andrew, as being of improper address and signature."

The same day, the Governor wrote to Major Strong, expressing his surprise, and that, knowing the contents of the letter which is returned, he found himself unable to instruct Colonel Browne how to amend it, "since the particulars of the offence were not stated, and were not discernible to me, nor, as I am assured, by him." He therefore asks "the favor of a precise statement of the offence committed." To which Major Strong replied on the 19th. After referring to army regulations, paragraph 449, he said, —

"The letter to which that was a reply was addressed to *your Excellency*, and therefore signed by General Butler himself, as claiming to be your Excellency's co-ordinate. Lieutenant-Colonel Browne's letter was addressed, not to the chief of staff at these headquarters, but directly to the Major-General commanding the department, and even then not in his official capacity."

On Dec. 20, a reply was made in a letter signed by Colonel Browne, from which we make the following extracts: —

"With the single exception of the President of the United States, no officer or person, whether State or national, civil or military, whether temporarily sojourning or permanently residing within the limits of Massachusetts, can be recognized within such limits as the 'co-ordinate' of the Governor of the Commonwealth in official dignity or rank."

He then expresses surprise that a gentleman of General Butler's acumen and professional training "should quote the regulations of the army of the United States, as dictating ceremonies of official intercourse to a magistrate who is no part of that army, and not subject to its regulations." His attention is also called to the order of the War Department of Sept. 16, by which Major-General Butler is placed under the orders of the Governor of Massachusetts, in respect to raising and organizing volunteers.

"In the present condition of national affairs, the Governor considers it impolitic and unpatriotic to embarrass the public service by undue nicety of etiquette; and he regrets that Major-General Butler's views of duty in this particular should not have corresponded with his own, so as to render the present correspondence unnecessary."

After disclaiming all intentional discourtesy, the letter thus refers to the letter quoted entire on a preceding page: —

"General Butler's letter of Oct. 12, written to Governor Andrew, but not addressed to him, except in so far as he is mentioned in the third person, after the fashion of dinner invitations, and the like, on private and social occasions, and not signed by the Major-General with any addition of rank or command, and frequently re-iterating the Governor's constitutional title and name, with significant and conspicuous marks of quotation surrounding them whenever repeated.

"It is customary to affix marks of quotation in manuscript to indicate passages or expressions borrowed from some other to whom they ought to be credited. But I am not aware, that a name given in baptism, or inherited from a parent, or a title conferred by the Constitution on a magistrate as his official description, are in any sense original ideas, or expressions which it is usual to designate by marks of quotation. Nor is this a matter in which a gentleman of Major-General Butler's learning and urbanity could have erred by mistake. . . . When a gentleman has violated the substance of courtesy, as did General Butler in that letter of Oct. 12, by a studious, indirect, insinuating, but not less significant, intentional act of impoliteness towards a magistrate whose only offence was fidelity to his duty, to the laws, and to the rights of his official position, he cannot be permitted, without comment, to arraign another for a supposed breach of military intercourse, simply formal, technical, and arbitrary, as he has assumed to arraign me in this matter through yourself."

This letter would have been addressed directly to General Butler, had the Governor not been advised that he was at Washington. He soon after returned, and, on the 28th of December, wrote to the Governor a letter in which he says, —

"I disclaim most emphatically any intentional or even accidental discourtesy to the Governor of Massachusetts.

"In the matter of the address in quotation, I but copied the address assumed by one of the numerous military secretaries who write me on behalf of the Governor, and it was because of the formality of that address. 'His Excellency Governor Andrew' is neither a baptismal, inherited, or constitutional title; and, after using it once in the letter alluded to, I carefully used the title of the Constitution, and marked it in quotation to call attention to the difference."

It appears by this, that General Butler "*carefully used the title of the Constitution, and marked it in quotation to call attention to the difference.*"

Mr. Parton, in his "Life of General Butler," says, —

"The person who made the copy sent to the Governor, with perverse uniformity, placed inverted commas before and after those words (His Excellency), as if to intimate that the author of the letter used them reluctantly, and only in obedience to a custom. It looked like an intentional and elaborate affront, and served to embitter the controversy. When, at length, the General was made acquainted with the insertion, he was not in a humor to give a complete explanation; nor, indeed, is it a custom with him to get out of a scrape by casting blame upon a subordinate."

This information, Mr. Parton says, he received "from a confidential member of General Butler's staff, the late General Strong," who was killed at Fort Wagner.

This letter appears to have closed the controversy regarding the letter of Oct. 12; but it introduced a new element of controversy. Respecting commissioning the officers of Battery No. 4, General Butler alludes to the objections which the Governor had interposed in regard to one of the persons recommended, and says, —

"If any base charge can be substantiated against either of them, I shall be happy to substitute others. I believe, however, that neither of them have ever done any thing worse than seducing a mother, and making a father wifeless, and children motherless; and that, you know, is no objection to a high military commission in Massachusetts."

On the 30th, the Governor addressed a note to General Butler, in which he quotes the words in the above extract, and requests to know what officer it is to whom he refers: —

"Moreover, may I ask whose mother is alluded to, and whose wife? and does the implied allegation mean that the crime of murder was added to that of seduction, although the words 'you know' assume the existence of greater knowledge than I possess? And, indeed, since the day I had the honor to detail yourself as a brigadier-general of the militia, at the beginning of the present war, to this day, and both inclusive, I cannot accuse myself of such an appointment. If I have done so, I beg you to expose it."

On the 1st of January, 1862, General Butler answered, —

"I referred, in my communication of the 28th ult., to the case of Wyman, appointed by your Excellency colonel of the Sixteenth Massachusetts Regiment. Unless the testimony of brother officers serving with Wyman is to be disbelieved, facts notorious are to be denied which have never been denied before.

"Colonel Wyman, while an officer of the United States army, held long adulterous intercourse with a Mrs. Brannan, the wife of a brother officer. This woman afterwards left her home under such circumstances as to induce the belief that she was either murdered by herself or another.

"This Wyman obtained leave of absence from the army, and joined his paramour in Europe; while there, he resigned his commission, because of a letter from the Adjutant-General of the army that he would be court-martialled if he did not, and remained abroad until after the breaking-out of the war, when he left her embraces, and returned to the army of the Commonwealth under your Excellency's appointment.

"This woman was the mother of children; and, if I should amend the language of my communication of the 28th ult., I should add, 'making a father worse than wifeless, and children worse than motherless.'

"I used the phrase 'you know,' because I have been informed, and I have reason to believe and do believe, that the substance of these facts was known to your Excellency at the time you made the appointment. Will your Excellency deny that you were then put upon inquiry as to them?

"I cannot expose this matter, because it has long since been made a matter of exposition in the public prints. I have no farther knowledge of Colonel Wyman, save that which may be learned by inquiry of any officer of the army who served with him. I have no disposition to injure or interfere with him, and have made this communication only in reply to your Excellency's statement."

As this was a grave, personal matter, touching the character of a brave and patriotic officer of Massachusetts, then at the front with his regiment, and who fell at the head of it, a few months afterwards, bravely fighting, we have thought it proper to copy this correspondence entire. The dead officer lies in Mount Auburn Cemetery. His services and his memory deserve that the defence of Governor Andrew, like the charge of General Butler, should be given without abridgment. Under date of Jan. 6, 1862, Governor Andrew writes to General Butler, —

"SIR, — At the first hour at my disposal for the purpose, I acknowledge the receipt of your letter of Jan. 1, in which you state that Colonel Powell T. Wyman, commanding the Sixteenth Regiment Massachusetts Volunteer Infantry, now stationed at Fortress Monroe, is the person to whom you had reference, when, addressing me under date of Dec. 28, you asserted that I ⋅ know ' that ' seducing a mother, and making a father wifeless and children motherless,' ' is no objection to a high military commission in Massachusetts.'

"In answer to your somewhat peremptory interrogatories, addressed to me in that letter of Jan. 1, I would state, for your information, that the first knowledge I ever had of Mr. Wyman was through a letter addressed by him to the Adjutant-General of Massachusetts, dated ' London, England, May 1, 1861,' stating that he was a citizen of Boston and a graduate of the West-Point Military Academy, and had served for ten years as an officer of artillery of the United States army, and tendering his services to the Executive of this Commonwealth in any military capacity. I am not aware that any acknowledgment was ever made of this communication.

"During the month of June, I received another note from Mr. Wyman, dated at the Parker House, Boston, he having, in the mean while, returned to America. This letter was assigned to a member of my staff, to whom Mr. Wyman was referred for consultation. It was at that time that I first heard that there was said to be a cloud of some sort upon Mr. Wyman's character; and, having little leisure myself to enter into quasi-judicial investigations as to personal character, I passed over his name in the appointments which I was then making. The nature of the reports against him were not then stated to me; and, although I was soon after advised of them, yet there are things stated, in your letter of Jan. 1, as 'notorious facts,' of which it is only through yourself that I have knowledge.

"Very shortly afterwards, Adam W. Thaxter, Esq., of this city, doubtless known to you as one of the most distinguished merchants of Boston, brought the name of Mr. Wyman very urgently to my attention, both personally and in a letter, dated June 20, in which he requested me to call on himself, if Mr. Wyman should 'need an indorser,' and stated, that, in his opinion, Mr. Wyman, if appointed a colonel, would 'do credit to his native State.'

"And, on July 1, Mr. Thaxter further presented to me a communication, in writing, signed by Captain Thomas J. C. Amory, of the Seventh Infantry, U.S.A., and Captain Lewis H. Marshall, of the Tenth Infantry, U.S.A., both of whom had served in the army with Mr. Wyman, and who were, if I remember, the only United States regular army officers then on duty in this city; and signed also by Charles G. Greene, Esq., Franklin Haven, Esq., William Dehon, Esq., William Parkman, Esq., Hon. George Lunt, Hon. Benjamin F. Hallett, Henry L. Hallett, Esq., P. Holmes, Esq., Edward F. Bradley, Esq., Joseph L. Henshaw, Esq., Peter Butler, Esq., Thomas C. Amory, Esq., and J. P. Bradlee, Esq., — all of these gentlemen of this city, who are doubtless known to you by reputation, and with some of whom I cannot doubt that you are personally acquainted, — in which communication, these gentlemen requested the appointment of Mr. Wyman as a colonel, and certified that they 'believed in him as a gentleman, a man of worth, an accomplished officer, and brave soldier; and that a regiment under his command would yield to none in the service for discipline, high tone, and efficiency; and also, that they felt convinced, 'under all circumstances,' he 'would do honor to his State and to his country.' These gentlemen further stated, that they made this request in full knowledge of the existence of the rumors and influences against Mr. Wyman's reputation; and nevertheless, with such knowledge, they earnestly 'urged' him, 'as one of those to whom the honor of Massachusetts may confidently be trusted.'

"About the same time, Mr. Wyman addressed to me a communication in writing, denying the truth of the prejudicial rumors in circulation against him, and, although admitting that it was true that he had formed a matrimonial connection with a lady who had eloped from her husband by reason of that husband's brutal treatment of her, yet stating also that he had not seen the lady for the year preceding, nor for the year after, her elopement. This communication, I find, upon referring to it, amounts also to a denial of the truth of much that is stated by you, in your letter of Jan. 1, as 'notorious facts,' derogatory to Mr. Wyman's character.

"Upon the basis of this statement, made by Mr. Wyman, and controlled by no responsible counter-statement or testimony whatsoever, and upon the formal assurance I received from the numerous gentlemen whom I have mentioned, that he was a good soldier and a good citizen, I did not feel myself justified in rejecting the services of a highly meritorious and thoroughly educated officer, upon unsubstantial rumors of an alleged moral error, which did not affect his military competency, and more especially at a time when the services of educated officers were so greatly needed for the command of our troops.

"I therefore appointed Mr. Wyman to be colonel of the Sixteenth Regiment, — an appointment which, under the circumstances stated, commended itself to my judgment, and which I have no reason whatsoever now to regret, and, under like circumstances, should not hesitate to repeat.

"As it was upon the faith of the assurances made to me by Mr. Thaxter and the other gentlemen in their communication of July 1 that the appointment of Colonel Wyman was made. I therefore conceive that your quarrel with this appointment should be with those gentlemen, rather than with myself; and therefore I propose to inclose copies of your correspondence with me, in this connection, to Mr. Thaxter, as representing them; and I must request you to address to them any future correspondence upon this subject, inasmuch as they are better acquainted than myself with Colonel Wyman, and his character, life, and connections, which I know chiefly through them. I desire to add, that, in all the intercourse which I have had with Colonel Wyman during the organization of his regiment, I never observed, on his part, the manifestation of any other qualities than those of an accomplished officer; and I should be very reluctant to give credit to your reproaches against his character, especially in view of the standing of those gentlemen by whom his character as a gentleman was certified to me.

"In conclusion, I would say, that I do not feel that any reason exists, *requiring* me to enter into such an explanation as the above; but when an officer of the rank of major-general in the army of the United States volunteers thinks it necessary to diversify his occupations by needless flings at a fellow-officer in the same army, seeking to strike *myself* through *him*, a sense of honor and duty, both to the Commonwealth and to the gentleman thus struck at, requires me to spare no proper pains to see that justice is fully done."

As reference is made, in the above letter, to a letter received by the Adjutant-General from Colonel Wyman, we would say, that our recollection of it is, that it was brought to our office by an old friend of Colonel Wyman, — James Oakes, Esq., a merchant of this city. The letter had been inclosed in one which he had received from Colonel Wyman. It was a tender of his services to the Governor of his native State, in any military capacity he might be pleased to place him. Before any action was taken upon the matter, Colonel Wyman arrived in Boston, and reported at the State House. He was a true Union man, and anxiously desired to serve his country. As before stated, he was killed before Richmond, June 30, 1862. No one in command of a regiment of Massachusetts, in so short a time, made himself more beloved by his officers and men, or exhibited higher military qualities, than Colonel Wyman. He was a modest, quiet, and reserved gentleman. He possessed the qualities of kindness and firmness in a high degree. He was of light frame, of middle age, had a pleasant, thoughtful face, a fine-formed head, and a warm, generous heart. There is not an officer or soldier remaining of the original Sixteenth Regiment who does not speak of him with an affectionate regard, surpassing ordinary respect; and many have said, that, if he had lived, he would have commanded the Army of the Potomac before the close of the war.

General Butler continued independent recruiting until two regiments of infantry, three companies of cavalry, and a company of light artillery, were raised by him in Massachusetts, notwithstanding the law gave to the Governor the exclusive right to organize regiments, and to commission the officers. The controversy lasted four months. The Governor had given General Butler the Twenty-sixth and the Twenty-eighth Regiments, which was the full proportion of this State, for his expedition. The troops raised by General Butler were sent from the State without commissioned officers, without rolls being deposited in the Adjutant-General's office, and without the knowledge of the Executive; all of which was against orders, good policy, and statute law. In the mean time, Massachusetts had sent forward to the front eight full regiments, besides many recruits for old regiments. The Governor had written of late frequently to the War Department about General Butler's course, but received no satisfactory answer. On the 21st of December, he enclosed copies of the entire correspondence up to that date to our Senators in Congress, accompanied by an earnest appeal for them to examine it, and afterwards to present it to the President. He said, —

"As I do not receive any reply from the officers of the Federal Government whom I have thus addressed, nor any redress or correction of the evils of which complaint is therein made, I am compelled thus to resort to your official intervention. However humble and unimportant might be the person who holds the place of chief executive magistrate of Massachusetts, the venerable Commonwealth which he serves should be treated with respect."

The letter refers to the blood shed by the children of this Commonwealth at Baltimore, at Ball's Bluff, and wherever else they have been called in arms, during the present year, and to the willingness the State has always been to bear her portion of the burdens of the war, and closes with this paragraph: —

"I am compelled to declare, with great reluctance and regret, that the course of proceeding under Major-General Butler in this Commonwealth seems to have been designed and adapted simply to afford means to persons of bad character to make money unscrupulously, and to encourage men whose unfitness had excluded them from any appointment by me to the volunteer military service, to hope for such appointment over Massachusetts troops from other authority than that of the Executive of Massachusetts."

To this letter Mr. Sumner wrote, Jan. 10, 1862, "I am authorized by the War Department to say, that, if you will send on your programme with reference to General Butler, it shall be carried out, and the department (of New England) given up. Please let me know your desires." This was received by the Governor on the 14th; and he immediately telegraphed, as an answer, "The President has my programme written, replying to his telegram of last Saturday. My letters should be *directly*, and not *indirectly*, answered by the President or Department."

The result of the controversy was, that the Department of New England was dissolved. The two regiments raised by General Butler, known as the Eastern and Western Bay-State Regiments, were afterwards designated the Thirtieth and Thirty-first Regiments Massachusetts Volunteers, and the officers were selected and commissioned by Governor Andrew; and, from that time until the end of the war, the War Department, under the Secretaryship of Mr. Stanton, did its business with the States through the Governors of States.

Before closing this subject, it is proper to state, that Governor Andrew, about the beginning of November, authorized the Adjutant-General to confer with General Butler in regard to organizing and equipping the Twenty-eighth (Irish) Regiment, which had been set apart as one of the two regiments which the Governor had offered him. At that time, parts of two Irish regiments had been recruiting, one of which was designated the Twenty-ninth, which was encamped at Framingham. It was, however, found expedient to take the men from Framingham, and mass them with the Twenty-eighth, which was in "Camp Cameron," at Cambridge. On the 7th of November, after the consolidation, the Twenty-eighth Regiment had seven hundred and fifteen men. On that day, the Adjutant-General addressed a letter to Major-General Butler, by direction of the Governor, calling his attention to the fact that the men had not been armed, uniformed, or equipped, which General Butler had informed the Governor he had authority from Washington to do. The regiment had received "no aid or attention" whatever, from his head-quarters. The Governor, therefore, wished to be informed immediately whether he considered the regiment as part of his command, or whether he did not wish to have it.

To which an answer was made, the same day, by Major Strong, that, as the Twenty-eighth Regiment had been thus far recruited by the State, it would be continued to be recruited by the State; but General Butler would take it as part of his command, if it could be ready by the 1st of December, and would add some recruits to complete it, if he could be permitted to indicate the officers who should command the men they had recruited. This being permitted, General Butler would at once "arm, uniform, and equip the regiment, as his authority requires him to 'organize' as well; but he will ask only an advisory power in the organization."

The Adjutant-General had a personal interview with Major Strong on the 9th, in which the whole matter was talked over.

There were, at that time, fifteen parts of companies at "Camp Cameron." After the personal conference with Major Strong, and on the same day, the Adjutant-General wrote to Major Strong, in which he referred to the personal interview, and said, —

"There are fifteen companies and parts of companies at 'Camp Cameron.' I propose to make ten companies of them, and fill up the ranks of each to the maximum standard; and I wish to know if General Butler will furnish men for the purpose. If you prefer, I will mass the men into eight companies, and then have two full companies sent from 'Camp Chase' (Butler's camp) to complete the regiment. General Butler can advise in regard to the officers. It is important that the regiment be filled immediately, and properly officered. I am authorized to adjust all matters relating to the regiment with General Butler and yourself. . . . I will, if you desire it, make out a complete roster; and you can lay it before General Butler for examination and approval. I would be glad to have him name persons whom he would like to have appointed, if he has any in his mind. His Excellency will leave for New York on Monday evening. I wish to have these matters definitely settled, if possible, before he leaves."

Nov. 11. — Major Strong wrote, in answer, that —

"It will be quite satisfactory to make the arrangement proposed, — viz., to make eight companies of the fifteen skeleton companies you mention, and to add two companies from 'Camp Chase' as soon as they are full, with the list of officers accompanying them, to be designated by General Butler, — this to be upon the understanding, that the Twenty-eighth Regiment is to be a part of the expeditionary corps soon to sail, and not a portion of the troops to be raised by General Butler, under order of Sept. 10, 1861; General Butler desiring to fill up the regiments destined for this purpose as soon as possible, besides those he is recruiting."

Major Strong further stated, that two regiments and two batteries "will sail the coming week;" also, that the "arrangement in regard to the Twenty-eighth Regiment is designed to be made wholly independently of the unhappy and unfortunate difference of opinion which has arisen between His Excellency the Governor and General Butler (which the latter much regrets), upon the right of recruitment, on the part of the United States Government, in Massachusetts." He also said, that

"General Butler would be happy to examine the roster, as proposed;" and, if not satisfactory, he would send other recommendations, as requested.

The letter was received by the Adjutant-General on the day on which it was written: and he returned his answer on the same day, as follows:—

"Yours of date is received, in relation to the Twenty-eighth Regiment. The fact which I wish to ascertain is this: *Will General Butler accept of the Twenty-eighth Regiment?* In your letter, he accepts it, with the following stipulation: '*On the express understanding, that the Twenty-eighth Regiment is to be a part of the expeditionary corps soon to sail, and not a portion of the troops to be raised by General Butler, under order of Sept.* 10, 1861.' This acceptance is not satisfactory. If General Butler accepts the Twenty-eighth Regiment for his division, it must be as one of the two regiments raised by Massachusetts as her quota of the six which were to be raised for his division in New England; and I wish to be informed, as soon as possible, whether General Butler will accept of the Twenty-eighth, with this understanding. The other propositions in your letter are satisfactory."

To this, Joseph M. Bell, Esq., acting aide-de-camp to General Butler, made immediate answer Nov. 11,—

"If the Governor will authorize two regiments — the Twenty-eighth and Twenty-ninth — to be organized by General Butler, with a veto power upon General Butler's selection of improper persons as officers, General Butler will accept the Twenty-eighth as one of them. This in answer to a communication of to-day to the Assistant Adjutant-General, who is absent."

The following note closed the correspondence:—

ADJUTANT-GENERAL'S OFFICE, BOSTON, Nov. 11, 1861.
To JOSEPH M. BELL, Esq., acting Aide-de-camp to Major-General Butler.

SIR,—Your letter of this date has been received. The proposition is respectfully declined.

Your obedient servant,
WILLIAM SCHOULER, *Adjutant-General.*

The Twenty-eighth Regiment consequently never became a part of Major-General Butler's command. When organized, it was sent to South Carolina, and was subsequently transferred to the Army of the Potomac.

In the foregoing pages, we have endeavored to give an impartial transcript of the correspondence between the Governor and General Butler, and of the other parties who incidentally took part in it. The original trouble grew out of the unauthorized interference by Secretary Cameron with recruiting in Massachusetts, by giving special permits to outside parties to recruit regiments here. No one had this right but the Governor of the State; no one had the right to appoint or to commission officers but the Governor. Upon him, and upon him alone, rested the responsibility of selecting proper officers to command our men. It was a responsibility which Governor Andrew had no right, and no wish, to avoid. The wisdom of having the entire control of raising, forming, and officering regiments placed in the hands of the Governors of States, must be apparent to every person who will give the subject a moment's consideration. They alone were responsible for their acts to the people of their several Commonwealths. To recruit men to meet the several calls of the President required in each State a well-arranged plan of operations, with a single will to guide and control it. It admitted of no interference by outside parties. There could be no State within a State. The Governor was the supreme executive officer of the Commonwealth, and there could be "no co-ordinate" power within its limits. He could not divide the responsibilities of his position with another, however honorable or distinguished, any more than he could divide the honors of his high office with another.

Whenever the State authority was interfered with by the Secretary of War, or by parties pretending to act under his orders, independent of the Governor of the State, confusion and strife ensued; out of these attempts grew embarrassing and contradictory orders, the evil of which is illustrated vividly in this correspondence. By interference, General Sherman lost his original expeditionary command, and Massachusetts the honor of contributing her part of the contingent to complete it. By interfering with the plans of the Governor, and his clearly established rights and responsibilities under the laws, the organization and completion of regiments were delayed. It interposed obstacles by interposing a pretended divided authority

In the foregoing pages, we have endeavored to give an impartial transcript of the correspondence between the Governor and General Butler, and of the other parties who incidentally took part in it. The original trouble grew out of the unauthorized interference by Secretary Cameron with recruiting in Massachusetts, by giving special permits to outside parties to recruit regiments here. No one had this right but the Governor of the State; no one had the right to appoint or to commission officers but the Governor. Upon him, and upon him alone, rested the responsibility of selecting proper officers to command our men. It was a responsibility which Governor Andrew had no right, and no wish, to avoid. The wisdom of having the entire control of raising, forming, and officering regiments placed in the hands of the Governors of States, must be apparent to every person who will give the subject a moment's consideration. They alone were responsible for their acts to the people of their several Commonwealths. To recruit men to meet the several calls of the President required in each State a well-arranged plan of operations, with a single will to guide and control it. It admitted of no interference by outside parties. There could be no State within a State. The Governor was the supreme executive officer of the Commonwealth, and there could be "no co-ordinate" power within its limits. He could not divide the responsibilities of his position with another, however honorable or distinguished, any more than he could divide the honors of his high office with another.

Whenever the State authority was interfered with by the Secretary of War, or by parties pretending to act under his orders, independent of the Governor of the State, confusion and strife ensued; out of these attempts grew embarrassing and contradictory orders, the evil of which is illustrated vividly in this correspondence. By interference, General Sherman lost his original expeditionary command, and Massachusetts the honor of contributing her part of the contingent to complete it. By interfering with the plans of the Governor, and his clearly established rights and responsibilities under the laws, the organization and completion of regiments were delayed. It interposed obstacles by interposing a pretended divided authority in the State. In the case of General Butler, whatever may be thought of his original authority to recruit six regiments of infantry in New England, it is clear that it was modified, and made to conform to the law of Congress, by subsequent orders of the War Department, — that he was to report to the Governor, and the regiments, so far as Massachusetts was concerned in raising them, were to be raised, organized, and officered as the Governor should direct. Two regiments were a liberal portion for Massachusetts to raise of the six authorized to be raised for his command. The Governor promised the President and Secretary of War to aid in their completion to the extent of his ability; but, having given his promise first to General Sherman to furnish certain regiments for him, he asked that his promise to General Sherman should be fulfilled before undertaking to recruit new regiments for General Butler. In part fulfilment of this qualified promise, however, he designated the Twenty-sixth Regiment, then nearly completed, and the Twenty-eighth Regiment, when completed, to form the contingent of Massachusetts for General Butler's command. Notwithstanding this, General Butler proceeded to recruit two new regiments of infantry, three new companies of cavalry, and one new company of artillery, in this State. He established a camp in Lowell, and another in Pittsfield. He promised persons commissions, which no one could issue but the Governor; he appointed recruiting officers, and enlisted men, and, in so doing, wholly ignored the act of Congress, and the orders and authority of the Governor. The Governor had either to succumb or resist; to sink the Commander-in-chief of the State and become a mere recruiting officer, to issue commissions to men whom he did not know or respect, or to sustain the whole dignity of his position as a magistrate, and his honor as a gentleman.

Those who knew Governor Andrew can feel no doubt as to the course he would pursue in such an exigency. Without any of the pride which mere place sometimes gives, without any of the arrogance which power sometimes nourishes, without desire of self-aggrandizement or unmerited personal favor, with an entire absence of that "insolence of office" which weak men often show, he was at the same time the proudest, the firmest, the most determined enemy of any thing like mere pretension, come from whatever source it might. He never took a position which he had not first well considered; and, when his position was taken, nothing but a clear conviction that he was wrong could make him change from it. Though no man cared less for power than he did, no man was more conscientious and scrupulous in the exercise of it. His authority as Governor he regarded as delegated to him by the people. He held it in trust, to be exercised for their benefit, and to be trampled upon by no man. Hence, what may have appeared to some who have read this correspondence as matters of no moment, and which might have been passed by without objection, the Governor viewed as an indignity to the office he filled, involving principles which could neither be compromised with honor, nor ignored with silence. By pursuing this firm and steady course, he was enabled in the end to preserve inviolate the rights of the State, the dignity of its chief officer, and the demands of public justice. It was these traits of character which made him honored and respected while living, and caused him to be mourned for when dead, even as the children of Israel, when bondmen in a strange land, mourned their captivity, and hung their harps upon the willows which grew by the waters of Babylon.

CHAPTER VI.

The Campaign of 1862 — Meeting of the Legislature — Ex-Governor Clifford elected President of the Senate — His Speech — Alexander H. Bullock elected Speaker of the House — Speech of Mr. Bullock — Of Caleb Cushing — Proceedings of the Legislature — Abstracts of Military Laws passed — Massachusetts Prisoners in Richmond — Clothing sent — Letter from Adjutant Pierson — Expedition of General Burnside — Capture of Roanoke Island — Massachusetts Troops first to land — Care of the Sick and Wounded — Dr. Hitchcock sent on — The Wounded in New York — Colonel Frank E. Howe — Establishment of the New-England Rooms — Care of the Sick and Wounded — The Army of the Potomac — The Wounded at Williamsburg — Letters of Colonel Howe — Every Assistance given — The Agencies of the State for the Care of the Men — The Office in Washington — Colonel Gardiner Tufts, Mrs. Jennie L. Thomas, Robert C. Carson, William Robinson, appointed Agents — Visits of the Adjutant-General, Colonel Ritchie, and Colonel John Q. Adams, to the Front — Report to the Governor — The Appearance of Washington — Reports of Edward S. Rand and Dr. Bowditch — First Massachusetts Cavalry at Hilton Head — Our Troops in North Carolina — Appointment of Allotment Commissioners — Their Valuable Services — Letters of the Governor — Rule for making Appointments — Illegal Recruiting — Colonel Dudley — Thirtieth Regiment — Captured Rebel Flags — Death and Burial of General Lander — Letters of Governor to Secretary of War — Secretary of the Navy — To the President on Various Subjects — Letter to General Burnside — Secretary Chase — The Retreat of General Banks — Great Excitement — Troops sent forward — Militia called out — The Position of our Regiments — The War in Earnest.

At the close of the year 1861 and the beginning of 1862, Massachusetts had filled every demand made upon her for troops, and most of them had been sent to the front. The Twenty-eighth, Thirtieth, and Thirty-first Regiments, nearly recruited to the maximum, were yet in camp; but they were sent forward in January and February, 1862. Massachusetts regiments and batteries were in front of Washington and at Fortress Monroe; five regiments were at Annapolis, ready to embark in General Burnside's expedition against North Carolina. One regiment and a battery were at Ship Island, in Mississippi, waiting orders from General Butler. In the Army of the Potomac, we were the strongest. Gunboats officered and manned by Massachusetts men kept watch and ward on the Southern coast, or carried the flag upon far-off seas. Officers remained here on recruiting service; and enlistments were made to complete new regiments, and to fill the depleted ranks of those at the seat of war. Wounded officers and soldiers were at home on furlough or discharged for disability. The "empty sleeve" was seen daily in our streets; and maimed veterans hobbled up the steps of the State House on crutches, on their return from distant hospitals, to show their honorable discharge papers, and tell in modest words of their toils and dangers.

The Legislature met at the State House, on Wednesday, Jan. 1, 1862. Hon. John H. Clifford, of New Bedford, formerly Governor of the State, was chosen President of the Senate, and Stephen N. Gifford, clerk. On taking the chair, Mr. Clifford referred to the present state of the country, to the war which existed, and to the duties which were imposed upon the Legislature. They were then in a new and untried exigency of public affairs, and subject to the solemn and momentous responsibilities which attach themselves to every position of public trust.

"We should fail, I am sure, to reflect the prevailing sentiment of the people of Massachusetts, and show ourselves unworthy the generous confidence of our respective constituents, if we could permit a word of party strife to be uttered within these walls. Whatever may be his professions, he is no true patriot, who, in this season of his country's peril, cannot rise to such a height as to lose sight of all those lines of political difference, which, in more peaceful and prosperous times, have divided the people of the Commonwealth, or who is not ready to sacrifice every thing but principle to make and keep them a united people. Already have the gallant sons of Massachusetts, native and adopted, of every class and condition, and holding every variety of opinion upon controverted questions of policy and principle, marched as a band of brothers to the field to uphold the common flag, or to fall in its defence."

Hon. Caleb Cushing, of Newburyport, senior member, called the House to order; in doing which, he made a short address, and referred to his services as a member in years that were past, and said, —

"At other times, the wordy warfare of party, the strifes of faction might be tolerated and endured, if not encouraged and applauded. Such is not the present hour. Higher and greater thoughts occupy us now. I confidently believe that you, gentlemen, will prove yourselves equal to the emergency; that you will rise to the height of your duties; and that, taking the Constitution for your loadstar and your guide through the troubles of the times, you will dedicate yourselves to the single object of contributing, with heart and soul, to uphold, to re-establish, and to perpetuate our sacred and beloved Union. That we resolve and determine to do, with the good help of God."

The House then made choice of Hon. Alexander H. Bullock, of Worcester, Speaker of the House: he received every vote cast. William S. Robinson, of Malden, was elected clerk. On taking the chair, Mr. Bullock also referred to the existing war, and to the duty of Massachusetts in regard thereto.

"More than thirty thousand of the men of Massachusetts are at this moment far from home, in arms, to preserve the public liberties along the Upper and Lower Potomac, among the islands and deltas of the Gulf, or wherever else they have been called to follow that imperilled but still radiant flag."

He closed with these words: "In the service of the State at all times, but especially at the present, the least of duties is a part of the impressive whole."

On Friday, Jan. 3, the two branches met in convention to administer the oath of office to the Governor and Lieutenant-Governor elect, and to listen to the annual address.

The Governor, in his address, made a broad survey of the military field of observation, and the part which Massachusetts had taken in the war during the year preceding. The amount of money expended by the State, for war purposes, was $3,384,-649.88, of which there had been reimbursed, by the United States, the sum of $987,263.54; leaving an unpaid balance of about $2,500,000. This was exclusive of the amount paid by the several cities and towns of the Commonwealth for the support of the families of soldiers, under the act passed at the extra session of 1861, which amounted, in the aggregate, to about $250,000, which was to be reimbursed from the treasury of

pledged to the solemn task of *war*, and with neither hand averted to uphold the institution which is the cause of all this woe; and that their bow shall not turn back, and their sword return not empty, until their grand deliverance shall be completed."

He speaks in fitting words of praise of the action of the Legislature of Maryland, in appropriating money to relieve the suffering condition of the widows and orphans of the Massachusetts men killed by the mob in Baltimore on the 19th day of April, and calls it "an oasis in all the resentment of the hour." The address concludes as follows: " Inspired by trust in God, an immortal hate of wrong, let us consecrate to-day every personal aspiration, every private hope, in one united apostrophe to our country and her cause, — ' Where thou goest, I will go; and where thou lodgest, I will lodge; thy people shall be my people, and thy God my God: where thou diest will I die, and there will I be buried.'"

The Governor the same day transmitted to the Legislature a letter from Secretary Seward, urging that expenditures be made by the State for the defence of its coast, which he had no doubt that Congress would sanction and reimburse; also, a letter, dated Dec. 20, from Brigadier-General Joseph C. Totten, Engineer Department, U.S.A., giving a detailed statement of the different surveys made in time past of the defences on the coast of Massachusetts; also, a letter addressed to His Excellency by Colonel Ritchie, of his personal staff, upon popular military instruction, in which a review was given of the different systems in Europe, and recommending that military art be encouraged and taught in some of our public schools, and higher seminaries of learning.

Jan. 6. *In the House.* — Mr. Cushing, of Newburyport, introduced an order that the Committee on the Militia consider the expediency of making provision for the families of citizens of the State engaged in the naval service of the United States during the existing war, similar to that made for those in the land service. The order was referred.

Jan. 7. *In the House.* — On motion of Mr. Maglathlin, of Duxbury, the Committee on the Militia were instructed to consider the expediency of the State paying the expenditures made by the cities and towns of the Commonwealth for uniforming and drilling volunteers during the present war.

Mr. Heard, of Clinton, offered an order, which was referred to the Committee on Federal Relations, that the Governor be requested to communicate with the President of the United States in regard to obtaining the release of Colonel Lee and Major Revere of the Twentieth Regiment, and of Captains Rockwood and Bowman of the Fifteenth Regiment, who are confined as hostages, in a felon's cell in Richmond, for captured rebel privateersmen.

Jan. 8. *In the Senate.* — Mr. Stockwell, of Suffolk, from the Committee on Printing, reported in favor of printing two thousand extra copies of the Adjutant-General's Report.

In the House. — Mr. Brown, of Taunton, introduced an order directing the Committee on the Militia to consider the expediency of amending the law of 1861, so that each city and town shall provide for the support of persons who may be dependent on volunteers of this State mustered into the United-States service, and that each city and town shall be reimbursed from the State treasury for the money so expended.

Jan. 9. *In the House.* — On motion of Mr. Stanwood, of Essex, the Committee on the Militia were instructed to report an amendment to the State-aid law, so as to extend its provisions to the families of Massachusetts soldiers who have enlisted in regiments belonging to other States.

Jan. 10. *In the House.* — Mr. Carver, of Newburyport, introduced an order instructing the Committee on the Militia to inquire what amount of money was paid to the three months' volunteers, while in the service of the State and before being mustered into the service of the United States, and what amount may now be due them for commutation pay.

Jan. 13. *In the Senate.* — A bill was reported from the Committee on the Militia, granting State aid to the families of the volunteers in the regiments raised in this State by General Butler. An attempt was made to suspend the rules and pass the bill through its several readings, but did not prevail.

In the House. — On motion of Mr. Davis, of Plymouth, it

PROCEEDINGS OF THE LEGISLATURE. 289

was ordered, that the Governor be requested to communicate to the House the correspondence relating to the recruiting of troops in this Commonwealth by General Butler.

Jan. 14. *In the Senate.* — The bill to give aid to the families of volunteers recruited in this State by General Butler was passed to be engrossed.

In the House. — Mr. Roberts, of Lakeville, offered an order, directing the Committee on the Militia to consider the expediency of making certain amendments to the State-aid law of 1861.

The Senate bill to give aid to families, &c., was passed through its various stages, under a suspension of the rules.

Jan. 17. *In the Senate.* — On motion of Mr. Northend, of Essex, the Committee on Printing were directed to consider the expediency of printing three thousand extra copies of the Adjutant-General's Report, in addition to those already ordered.

In the House. — On motion of Mr. Manning, of Reading, it was ordered, that the Committee on the Militia consider the expediency of amending the militia law, so as to make all the enrolled militia do military duty.

Jan. 20. *In the House.* — On motion of Mr. Pierce, of Dorchester, it was ordered, that the Committee on the Militia inquire whether the blankets, which were contributed by the people of the State to relieve the necessities of the volunteers in the service, were delivered to the soldiers as gifts, or were charged to them at the market price.

Mr. Chandler, of Boston, moved that the same committee consider the expediency of authorizing the Governor to enter into contracts immediately for the manufacture of heavy ordnance for the coast defences of Massachusetts, and also for instituting a camp of instruction for artillery.

Jan. 23. *In the Senate.* — A message was received from the Governor, returning the bill to grant State aid to the families of volunteers recruited by General Butler, with his reasons for not signing it. The Governor was in favor of granting the aid as contemplated; but the bill was imperfectly drawn. He pointed out the errors which it contained. The message was laid upon the table.

In the House. — Mr. Burbank, of Boston, from the Committee on the Militia, reported that the troops in the three months' service had been paid by the Commonwealth, from the time of being ordered out by the Governor until mustered into the United-States service, $9,580.63. There was nothing more due them, and nothing more had been claimed by them.

On motion of Mr. Pierce, of Dorchester, the Committee on the Militia was requested to consider the expediency of requiring the State Treasurer, or some suitable person, to act as allotment commissioner for such sums as the soldiers in the field may allot of their pay for themselves or families.

Jan. 30. *In the House.* — A message was received from the Governor, calling the attention of the Legislature to the illegal enlistment of men in Massachusetts by persons coming from other States. Laid on the table, and ordered to be printed.

Jan. 31. *In the House.* — Mr. Pierce, of Dorchester, reported a resolve appropriating $500,000 for the manufacture of ordnance for coast defences.

Feb. 3. *In the House.* — The above resolve was debated, and passed to a third reading by a unanimous vote.

Feb. 7. — Mr. Burbank, of Boston, from the Committee on the Militia, reported a bill concerning the custody and distribution of funds of the Massachusetts volunteers.

On motion of Mr. Curtis, of Roxbury, it was ordered, that the Committee on the Militia be authorized to send for persons and papers on the matter of blankets and other articles contributed for the use of the soldiers.

Feb. 11. *In the Senate.* — The veto message of the Governor, of the bill granting State aid to the families of volunteers recruited by General Butler, came up by assignment. The Governor had informed the Militia Committee, that, since the message was sent in, the Secretary of War had placed these troops to the credit of Massachusetts, and under the authority of the Governor, the same as other regiments; and therefore no further legislation was necessary, as they would come within the provision of the law of 1861. The whole subject was then laid upon the table.

Feb. 15. *In the Senate.* — Mr. Thompson, of Hampden, from the Committee on the Militia, submitted a report upon all the orders which had been referred to them concerning State aid to soldiers' families. The report was accompanied by a bill, which provided that State aid should be paid to the families of Massachusetts soldiers who were in the New-York regiments, and whose families resided in this State. It also provided that the same should be paid to the families of Massachusetts men who should thereafter enlist in the navy.

Feb. 20. *In the House.* — Mr. Chandler, of Boston, from the Committee on Federal Relations, to whom was referred the resolve requesting the Governor to communicate with the President in favor of an exchange of prisoners, recommended that the resolve ought to pass. Mr. Chandler made a long and able report in favor of the object sought for in the resolve, which was ordered to be printed.

Feb. 26. *In the Senate.* — A long debate ensued upon the bill granting State aid to families of volunteers. That part of it relating to families of men in the navy was stricken out. Pending the consideration of other amendments, the Senate adjourned.

March 1. *In the Senate.* — The bill concerning State aid, &c., was amended, and passed to be engrossed.

March 3. *In the Senate.* — Mr. Northend, of Essex, announced the death of Brigadier-General Frederick W. Lander, and delivered a short but touching eulogy upon his life and character. He also introduced a joint resolution in honor of the deceased, which was passed unanimously.

March 5. *In the House.* — A message was received from the Governor concerning three rebel flags, which had been captured by the Massachusetts regiments in the battle at Roanoke Island, N.C. A resolution was adopted to have the flags placed in the House of Representatives during the remainder of the session. Patriotic speeches were made by Mr. Field, of Stockbridge, and by the Speaker of the House, Colonel Bullock.

March 6. *In the House.* — The Senate bill granting State

aid to the families of volunteers was discussed during the greater part of the day, and was passed to a third reading, yeas 100, nays 73.

Nothing further of material interest to the volunteers, or in relation to the war, was considered during the session. The acts passed by the extra session the year before left little more to be done for the soldiers.

The session continued until the 30th of May, when both Houses were prorogued, having passed 226 acts and 117 resolves.

Among the laws passed by the Legislature at this session was one declaring that the term of enlistment of a person in the military or naval service shall not be taken as part of the period limited for the prosecution of actions of such persons, and that, if defaulted, he may sue out a writ of review, and that, when absent, the court may continue or suspend the suit; also, a resolve authorizing the Governor to build one or more iron-clad Monitors for coast defences; also, authorizing the Treasurer to receive and distribute moneys remitted by Massachusetts volunteers, and to notify the treasurer of the town in which the family of the soldier resides, who was to notify the party to whom the money was due, and to pay the same free of charge. All such money was exempt from attachment, by trustee process or otherwise. If the money remained in the State treasury over thirty days, interest was to be allowed. A resolve was passed appropriating five hundred and fifty dollars to reimburse expenditures made for the relief of the Massachusetts prisoners of war at Richmond and elsewhere; also, a resolve authorizing the Governor to take measures for the removal of the sick and wounded soldiers of Massachusetts to their homes, the expenses of which were to be paid from the treasury of the State; also, a resolve authorizing the Governor to arrange for the reception and treatment in State hospitals of such of our wounded and sick seamen and soldiers as they can accommodate, to be paid for by the State; also, an act authorizing towns to raise and appropriate money for the aid of the families of the soldiers, not to exceed one dollar a week for the wife, and one dollar a week for each child and parent, provided that the whole sum shall not exceed twelve dollars per month for all the persons named, the money thus expended to be annually reimbursed to the cities and towns from the treasury of the State; also, a resolve thanking Adeline Tyler, of Baltimore, for the kind, humane, and Christian services rendered by her to our soldiers who were wounded in Baltimore, April 19, 1861; also, resolves acknowledging the liberal appropriation of the State of Maryland for the relief of the wounded, and to the families of the killed, of the Sixth Regiment in Baltimore, on that memorable day.

The clothing and blankets forwarded to Richmond for the comfort of the Massachusetts prisoners confined there was contained in thirty-six cases. Lieutenant Charles L. Peirson, adjutant of the Twentieth Regiment, was one of the prisoners at Richmond. He was permitted by the rebel authorities to receive and distribute the articles. In a letter addressed by him to the Quartermaster-General of Massachusetts, dated Richmond, he says, —

"I have distributed the articles, and find the invoice correct. I find the number of prisoners to be nearly four hundred. By strict economy in the distribution, they are all, with hardly an exception, completely clothed. There are, however, some sailors of the crew of the 'Massachusetts' who are badly off. I hope soon to see them provided for. I have sent part of the clothing forward to those Massachusetts soldiers who are in New Orleans and Tuscaloosa. One hundred and seventy-five, including some of the Fifteenth and Twentieth men, are to be sent to Salisbury, N.C., to-morrow; and the remainder will follow in a short time. Mr. Faulkner called upon me yesterday, and assured me that the rebel privateers in New York were much better cared for than Colonel Lee and his associates in Henrico County jail, and promised to use his influence to render their condition more comfortable. I hope soon to represent Massachusetts under the stars and stripes."

The military expedition under General Burnside, to invade North Carolina, commenced embarking on board transports at Annapolis, on the fifth day of January, 1862, and sailed from that port on the ninth and tenth. The military force was divided into three brigades, of five regiments each. One-third of the whole force was from Massachusetts; comprising the Twenty-first, in the Second Brigade, commanded by General Jesse L. Reno, and the Twenty-third, Twenty-fourth, Twenty-fifth, and Twenty-seventh Regiments, in the First Brigade, commanded by Brigadier-General John G. Foster. The most intense interest was felt in Massachusetts for the safety and success of this expedition. The report reached Boston, on the twenty-third day of January, that shipwreck and disaster had befallen the fleet, which gave pain to many hearts. The report, however, proved groundless, although the ships had encountered a succession of severe storms for nearly two weeks the ships were at sea; great difficulty was encountered in crossing the bar at Cape Hatteras, which was at length successfully surmounted. When the fleet came to anchor off Roanoke Island, an escaped slave came on board the ship to General Burnside, with whom he had a long interview, and gave much valuable information in regard to the best place to land, and the force of the enemy on the island.

The troops disembarked on the seventh day of February. A detachment of General Foster's Brigade, and the Twenty-fifth Massachusetts, was the first regiment to land and invade the soil of North Carolina. The capture of the island, the bravery exhibited by the troops, and the large number of prisoners taken from the rebels, made it one of the most successful and brilliant exploits, up to that time, of the war. The Massachusetts regiments were conspicuous for their bravery and good conduct, and captured three rebel regimental colors. On the reception of the news of Burnside's success, great joy was felt throughout the Commmonwealth, although many homes were made desolate by the death of members who had fought, and won the victory. The news of the battle reached Massachusetts on the fifteenth day of February; the battle having been fought on the eighth. The Legislature was in session; and a number of the members requested the Governor to send a special agent to the island to take care of the wounded. He at once selected, with great judgment, Hon. Alfred Hitchcock, of Fitchburg, a member of the Executive Council, and one of the most experienced and skilful surgeons in the State. The doctor reached the island in the quickest possible time, where his services as a surgeon were put in immediate requisition. He remained there several weeks, and assisted in preparing the convalescents for transportation to New England.

On the seventh day of March, one hundred and twenty-five sick and wounded soldiers were placed on board a steam transport, by order of General Burnside; and Dr. Hitchcock was placed in charge of them, with full power to provide for their wants, and procure transportation to their several homes. They reached Baltimore on the evening of the 9th of March. On arriving at New York, the wounded soldiers were welcomed by Colonel Frank E. Howe, our Massachusetts agent, and amply supplied with whatever was necessary for their wants. The Massachusetts men, seventy-one in number, were at once forwarded by rail, and reached their homes or hospitals before the thirteenth day of March. At the New-York and New-Haven depot, in New-York City, a cruel and unjustifiable detention occurred in the embarkation of these wounded men, which elicited some very sharp criticisms in the loyal papers of that day, and in letters of Dr. Hitchcock and Colonel Frank E. Howe to Governor Andrew.

Colonel Howe writes to the Governor, from New York, March 11, "Received telegram from Dr. Hitchcock at two o'clock at night, got up immediately, did all I could for him and his poor men. Dr. Hitchcock is a *remarkable man*. It was very rough for him and all his men. I have spent a good many dollars to-day." Also telegraphs the Governor the same day, "Dr. Hitchcock leaves with his men in half-past-three-o'clock train. They will need litters, carriages, and refreshments."

During the month of March, a large number of other sick and wounded soldiers were forwarded by General Burnside. March 25, Colonel Howe telegraphs to the Governor, "One hundred wounded men from Burnside left Baltimore this morning, mostly Massachusetts men. Shall take good care of them." Same day, he writes to the Governor, "Dr. Upham has just arrived, with thirty Massachusetts men, — Major Stevenson, Lieutenant Nichols, Lieutenant Sargent, Sergeant Perkins, and others. We shall get them off to-morrow morning by the eight-o'clock train. A hundred and fifty men, who left Baltimore this morning, have not yet arrived." On the fourth day of April, Surgeon-General Dale made a report to the Governor, in which he submitted a plan of forwarding the sick and wounded men of the Massachusetts regiments, which would obviate much of the confusion and delay heretofore experienced. He says that Colonel Howe had leased in New York a large, commodious, and well-ventilated store, on Broadway, for the accommodation of the returning sick and wounded, and that Dr. Satterlee, the army purveyor stationed there, had provided them with one hundred and fifty iron bedsteads, with bed-sacks, blankets, sheets, and pillow-cases. He would also furnish medicines, dressings, and every thing necessary for the comfort of the sick and wounded in this temporary building. Colonel Eaton, U.S.A., would furnish subsistence, and Colonel Tompkins, United-States Quartermaster, would furnish transportation. Nothing is wanted of the State, except an ambulance wagon.

Colonel Howe writes, April 6, "The store is nearly ready. Every thing is in it but baths and cooking ranges, and those I am at work on day and night, and am ready to take in and care for the wounded soldiers from *any* and *every* where. Plenty of money, heaps of hearts ready and determined. I have got all the United States officials with us, and as many of the surgeons as we want. The community is with us, and we feel sure that we have the Almighty with us."

About the middle of March, General McClellan began his movement against Richmond, by a change of base from before Washington to the James River. It was not until the middle of April that the Army of the Potomac was ready to advance. Yorktown was captured April 26; and the battle of Williamsburg was fought May 5, in which Hooker's brigade bore a conspicuous part, and the Massachusetts First and Eleventh Regiments suffered severely.

From that time until the retreat of McClellan, in August, the Army of the Potomac stood with its face towards the rebel capital, every foot of its onward march contested by the rebels, and almost every mile of its advance a battle-field. Many of the Massachusetts dead were embalmed, and sent home to their relatives for burial by the graves of their kindred. Many of the wounded were forwarded to the North; the military hospitals at Washington, Fortress Monroe, and elsewhere being filled to repletion. On the 13th of May, the first instalment of the wounded at Williamsburg reached New York. Colonel Howe on that day telegraphs to the Governor, "I am compelled to send off thirty-three wounded to-night, by eight-o'clock train, all able to walk, — all from Williamsburg. Twenty-six of them belong in Boston. The transport 'Daniel Webster' in, with three hundred more." Next day, — May 14, — he telegraphs, "I send, by eight-o'clock train, six bully Chelsea boys, of the First Regiment, in care of a Councilman, John Buck, also five more brave fellows. All will have to ride from the depot. We are with the sick and wounded day and night, ladies and all. Have one hundred at rooms, and one hundred and fifty coming in this morning. Not one complains." Every assistance in the power of the Governor, the Surgeon-General, and other State officers, was rendered the brave men, upon their arrival in Boston. Among the many despatches received at this time is one dated New York, May 18, to the Governor: "Have sent forty-eight men, — Twenty-third Regiment, — by five-o'clock train, to Boston, from Burnside's Division, all able to travel." This, on being referred to Surgeon-General Dale, was returned to the Governor, with this characteristic indorsement: "The men came four hours ago; 'and I am sorry I was not informed of it, though none of them required medical assistance, probably; *yet* it is better to be there when they arrive. It looks more friendly, and as if the State was solicitous about them. No harm done now, however."

From this period until the end of the war, the number of our sick and wounded soldiers increased; and the duties of the several State agents were rendered more important and arduous. The Governor was fortunate in the selection of gentlemen to fill these places, and discharge these duties. The most important of these agencies was the one established in Washington, of which Colonel Gardiner Tufts, of Lynn, was placed in charge. A brief sketch of its origin and subsequent growth deserves a place in this volume, and may as well be given now as hereafter.

When our Sixth Regiment reached Washington, April 19, 1861, it was ordered to the Capitol, and quartered in the Senate wing. No provision had been made for the wounded; but by advice of Major McDowell, U.S.A., they were taken in carriages by the Massachusetts residents, who met the regiment at the depot, to the Providence Hospital. This institution is under the direction of the Sisters of Charity. Here the first wounded in the war were kindly and tenderly cared for. On the same evening, a meeting of the Massachusetts residents was held, to organize a society to look out for the wants of the Massachusetts soldiers. We have before us the original copy of the constitution which was adopted, with the names of the original members, who signed it. The preamble is in these words: —

"The undersigned, now or formerly citizens of Massachusetts, in order to secure, by organization and mutual co-operation, proper care for the wounded and disabled, and decent interment for the dead, of the Massachusetts troops which are now or may be on duty in this vicinity, do form ourselves into a society, to be called the Massachusetts Association."

This preamble expresses, in clear language, the object of the association. This was the first organization of the kind formed in the war. The names of the original signers were Ben. Perley Poore, George W. McClellan, Charles F. Macdonald, Arthur W. Fletcher, Arnold Burgess Johnson, Ira Murdock, William Stimpson, I. O. Wilson, Nathan S. Lincoln, Edward Shaw, Henry O. Brigham, H. H. Pangborn, J. Wesley Jones, Z. K. Pangborn, Judson S. Brown, B. Fanuel Craig, B. W. Perkins.

The meeting for the choice of officers was held in the old Senate Chamber, in the Capitol. George W. McClellan, Second Assistant Postmaster-General, was elected president; Z. K. Pangborn, vice-president; Charles F. Macdonald, surgeon and treasurer; and A. B. Johnson, secretary. This society appointed Miss Lander, of Salem, to distribute proper articles for the sick and wounded. Before the end of April, it was in successful operation. Upon the arrival of our Eighth Regiment at Washington, Lieutenant Herrick, of the Beverly company, whose foot was severely wounded by the accidental discharge of a musket in the rotunda of the Capitol, was taken to the supreme-court room, where his foot was amputated. It was then decided to fit up the room as a field hospital; and it became the first army hospital established in the Rebellion. Its beds were soon all occupied; and the care of sick and wounded devolved upon the members of the association, who were promptly seconded by the Massachusetts ladies then in Washington. Miss Lander, of Salem, sister of the late General Frederick W. Lander, was a leader in these good works. She "headed the advance-guard of that corps of mercy." This volunteer association fulfilled its mission. As the war went on, many of the most active members entered the army and navy. The demands for hospital accommodations now required the action of the Government, and an organized system. In the summer of 1862, when the sick and wounded were returned in great numbers from the peninsula of Virginia, the Governor decided to appoint Gardiner Tufts the agent for Massachusetts in Washington; and, on the 18th of July, Mr. Tufts was commissioned for that purpose.

His instructions were prepared at the State House, and forwarded to him. He was to prepare a weekly report of the disabled Massachusetts soldiers in Washington, with the company and regiment to which they belonged. As far as practicable, he was to visit the hospital in person, and supply all proper wants of our men. He was to communicate with the families of the patients, stating their wants, and how the needed supplies could be forwarded. He was to have an oversight of the burial of the dead, and, when requested by their friends, to have the bodies forwarded, at the expense of the parties requesting it. He was to aid the soldiers with money in returning home, if they had not sufficient for their wants themselves. The instructions were very comprehensive, and drawn with marked ability. They covered every service which an agent could do, or a soldier require.

Mr. Tufts entered upon his duties July 28, 1862. There were, at that time, forty-four army hospitals in the District of Columbia, Fairfax, and Falls Church, Va. The battles of Cedar Mountain, second Bull Run, Chantilly, and Centreville, soon after increased the sick and wounded to sixty hospitals, which were filled. The first business of the agent was to ascertain the number of Massachusetts soldiers among the sick and wounded, also their condition, the regiments to which they belonged, and what assistance they required. Nearly five hundred of our men were in these hospitals; and the whole number upon the books of the agency, as having been in the hospitals in that department, during the war, was seventeen thousand four hundred and eighty-eight, of which seven hundred and thirty-six died. Soon after the appointment of Mr. Tufts, another society, composed of Massachusetts men, living in the district, was organized, under the name of the "Massachusetts Soldiers' Relief Association," the members of which visited the hospitals regularly, and ascertained the name and condition of every Massachusetts soldier, and relieved his wants. This organization ceased some time in 1863; and the labor which the members had performed devolved upon the State agent, who was empowered to employ persons to visit the soldiers, for which they were paid by the Commonwealth. By systematic effort, the agent, during the entire war, was enabled to ascertain the exact condition of every patient belonging to the State, and to have a perfect record in his office. The greatest number of persons employed at any one time was eighteen. This was in December, 1864. All accessible battle-fields were visited by the agent, a knowledge of our wounded obtained, and assistance rendered. In May, 1864, when General Grant began his memorable advance toward Richmond from the Rapidan, a field-agency was established, following the army, which continued in successful operation until the end of the war. During the general exchange of prisoners, which began in December, 1864, a force of the agency was maintained at Annapolis, Md., and information of great value obtained in regard to our men who had suffered and who had died in rebel prisons, and much needed assistance was rendered.

Up to Jan. 1, 1867, over twenty-five thousand letters had been written at the agency at Washington, which covered twenty thousand pages of letterpress. During the same period, about five hundred and sixty thousand dollars had been collected from the Government for soldiers or their heirs without charge. During this period, the total amount of money transactions of the agency was $721,722.87. The total number of names of Massachusetts soldiers invalided during the war at the agency was 36,151, the names of whom had, from time to time, been reported by Mr. Tufts to the State authorities. Many more interesting facts connected with the agency might be given; but those already stated are sufficient to show its importance, and to make manifest the arduous and faithful labors of the agent, in grateful recognition of which the Governor appointed Mr. Tufts an assistant adjutant-general, with the rank of lieutenant-colonel. The entire cost of the agency to the Commonwealth was thirty-five thousand dollars. We cannot close this brief sketch without expressing our acknowledgments to Colonel Tufts, for the services rendered by him to the sick and wounded soldiers of the Commonwealth; and also to Mrs. Jennie L. Thomas, of Dedham, who was appointed in October, 1862, to assist Colonel Tufts in his humane labors, and whose devotion to the cause and kindness to the worn and weary of Massachusetts soldiers, suffering from honorable wounds or from fevers engendered by exposure in the Wilderness of Virginia, the morasses of the Carolinas, and the swamps of Mississippi and Louisiana will never be forgotten by them.

Agencies were also formed in Baltimore and Philadelphia. William Robinson was appointed to take charge of the first named, and Robert C. Carson of the last. Mr. Robinson had been kind to our soldiers who were wounded on the 19th of April; and Mr. Carson had been distinguished for his attention to our men on their way to the front, and on their return, while in Philadelphia. Mr. Robinson died before the close of the war; Mr. Carson was appointed assistant quartermaster-general, and commissioned by the Governor lieutenant-colonel. These two agencies were of much assistance to the State authorities, and of material service in many ways, especially as useful auxiliaries to the two great agencies in New York and Washington, at the heads of which were Colonel Howe and Colonel Tufts.

In addition to the agencies established by the Governor to guard the rights and protect the suffering soldiers of Massachusetts, members of his staff, at various times, were sent to the front to look after them, to report their condition, and ascertain if any thing could be done by the State to render them more comfortable. The Governor also frequently visited the Massachusetts regiments, and made himself personally acquainted with their condition. During the year 1862, which was one of much disaster and suffering, the Adjutant-General, Colonel Ritchie, Colonel John Q. Adams, and Dr. Bowditch, were sent to the front and visited our men, and reported to the Governor all matters of interest in relation to them. An abstract of these reports we now present.

The Adjutant-General left Boston on the 21st of January. He remained in New York one day, and visited the Twenty-eighth Regiment, which was in the old fort on Governor's Island, New-York Harbor. The cold and gloomy casemates, in which they were quartered, and the badly provided commissariat, caused much suffering and discontent among the men. He hurried on to Washington that night, and the next morning, accompanied by Senator Wilson, called at the War Department, and had an interview with Adjutant-General Thomas, and acquainted him with the condition of the regiment. The latter promised to lay the subject before the Secretary of War immediately. The Adjutant-General says, " I waited three days before I could see him again; and it was not until I received your Excellency's letter, inclosing a copy of a letter from Captain Barrett complaining of the treatment of this regiment, that I was enabled, with Senator Wilson's assistance, to have action taken by the War Department. Secretary Stanton issued orders immediately, by telegraph, to the commander of the fort and to the colonel of the regiment, which I subsequently ascertained were of great service in obtaining the necessary comforts for the men. On my return to New York, a fortnight after, I found the regiment in good condition." The Twenty-eighth sailed, on the 16th of February, from New York, to join General Sherman at Port Royal, S.C.

The Fifth Battery was encamped on Capitol Hill, and had

been assigned to General Franklin's division. The officers had preferred to be put in General Fitz John Porter's division, as he had many Massachusetts regiments in his command. This he effected with the aid of Messrs. Elliot and Gooch, members of Congress. He next visited the camps of the Seventh and Tenth Regiments at Brightwood, about six miles from Washington. He says, "Although the weather had been bad, and the roads were in a condition hardly conceivable by a New-Englander, I found the officers and men in good health and excellent condition. There was but one man sick in the Seventh, and the Tenth had not a single person in the hospital. The men lived in comfortable log huts, which they had built themselves, and were quite well satisfied with their quarters. After spending some pleasant hours with the officers, and making an inspection of the men's quarters, I returned to Washington, much pleased with the day's labors." The journey was made on horseback; and he was accompanied by Captain Dudley, U.S.A., then stationed in Washington, but who was shortly after appointed by the Governor colonel of the Thirtieth Regiment; and by Major Fletcher, United-States paymaster. The next two days, he remained in Washington, transacting business at the War Department, and endeavoring to secure the acceptance of Maxwell's company of sharpshooters, but failed to accomplish it. The report then proceeds:—

"Having obtained a pass from General McClellan, I proceeded to the Virginia side to visit the Massachusetts troops beyond the Potomac. I passed over the Long Bridge about nine o'clock, and was surprised at the number of wagons, equestrians, and pedestrians, moving through the mud into Virginia. At the end of the Long Bridge is Fort Runyon, garrisoned by a company of the Massachusetts Fourteenth [shortly afterwards changed to the First Heavy Artillery]. The other companies of this command are near, at Forts Albany and Hamilton; the main body being at Fort Albany, the headquarters of Colonel Green."

Here he spent an hour, and then rode on to visit the Ninth, Eighteenth, and Twenty-second Regiments, and the Third and Fourth Batteries in General Porter's division. The roads were shocking. He stopped at General Blenker's headquarters, which were in what had formerly been a cross-roads tavern. He was kindly received, and was introduced to a number of the staff officers. They were all foreigners, among whom was Prince Salm-Salm, who has since become famous for his exploits in Mexico, under the late Emperor. Blenker's brigade was composed almost entirely of German regiments. The Massachusetts regiments named above were encamped near Hall's Hill. The camps of many of the regiments were decorated with evergreens; beautiful arches, made of pines and cedars, adorned the company streets. On a large, open field, between the German and the Massachusetts camps, he witnessed a spendid sham-fight, in which upwards of five thousand men, of all arms of the service, took part. After making a pleasant call at the headquarters of the Eighteenth and Twenty-second Regiments, where he found the men in good health, and supplied with every necessary for camp life, he passed on over Hall's Hill and Minor's Farm, through fields made desolate by war, to the camp of the Ninth Regiment, stationed within a mile of Fall's Church, which was plainly in sight, though it was within the rebel lines, where pickets were plainly visible. "Between Hall's Hill and the camp of the Ninth is a large field, where a skirmish had taken place some months before. The graves of the men who had fallen, and the skeletons of dead horses, half buried, mark the spot."

He found Colonel Cass in his tent, and received from him a warm and hearty welcome. The regiment was full, and not a sick man among them. General Morrell, who commanded the Brigade, came over to Colonel Cass's quarters in the evening, and stopped several hours.

"That night I slept under canvas; and, although it rained incessantly, not a drop came through. The next morning, I saw the regiment in line; and, notwithstanding the snow and rain which continued to fall, the ranks were full. I saw most of the officers, and passed many pleasant hours with this regiment. On my return, Colonel Cass accompanied me as far as Fort Albany. On our way, we called on Major-General Porter, and arranged with him about receiving our Sixth Battery. We also called at the headquarters of Brigadier-General Martindale, but he was absent; but I was glad to find, in a tent near by, our old friend Dr. Lyman; also, Captain Batchelder, late of the Twenty-second Regiment, now on Martindale's staff. We then proceeded over fields of fallen timber, and across ravines, for about four miles, to Fort Cass, which was constructed last summer by the Ninth, and named in honor of their colonel. After warming ourselves and drying our clothes, we started across the country towards Fort Albany, passing through several camps; among them, that of the Nineteenth Indiana, commanded by an old veteran friend of mine, Colonel Meredith. At Fort Albany, we parted with Colonel Cass; he returning to his regiment, and we to Washington, and reached our hotel about six o'clock."

We never saw Colonel Cass in life again. He was mortally wounded before Richmond, and died July 12, 1862. The report continues, —

"I had been two days on horseback, through a continued storm of rain and snow, with mud up to the stirrups part of the way; and yet I never had a more delightful journey."

Two more days were passed in Washington, transacting business at the War Office. On the third day, accompanied by Colonel Coffin, of Newburyport, went on board a steamer, and were taken to Budd's Ferry, about fifty miles down the Potomac, on the Maryland side. Here were the First and the Eleventh Regiments, which formed part of General Hooker's brigade. We quote again: —

" On the opposite side from the landing, one of the rebel batteries was distinctly visible. The roads from the landing to the camps of our regiments were the worst I ever saw. At one place, a wagon of the Second New-Hampshire Regiment was stuck fast in the mud. The forward wheels were completely out of sight, and the thin, red mud was running into the bottom of the wagon. We soon came to a detachment of the First Regiment, under command of my friend, Captain Chamberlain, of Roxbury, making a corduroy road. After a tiresome ride on horseback of two hours, we came to General Hooker's head-quarters."

We had a pleasant interview with the General, and then went forward to the regiments, where we met with a hearty welcome. Colonel Cowdin was acting Brigadier-General. The regiments were comfortably quartered, and there were but few in the hospitals. We remained in Colonel Cowdin's quarters all night, made an inspection of the regiment next morning, and, taking a friendly good-by of officers and men, rode back to the ferry, and reached Washington that night.

"The next day" (says the report), "I went to see General Barry, chief of artillery, with Captain Davis, of Lowell, to have his company, which has been at Fortress Monroe ever since May last, changed to a light battery, as recommended by Major-General Wool."

The change was made the next day, and the company was from that time known as the Seventh Light Battery Massachusetts Volunteers. On the following day, we went to Baltimore, where the Seventeenth Regiment and the First Light Battery were stationed. We received a hearty welcome from officers and men; visited the barracks and the hospital. There was more sickness in the regiment than in any others we had visited, which we attributed to its close proximity to a large city. The number in hospital was thirty. The report says, —

"The officers take good care of the health of the men. Both the regiment and battery are highly esteemed by the loyal citizens of Baltimore, several of whom I saw, and conversed with."

On the same evening, we left Baltimore in a steamer for Fortress Monroe, and arrived there the next morning. We paid our respects to Major-General Wool, who was in command of the department. He spoke warmly in praise of our State, and of the Massachusetts troops in his command. We quote again : —

"I remained three days at Fortress Monroe and Newport News, and had an excellent opportunity of becoming acquainted with the condition of our Sixteenth and Twenty-ninth Regiments. Here, as elsewhere, I found our men in general good health, and earnestly desiring to advance on the enemy. Colonel Wyman is almost idolized by his regiment (the Sixteenth), which he has brought to a high state of discipline. Colonel Pierce had taken command of the Twenty-ninth a short time before my arrival. From all I can learn, his appointment seemed to give general satisfaction; and I believe he will be an efficient and popular officer. The New-York Ninety-ninth is stationed near Fortress Monroe, and commanded by my old friend, Colonel

Wardrop.* As nearly one-half of his regiment is composed of Massachusetts men, I regret he does not hold a Massachusetts commission. Captain Davis's company, to which I have before alluded, is stationed inside of the fortress, and is permanently attached to the garrison."

We remained at Fortress Monroe three days, and then returned direct to Boston. We succeeded in getting from the regiments correct rolls of desertions, discharges, and deaths, since they had left the Commonwealth. These rolls were of great value in correcting the descriptive rolls at the State House, and in preventing frauds in paying the State aid to the families of soldiers. We were absent from the State about three weeks.

It was difficult to realize the change which the war had made in Washington and vicinity. Soldiers were everywhere. From the dome of the Capitol, a splendid view was obtained of the different camps, in which were stationed a hundred thousand armed men, — the nucleus of what afterwards became the Grand Army of the Potomac. The railroad from the Susquehanna was guarded by soldiers, along the entire line, to Washington. Pennsylvania Avenue was patrolled by detachments of infantry and cavalry. New regiments arrived daily, marched up the avenue, crossed the Long Bridge into Virginia, selected their camp-ground under orders of brigade commanders, pitched their tents, lighted their camp-fires, and became a part of the living mass wherein were centred the best hopes of loyal America, and for whom the prayers, from a million family altars, ascended daily to heaven. No one can fully realize the grandeur of the army, and the magnitude of the Rebellion, who never visited Washington in the years when it was being fought.

On or about the 20th of July, the Governor despatched Colonel Ritchie, of his personal staff, to the James River, to make a personal examination into the condition of the Massachusetts regiments in General McClellan's army, which had fallen back from before Richmond to the James River, near Harrison's Landing and Malvern Hill. On the 28th of July, Colonel Ritchie had

---

* Colonel Wardrop commanded the Third Regiment of Massachusetts Militia, in the three months' service.

reached Harrison's Bar, James River, Va., where he wrote a long and interesting letter to the Governor. It appears that Colonel Ritchie went by way of Washington, where he found General Burnside, who had been summoned from North Carolina to a consultation with General Halleck; "and they both left, that same day, for this place, to confer with General McClellan. This move on the part of General Halleck was intended to be kept a great secret, and he left Willard's almost in disguise; but, though no one at Fortress Monroe or this point knew of the visit, it was duly recorded by those admirable spies for the enemy, the New-York papers. Generals Halleck, Burnside, Reno, Parke, Cullom, and Sedgwick have all made most earnest inquiries concerning the success of the recruiting in Massachusetts, and expressed the greatest satisfaction at your determination to fill up the old regiments first. At the same time, I find that the almost universal feeling of the army is against the system of bribing men to do their duty by large bounties, and in favor of an immediate draft." General Burnside offered Colonel Ritchie passage to Fortress Monroe in his flag-boat, which offer was accepted; and, finding that our Twenty-first and Twenty-eighth Regiments were at Newport News, he determined to visit them at once. Captain Davis (Seventh Battery) had left Fortress Monroe, that morning, with a force of infantry, to reinforce against an apprehended attack. It was represented to be in splendid condition.

The Colonel then writes, —

"It may be useful to remark, that General Dix, in command at Fortress Monroe, exercises a discretionary power, or revising power, at Old Point, as to passes from the Secretary of War; and the *visé* of the provost-marshal is absolutely necessary to enable any one to get up this river. I will also notice, for the information of any of the staff whom your Excellency may see fit to send out here at any time, that, contrary to General Reed's opinion, I find my uniform an 'open sesame,' while a civilian's dress would stop a man at every step."

Colonel Ritchie found, at Newport News, three divisions of Burnside's corps, and General Stevens's division, from Hilton Head. General Burnside expected to have, in a short time, thirty thousand men; but it was a curious fact, that not a regiment had been sent up the river to Harrison's Landing. He found the Twenty-first Regiment, which had come from North Carolina, "in fine condition," and only requiring a hundred and fifty recruits to fill it up. Colonel Clarke, who commanded the Twenty-first, informed Colonel Ritchie, that "he had forwarded his recommendations for promotions, and had nothing more to add, excepting that he hoped your Excellency would not give any commissions to officers who had resigned. I will add here, that this is a point upon which I find the greatest sensitiveness, in every direction. The number of resignations have been scandalously large; only those are accepted which are considered beneficial to the service; and it would have a most disastrous effect to send back men with increased rank, or with any rank, who have shirked the hardships and exposures of the army."

Colonel Ritchie next visited the Twenty-eighth Regiment, which was composed, in great part, of men of Irish birth, and which had been brought up from South Carolina to reinforce the Army of the Potomac. It was stationed at Newport News, and formed part of General Stevens's division. Of this regiment, the Colonel writes, —

"They have made full returns of the number of recruits required. Colonel Monteith is under arrest, and is now before a court-martial. He has been very ill, and is such a sufferer as to be unfit for duty. The lieutenant-colonel has resigned. Major Cartwright is in command, and is an excellent officer. The regiment is composed of splendid material; but it requires two new field officers, of energy and capacity, and who are also gentlemen, to bring up its *morale* and discipline, which is, at present, very unsatisfactory."

Colonel Monteith was a citizen of New York. He was strongly recommended by James T. Brady, Esq., of that city, and by prominent Irish gentlemen of Boston. The Governor had no acquaintance with Colonel Monteith, but commissioned him upon the representations made of his fitness by the gentlemen referred to. In five days after Colonel Ritchie wrote the report from which we quote, — viz., on the 5th of August, — Colonel Monteith was discharged. Colonel Ritchie left Fortress Monroe on Saturday, the 26th, for Harrison's Landing, in the mail-boat, taking a gunboat as convoy from James Island, about sixty miles up the river. The passage was somewhat hazardous, and very exciting. On landing, he says, —

"I should have been miserably helpless, had not General Devens sent down his orderlies, with horses and wagon, and Lieutenant Church Howe, aide-de-camp to General Sedgwick, to show me the way. We had to take refuge at this general's headquarters. This gave me a chance of talking with him. He spoke most warmly of the Fifteenth, Nineteenth, and Twentieth, which are in his division, Sumner's corps. The officers he particularly commended were Hinks, whom he has repeatedly urged for a brigadier-generalship; Palfrey, who, he says, is a most excellent officer; and Major Paul Revere, who, he says, ought to have a regiment. General Sumner says that he has offered Revere the inspector-generalship of his staff. Revere hesitates, as he has made application for a position in one of the new regiments."

The brigade commanded by General Devens included the Seventh and Tenth Massachusetts Regiments. The brigade was in Keyes's corps. These were next visited by Colonel Ritchie. The Seventh had been but little exposed in action, and was "in magnificent condition. The colonel is held in high esteem." The lieutenant-colonel was regarded as inefficient; the major, a most excellent officer. A board had been appointed to examine the lieutenant-colonel, and he would probably resign. He was discharged Oct. 4, 1862. A great many officers and men were at this time in hospitals, and a good many enlisted men had deserted. General Marcy, of General McClellan's staff, "urged the importance of some appeal, by the Governors of States, to the authorities of cities and towns, and the people in general, to force deserters to return to their duties, and give such information concerning such men as to get them returned." Colonel Ritchie reports at great length in regard to filling the existing vacancies in the Seventh and Tenth Regiments, and gives a full and impartial review of the qualifications of those who were naturally looking for promotions. The Tenth Regiment wished to have an army officer appointed colonel in place of Colonel Briggs, wounded, and promoted brigadier-general. Captain Dana, of the regular army, was the choice of nearly all.

"Dexter F. Parker, who has resigned his commissariat to go into the line is highly recommended by General Devens, for a majorship in the Tenth. Captain Parker said he would not go into the regiment; but, on the suggestion that the regiment might get Captain Dana for colonel, Parker said, that, in such a case, he would be too glad to go into it; that he knew Dana well, and considered him one of the entirely honest and reliable men and gentlemen in the Quartermaster's Department." Captain Dana was not commissioned colonel of the Tenth, but Henry L. Eustis, a graduate of West Point, was. Captain Parker was commissioned major, and served until he was mortally wounded in General Grant's advance from the Rapidan, and died May 12, 1864. The remaining part of Colonel Ritchie's report relates to matters not of general interest, though of importance to the Governor, in furnishing information to guide him in making appointments to fill the vacancies in the Massachusetts regiments in the Army of the Potomac.

Edward S. Rand, Esq., of Boston, who had a son, an officer, in the First Regiment of Massachusetts Cavalry, in April, 1862, visited the regiment, then stationed at Hilton Head, S.C. Of this regiment, much complaint had been made, even before it left the State, concerning the severity of the discipline imposed by Colonel Williams. These complaints reached the State House; and Mr. Rand was requested by the Governor to inquire into them, and report the facts upon his return. The report made by Mr. Rand was in the highest degree complimentary to Colonel Williams, and to the condition of the regiment, which had been brought to an excellent state of efficiency. The charges of undue severity and cruelty, made by interested parties, were declared to be entirely groundless. The men were satisfied, were well cared for, and in good health. In conclusion, he says, —

"I cannot omit mentioning a custom introduced by Colonel Williams, which I could wish prevailed in all the regiments of our vast army. At the close of the dress-parade, each day, and before the parade is dismissed, the chaplain, who has been standing in the rear of the colonel, advances to the front, and, while officers and men stand uncovered, offers a short and earnest prayer to Him who is the only shield from danger, and the only Giver of all victories."

Mr. Rand also visited the camp of the Twenty-eighth Massachusetts Infantry, who were encamped near the cavalry. The camp was kept clean, and the general health of the men good, for which, he says, —

"Much praise is due to the skilful and attentive surgeon, Dr. O'Connell, for his faithful discharge of duty, his care of the men; and perhaps the highest praise will be found in the fact that in the hospital were but four patients, all convalescent."

Dr. Henry I. Bowditch, of Boston, who also had a son, an officer, in the regiment, visited the regiment about the same time. On his return, the Governor requested him to state, in writing, his opinion in regard to the regiment, and upon the general question of the best way to preserve the health of the soldiers on duty in the extreme Southern States. Of the condition of the regiment, he fully confirms the favorable report of it made by Mr. Rand. He says, —

"The drills are actively carried out, and the highest officers in the army agree that, at times, they are equal to any in the regular cavalry. Three times a week, the colonel has recitations, at which the highest principles of military tactics are enforced. To sum up my opinion in one sentence: I have very near and dear relatives, and many young friends, in that regiment; I should greatly regret, if, from any cause, any of them should be compelled to leave the service of such a commander."

Colonel Williams, at the time of his appointment, was a captain of cavalry, U.S.A. He was a graduate of West Point, and distinguished as a cavalry officer. He was a Virginian by birth, but never hesitated which was the path of duty for him to tread. He was a strict disciplinarian, but he was kind to his men. During the last two years of the war, Colonel Williams was assistant adjutant-general of the army, and was brevetted brigadier-general, for brave and meritorious services.

John Quincy Adams, who was appointed on the personal staff of the Governor to fill the vacancy occasioned by the resignation of Colonel Horace Binney Sargent, who was appointed lieutenant-colonel of the First Massachusetts Cavalry, was directed by the Governor, in September, to visit the Massachusetts regiments in the Department of North Carolina, and to report their condition on his return. These regiments were the Seventeenth, Twenty-third, Twenty-fourth, Twenty-fifth, and the Twenty-seventh. The Seventeenth he found in camp upon a fine plain across the river, westward from Newbern. It was stationed there to guard the ends of two bridges which span the river. The regiment was in excellent order, and the men looked hardy and cheerful, and were under the command of Lieutenant-Colonel Fellows. Colonel Adams requested a report showing the exact condition of the regiment on that day, — their wishes, wants, notes, or information in any way appertaining to their condition, — in order that he might lay the same before the Governor. But the regiment was ordered on an expedition up the Roanoke River, and Lieutenant-Colonel Fellows promised to send the report home by mail. Colonel Amory, of this regiment, had been for some time acting as brigadier-general. Colonel Adams witnessed a review of the regiment, and afterwards made a thorough inspection of each company. He says, —

"I examined every musket personally, and almost every equipment, and can say, with perfect satisfaction that their condition, in almost every case, was admirable. The arms, particularly, were as clean and bright as when they were issued. The regiment was then drilled by Lieutenant-Colonel Fellows in various evolutions, concluding with the drill as skirmishers, in all which the men showed careful and faithful training, and most commendable proficiency."

The Twenty-third Regiment, Colonel Kurtz, had been stationed, since May preceding, in the town of Newbern itself, where it performed the duties of provost guard, Colonel Kurtz acting as provost-marshal. He could not, therefore, speak of the condition of their camp-equipage; but the barracks, which he visited, were clean and orderly, and the appearance of the men tidy and excellent. He also reviewed the regiment, and inspected their arms and equipments, which were in perfect order. "Altogether," he says, "the condition of the regiment was very satisfactory, and reflects great credit upon their officers."

Colonel Adams next visited the Twenty-fourth Regiment, Colonel Stevenson, who had been for some time acting as brigadier-general; and the command had devolved upon Lieutenant-Colonel Osborne. The regiment was in camp on a fine, dry plain, about a quarter of a mile from the town. Every thing was in perfect order, as he found upon careful inspection of the arms and equipments, and of the camp. "Both officers and men might well be a source of pride to the Commonwealth."

On the morning of the second day of his stay in Newbern, he rode out to the camp of the Twenty-fifth Regiment, Colonel Upton; but neither he nor the lieutenant-colonel nor the major were in camp at the time; but the adjutant was there, and with him he examined carefully the camp, which was on a fine, beach plain of very large extent, and admirably adapted for a drill and parade ground, about half a mile from the centre of Newbern, and westerly from the camp of the Twenty-fourth Regiment. He says, —

"I was entirely satisfied with the appearance of the camp, and the aspect of the men. Great neatness was evident in the cleanliness of the company streets, and the men seemed tidy, cheerful, and contented. I attended a dress parade of this regiment with General Foster, and found their appearance admirable, and their drill excellent."

Colonel Adams says General Foster told him, —

"The first thing an officer should do is to try to make every man of his regiment a dandy, proud of his appearance, the glitter of the musket, and the polish of the brass on his equipments. When you see such a man, be sure he is a good soldier."

The Twenty-seventh Regiment, Colonel Lee, he found under the command of Lieutenant-Colonel Lyman. Colonel Lee was acting as brigadier-general. There were only five companies in camp, the remaining five being engaged in picketing the railroad to Beaufort, and thus scattered, in small squads, along twenty miles of road. Colonel Adams could not see them. Those in camp looked as well as any companies he had seen.

These comprised all the Massachusetts regiments in that department; and as each had made regular reports to the

Adjutant-General of the Commonwealth, showing their exact condition, nothing more was necessary to be done. Colonel Adams says, —

"Major-General Foster repeatedly assured me, that he considered them as good as any regulars in the army; and he was never weary of extolling the energy, efficiency, accomplishments, and bravery of Massachusetts officers, and the intelligence, docility, discipline, and courage of Massachusetts privates."

Colonel Adams concludes his report in these words: —

"I was much impressed with the untiring energy and interest with which General Foster looked after every thing within his reach; and I was pleased at the high commendation he bestowed upon Colonels Stevenson, Amory, and Upton, in especial. I was the bearer of a recommendation from him to the Secretary of war, that Colonels Amory and Stevenson should be appointed brigadier-generals. He desired me to solicit your recommendation for them also."

During the early part of the year 1862, three allotment commissioners were appointed by the President, as provided by acts of Congress, passed July 22, 1861, and Dec. 24, 1861. These acts provided, —

First, for the transmission, free of expense, of portions of the soldiers' pay to their families or friends, as had been done under the half-pay system in the navy.

Second, for the appointment, by the President, for each State which chose to adopt this system, of three commissioners, without pay, who should visit the troops, and invite each soldier to avail himself of this opportunity.

In February, 1862, President Lincoln, upon the recommendation of Governor Andrew, appointed, as commissioners for Massachusetts; Henry Edwards, of Boston; Frank B. Fay, of Chelsea; and David Wilder, Jr., of Newton. They immediately proceeded to visit all the Massachusetts volunteers, — in the Army of the Potomac, under General McClellan; in the Shenandoah Valley, under General Banks; and at Warrenton, under General McDowell: and, when the Army of the Potomac moved to James River, they accompanied it to Fortress

Monroe, and to Yorktown. Allotments were made by the First, Second, Seventh, Tenth, Eleventh, Twelfth, Thirteenth, Fifteenth, Sixteenth, Eighteenth, Nineteenth, Twentieth, Twenty-second, and Thirty-second Regiments, and the Third and Fifth Light Batteries, and, subsequently, by the Thirty-third, Thirty-fourth, Thirty-seventh, Thirty-ninth, and Forty-first Regiments, and the Ninth, Tenth, and Eleventh Light Batteries; at a still later period, allotment rolls were made up for the Third, Fourth, Fifth, Sixth, Eighth, Forty-third, Forty-fourth, Forty-fifth, Forty-sixth, Forty-seventh, Forty-eighth, Forty-ninth, Fiftieth, Fifty-second, Fifty-third, Fifty-fourth, and Fifty-fifth Regiments, — making, in all, forty-one different organizations which were visited, either in the field, or at the camps at home, before the men were sent forward. The Legislature of Massachusetts passed an act, March 11, 1862, to carry out more perfectly the system of payments. Mr. J. P. Wainwright, as a volunteer agent of the commissioners, aided in getting the soldiers to make allotments, and, in the fulfilment of this work, visited the Massachusetts regiments in the Department of the Gulf. Communications were made by the commissioners to the officers of the Massachusetts regiments, pressing upon them the advantages, to the soldiers and to their families, of the system. No allotments were received, however, from regiments not visited, except, in a solitary case, of the Twenty-fourth, — Colonel Stevenson's regiment. Much of the success in securing allotments in regiments depended upon the interest felt, and the encouragement given, by its officers. For instance, in one company, containing eighty-three men, seventy-four, following the example of a worthy captain, allotted a portion of their pay; and thirty-three of these, mostly young men, placed it in the State Treasury on interest, subject, at any time, to their order, properly approved by the commanding officer of their company; and two regiments allotted about seven thousand five hundred dollars a month each.

The allotment system was simply this: The sums allotted were deducted by the paymaster on each pay-day, and forwarded to the State Treasurer for distribution, or by separate checks to the family, according to the system adopted by the State. Our Massachusetts system proved most satisfactory, as it avoided all risk of chance of omission by transmission of a check by mail, and secured payment directly to the family at home. The payments to the soldiers, from the General Government, were to be made at or near the close of every two months, commencing with January. But, owing to sudden or hazardous movements and other causes, these payments were often delayed, and both the men and their families were much distressed. To remedy this evil, — in part, at least, — and secure, if possible, the retention of a large share of the soldiers' wages at home, the Massachusetts Legislature, in 1863, at the suggestion of Governor Andrew, passed an act, authorizing the State Treasurer to assume the payment of all the Massachusetts volunteers, provided that Congress would permit this to be done. For some reason, permission was not given, much to the regret of the soldiers and the Massachusetts authorities. The act passed by the Legislature of Massachusetts, March 11, 1862, provided that the Treasurer of the Commonwealth should receive and distribute, without expense to the soldiers or their families, all money which our volunteers might forward for this purpose; and that the distribution should be made to parties in the State by the Treasurer of the Commonwealth, through the town and city treasurers, who were to notify the persons 'to whom the money was assigned, and, if they failed to call for it, return the money to the State Treasurer, who placed it on interest, until further order from the soldier. Persons living out of the State, to whom money was assigned, were to be notified; and, upon the return of a proper order or draft, the amount was forwarded, by a check upon a bank in Boston or New York, as would best serve the interest of the claimant. In many cases, the money was directed by the soldier to be placed at once in the State Treasury, where it drew five per cent interest, thus virtually making the State Treasury a savings bank.

It appears, from the report of the State Treasurer for 1866, that the first allotments forwarded to him were in April, 1862; and that —

The whole amount, for that year, including about
$40,000, placed on interest, was $202,905.56
In 1863, including $90,000 on interest, was. . . . 698,297.76
Also, allotments of State bounties 190,012.50
In 1864 and 1865, including State bounties 2,144,136.65
In 1866, for deposits by State paymaster 2,294.65

Total $3,237,647.12

At the close of the year 1866, all this money, excepting $76,269.15, which remained on interest to the credit of eight hundred and seventy soldiers, had been distributed; and the balance awaited the appearance of the men, or their legal representatives, to whom it will be paid.

It is evident, from these figures, that the system of allotment, and the very able and satisfactory manner by the commissioners and the State Treasurer, was of very great utility. It secured to many men and to their families much money which would otherwise have been wasted; and it induced and encouraged a habit of saving, the effect of which may have a material, beneficial influence upon those who practised it. It also lessened the taxes which would otherwise have been imposed upon the Commonwealth. To the members of Congress, who inaugurated this admirable system, and to Governor Andrew and the Legislature, who encouraged it, and especially to the commissioners, who gratuitously, at great expense of time and money, performed this onerous service, the soldiers and the State owe a debt of gratitude.

The letters written by the Governor, during the year, relate chiefly to military matters, — many, in the early part of the year, to the appointment of regimental and company officers. Governor Andrew had established a rule for making appointments, from which he seldom departed during the Rebellion. This rule was based upon the principle of selecting the best men he could find, without regard to personal or political affinities. Whenever he could obtain the services of an experienced and educated officer to command a Massachusetts regiment, he commissioned him. The selection of officers for commands he regarded as the most solemn duty which the war imposed on him. We have often heard him say, when asked to appoint persons whose claims upon his favor were based upon the fact that the candidate and his family exercised a local, political influence, —

"Such considerations impress me with no force. The appointment is in no manner a political one. The man I shall commission is he who can best command his men, care for their health, lead them bravest in battle, and, by his intelligence and capacity, save life and limb from needless sacrifice. This I owe alike to the men themselves, to their families they leave behind, and to common humanity."

Of course, he did not, at all times, make the best choice; but he endeavored to, and thought he had succeeded. We remember one rather remarkable case, where the Governor erred in making selection of a captain in the Twenty-second Regiment. The Governor believed the person whom he selected to be best fitted for the command. The Adjutant-General believed, and so reported, that the gentleman who was to be a lieutenant in the company should be made captain. The Governor, however, did not change from his original purpose; and the commissions were made out as originally determined upon. The person commissioned captain never attained higher rank: the one commissioned lieutenant rose to be a major-general of volunteers, and gained a reputation second to none, as an able and accomplished volunteer commander, in the Army of the Potomac, — we refer to Major-General Nelson A. Miles, now colonel of infantry in the United-States army, who began his military career as first lieutenant in the Massachusetts Twenty-second Regiment, and whose military record reflects great honor upon his native State.

Governor Andrew, however, seldom erred in his judgment of men; and we have no question that the officers selected by him will bear a favorable comparison with those of any other State. When a vacancy occurred after the regiment left the State, his rule was to wait until a recommendation of a person to fill the vacancy was received from the officer in command of the regiment, which recommendation required the approval and indorsement of the officer in command of the brigade. If the person recommended appeared, by the roster, to be junior to others of the same rank, the colonel was written to for his reasons for deviating from the military rule of seniority: if the reasons returned were satisfactory and properly indorsed, the promotion was made, and the commission issued; but, if the reasons given were not satisfactory, — if they disclosed favoritism, family influence, or unjust prejudice, — the appointment was not made, but the officer properly in the line of promotion was commissioned. The Governor's mind was eminently just; he despised trickery and treachery, and all the small devices to which mean natures resort to gain their ends.

On the 11th of January, the Governor writes to Montgomery Blair, Postmaster-General, calling his attention to a bill reported in the United-States Senate by Senator Wilson, "providing, among other things, that vacancies occurring in regiments of volunteers mustered into the United-States service shall be filled by presidential appointment," and gives strong reasons why it should not become a law. He concludes by saying, —

"It is simply impossible that the volunteer officers can be well selected at Washington. I make mistakes, make some exceptionable appointments, find it out, and try to avoid similar errors again; and I know how difficult is the task. Knowing its difficulty, I write you this note, though the passage of the bill would relieve me personally from much irksome and anxious duty."

The bill here referred to never became a law; and appointments continued to be made by the Governors of States, until the end of the war. On the same day, he writes a long and interesting letter to Major-General McClellan, thanking him for the "assurance of your valuable aid in establishing our coast defences, furnishing instructors for our volunteer artillerists," and asking his influence to have a company accepted, "the rank and file of which will be mechanics, riggers, carpenters, smiths, &c., for the special duty of garrisoning Fort Independence, putting the fort in order, mounting and serving the guns." This company was, long afterwards, raised and accepted, of which Stephen Cabot was commissioned captain, and became the nucleus of the Fort Warren Battalion.

On the 13th of January, the Governor writes three letters, in regard to our coast defences, — one to the President, one to our Senators and Representatives in Congress, and one to Secretary Seward, — in which he argued the importance of the subject, and that the General Government authorize it to be done by the State, as "the State can do it with more expedition and economy than it can be done otherwise." These letters were taken to Washington by Colonel Charles Amory, master of ordnance of Massachusetts.

Jan. 18. — Colonel Browne, by direction of the Governor, writes to Henry N. Hooper, of Boston, respecting an exchange of prisoners : —

"Every thing that the Governor can do by prayers, entreaties, arguments, and remonstrances, to induce the Federal Government to *do justice* to our prisoners by instituting a proper system of regular exchanges, has been done in vain. The Federal Administration have obstinately refused to institute such a system; and it is only by individual effort that our fellow-citizens can extricate their fathers, brothers, and sons from that Southern captivity."

Jan. 22. — Governor writes to Hon. Roscoe Conkling, United-States House of Representatives, and now United-States Senator : —

"I have received, and perused with lively gratification, your speech, delivered on the 6th inst. For its lofty eloquence, and its tribute to the valor and devotedness of our soldiers, — particularly of the men of the Fifteenth and Twentieth Regiments, — I beg to tender you the homage of respectful and hearty gratitude."

Jan. 27. — Governor writes to Edwin M. Stanton, who was recently appointed Secretary of War, in place of Mr. Cameron, —

"I have the honor to introduce John M. Forbes, Esq., of Boston, one of the most eminent citizens and business men of Massachusetts. He takes great interest in the subject of coast defences, of which Mr. Seward wrote me, last October, but which, I believe, is now in the care of your department. It is very desirable that Massachusetts should act promptly in every way in which her action is needful; and I desire not to be remiss in any duty, but rather to anticipate than delay. Any views imparted to Mr. Forbes would be received for the common good."

Same day, to Hon. Salmon P. Chase, Secretary of the Treasury: —

"I have the honor to give notice, that Massachusetts assumes, and will pay, her quota of the direct national tax; and I inclose you a copy of the resolve of the General Court, giving me authority to that end."

Reference having been made, in the newspapers, to the letter written by General Butler, reflecting upon the personal character of Colonel Powell T. Wyman, of the Sixteenth Regiment, and the answer which the Governor made to it, it would appear that Colonel Wyman, on the 24th of January, wrote to the Governor, as we find a letter written by the Governor, Jan. 27, to Colonel Wyman, from which we extract the essential part: —

"Nothing contained in General Butler's letter lessens my estimation of your qualities as a soldier and a gentleman; nor, to my knowledge, is there any officer connected with my staff who entertains any other feeling towards you than such as was manifested continually during your intercourse with us, while organizing your regiment. I have heard but one expression of sentiment with regard to the affair; and that has been of very cordial sympathy with you, under the infliction of so wanton, unprovoked, and unmerited an attack."

On the 30th of January, the Governor was suddenly called to Washington, and was absent about ten days. It was while in Washington at this time that the troops raised by General Butler in Massachusetts were placed in the charge of the Governor, and the irregular and illegal manner of raising regiments ended; and the "Department of New England" was discontinued.

In January and February, persons representing themselves recruiting officers for a Maryland regiment came to Boston, and, by their misrepresentations of large pay and little service, induced some thirty or forty men to enlist, and go with them to

Baltimore. Upon arriving there, they found how miserably they had been imposed upon. The promises held out were delusive, and the men whom they had trusted were cheats. They were left without money to support themselves; and many letters were received by the Governor and the Adjutant-General, asking that transportation be furnished to return to Massachusetts. Strenuous efforts were made by the Governor to have the men released from the trap in which they had been caught. We find among his letters, at this time, many relating to this unfortunate occurrence. He wrote to General Dix, then commanding at Baltimore; to the Secretary of War; to our members of Congress; to the Governor of Maryland; and to the men themselves. In a letter to one of our members of Congress, he thus describes the transaction: —

"It has been done by the most dishonorable and outrageous fraud; and my efforts have been baffled, and these men and others have been entrapped into organizations in which they find only discomfort and misery; and I think that their condition appeals strongly to the sympathy, as well as to the sense of justice, of the War Department."

He had the satisfaction in a few weeks to know that his efforts had been successful. The men were released, and afterwards enlisted in Massachusetts regiments.

Feb. 18. — The Governor writes to the Secretary of War, —

"I am informed by Colonel Dudley, that, from conversations he has had with Major-General Butler, he is satisfied, and feels it his duty to report to me, that, if I commission any other person than Mr. Jonas H. French as lieutenant-colonel, he will compel him (Colonel Dudley) to recognize Mr. French as such, and to repudiate the gentleman I appoint, notwithstanding the commission. Colonel Dudley states, that, as a pretence for this action, General Butler states to him that he proposes to rely on Special Order No. 11, of the current series of your department, which is of course inoperative, so far as it undertakes to designate officers over a body of men which it rests with me alone to organize by the appointment of commissioned officers, but which, nevertheless, Major-General Butler cites, in opposition to *the law*. I respectfully suggest to you, that that order should be annulled, and that General Butler should receive, from his commander-in-chief, directions suitable to the occasion, and to the demeanor thus assumed by him."

Colonel Dudley, who is here mentioned, was a captain in the United-States army, — a Massachusetts man, — and had been commissioned by the Governor colonel of the Thirtieth Regiment.

At this time, the Governor had offered the lieutenant-colonelcy of the regiment to William S. Lincoln, of Worcester; but, from some cause, a change was made, and William W. Bullock, of Boston, received the appointment, and served with the regiment until ill health compelled him to resign, Nov. 25, 1863.

The following is the answer of the Secretary of War to the letter above quoted: —

"This Department recognizes the right of a Governor to commission volunteer officers. If General Butler assumes to control your appointment, or interfere with it, he will transcend his authority, and be dealt with accordingly. The Adjutant-General will transmit to General Butler an order that will prevent his improper interference with your legitimate authority."

Feb. 19. — The Governor telegraphed Hon. John B. Alley, member of Congress, —

"The gentlemen said to have been designated by the President, as allotment-commissioners for Massachusetts troops, have received no notice of their appointment. Will you ascertain why, and see that notice is immediately forwarded? Telegraph, if you succeed."

Feb. 20. — The Governor's private secretary, Colonel Browne, writes to Colonel Dudley, —

"Governor Andrew directs me to inclose to you the within photographic likeness of the young gentleman, Mr. Joseph W. Morton, of Quincy, of whom he spoke to you, and who is acting as a non-commissioned officer in the Thirtieth Regiment. He hopes you may find him qualified to be recommended for appointment to a first or second lieutenancy. He is represented to be a person of careful education, extensive travel, and general capacity."

It is proper to state here, that the Thirtieth and Thirty-first Regiments of Infantry, recruited by General Butler in this

Commonwealth, and originally designated by him as the Eastern and Western Bay-State Regiments, were sent from the State to Louisiana without a single commissioned officer. Persons selected by General Butler had been designated by him to act as officers. As many of these persons acted in good faith, and were believed to be competent to command men, Colonel Dudley, of the Thirtieth, and Colonel Gooding, also an army officer, who was commissioned colonel of the Thirty-first, were directed by the Governor, upon joining their regiments in Louisiana, to make a careful examination of the qualifications of the gentlemen acting as officers, and to report to him the names of those who were qualified, that they might receive their commissions. This duty was performed, and, in due time, the officers were properly commissioned. The young gentleman, Mr. Morton, referred to in the above letter, was afterwards commissioned by the Governor in one of the cavalry companies raised by General Butler, and serving in the Department of the Gulf. He was a good officer, and died at his home in Quincy, before the end of the war, from disease contracted in the service.

Feb. 20. — The Governor writes to Mr. Stanton, —

"I earnestly desire authority to change the battalion at Fort Warren to a regiment. It consists of six companies, and needs the staff officers pertaining to a regiment. Major Parker has repeatedly urged this, and is by my side while now writing."

The battalion here spoken of was raised by Francis J. Parker, of Boston, for garrison duty at Fort Warren, and remained there until the retreat of General McClellan, in the summer of 1862, from before Richmond, when it was sent forward to the front, at a day's notice, to meet the pressing exigency, which then existed, for additional forces. Previous to this time, Mr. Stanton persistently refused to allow the battalion to be recruited to a regiment. After it had left the State for the seat of war, permission was given, and four new companies were added to it, and it was designated and known, to the end of the war, as the Thirty-second Regiment, Massachusetts Volunteers.

Feb. 27. — The Governor writes to Colonel Tompkins, United-States Quartermaster at New York, —

"The Rev. A. L. Stone, pastor of the Park-street Church in this city, desires to visit Port Royal for the purpose of gathering information concerning the moral and spiritual condition of the 'contrabands' in that quarter. He is a suitable person to accomplish such a mission. May I hope that you will do what you can to facilitate Mr. Stone's transit to and from Port Royal?"

Feb. 28. — The Governor writes to the Adjutant-General of Massachusetts, —

"I have just, this afternoon, had time to read your interesting report, and I beg you would do what it reminds me of; namely, send to Captain Davis, at Fortress Monroe, and learn what is the present state of his company. General McClellan agreed to change it to artillery; but as yet I have received no orders about it."

This letter refers to the report made by the Adjutant-General of his visit to the front, of which an abstract is given in preceding pages in this chapter.

March 3. — The Governor addressed a letter to Hon. A. H. Bullock, Speaker of the House of Representatives, calling his attention to a general order issued that day by the Adjutant General of the State, concerning three rebel flags taken at the battle of Roanoke Island by the Massachusetts regiments, and says, —

"Such trophies are always prized by the soldier. They are earnest proofs of his efforts and achievements in the performance of his perilous duties. I confess that I received these with the utmost sympathy; and I can but pay to the men who won that day my humble but hearty and admiring gratitude."

The Governor then states that the House of Representatives would probably like to pay to our soldiers the honor of having the flags displayed for a time in their hall, and that any direction as would enable this to be done he would gladly concur in. The flags were subsequently presented to the House, and were displayed there until the end of the session.

March 3. — The Governor writes to Right Rev. Bishop Fitzpatrick that he had no power "to order private McDonald's discharge: that rests alone with the Federal authorities. I will, however, be happy to unite with you in presenting to the Secretary of War, or the General-in-chief of the army, any statement of reasons for requesting the discharge which is desired."

March 4. — The Governor writes to Colonel Kurtz, Twenty-third Regiment, at Newbern, N.C., —

"I wish to learn the place of burial of James H. Boutell, late private in Co. K, Twenty-third Regiment. He died in the service, and is supposed to have been buried at Hatteras; also, the best means for his friends to get his remains to Massachusetts. His wife, Mrs. Abbie P. Boutell, resides in Wrentham."

March 9. — The Governor writes to Mr. Stanton, Secretary of War, —

"I beg leave to report to you, that the honor you paid to the memory of General Lander, by causing his remains to be returned, under a suitable escort, to his native State, was rendered complete by the faithful and decorous manner in which the sad duty was fulfilled by Captain Barstow, and the officers and soldiers accompanying him. The Commonwealth of Massachusetts, and the city of Salem, the place of General Lander's nativity, have received with much sensibility the manifestation of grateful respect, on the part of the War Department, toward a soldier and gentleman whose fame, now a part of his country's history, is one of the precious possessions of those from whom he went forth to her service and defence. His body now rests in silence beneath the soil on which his youth was spent, and to which it was committed with every demonstration of regard on the part of the executive and legislative branches of the government of the Commonwealth, and on the part of the municipality of Salem, in the presence of many thousands of his fellow-citizens, and with appropriate military honors. With the fervent hope that we who survive him, and are charged with leadership in our patriotic army, will vindicate on the field an equal title with his to gratitude and admiration, and with sentiments of the utmost regard, I am, sir, ever

"Your obedient and humble servant,
"JOHN A. ANDREW, *Governor of Massachusetts.*"

No words of ours can add to the respect and esteem with which General Lander was held by the people of this Commonwealth; and no words of eulogy can be added which would give significance and strength to the letter we have just quoted.

March 28. — The Governor wrote to Mr. Fox, Assistant Secretary of the Navy, by which it appears that Mr. Fox had sent to the Governor a copy of a letter "taken out of a pocket of a secesh pea-jacket" by Commodore D. D. Porter, commanding the fleet at the mouth of the Mississippi River, and which related to a Mrs. Sarah A. Blich, of Holmes Hole, who, it appeared, had been giving information to the rebels at New Orleans. Inquiry was made by the Governor, and it was ascertained that a person of that name resided there. He writes, —

"She is a native of New Orleans, and was married to Blich last spring. Her maiden name was Sarah A. Stickney. She has a brother in the South, named William Stickney, who is undoubtedly the writer of the letter in question. · Her husband, Blich, is a seafaring man, and sailed recently on a voyage to Rio Janeiro; he has a brother who keeps a jewelry shop at Holmes Hole, and is now there. Mrs. Blich is known to have used very violent language of a treasonable character during the progress of the rebellion, and is believed by my informants to be disposed to aid the rebels by information or otherwise. My informants think it more than probable that she has been a medium of communication with the rebels as intimated in her brother's letter. I have not been able to ascertain who is the person named 'Dora,' to whom the letter is addressed; but I expect within a few days to obtain information on that point also."

Nothing further in relation to this matter appears in the Governor's correspondence.

On the ninth day of April, the Governor writes to Colonel Frank E. Howe, New York, that Surgeon-General Dale had made arrangements by which to have an ambulance kept at the city stables, and that city horses would be furnished, without expense, to be used for our wounded soldiers, whenever required. An ambulance, therefore, was purchased; and Colonel Howe was authorized to purchase one, to be used for our wounded in New York.

April 8. — The Governor writes to the President of the United States : —

"I have the honor, by the hand of Hon. Francis W. Bird, who is specially deputed therefor, to place in your hands an engrossed copy of the resolves of the General Court of Massachusetts, in approval of your recent message to the Congress of the United States, in favor of national co-operation with any State of this Union, in the abolishment of slavery. I deem it due to the solemnity, interest, and importance of the occasion, and to the earnest devotion of this ancient Commonwealth, alike to the Union, the fame, and the happiness of these States and people, as well as to her hereditary love of liberty, that this expression of her hearty concurrence with your great act, should receive the most formal and cordial utterance. . . . I devoutly pray that the good providence of God will conduct your administration and this nation through all the perils they encounter, and establish our country on eternal foundations of impartial justice to all her people."

April 9. — The Governor telegraphs to the Secretary of War, —

"Accept my congratulations on victories at Corinth, and the Mississippi. Do you desire extra surgeons from Massachusetts for the care of wounded, there or elsewhere? If so, there are several here, of professional eminence, who, under the direction of our State Surgeon-General, are prepared to start immediately to any point of active operations, giving their professional services gratuitously, from motives of patriotism."

April 12. — The Governor writes to General Burnside, at North Carolina, congratulating him upon his well-deserved promotion, which has given "sincere as well as universal pleasure." He then refers to a letter which he had received from Brigadier-General Foster, that seven hundred and fifty recruits were needed to supply the losses in the four Massachusetts regiments in his brigade. But just at this time, an order had been issued from the War Department, discontinuing recruiting in every State, and requiring recruiting parties to close their offices, and join their regiments. The Governor telegraphed to Mr. Stanton for permission to recruit for the Massachusetts regiments under General Foster, and leave was granted. At this time, the general superintendence of recruiting, in the different States, had passed into the hands of the War Department; and army officers were detailed, in various States, as military commanders, who assumed control of all enlistments, mustering, subsistence, and transportation of men. The military commander in Massachusetts, in April, 1862, was Colonel Hannibal Day, U.S.A.

This change in mode of recruiting was not satisfactory at first; but, after it was in operation some time, certain modifications were made by the War Department, and the State and United-States authorities worked in harmony together. The men asked for by General Foster were soon recruited, and forwarded to North Carolina.

April 19. — The Governor writes to Mr. Chase, Secretary of the Treasury, calling his attention to a communication of the Treasurer of Massachusetts, which he inclosed to him, and says, —

"The prominent fact to which I beg to allude with emphasis is, that, after the passage of the tax act, we very much more than paid our share of it by heavy expenditures, made at Mr. Cameron's request, and on which we are losing the interest. I ask, therefore, that at least as much as the amount of the tax assessed on Massachusetts should be paid to us before we pay this tax. This is safe for the United States, and only just to Massachusetts."

On the same day, the Governor wrote to the Secretary of the Navy, introducing Hon. Joel Hayden, of the Executive Council, and Edward S. Tobey, President of the Boston Board of Trade, who were deputed to confer with him in relation to iron-clad ships. These gentlemen had a plan for iron-plating four steamers, belonging to the Government, at Charlestown and the Kittery Navy Yards, which, the Governor said, "would render them invulnerable, and present them ready for action and in sea-going trim *in fifty days*. If those vessels belonged to us," he continues, "we would undertake to prepare some of them for service in this way; but they belong to the United States. If you will turn over to us one or two of them, we will be glad to take them, and have the work done; and we desire that the four should be thus treated." The proposition here made was not complied with.

As one of the many evidences of the firmness of purpose and justness of decision of Governor Andrew, we give an extract from a letter, dated April 29, to Brigadier-General Doubleday, then on duty at Washington. A lieutenant-colonel of one of our regiments had been accused, by the colonel, of certain delinquencies; and charges were preferred to bring the case before a court-martial. In a hasty and inconsiderate moment, the lieutenant-colonel resigned, rather than stand trial. After the resignation was accepted, the officer repented of his hasty act, and sought to be restored by the Governor. Before acting upon this request, he wrote to General Doubleday, to make inquiry into the charges, and inform him what he thought of them. From this letter we quote: —

"While I feel kindly towards Lieutenant-Colonel Oliver, I wish only for exact justice, and would not restore him to the regiment, unless he was unjustly accused. I am jealous of the honor of the Massachusetts corps, sensitive to every thing which affects them, desirous of doing exactly right, hit where it will. The matter lies in a narrow compass; and I wish to reach a speedy conclusion, founded upon a basis of established proofs, which shall satisfy the demands of justice, truth, and honor."

Lieutenant-Colonel Oliver was not restored to the regiment from which he resigned, but was afterwards commissioned major in the Second Regiment Heavy Artillery, which shows that the Governor had been satisfied that the charges against him did not affect his standing as an officer and gentleman.

April 30. — The Governor received the following despatch from Major-General Wool, dated —

"HEADQUARTERS DEPARTMENT OF VIRGINIA,
FORTRESS MONROE, April 29.

"I have just received your communication of the 26th inst. The Government have made arrangements to send the sick and wounded of the Army of the Potomac to Washington, Baltimore, Philadelphia, New York, and Boston. Agents have been detailed to superintend forwarding them."

This is the first despatch received at the State House in relation to the sick and wounded of General McClellan's army, from which, for months following, the brave and ghastly sufferers of that memorable campaign returned, to fill the homes of their friends, and the hospitals of the Government. In connection with these wounded and suffering men, we find a letter written by the Governor, May 1, addressed to all officers of

Massachusetts corps volunteer officers in the field, commending to their courtesy and co-operation Dr. Alfred Hitchcock and his assistant, Mr. J. W. Wellman, who were detailed to visit the Massachusetts troops at Yorktown, Newbern, or elsewhere, and to render such aid as might be practicable to the sick and wounded in the field or hospitals, and transporting them to their homes. Of Dr. Hitchcock's services, while thus detailed, we have already spoken, but shall have reason to speak of them again, when he visited, by direction of the Governor, the sanguinary but victorious field of Antietam.

The first mention we find, in the Governor's letters, of raising colored troops, is in a letter addressed by him to Mr. Francis H. Fletcher, Pratt Street, Salem, in which he says, —

"No official information has been received at this department from the United-States Government, concerning the plan, which is now mentioned with favor, of raising colored regiments for garrison duty in the Gulf and cotton States; nor is any thing known at this department of the intentions of the United-States Government in that regard, beyond what is published in the public prints. General Saxton, who is mentioned in the newspapers as being detailed to organize such a force, is a native of Massachusetts, and a most worthy and humane gentleman, as well as a skilful officer; and, if the report is correct, it is a very judicious selection for such a duty and command."

It appears that Mr. Fletcher was a candidate for a commission in such regiments; and the Governor offered him a letter to General Saxton, and such other assistance as was in his power, to obtain what he desired.

Dr. Le Baron Russell, of Boston, at the request of a committee of teachers and other friends of education in Massachusetts, visited Washington, for the purpose of arranging some plan, under the sanction of the Federal authority, to enable Massachusetts teachers and agents to participate in the humane and benevolent work of improving the intellectual and moral condition of the emancipated slaves within certain of our military posts. He carried letters from the Governor to the Secretary of War and other official persons, highly approving the purpose of his mission. This appears to have been the commencement of the educational labors among the liberated slaves, which has been attended with so much good.

On the 19th of May, the Secretary of War telegraphed to the Governor to know if he could raise four more new regiments at short notice, to which he replied affirmatively; but, in the letter expressing his readiness to comply with the Secretary's demand, he says, —

"If our people feel that they are going into the South to help fight rebels, who will kill and destroy *them* by all the means known to savages, as well as civilized man, — will deceive them by fraudulent flags of truce and lying pretences, will use their negro slaves against them both as laborers and as fighting men, while they themselves must never *fire at the enemy's magazine*, — I think that they will feel that the draft is heavy on their patriotism. But, if the President will sustain General Hunter, — recognize *all* men, even black men, as legally capable of that loyalty the blacks are waiting to manifest, and let them fight with God and human nature on their side, — *the roads will swarm, if need be, with multitudes whom New England would pour out to obey your call.*"

A copy of this letter was sent to the Governors of the New-England States, in the thought that mutual conference might be useful, and tend to unite and concentrate opinion in New England upon the subject to which it relates.

On the 25th of May, received from Mr. Stanton the following telegrams: —

"Send all the troops forward that you can, immediately. Banks is completely routed. The enemy are, in large force, advancing on Harper's Ferry."

"Intelligence from various quarters leaves no doubt that the enemy, in great force, are advancing on Washington. You will please organize and forward immediately all the volunteer and militia force in your State."

Upon the receipt of these telegrams, orders were immediately issued by the Adjutant-General for the militia of the Commonwealth to report at once for duty on Boston Common, to proceed to Washington; and four thousand men were in Boston, and ready to start, on the 27th. But, on the morning of the

27th, the Governor received the following, dated midnight, May 26, from the Secretary of War: —

"Two despatches have been received from General Banks, one dated at Martinsburg, the other between Martinsburg and Williamsport, which state that he has saved his trains, and the chief part of his command, and expected to cross the Potomac at Williamsburg in safety. We hope he may accomplish his purpose."

In consequence of the favorable change of affairs in General Banks's command, the order to send forward the militia was countermanded, and the men returned to their homes, most of them disappointed that they were not to go forward.

The battalion raised for garrison duty at Fort Warren, composed of six companies of three years' men, left, on the 27th, for the front, under command of Lieutenant-Colonel Francis J. Parker; and orders were received to recruit four new companies, and make it a regiment, which was speedily done.

This was what was called afterwards "the great scare," and many people blamed Mr. Stanton for the semi-sensational character of his telegraph messages. They certainly created the wildest excitement throughout the Commonwealth; and Boston, in a degree, resembled Edinburgh on receipt of the fatal news of Flodden Field.

June 2. — Governor telegraphs General Banks, Williamsport, Md.: —

"Telegram received yesterday. Surgeon-General Dale has arranged to supply your requisition immediately. I greet you cordially. All honor to our brave Massachusetts men!"

This was a request to send forward additional surgeons to take care of the wounded in General Banks's command.

On the 4th of June, the Governor wrote Colonel George H. Gordon, Second Massachusetts Volunteers, who had command of a brigade under General Banks, —

"Permit me, in closing, to congratulate you upon your nomination to the rank of brigadier-general, and also upon the brilliant success achieved by the withdrawal of our forces, with so little loss, from the heart of the enemy's country, and against a force so completely overwhelming."

www.ingramcontent.com/pod-product-compliance
Lightning Source LLC
Chambersburg PA
CBHW030303240426
43673CB00040B/1039